Exploiting Machine Learning for Robust Security

Minakshi
King Khalid University, Saudi Arabia

Anchit Bijalwan
British University, Vietnam

Tarun Kumar
Galgotias University, India

IGI Global
Scientific Publishing
Publishing Tomorrow's Research Today

Vice President of Editorial	Melissa Wagner
Director of Acquisitions	Mikaela Felty
Director of Book Development	Jocelynn Hessler
Production Manager	Mike Brehm
Cover Design	Phillip Shickler

Published in the United States of America by
IGI Global Scientific Publishing
701 East Chocolate Avenue
Hershey, PA, 17033, USA
Tel: 717-533-8845
Fax: 717-533-7115
Website: https://www.igi-global.com E-mail: cust@igi-global.com

Library of Congress Cataloging-in-Publication Data

LCCN: 2024054456 (CIP Data Pending)
ISBN13: 9798369377581
Isbn13Softcover: 9798369377598
EISBN13: 9798369377604

British Cataloguing in Publication Data
A Cataloguing in Publication record for this book is available from the British Library.

Table of Contents

Detailed Table of Contents

authors then fine-tune pre-trained Inception-ResNet v2 and DenseNet models on a large- scale dataset comprising various types of malware and benign software.

The rapid evolution of malware poses a significant threat to cybersecurity, necessitating advanced techniques for effective detection and classification. Traditional methods, such as signature-based and heuristic-based detection, struggle to keep pace with the sophisticated evasion techniques employed by modern malware. This chapter explores the integration of machine learning techniques into malware analysis to address these challenges. It delves into the types and behaviors of malware, the principles of machine learning, and the processes of data collection, preprocessing, and feature extraction. Through real-world case studies and comparative analyses, the chapter highlights the advantages and limitations of these models in real-time applications. Additionally, it discusses the future directions and potential of machine learning in adapting to emerging malware threats. By providing a comprehensive overview, this chapter aims to equip readers with the knowledge and tools necessary to leverage machine learning for robust malware detection and classification.

Malware is a global problem. Malware's impact according to studies is escalating. In the fight against malware, Malware detection and analysis techniques are the most important defense tools. That which makes a detector good, or terrible, is largely determined by its techniques of operation. Thorough understanding of the many types of malware detection procedures is essential. This chapter investigates malware detection and analysis techniques, first and second-generation malware (i.e. encrypted, metamorphic, polymorphic, oligomorphic), and the study of machine learning algorithms for malware detection techniques.

As networks and Internet of Things (IoT) devices become more complex and interconnected, robust security protocols are essential. Sophisticated cyber-attacks often outpace traditional measures, necessitating the use of modern technologies like machine learning (ML). This chapter will explore how ML techniques can enhance the security of networks and IoT ecosystems. By employing ML for anomaly detection, intrusion detection, and predictive analytics, entities can proactively address security vulnerabilities. The chapter will cover various ML approaches, their application to network and IoT security, related challenges, and future directions. It aims to provide valuable insights for scholars, practitioners, and policymakers in cybersecurity and IoT deployment.

The rapid surge in cybercrime during the COVID-19 pandemic has become a pressing concern for mental health professionals. The increased reliance on digital technologies for work, education, and healthcare has led to a rise in cyber-attacks, with perpetrators exploiting vulnerable individuals through methods like phishing scams and online harassment. These incidents can have severe psychological consequences, such as heightened anxiety, depression, and post-traumatic stress. To address this challenge, the text explores the dynamic interplay between cybersecurity practices and the preservation of mental health and well-being. It examines various cyber threats, including cyberbullying, doxing, and revenge porn, and their emotional and mental impacts on victims, such as anxiety, depression, and social withdrawal.

Preface

The meteoric rise of cloud computing has revolutionized industries across the globe, offering unparalleled opportunities for scalability, agility, and cost savings. Yet, this transformative technology brings with it a labyrinth of security challenges that demand innovative and robust solutions. In this era of rapid technological advancement, securing cloud environments against evolving threats is no longer optional but imperative. With this book, *Exploiting Machine Learning for Robust Security*, we aim to address this pressing need by providing a comprehensive exploration of how machine learning (ML) can be leveraged to fortify cloud security.

As editors, we bring diverse perspectives from our academic and professional experiences. Minakshi from King Khalid University, Saudi Arabia; Anchit Bijalwan from the British University, Vietnam; and Tarun Kumar from Galgotias University, India, have collaborated to curate this book as an authoritative resource for both practitioners and researchers. It is our shared belief that machine learning holds immense potential to transform traditional approaches to cloud security, enabling organizations to stay ahead of sophisticated cyber threats.

The primary objective of this book is to empower readers with the knowledge and tools necessary to secure data, applications, and infrastructure in cloud computing environments. We delve into foundational cloud security frameworks, service models, access control methodologies, encryption protocols, and monitoring technologies, all through the lens of ML applications. Each chapter has been carefully structured to provide in-depth insights into:

- Identifying and mitigating unique vulnerabilities such as data breaches, regulatory violations, and crippling cyberattacks.
- Implementing secure cloud migration practices and robust incident response mechanisms.
- Ensuring business continuity through effective disaster recovery planning and resilience strategies.

To bridge the gap between theory and practice, the book includes real-world case studies that illustrate how organizations across various sectors are deploying ML-driven security measures. These examples highlight the adaptability and scalability of cloud security solutions tailored to diverse business needs and operational models.

CHAPTER OVERVIEW

Chapter 1: This chapter discusses the integration of machine learning in cybersecurity, examining its applications and challenges. It covers key areas including intrusion detection systems, malware detection, user authentication, and biometric security. The text explores both defensive applications of ML in security and potential vulnerabilities, emphasizing the need for privacy-preserving techniques and ethical considerations. It concludes by highlighting future trends, particularly in deep learning and reinforcement learning, while stressing the importance of proactive defense strategies against evolving cyber threats.

Chapter 2: Exploring the growing reliance on machine learning in combating contemporary cybersecurity challenges, this chapter provides a systematic review of its applications. It examines advanced attack detection through adversarial machine learning, ML's role in cryptography and blockchain, and privacy-preserving measures aligned with data protection laws. By bridging theoretical insights with practical applications, this chapter equips researchers and practitioners with the knowledge to develop robust, ML-based cybersecurity solutions.

Chapter 3: Intrusion Detection Systems (IDS) serve as a critical line of defense in cybersecurity, and this chapter provides a comprehensive analysis of their types, including signature-based and anomaly-detection systems. It addresses prevalent threats, strategies for incident handling, and attacker evasion techniques. Incorporating machine learning, deep learning, and optimization algorithms, the chapter offers insights into enhancing IDS effectiveness, supported by discussions on relevant datasets and system performance metrics.

Chapter 4: With cyber threats becoming increasingly frequent and sophisticated, this chapter explores the automation capabilities of machine learning in mitigating risks. By analyzing anomalies, detecting phishing attempts, and enhancing multi-factor authentication (MFA) systems, ML demonstrates its effectiveness in securing digital ecosystems. Practical examples include behavior-based identity verification and streamlined MFA solutions tailored to organizational needs.

Chapter 5: The chapter discusses the intersection of machine learning (ML) and big data, highlighting the challenges and opportunities in ensuring security and privacy. It emphasizes the vulnerabilities of ML systems and the importance of robustness against malicious attacks. The paper explores the ML process pipeline, detailing potential security issues at each stage. It calls for ongoing research and innovation to enhance ML longevity and safety, stressing the need for effective countermeasures and constant evaluation in dynamic environments.

Chapter 6: This chapter introduces a novel approach to malware detection, leveraging advanced deep learning models like Inception-ResNet v2 and DenseNet. Through techniques such as byte-level n-gram frequency analysis and opcode sequence extraction, these models demonstrate their capacity to identify subtle malware patterns. Pre-trained on large-scale datasets, these architectures highlight the integration of cutting-edge deep learning methodologies in combating malicious software.

Chapter 7: This chapter provides an in-depth study of malware detection, categorizing various techniques—from traditional methods to advanced machine learning algorithms. It explores the evolution of malware types, including encrypted, metamorphic, polymorphic, and oligomorphic malware, offering insights into the operational mechanisms of effective detection systems.

Chapter 8: Focusing on the integration of machine learning in malware analysis, this chapter examines traditional detection methods and their limitations. It explores data collection, preprocessing, and feature extraction techniques, supported by real-world case studies. The discussion extends to the future of machine learning in malware detection, emphasizing its adaptability to emerging threats and its potential for real-time application.

Chapter 9: As IoT ecosystems and networks become increasingly complex, this chapter emphasizes the role of machine learning in strengthening their security. By employing ML for anomaly detection, intrusion detection, and predictive analytics, the chapter outlines proactive measures to address vulnerabilities. Challenges and future directions in this domain are explored, providing valuable guidance for practitioners and policymakers.

Chapter 10: The surge in cybercrime during the COVID-19 pandemic has significant implications for mental health. This chapter examines the psychological impact of threats like phishing, online harassment, and cyberbullying. It emphasizes the importance of cybersecurity practices in mitigating these effects and explores strategies to safeguard mental well-being in an increasingly digital world.

Chapter 11: This chapter investigates the intersection of cybersecurity and mental health, highlighting the emotional toll of cyber threats and the need for safe online spaces. It discusses the best practices and technologies for protecting user data and preventing information leakage. Through case studies and practical advice, the chapter offers guidance for policymakers and mental health professionals in fostering secure digital environments.

Chapter 12: Focusing on the integration of Web of Devices (WOD) for mental health monitoring, this chapter explores how connected devices facilitate real-time data collection and analysis. It examines the role of WOD in early detection and treatment of mental health disorders, emphasizing the interplay between security technologies and psychological well-being.

Chapter 13: This chapter highlights the crucial intersection of cybersecurity and mental wellness, addressing threats like cyberbullying, harassment, and identity theft. It advocates for collaborative efforts among mental health professionals, technologists, and educators to create secure digital spaces. Strategies for prevention, content moderation, and community partnerships are discussed, offering a vision for a safer online environment.

Chapter 14: This chapter focuses on the challenges of combating online child abuse in India, emphasizing the need for comprehensive awareness and prevention strategies. Through surveys and stakeholder discussions, it examines the dynamics of child abuse and the effectiveness of cybersecurity measures. The findings aim to enhance understanding and contribute to the existing literature on protecting vulnerable populations.

Chapter 15: Traditional spam filters often fall short in detecting sophisticated spam patterns. This chapter explores the use of artificial neural networks (ANNs) for identifying subtle spam tactics while distinguishing legitimate emails. The investigation underscores the impact of spam on community trust and online safety, offering insights into building resilient spam detection systems.

This publication is intended for a broad audience, including cloud security professionals, students, researchers, academicians, faculty members, cloud architects, IT managers, decision-makers, and regulatory compliance experts. By addressing the multifaceted challenges of cloud security, we aim to provide actionable insights and strategies that resonate with readers at all levels of expertise.

Machine learning's role in cybersecurity is not just reactive but predictive, offering proactive solutions to emerging threats. As cloud adoption continues to grow, so does the necessity for innovative security measures that evolve in tandem with the threat landscape. With this book, we aspire to contribute to this critical discourse and inspire advancements in securing cloud environments.

We extend our heartfelt gratitude to the contributors whose expertise and dedication have enriched this publication. It is our hope that this book will serve as a valuable resource for organizations and individuals seeking to navigate the complexities of cloud security with confidence and competence.

Minakshi
King Khalid University, Saudi Arabia

Anchit Bijalwan
British University, Vietnam

Tarun Kumar
Galgotias University, India

Chapter 1
Exploiting Machine Learning for Robust Security

Tarun Kumar
https://orcid.org/0000-0002-8507-8522
Galgotias University, India

Minakshi
https://orcid.org/0000-0001-7586-6309
King Khalid University, Saudi Arabia

Shree Harsh Attri
https://orcid.org/0000-0001-6915-0048
Sharda University, India

ABSTRACT

The chapter discusses cybercrime's significant global economic impact, resulting in a 0.9% GDP loss and approximately $600 billion in damages in 2017. It outlines the evolving cybersecurity threat landscape, focusing on dangerous types like malicious software, automated attacks, and advanced persistent threats that challenge traditional security measures. The chapter highlights artificial intelligence and machine learning's emerging roles in cybersecurity, showing how these technologies enhance security automation, response times, and risk assessment. Deep learning shows particular promise in real-time processing and classification, offering solutions for malware and social engineering detection. The chapter emphasizes the need for ongoing research while noting challenges in integrating machine learning into cybersecurity practices. Additionally, it underscores the historic scientific value of intelligent cybersecurity advancement and the importance of establishing clear

DOI: 10.4018/979-8-3693-7758-1.ch001

research milestones.

1. INTRODUCTION TO MACHINE LEARNING IN SECURITY

In 2017, the global economy suffered an estimated 0.9% loss of gross domestic product (GDP) to cybercrime, leading to a reported $600 billion in losses. Today, the most dangerous forms of cybersecurity threats include malicious software, automated attacks, and advanced persistent threats. All of these, due to their dynamic and intelligent nature, can defeat traditional security measures. Recently, artificial intelligence and machine learning techniques have become trending application areas in cybersecurity, offering security automation, faster response, risk assessment, and intelligent predictive measures (Manoharan & Sarker, 2023). Deep learning in particular has provided groundbreaking real-time processing and classification capability where conventional feature matching approaches are least likely to succeed. These increasingly popular and versatile technologies have enabled novel security applications ranging from malware detection to social engineering detection. Subsequently, ongoing research is increasingly focusing on these technologies; though this domain is evolving rapidly due to practical implementations, it is important to summarize and analyze these trends in a formalized way to promote further research in the direction where it is actually required. Figure 1 shows the role of machine learning in cybersecurity.

Figure 1. Role of machine learning in cybersecurity

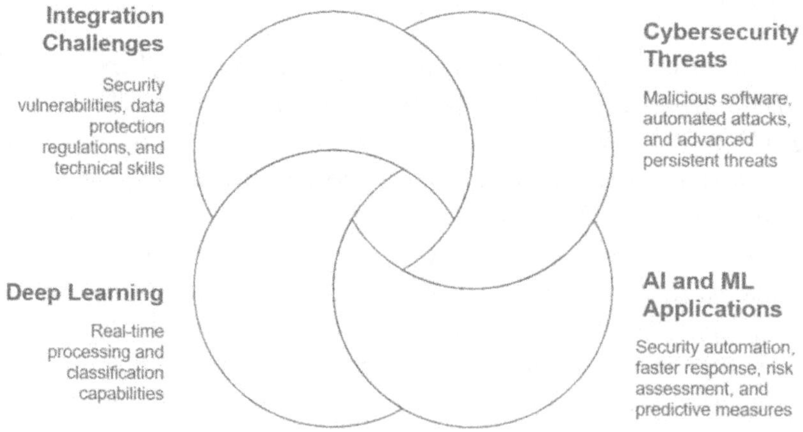

Every technology may not be equally suitable for a particular application. Cybersecurity, as a field, provides an excellent testbed for the development and real-time deployment of machine learning technologies due to ever-growing threats and dirty data that can be used offline and online (Naseer, 2021). However, integrating machine learning into functional cybersecurity practices represents a significant challenge due to potential security vulnerabilities, data protection regulations, and technical skills required. Milestones in intelligent approaches for cybersecurity research and applications are yet to be defined or compiled, and this area holds historic scientific value.

2. FUNDAMENTALS OF CYBERSECURITY

As digitization continues to pervade the global landscape, ensuring cybersecurity has become more critical than ever. It is important to understand some consolidation data that helps in this field. Establishing the fundamentals of cybersecurity is vital to comprehending the dynamics of security and elucidates how threats can be identified, cyber risks assessed, and different strategies of mitigation developed for reducing the risks. At a higher level, cybersecurity is concerned with safeguarding all the digital information gathered, processed, and communicated by different systems for varied stakeholders. This information needs to be kept intact and confidential to ensure trust in different systems and communication among them. It thus becomes evident that cybersecurity relates to securing the communication channels that would ultimately ensure its privacy (Montasari et al., 2021). Moreover, policies and practices regulating the use of technology by individuals or organizations in a digital ecosystem also govern the concept of cybersecurity. Technology and public policy thus operate in the convergence space of cybersecurity, which further gets influenced by the behavior of individuals or groups. The war against cyber risks must address these multiple challenges - from technology and public policy perspectives as well as convergence areas. The availability of stronger cryptographic tools has also contributed to this evolution. State and corporate espionage has targeted leading firms, pursuing access to proprietary techniques and trade or defense details. In this technical universe, terms like 'cyber safety' or 'information security' are used as a boxed frame focused by users, an effort that plans on understanding, protecting, recognizing, responding to, and recovering from cyber breaches (Ozkan-Okay et al., 2024). Figure 2 shows the key components and challenges.

Figure 2. Key components and challenges

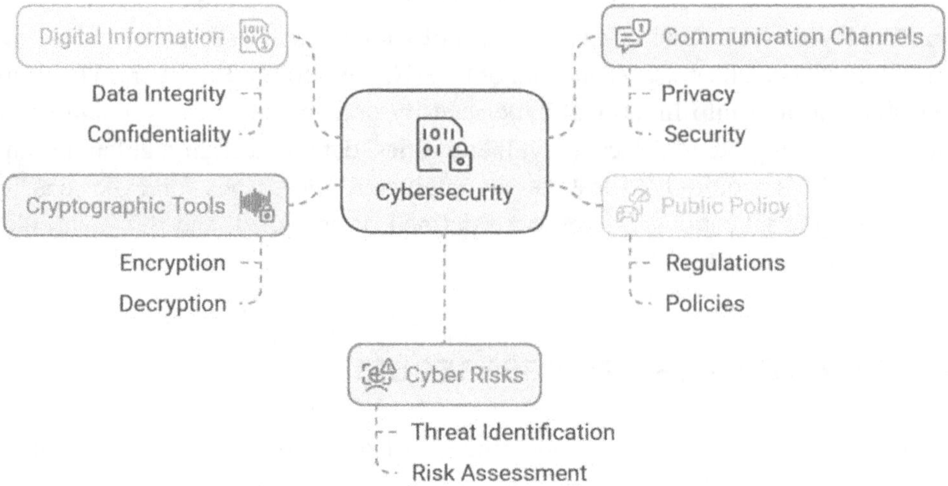

Standard entrepreneurs, specialists, and identifiers have also reported a few situations where the government has minimized foreign essential infrastructure malware or hindered the overseas activities of international lawbreakers. However, in the systems of senior policy officers, as well as in the latest policy strategy papers, intelligence dialogues, and public tests, there remains a divide between active cyber protection and traditional network self-defense.

3. PRINCIPLES OF ROBUST SECURITY

Robust security should be characterized by the ability to work in the presence of failure by having a high degree of fault tolerance, gracefully adapting to new situations, and being redundant. Security is more than just a checklist of security features and a set of policies and procedures. Security also depends on the human factors contributing to system security. Figure 3 shows the principles of robust security.

Figure 3. Principles of robust security

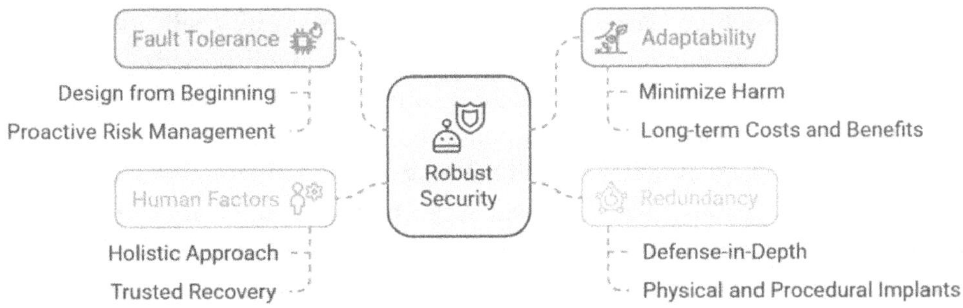

The fundamental principles in security are: design right from the beginning with robust security features, proactively consider all the risks in designing security features explicitly rather than just ignoring them, minimize the potential harm due to successful attacks; consciously consider the long-term costs and benefits that security may impose, balance the trade-offs associated with providing resources, and drawing an effective line between the worst-case scenario-based security approach and the remaining levels of acceptable security failures primarily dependent on human factors (Nassar & Kamal, 2021). One must follow defense-in-depth architecture, giving physical and procedural implants in addition to traditional electronics and software means for securing data and resources.

The intent to minimize the overall risk as part of risk management directly implies resiliency and robustness in security protocols. It is a necessity to adopt a holistic approach that would encompass all the types of solutions that are deemed necessary to counter the various threats, combining responsive technical solutions with others for influencing the human factors early on to avoid security incidents. Trusted recovery through alerting and auditing methods; continuous auditing can recover reliably from intrinsic environmental risks (Trim & Lee, 2022). Notice the difference between proactive risk management and the traditional point-based security analysis and auditing. The essence goes beyond detection and reaction to reducing the potential scope for the damage caused due to a successful attack. In order to preclude the potential scope and also mitigate a broader range of risks, one can't merely rely on security strings thinking to make full use of data and not just its storage (Goriparthi, 2023).

4. MACHINE LEARNING MODELS FOR SECURITY

A variety of machine learning models are used in security applications, which can be broadly divided into three paradigms: supervised, unsupervised, and reinforcement learning. Each of these use cases is often applied to two primary security functions, i.e., threat detection and response. Fundamentally, these models can be characterized by their different situational dependencies. Unsupervised and deep learning models, for instance, are designed to be less dependent on the specific instance or situation at hand. The performance of a deep learning model is more sensitive to the quality and diversity of the training data (Kumar & Attri, 2024).

Supervised learning is popular for a diverse set of security applications, providing a variety of different strengths and weaknesses with a range of possibilities and deployment conditions. Given all of the possible combinations that exist between these models and security applications, it is very difficult to make broad pronouncements on their real-world performance. Performance metrics for these models are used to generate a range of different indicators. Performance measures are needed to provide concrete benchmarks and evaluate model predictions. For purposes of this review, three primary performance measures are used: sensitivity or true positive rate, specificity or true negative rate, and the receiver operating characteristic curve, which provides a threshold-insensitive overview of the interrelationship between false positive rate, true positive rate, and a predetermined false positive rate (Khan & Ghafoor, 2024). The predictive capabilities of machine learning are highly influenced by the quality of the training, validation, and test datasets, and therefore, the variety of the used adversarial techniques establishes the accuracy of the machine learning model predictions. Figure 4 shows the machine learning models in security.

Figure 4. Machine learning models in security

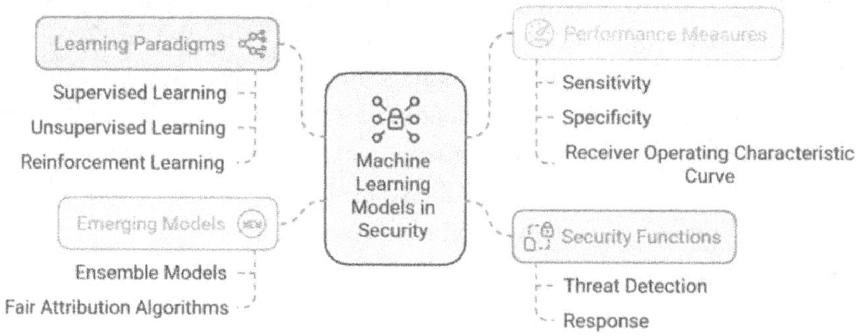

Several new emerging models offer the likelihood of employing more developed prediction models to combine the strengths of various previously discussed models, allowing the most performant techniques to be combined according to previously proven optimal architecture and trained across larger and more diversified datasets. The advent of ensemble models and fair attribution algorithms is currently generating a significant uptick in the expected functional promise of machine learning in general, and of deep learning in particular, toward investing in novel approaches in the predictive capabilities of security systems (Nguyen & Reddi, 2021). These advances point to a coming industry fusion between machine learning and traditional security technologies, offering a new era of machine learning and deep learning-based security technologies.

4.1 An Overview of Security-Specific Applications in Machine Learning

Within the expanding landscape of applications for machine learning techniques, there exist numerous applications that focus primarily on security concerns. Many machine learning applications are intended to be put to work in order to make digital infrastructure increasingly secure. These security-specific applications can be divided into a number of focus areas: prediction of threats to IT systems, the learning and deployment of automated cyber defenses, generation of fake data in order to degrade the quality of an attacker's machine learning model, the prediction of cyber events in real time, the inference of whether someone using an IT system has authorization to take a particular action, the automatic evaluation of whether an event is suspicious and needs to be investigated, the understanding of whether a piece of software is harmful to other pieces of software, and the categorization of suspicious events into several classes according to the threat level.

There are several important areas of established security research that involve the application of machine learning, including automated intrusion detection, user and entity behavior analytics, malware binaries classification, and attack strategy prediction. An important point to note is that the established security practice is based largely on non-ML techniques, which include first-generation signature-based firewalls and antivirus, behavioral firewalls, and filters with whitelisting/blacklisting, all the way up to complex digital identity infrastructures and particularly crafted communication protocols. These all aim to protect the client and asset from the inside. Consequently, rather than replacing these, security-specific ML applications are used in tandem with these security technologies in order to augment a defense-in-depth, layered security strategy. Unfortunately, research has pointed out that malice found in the users of the IT infrastructure is the least detectable and thus the most likely attack vector. In order to increase the detection of this attack vector, humans must be coupled with technology.

4.2 Intrusion Detection Systems

An Intrusion Detection System (IDS) is crucial for augmenting the network security arsenal as the number and complexity of security breaches and attacks over diverse networked systems are increasing rapidly. It only becomes more consequential when we can distinguish between normal and malicious activities in the short expanse of network traffic provided. Early entries into the system bring up the need for threat detection systems with more proactive mechanisms, which can instantaneously detect the presence of a threat and inform response mechanisms to react to it. IDS are built on the backends of machine learning algorithms. Machine learning-based algorithms have a significant impact on the real-time capability of detection systems.

Intrusion detection can be performed in multiple ways, where most of these methods will categorize under these two main approaches: anomaly detection and signature-based detection. These two are the main approaches in threat detection, where anomaly detection algorithms can only sense new types of threats, while traditional signature-based detection algorithms can do that job when we update their database with new signatures. Each approach has its pros and cons. The signature-based detection approach is more complete and faster, as anomalies detect a slow rise, especially in large organizations. It is also assumed that the detection of known threat methods of attack is effective. It is also known that it is very efficient to identify malicious activities by comparing the recorded events with a knowledge base of well-known attacks. However, the continuing growth of continual variation of threats demands further study to be carried out to add machine learning.

4.2.1 Anomaly Detection

Intrusion detection systems are one of the aspects of security systems. An anomaly-based detection system is used to detect patterns of intrusion attacks in data or networks within a computer system. Typically, this is network traffic or behavior of a system based on the normal behavior pattern. This approach identifies if at any moment in time behavior deviates from what is typically observed. One of the main goals of this model is to detect any attack patterns that occur in the system. An improved method to detect this behavior uses statistical analysis as the basis of inspection, scanning, and analysis of pattern recognition. Machine learning, such as clustering techniques to detect abnormalities or classification algorithms to provide for the assignment of classes, can be used for such purposes.

While anomaly-based approaches may provide benefits in detecting attacks within network traffic, the very nature of the evolving online attack paradigm is changing. The concept of an outlier detects the incidents of anomalies on network traffic or network system data and can be extended into this paradigm. Importantly, methods for anomaly detection will typically detect a number of attacks. A major issue here is the objective setting of the level or the critical areas and trade-offs when they are set. The additional complication for such systems on real-time networks is that setting such values in the presence of sensor noise or network anomalies can create spurious warnings and errors, creating false positives and negatives. This is often more problematic in anomaly detection than in more commonly seen data classification examples, where feedback for new examples can be done with more precise diagnostic information. Techniques to help alleviate this problem are often found in real-time anomaly detection systems by using hidden variable models, more sophisticated loss functions on input and output values, continuous learning and adaptation for threshold values, and allowance for time clustering of warnings and false positives. In real-time setups, care must be taken against the false positive problem of not inadvertently merging together distinct anomalies, thus the potential problems of lack of precision and recall in captured warnings and errors.

4.2.2 Signature-Based Detection

Signature-based detection is a widely used traditional method in intrusion detection systems (IDSs). It is designed to find known threats and events within network traffic. Signature-based detection operates based on prototypes of known risks such as viruses, worms, and other malware that are already programmed into the system as a screening process. It functions by sifting through traffic for a prearranged catalog of events or patterns that can be commonly connected with recognized cyber threats. With the power of pattern recognition, such systems can help identify threats very rapidly. However, due to the inherent tendency of signature-based systems to usually overlook viruses, it does not acknowledge threats that have already been processed; this technology is unfit for countering different or never-seen-before dangers.

The system is built on a pattern database using cryptographic decryption algorithms, a collection of attack chapters, including the classes for each instance in the dataset, the definition of a particular class as legitimate, a collection of classes for attack types, and the specification of a rule that measures the similarity between the two vector instances. Signature-based detection recognizes known threats. In other words, it operates on finding known risks. Anomalous attacks are usually undetected when IDS solutions do not make use of any symptoms. At first, signature-based detection is scarce in developing environments technologically, but it is efficient in recognizing very detailed attacks. There are integrated security solutions and tools available that use digital signatures cryptographically. Signature-based detection is a foundational element and a significant part of a systematically diversified strategy for protecting against malicious communication (Kumar et al., 2024).

4.3 Malware Detection

Malware is typically defined as software that purposely damages or exploits computer systems. The diversity in its forms varies, ranging from spyware and adware to causing service disruption and data theft, to the most harmful strains, such as ransomware, cryptominers, and other targeted threats. As malware becomes more sophisticated, developing a method of detecting and preventing it is essential to avoid its many negative effects. This is why a huge part of the machine learning community is interested in creating malware detection models, even though designing secure systems is a difficult task in itself.

Machine learning can counter many types of malwares, such as exploiting domain generation algorithms, malware distribution networks, and malware families. Moreover, it can be a good choice to reduce malvertisement and e-fraud issues. The naive approach for medical applications is to build these models as supervised learning activities because specialists in these domains can offer a binary scenario when calculating pathologies using multiple profiling techniques. Furthermore, the idea is to also bring in unsupervised learning in these cases together with supervised learning to design a model capable of classifying some known and unknown threats. This is used as a backup plan to help identify threats if a new malware strain is released to networks quickly. Today, organizations use specific environments such as sandboxes, live scanning systems, software protection mechanisms, or antivirus engines to test thousands of malware samples. While malware detection systems with dynamic behavioral analysis give the subtle variants of malware more robust vigilance, they are able to handle the generation of polymorphic and metamorphic malware. Up until now, malware detection systems have been generally well received and have proven their caliber in trials and testing.

4.4 Phishing Detection

Phishing attacks, financially threatening individuals and organizations are now a major concern. Sophisticated preventive measures can be exploited by cybercriminals to conduct phishing campaigns that bypass the existing signature-based detection systems, making users easy targets. As a result, much effort has been put into research towards machine learning models that are, at a technological level, reliable for phishing detection, and security practitioners have used machine learning as one of the tools in their arsenal for defense and protection against such malicious activities. Predictive or descriptive machine learning models have demonstrated substantial impacts in addressing phishing threats and predicting when, how, and where criminals might infiltrate and execute their insidious operations.

Machine learning-based models are employed in numerous phishing detection methodologies. For example, an online application of a machine learning model utilizes feature extraction and classifiers to predict the phishing URL. Similarly, clustering-based techniques are used to predict phishing websites by employing a machine learning model. Moreover, machine learning and feature extraction techniques help classify phishing-based electronic mail addresses. In another study, machine learning and feature extraction techniques are used to identify spear phishing electronic mail, which aids in predicting and preventing current spear phishing threats. Correspondingly, a mechanism for knowing the phishing potential of social engineering traits using the authentication values of websites is proposed. In addition to that, a machine learning-based phishing detection model is designed for detecting phishing websites based on assessing the content of webpages. Subsequently, the combination of machine learning and artificial intelligence is proposed in the phishing detection distribution system of webpages.

4.5 User Authentication and Access Control

An important aspect of securing resources is to ensure that only authenticated users are accessing them. For that, we use user authentication systems. Existing traditional user authentication systems use password-based and token-based schemes. Although multi-factor authentication was introduced to bypass the limitations of traditional authentication, the memorability of the scheme has not been significantly improved. Biometric-based user authentication systems have also been introduced to address this limitation. However, conventional systems have shown vulnerability when storing user biometric templates centrally, and also the possibility of types in the same physiological or behavioral features in different users. In the context of machine learning, various techniques have been developed to enhance user authentication and minimize unauthorized access to resources. However, user authentication systems suffer from demographic, psychological, and behavioral factors which can leave them vulnerable to in-depth phishing. Moreover, existing intelligent and adaptive systems learned from the user's data have been shown to be vulnerable to various kinds of attacks on data and models.

In order to overcome the limitations encountered in traditional user authentication systems, intelligent and adaptive solutions are inevitable. User behavioral profiling is used for user authentication. The biometric-based approach uses physiological measurements, which provides high individuality. Moreover, navigation behavior is also proposed in the biometric context to prevent replay attacks. Some of the advanced methods have been proposed based on human physiological responses and sensor responses. Leveraging user authentication as an adaptive and intelligent security solution, machine learning algorithms are also proposed to identify consumer anomalies. Access control processes utilize intelligence to determine the permissions a user has for different system resources based on role-based systems. Moreover, blockchain technology employs access permission as its first line, which must be verified before a new block is created and broadcast in the network. It is emphasized that user access to data resources is verified as part of the layered security.

Secure user authentication and access control metrics are discussed to describe models and security mechanisms (Kumar et al., 2024). Resorting to secure communications, the dynamic fingerprint of the device user is based on information from the component-based unique system that is stored in the distributed ledger. Although different methods demonstrate how secure user authentication can protect data resources, they require tremendous computational resources to secure fingerprint identification used for this purpose, and trust relationships resulting from social engineering can contribute to revealing the identity of the user. In today's world, several methods of user authentication and access control are employed. Behavioral analysis has shown to control system access dynamically. To increase security performance, these systems are integrated with biometric, fingerprint techniques, or iris scanning. Nevertheless, threats and attacks are on the rise with advanced techniques, and a more secure dynamic decision process is required to detect intruders or malicious activities. Behavioral authentication, if adopted as a standalone technique, will enhance the interaction aspect of the authentication process, deploying security models to enforce the overall guarantee of protectiveness. Behavioral analysis identifying human sentiment and emotion monitors erratic behavior on the network and detects tombstoning, which is still a growing field in computer security. Trends in various behavioral authentication models of biometrics can authenticate and ensure security mechanisms based on behavior.

5. ADVERSARIAL ATTACKS AND DEFENSES

Machine learning-based approaches face numerous security threats. The security and robustness of machine learning algorithms are often compromised by what are known as adversarial attacks. These attacks refer to subversions of ML systems designed to achieve outcomes that are undesirable to the systems' owners or operators. The primary adversarial attacks against ML systems include evasion attacks that generate misclassifications in supervised learning systems by slightly modifying the input, and poisoning attacks that add adversarial samples to the training set of a learning algorithm to compromise the classifiers or the clustering models. All these challenges require an urgent need for developing efficient and effective learning defense strategies to guarantee and enforce the security of modern machine learning models. Handling the adversarial behavior against machine learning techniques has attracted the attention of several researchers in recent years, and there is a continuous arms race between the attackers and defenders. From a conceptual perspective, the most effective way of adversarial defense is to understand and study adversarial behavior, and provide enough precaution in algorithm development, feature extraction, and network architecture design to show resilience against potential adversarial challenges in practical applications. In fact, substantial empirical evidence accumulates on the effectiveness of some adversarial defense mechanisms. However, for a comprehensive defense strategy, robust evaluation of machine learning algorithms based on large-scale, diverse, and increasingly complicated datasets is yet to be accommodated in practice (Rosenberg et al., 2021).

6. INTRUSION DETECTION SYSTEMS USING MACHINE LEARNING

The majority of employed and deployed intrusion detection mechanisms make use of machine learning technologies to identify malicious assaults and deliver a rapid response. Also, machine learning technologies are able to make predictions based on provided data to prevent unauthorized access. Intrusion detection systems are commonly classified into wide categories based on internal workings, e.g., network-based, distributed, host-based, and network-based intrusion detection systems. Network-based intrusion detection systems focus on anomaly detection in network communication and rely upon known patterns. Host-based intrusion detection systems are responsible for analyzing events, operations, logs, and application data to securely manage operating systems and applications, with less focus on network communication. Moreover, network-based intrusion detection system intelligence is implemented in data analysis in contrast to host-based systems and is satisfied with the produced intelligent outputs. Interestingly, network-based intrusion detection systems are developed entirely in software solutions, hardware implementations, and hybrid solutions, and are mechanisms to support national or local levels. Intrusion detection systems can be reactive, where the system responds to the attackers' invasion attempts, and they can also be predictive (Alsajri & Steiti, 2024). There is various classification systems used in intrusion detection systems, and once machine learning techniques are employed as the basic intrusion detection mechanism in research, the intrusion detection system will be classified on the basis of those techniques. Also, intrusion detection systems can be classified based on malicious event targets, such as misuse detection or anomaly detection systems. Misuse detection systems alert whenever they see any repetition of malicious activities historically, whereas anomaly detection systems are capable of detecting any deviation from normal activity, and hence it may be a malicious activity typically. All created systems employing machine learning are not the same in performance, as we have many results indicating the effectiveness and accuracy of the system (Arvindhan et al., 2022). This can be proven by validating more than one machine learning technology in real deployment scenarios and explaining the limitations of technology to highlight the potential in another field. Additionally, more research is done in comparing the capabilities of different machine learning algorithms that are used in the same technique to focus on the algorithm that increases the effectiveness of the system, mainly for intrusion detection. Intrusion detection systems benefit from machine learning because of ineffective performance within real-time data analysis and knowledge of future conditions evaluation. Anomaly detection gives attention to accurate detection, with the technique increasing the performance of the system depending on real experiences (Jaisingh et al., 2024). The experimentation of the employed machine learning algorithm in the intrusion detection system helps in identifying the performance of the system to be benchmarked. The intrusion detection system with machine learning always increases the efficiency of the system, especially with the techniques that have the self-behavior of learning methods. An increase in performance with accuracy and retraining methods for newly recorded malicious activities helps the system to be effective over large periods of time. The evaluation of feature selection with machine learning increases the efficiency of the system by focusing on the results in the confusion matrix estimated to be the performance-based condition. Feature selection helps in reaching the required privacy agreement because it decreases the features in the system, and the attacks can be done with reduced limitations.

7. SECURE COMMUNICATION SYSTEMS

Secure communication systems are vitally important for sensitive data transmission over wired and wireless networks. Modern cryptography and security protocols ensure confidential and authenticated message exchange among the communication parties. Hence, an adversary is always keen to compromise secure communications. Figure 5 shows the enhancing secure communication system.

Figure 5. Enhancing secure communication system

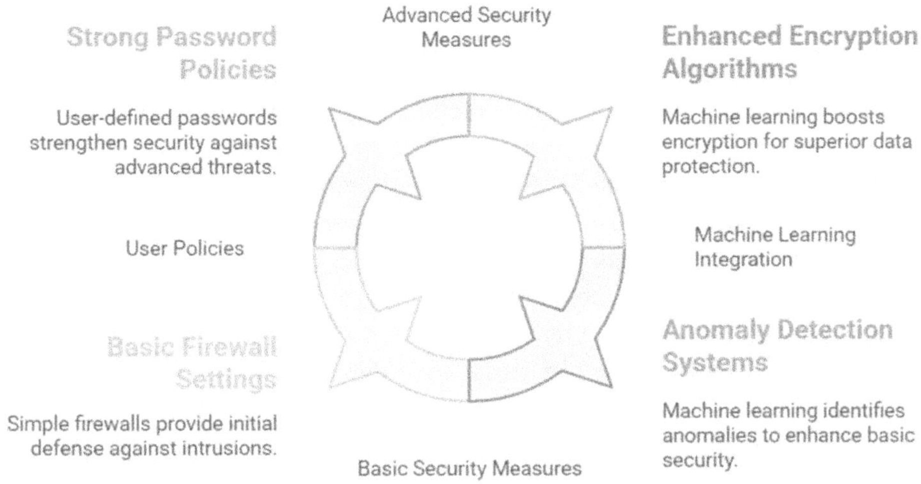

A communication channel between two entities can be attacked using various attack vectors, such as eavesdropping, jamming, man-in-the-middle, message control, message redirection, traffic analysis, and many more. To prevent attacks, security experts need to integrate robust security techniques into communication systems from communication aspects (Javed et al., 2025). One effective way to integrate robust security is by using machine learning. For example, machine learning can be used to enhance encryption algorithms, detect intrusion and anomalies during communication transactions in both wired and wireless networks, and secure multiparty computation and secure data sharing in the database. Almost all security mechanisms depend on communicating with users, so users must follow some security policies, such as using strong passwords or quick disconnections. Policies help to give direct feedback to technology. In turn, technology helps security practitioners, experts, and managers create more secure policies and guide the organization's security community towards best practices for security. This is especially true for secure communication because the vulnerabilities of communication ports and availability issues are well documented. Machine learning can enhance all communication security practices (Dumka et al., 2019).

8. BIOMETRIC SECURITY AND MACHINE LEARNING

Biometric security and machine learning involve human biometrics such as DNA, fingerprints, face, eye iris, retina, voice, gait, keystrokes, body odor, body shape, vein patterns, skin reflectance, and hand geometry, which can be used for identity verification for various purposes. Biometric systems that focus on one or more of the above biometric modalities for user authentication have started to gather significant attention. It has also been shown that a person wearing different clothes and under different illumination conditions can still be effectively recognized by facial recognition biometric modalities. However, the research community adopts a consent perspective regarding facial modification biometrics. Machine learning-based approaches used in these biometrics have significant potential to improve not only the accuracy of these systems but also the time to process and find a match (Dini et al., 2023).

From the experimental results obtained from various research, we have been able to explore the core issues in the use of biometrics in security. Ethical pressures to incorporate biometric technology in security are hindered by concepts such as loss of privacy and data misuse. Most authentication systems claim to guarantee their performance based on human biometric characteristics; however, in real-world environmental situations, the performance can be significantly different. Biometric data is being stored based on banking systems, and automatic teller machines are beginning to use biometric data for authentication systems. Airports and border checks also use biometric data for individuals to cross borders and to inform future practices and signals. Another major challenge reported not only in this class project but also in experimental papers from the field of biometric security is the security of the biometric system against spoofing attacks. Figure 6 shows the integration of biometric security and machine learning.

Figure 6. Biometric security and machine learning integration

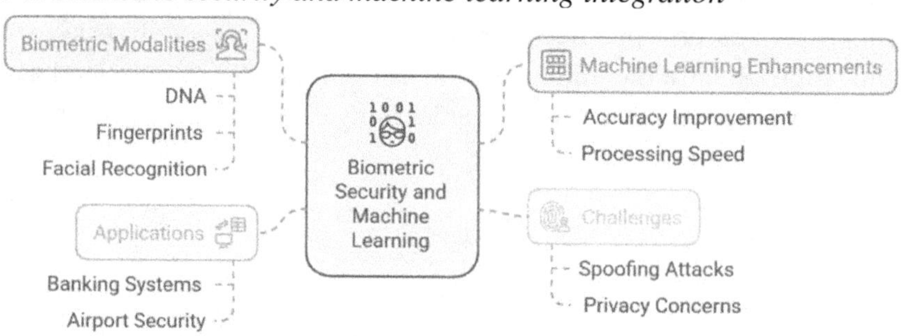

Combining results from intra- and inter-biometric systems can address the limitations of biometric systems, increase overall recognition accuracy, and enhance system reliability. The current trends and advancements in the field of human security have changed significantly and rapidly, making use of the latest machine learning methods, as will be seen in the next chapter. The development of machine learning methodologies in the area of security will reshape human user authentication by combining different methodologies to create secure systems.

9. PRIVACY-PRESERVING MACHINE LEARNING TECHNIQUES

One of the striking features of any learning process, including that of machine learning and artificial intelligence, is that it learns from data. This is great if the data are clean, sufficiently representative, and have a good basis for drawing reliable conclusions. But often the data are messy, subject to manipulation, not complete, or up to a sufficiently high standard, so that conclusions from its analysis are liable to result in dubious, misleading, or even worse, disastrous consequences (Kumar et al., 2024). Yet it is increasingly, if not already, unacceptable for an ML model to directly process people's data. From commentary to speculation, research to regulation, concern about data abuse is growing. While there is no consensus on what good standards of data management might look like, it is fair to say there is decreasing tolerance for organizations that fail to handle personal data in a trustworthy way. These concerns are given weight not just by public sentiment but by regulations as well. From a corporate ethics standpoint, respecting user privacy and complying with privacy regulations are core to the responsible use of AI and ML (Rawat et al., 2023). Further, the technical developments that have recently garnered much attention around the use of existing AI and machine learning on personal data without that data being shared may prove a source of much value with regard to compliance with privacy regulations and respecting privacy norms.

Some techniques that have been tested take existing AI and ML and design a training process that deduces the outcome of a model without the data being available outside a user's devices. Federated learning, differential privacy, and a raft of varied encryption techniques have all been used in applications up to proof of concept/testing stage and use existing AI to apply these techniques. However, each of these techniques has its strengths and weaknesses and different approaches to mathematically framing the problem, which may be more or less appealing depending on the use case. The same is also true from a regulatory and business standpoint. While it might be reductionist to say that there is a trade-off between allowing data to affect decision-making and protecting user privacy, there is certainly a trade-off between the most efficient way of allowing data into machine learning models and the most protective of user privacy. The machine learning community has been hardening its creations against powerful adversaries, but these have been created in simulation. In conventional technical cybersecurity wisdom, the best defense is not to be an appealing target. Regulatory policy and the landscape in which technical solutions operate are not an appealing way of ruling out nefarious adversaries either by shaping incentives or reducing the number of people acting adversarially (Caviglione et al., 2023).

10. ETHICAL CONSIDERATIONS IN MACHINE LEARNING FOR SECURITY

Ethical considerations are taking on an ever more prominent role in discussions of machine learning for security. Machine learning promises to automate key functions of security analysis, but a common concern is that algorithms encode and perpetuate human prejudices rather than liberating decision-making from them. In the security community, this fear appears in the significant debates over the utility of predictive policing policies, as arguing that law enforcement algorithms may actually reduce crime is challenging if these algorithms integrate and amplify existing inequalities. Security applications, in particular, underscore for the general public the ways in which decision-making on the basis of learned models may have real implications for social justice. In response, a great deal of work is being performed at the intersection of ethics and machine learning to study how ML can be made more transparent, accountable, and fair in its applications (Dhanya et al., 2023).

Ethical ML initiatives set the stage for the expansion of existing principles to the particularities of machine learning applications in security. This development is notable in part because AI has come to be seen as an existential issue, driving many tech companies and researchers to establish strict governance structures to ensure they are not complicit with malevolent use. Among the researchers and practitioners, a contentious debate has emerged about the ethics of data, particularly as related to the implications of surveillance and other privacy-infringing practices. Information about issues and case studies where machine learning algorithms go awry creates windows of opportunity for malicious users and weaponizes the lack of public understanding of AI capabilities. If members of the public have little understanding and knowledge in machine learning, they may easily be made to believe a wide number of things about machine learning capabilities, intentionally or otherwise, through adversarial shaping of the media. By engaging directly in envisioning the future development of machine learning applications, security may be positively and ethically influenced for the better (Tripathi et al., 2021). While analyses of data governance and the response to AI bias focus in part on practitioners and their treatment of data and models, the range of explanatory factors implicated in surveillance raises deep and specific moral questions around technology visioning and the role of the user and markets. Ethical considerations, perhaps belatedly, should act as guides in determining what we develop with machine learning as much as they exist to guide us on how to develop it (Dhakal et al., 2024).

11. FUTURE TRENDS AND CHALLENGES

This chapter presents the state-of-the-art development on using machine learning to achieve robust security. It is anticipated that future deep learning, like generative adversarial networks and reinforcement learning, will likely play a significant role in providing security to various systems. However, the attachment of real human brains and machines raises bigger challenges in designing moral, ethical, and legally conformant machines. The convergence of AI, robotics, and allied fields with ethics, regulations, and social sciences will likely raise many ethical dilemmas and regulatory and legal issues in designing autonomous secure systems (Mohammed et al., 2022). Armies and corporations are increasingly penning deals on artificial intelligence, but are they using controversial technology ethically? The wider world of science and technology is debating how cutting-edge technology will change humanity.

This chapter does not have any adversarial mindset other than showing how simple it has become to breach systems using malicious deep learning and also how secure we can be using benign deep learning. This survey on malicious deep learning and benign deep learning can certainly help in shaping future security and can make systems strong enough to defeat the bad effects of toxic AI. Nearly all core critical infrastructure systems have been digitalized. As the next industrial revolution becomes a practical reality, despite the increasing complexity of these everyday-critical systems, cybercriminals are becoming more innovative than ever. Their know-how is advancing to an extent faster than today's cybersecurity technology. The ever-changing threat landscape raises the question: how proactively can we defend ourselves? Let us try to look at the future, which will see the marrying of a range of secure and machine perception techniques.

12. CONCLUSION

In conclusion, this chapter emphasizes that while malicious deep learning presents a significant risk to system security, benign deep learning offers avenues for robust defense. The exploration of these two facets illustrates the imperative to strengthen our defenses against the advancing tactics of cybercriminals. As critical infrastructure continues to undergo digital transformation, the urgency of enhancing cybersecurity measures becomes even more pronounced. With the cyber threat landscape evolving rapidly, proactive strategies will be essential. Looking ahead, a synergistic approach that integrates various secure techniques with advanced machine perception capabilities may hold the key to safeguarding our systems in an increasingly complex digital environment.

REFERENCES

Aloqaily, A., Abdallah, E. E., AbuZaid, H., Abdallah, A. E., & Al-hassan, M. (2025). Supervised Machine Learning for Real-Time Intrusion Attack Detection in Connected and Autonomous Vehicles: A Security Paradigm Shift. *Informatics (MDPI)*, 12(1), 4. DOI: 10.3390/informatics12010004

Alsajri, A., & Steiti, A. (2024). Intrusion Detection System Based on Machine Learning Algorithms: (SVM and Genetic Algorithm). *Babylonian. Machine Learning*, 2024, 15–29.

Arvindhan, M., Bhatia, M., Sinha, N., & Kumar, T. (2022). Coronavirus Visual Dashboard and Data Repository: COVID-19. In *Applications of Computational Methods in Manufacturing and Product Design: Select Proceedings of IPDIMS 2020* (pp. 269-279). Singapore: Springer Nature Singapore.

Caviglione, L., Comito, C., Guarascio, M., & Manco, G. (2023). Emerging challenges and perspectives in Deep Learning model security: A brief survey. *Systems and Soft Computing*, 5, 200050. DOI: 10.1016/j.sasc.2023.200050

Dhakal, S., Parvez, A., Das, P., Saxena, S., & Memoria, M. (2024). An analysis of AI-driven technologies for enhancing security along the India-Nepal border. In *2024 International Conference on Computing, Sciences and Communications (ICCSC)* (pp. 1-6). IEEE. DOI: 10.1109/ICCSC62048.2024.10830380

Dhanya, K. A., Vajipayajula, S., Srinivasan, K., Tibrewal, A., Kumar, T. S., & Kumar, T. G. (2023). Detection of network attacks using machine learning and deep learning models. *Procedia Computer Science*, 218, 57–66. DOI: 10.1016/j.procs.2022.12.401

Dini, P., Elhanashi, A., Begni, A., Saponara, S., Zheng, Q., & Gasmi, K. (2023). Overview on intrusion detection systems design exploiting machine learning for networking cybersecurity. *Applied Sciences (Basel, Switzerland)*, 13(13), 7507. DOI: 10.3390/app13137507

Dumka, A., Memoria, M., & Ashok, A. (2019). Security and challenges in mobile cloud computing. In *Security Designs for the Cloud.* IoT, and Social Networking. DOI: 10.1002/9781119593171.ch3

Goriparthi, R. G. (2023). AI-Augmented Cybersecurity: Machine Learning for Real-Time Threat Detection. *Revista de Inteligencia Artificial en Medicina*, 14(1), 576–594.

Jaisingh, W., Nanjundan, P., & George, J. P. (2024). Machine Learning in Cyber Threats Intelligent System. In *Artificial Intelligence for Cyber Defense and Smart Policing* (pp. 1–20). Chapman and Hall/CRC. DOI: 10.1201/9781003251781-1

Javed, H., El-Sappagh, S., & Abuhmed, T. (2025). Robustness in deep learning models for medical diagnostics: Security and adversarial challenges towards robust AI applications. *Artificial Intelligence Review*, 58(1), 1–107.

Khan, M., & Ghafoor, L. (2024). Adversarial Machine Learning in the Context of Network Security: Challenges and Solutions. *Journal of Computational Intelligence and Robotics*, 4(1), 51–63.

Kumar, T., & Attri, S. H. (2024). The machine translation systems demystifying the approaches. In *A handbook of computational linguistics: Artificial intelligence in natural language processing* (pp. 160–191). Bentham Science. DOI: 10.2174/9789815238488124020011

Kumar, T., Kumar, P., & Namasudra, S. (2024). User revocation-enabled access control model using identity-based signature in the cloud computing environment. *International Journal of Interactive Multimedia and Artificial Intelligence*, 9(1), 127–136. DOI: 10.9781/ijimai.2024.05.001

Manoharan, A., & Sarker, M. (2023). Revolutionizing Cybersecurity: Unleashing the Power of Artificial Intelligence and Machine Learning for Next-Generation Threat Detection. https://www. doi. org/10.56726/IRJMETS32644

Mohammed, A., Kumar, S., Mu'Azu, H. G., Kumar, R., Shah, P., Memoria, M., Rawat, A., & Gupta, A. (2022). Data Security and Protection: A Mechanism for Managing Data Theft and Cybercrime in Online Platforms of Educational Institutions. *2022 International Conference on Machine Learning, Big Data, Cloud and Parallel Computing, COM-IT-CON 2022*. DOI: 10.1109/COM-IT-CON54601.2022.9850702

Montasari, R., Carroll, F., Macdonald, S., Jahankhani, H., Hosseinian-Far, A., & Daneshkhah, A. (2021). Application of artificial intelligence and machine learning in producing actionable cyber threat intelligence. Digital forensic investigation of internet of things (IoT) devices, 47-64.

Naseer, I. (2021). The efficacy of Deep Learning and Artificial Intelligence Framework in Enhancing Cybersecurity, Challenges and Future Prospects. Innovative Computer Sciences Journal, 7(1).

Nassar, A., & Kamal, M. (2021). Machine Learning and Big Data analytics for Cybersecurity Threat Detection: A Holistic review of techniques and case studies. *Journal of Artificial Intelligence and Machine Learning in Management*, 5(1), 51–63.

Nguyen, T. T., & Reddi, V. J. (2021). Deep reinforcement learning for cyber security. *IEEE Transactions on Neural Networks and Learning Systems*, 34(8), 3779–3795. DOI: 10.1109/TNNLS.2021.3121870 PMID: 34723814

Ozkan-Okay, M., Akin, E., Aslan, Ö., Kosunalp, S., Iliev, T., Stoyanov, I., & Beloev, I. (2024). A comprehensive survey: Evaluating the efficiency of artificial intelligence and machine learning techniques on cyber security solutions. *IEEE Access: Practical Innovations, Open Solutions*, 12, 12229–12256. DOI: 10.1109/ACCESS.2024.3355547

Rawat, G., Kanti, P., Memoria, M., Kumar, R., & Choudhury, T. (2023). Ace of cyber security and it's emerging trends on latest technologies. In 2023 3rd International Conference on Innovative Sustainable Computational Technologies (CISCT) (pp. 1-6). IEEE. DOI: 10.1109/CISCT57197.2023.10351359

Rosenberg, I., Shabtai, A., Elovici, Y., & Rokach, L. (2021). Adversarial machine learning attacks and defense methods in the cyber security domain. *ACM Computing Surveys*, 54(5), 1–36. DOI: 10.1145/3453158

Trim, P. R., & Lee, Y. I. (2022). Combining sociocultural intelligence with Artificial Intelligence to increase organizational cyber security provision through enhanced resilience. *Big Data and Cognitive Computing*, 6(4), 110. DOI: 10.3390/bdcc6040110

Tripathi, P., Ankit, K., Sharma, R., & Kumar, T. (2021). Facial expression recognition through CNN. In 2021 6th International Conference on Communication and Electronics Systems (ICCES) (pp. 1-5). IEEE. DOI: 10.1109/ICCES51350.2021.9488963

Chapter 2
Machine Learning in Cybersecurity: Challenges, Applications, and Future Directions

D. Prabhu
Vel Tech Rangarajan Dr. Sagunthala R&D Institute of Science and Technology, India

P. Aparna
https://orcid.org/0009-0007-7510-2561
RMK College of Engineering and Technology, India

L. Sudha
https://orcid.org/0000-0003-4974-7482
SRM Institute of Science and Technology, India

Siva Subramanian R.
https://orcid.org/0000-0002-7509-9223
RMK College of Engineering and Technology, India

Pandi Kumari M. R.
https://orcid.org/0009-0004-9446-9367
Panimalar Engineering College, India

V. Sathya
Vel Tech Rangarajan Dr. Sagunthala R&D Institute of Science and Technology, India

A. Adaikkammai
RMD Engineering College, India

ABSTRACT

This survey paper explores how machine learning (ML) has been useful in handling modern security issues. In today's dynamic world of cybersecurity threats, conventional means of protection are not sufficient to counter modern day threats. This field introduces new approaches to improve threat identification and mitigation measures. The paper is introduced with an analysis of modern threats in the sphere of cybersecurity and the use of machine learning. Basic concepts of ML and how they can be used in cybersecurity are described to build the necessary background for

DOI: 10.4018/979-8-3693-7758-1.ch002

the next topics. The paper explores topics such as detecting and mitigating advanced attacks using adversarial machine learning and machine learning in cryptography and blockchain. The methods for protecting the privacy of data in ML are discussed to meet the requirements of data protection laws. With this in mind, this systematic review shall provide key insights to enable researchers and practitioners in the development of effective and robust machine learning based cybersecurity solutions.

1. INTRODUCTION

1.1 Overview of the Evolving Cybersecurity Landscape

In the modern world where nearly every business activity is conducted online, cybersecurity has emerged as a major issue due to increasing sophistication of cyber threats (Saloni Khurana, 2017). It is important to understand that the cybersecurity environment is a war between the defenders and invaders, where the latter apply advanced tactics. Although traditional security measures are important here, they do not effectively address the fluidity of threats in cyber-world. Such a rapidly changing environment requires fresh solutions, and machine learning (ML) has become a promising means to improve cybersecurity (Parikh, T. P., & Patel, A. R. 2017).

1.2 Importance of Machine Learning in Addressing Cybersecurity Challenges

AI is a broad field subdivided into many branches which include machine learning that deals with creating algorithms on how a computer can learn and make decisions with the help of data. Indeed, because of these capabilities of pattern identification, outcome prediction, and learning, it is especially suitable in the context of cybersecurity (Das, R., & Morris, T. H. 2017). With the help of ML it is possible to process vast amounts of data and find threats and anomalies and react to attacks immediately; the approach is proactive in nature. Another crucial advantage of utilizing machine learning in the sphere of cybersecurity is flexibility. Unlike conventional rule-based systems, it can learn from initial inputs and the growing threats without the need for reprogramming (Yavanoglu, O., & Aydos, M. 2017). This flexibility is important because the threats in cyberspace evolve from time to time. For example, in the case of ML models, they can identify zero-day exploits, that is, new, previously unknown types of vulnerabilities, by recognizing behavior patterns that differ from the norm.

Overall, the employment of machine learning in cybersecurity transcends multiple levels of processes. In anomaly detection, ML models analyse the current network behavior and alert the users to any change that can be deemed a threat or a breach of security. In malware analysis, classification and identification of malware is achieved using ML techniques, with the knowledge that malware authors are always devising new ways of evading detection (Gupta, B. B., & Sheng, M. 2019). Furthermore, it is stated that ML improves threat intelligence concepts by collecting and analyzing big data from various sources to support information security specialists.

Thus, the use of machine learning in cybersecurity is beneficial, but it has its drawbacks too. The critical challenges that need to be solved are data quality and availability, model interpretability and robustness, and adversarial attacks on ML systems. However, there are certain ethical issues that need to be addressed before ML can be unleashed in the cybersecurity domain, especially with respect to privacy.

1.3 Structure and Scope of the Survey Paper

This survey paper seeks to give an overview of the use of machine learning in cybersecurity. It covers the existing cybersecurity environment, basic concepts regarding ML approaches that can be used in cybersecurity applications, and different deployment of ML in threat identification and prevention. Therefore, by comparing case studies and the future development of machine learning in cybersecurity, this paper aims to present applicable uses and their related prospects and risks both to researchers and practitioners in the field.

2. THE EVOLVING CYBERSECURITY LANDSCAPE: CHALLENGES AND OPPORTUNITIES

2.1 Current Cybersecurity Threats and Vulnerabilities

The world of cybersecurity is ever evolving with new threats and risks that are out of place presenting issues to traditional security measures. It is important to understand that the threats in the cyber world today are far more advanced and diverse than they used to be. These are ransomware that locks the victim's data until the attacker is paid a certain sum of money, phishing where the enemy tries to fool a victim into surrendering some information, and Advanced Persistent Threat (APT) that is usually a long and focused attack usually associated with state-sponsored organizations. Due to the fact that there are always unpatched software and hardware as well as misconfigured devices, the system offers points of attack. An ever-increasing variety of connected devices, and especially the IoT ones which are often not built with strong security in mind, have prolonged the attack vectors, thus making the networks more vulnerable to threats (Aslan et al 2023). Figure 1 shows the challenges and opportunities evolving in cybersecurity landscape.

Figure 1. The evolving cybersecurity landscape: Challenges and opportunities

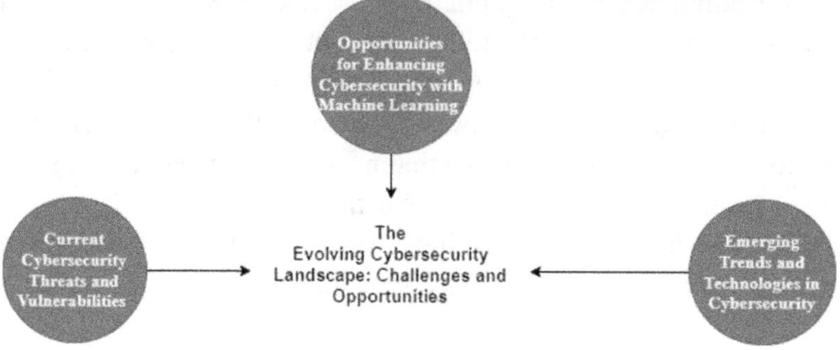

2.2 Emerging Trends and Technologies in Cybersecurity

As a result of the above threats, new trends and technologies are progressively developing in the field of cybersecurity. Zero Trust Architecture used on the 'never trust, always verify' model is becoming popular, focusing on tight identity checks for all users and devices. Cybersecurity is more effective with AI and ML currently being implemented to be more predictive and adaptive to the threats. Blockchain solutions are being researched for application in increasing the credibility of data and improving transaction security. Also, there is an increasing interest in the automation of cybersecurity operations as people are a weak link and investigations take too much time. Still, the threats are evolving, and so the attackers use AI for creating deepfakes or automating attacks and other unlawful intentions.

2.3 Opportunities for Enhancing Cybersecurity With Machine Learning

Machine learning is one of the most promising tools that can be helpful in improving cybersecurity and tackling its major issues. The trained machine learning algorithms can then handle a large data set to help flag out areas that require scrutiny in the event of a cyber threat. This capability is especially beneficial in identifying new types of threats that have not been discovered yet, such as zero-day exploits.

In the anomaly detection method, the erasures of the typical behavior by the use of ML can allow organizations to identify the suspect behavior of an Entity faster than normal in comparison to the identification of the same by anti-virus programs. In malware analysis, it is possible to use ML models to, respectively, classify and identify new strains of the virus and their modifications based on the machine learning algorithm that would continually develop from the prior example while malware writers perform the same. In addition, it can increase threat intelligence since it integrates data from different sources to give insights that can act as predictors of threat occurrences.

Besides, the use of machine learning also finds its use in other security aspects such as intrusion detection, frauds, and endpoint security (Sreelakshmi et al 2024). This makes use of ML models a flexible approach to creating defense as it has the potential of adapting to new threats as they arise. However, the consideration of ML in cybersecurity also has its challenges some of them are data quality issue, interpretability of the model and adversarial attacks on the integrated ML systems. Solving these issues remains to be vital for enhancing the ability of utilizing ML for enhancing cybersecurity. In general, applying machine learning to cybersecurity will help to design better and more effective security measures for the growing field of machine interactions.

3. MACHINE LEARNING FUNDAMENTALS FOR CYBERSECURITY APPLICATIONS

3.1 Introduction to Machine Learning Concepts and Techniques

Machine learning (ML) is an important subfield of artificial intelligence that is characterized by the ability to learn from data and make decisions (Maithili et al 2024). Unlike typical programming where instructions are coded and executed, the ML algorithms learn from the given data to generate an outcome on their own. Some of the most common techniques are classification, regression, clustering, and feature reduction. All these techniques can be applied to numerical data, categorical data and even text data and as such they are useful tools in the cybersecurity field. Figure 2 shows the machine learning fundamentals for cybersecurity applications.

Figure 2. Machine learning fundamentals for cybersecurity applications

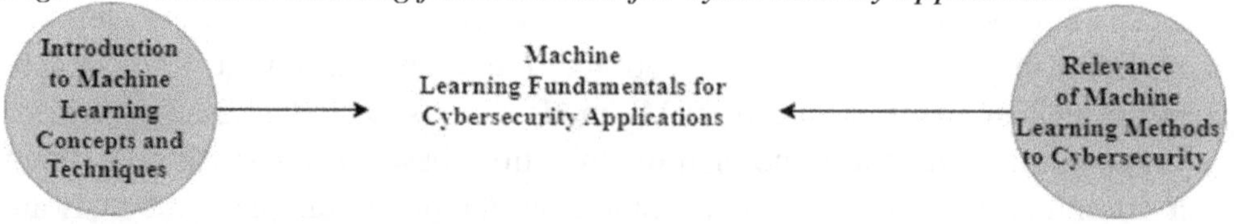

3.2 Supervised, Unsupervised, and Reinforcement Learning

ML can be categorized into three main types: kinds include supervised learning, unsupervised learning, and reinforcement learning (Nithya et al 2023).

Supervised Learning: This approach entails feeding the network a set of training data for which the output is already known. Some of the examples of supervised learning problems are Classification (like identifying whether an email is spam or not) and Regression (like estimating the time it will take to fix an incident). The applications of supervised learning in cybersecurity include situations where the model is trained to distinguish, for instance, between a genuine virus and harmless software (Saravanan et al 2023).

Unsupervised Learning: On the other hand, in unsupervised learning, the input data are not labeled. It is aimed at revealing the structures or regularities of some certain data. Examples of its use include clustering (for example, grouping similar network activity) and anomaly detection (detection of behavior that differs from a normative mode). Unsupervised learning on the other hand comes in handy for identifying new threats, or any other activity that is deemed to be out of the norm, and the model has no prior information about it being a threat.

Reinforcement Learning: This type of ML uses models' interaction with an environment and learning to make decisions based on the received rewards or penalties. Reinforcement learning is ideal in conditions where there is a lot of change and the model is expected to learn and get better over time. Finally, in cybersecurity, reinforcement learning can be used for automated response to incidents which allow the system to improve the strategies of addressing threats with time (Sivamayil et al 2023).

3.3 Relevance of Machine Learning Methods to Cybersecurity

The use of ML in cybersecurity is based on the fact that it enhances the identification and analysis of large amounts of data and is multidisciplinary. Introduction of ML in the security systems can help recognize patterns of any abnormalities that are an indication of a potential threat. For instance, supervised learning is used to learn from existing known samples of malware and identify similar samples while unsupervised is used to analyse behavioral characteristics of new unknown malwares. The ability of reinforcement learning is to improve current mechanisms of automating defence and become capable of preventing new types of attack and respond flexibly (Bharadiya, J. 2023).

ML also enriches threat intelligence through the integration of data from various sources and generating a broader picture of threats. This capability is vital in anticipating and averting cybercrimes. Besides, while developing Al techniques, the ML models can be updated over time, whereby new information is readily incorporated to counter the evolving threats. However, integrating ML in cybersecurity also has its own problems that include lack of quality data for training the ML, the interpretability of the models and attacks aimed at deceiving the ML. Overcoming these issues is crucial for obtaining the best results from ML in the sphere of cybersecurity.

In summary, machine learning presents robust opportunities in improving cybersecurity, enabling dynamic and predictive measures against constantly emerging threats.

4. ANOMALY DETECTION AND THREAT INTELLIGENCE WITH MACHINE LEARNING

4.1 Machine Learning Approaches for Anomaly Detection

Anomaly detection in cybersecurity mainly helps detect a pattern that differs from a common baseline, and this generally contributes to the identification of threats and malicious activities (Aruna Bajpai et al 2024). When it comes to anomaly detection, the ML algorithms provide multiple options, which help to increase the efficiency of identifying new and elaborate threats. Common ML techniques for anomaly detection include:

Statistical Methods: These methods include setting up a normal baseline and raising alerts in case of abnormal behavior. Examples include Gaussian Mixture Models (GMM) and z-score analysis.

Clustering Algorithms: The grouping of similar data points is done with the help of unsupervised learning algorithms such as k-means, DBSCAN, and hierarchical clustering. Outliers are defined as points that do not belong to any cluster or are poorly matched with some of them.

Neural Networks: Autoencoders and recurrent neural networks (RNNs) are employed to learn a compressed representation of normal data. Anomalies are observed when many errors occur during the reconstruction and the patterns are unfamiliar.

Isolation Forests: This technique works on the basis of highlighting outliers rather than working on regular data samples. This covers the observations by randomly partitioning the data and the length of the paths in the trees as its measure of isolation with lower path length as anomalies. Figure 3 shows the anomaly detection and threat intelligence with machine learning.

Figure 3. Anomaly detection and threat intelligence with machine learning

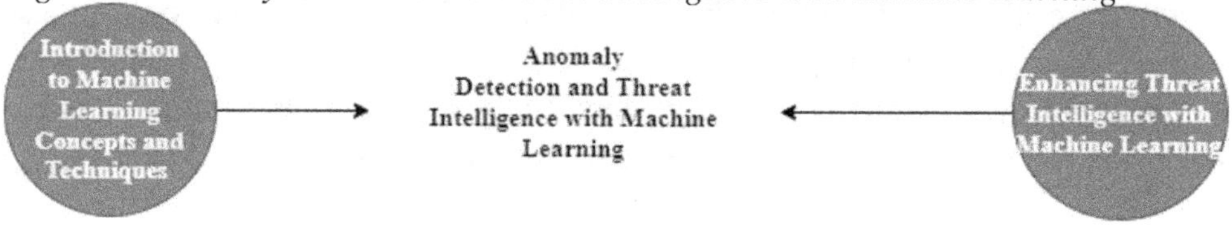

4.2 Enhancing Threat Intelligence with Machine Learning

Threat intelligence is the process of collecting and analyzing data that is in regard to possible threats to prevent the attacks. Threat intelligence is most benefited by using machine learning that automates data analysis and reveals patterns in the data. Key ML applications in threat intelligence include:

Data Correlation: Machine Learning algorithms can easily integrate the data from different sources such as logs from the network, data from the endpoints and threat intelligence feeds.

Predictive Analysis: The use of ML models can be used to prevent future threats because the information acquired in the present can be used to identify trends that may lead to threats in the future. It also gives the organizations the opportunity to detect even potential risks which can be dealt with before arising (Anita et al 2024).

Natural Language Processing (NLP): AI in NLP can handle large volumes of unstructured data from social media platforms, forums, and other web markets to detect new threats and threats actors.

These examples show the potential of using ML-based anomaly detection and threat intelligence in achieving enhanced endpoint security in organizations and improving the way threats are detected and acted upon. Using ML in cybersecurity systems increases the effectiveness of the systems of protection adaptability to handle the changing threats. Of course, this requires the constant retraining of the models with a range of new parameters to keep their effectiveness levels high in relation to newly emerged threats.

5. MALWARE ANALYSIS AND CLASSIFICATION USING MACHINE LEARNING TECHNIQUES

5.1 Machine Learning Methods for Malware Detection

Malware detection is one of the important purposes of cybersecurity, its goal being to detect malicious software and prevent its further use (Okada, S et al 2021). The technique of using artificial intelligence has improved the identification of malware by automating the process. Common ML methods for malware detection include

Signature-Based Detection: Also known as the signature-based method where patterns of well-known viruses are detected. ML improves this in one aspect by detecting pattern similarities of known malware (Priyanshu Anjney et al 2023).
Behavioral Analysis: Machine Learning models used to analyse the behaviour of the software in order to find out any insecure activities that had been performed. HMM and LSTM are among the techniques employed to model & recognize moving patterns that are specific to malware.
Static Analysis: This entails a process of examining the code of a given program without the actual running of the program. In ML classifiers such as Random Forest, Support Vector Machines (SVM) binaries can be classified using features from the code.
Dynamic Analysis: More of an analytical tool since it helps observe the behavior of software in a controlled environment. Thus, at runtime, ML models can analyse system calls, network traffic, and other operational activities to identify malware.

5.2 Techniques for Malware Classification

Malware classification involves grouping the detected malware into families depending on their codes, behaviors, or both. Effective ML techniques for malware classification include:

Feature Extraction and Engineering: There is a need to select the appropriate features from the actual code of the malware or its output. Examples of such methods include the use of opcode frequency analysis and API call sequences.
Clustering Algorithms: Supervised learning methods such as k- means or hierarchical clustering, cluster the similar malware samples. These clusters can show new malware families or new variants of previously known families.
Deep Learning Models: CNNs and RNNs are used for automatic extraction of the features from raw data and for the detection of the malware. They are mostly useful in cases that require the detection of slight resemblances and similarities.
Ensemble Methods: Specifically, the use of multiple ML models in classification to enhance the accuracy of the outcomes achieved. Methods such as stacking and boosting combine the strengths of each model to improve overall results.

6. SECURING NETWORKS AND IOT SYSTEMS WITH MACHINE LEARNING

6.1 Challenges in Securing Networks and IoT Systems

Protecting networks or IoT is difficult due to the complexity of the networks as well as the number of devices that are connected to the internet. Key challenges include:

Scalability: Due to the high number of devices and an increasing amount of data on the whole network, its management and the protection of all the network components become more rather difficult.
Heterogeneity: Networks and IoT systems include a large number of devices, and these devices are used differently, have different modes of functioning, mechanisms of communication, and security measures.
Resource Constraints: The IoT devices are often resource limited with restricted computational and memory capabilities for running breakthrough security features.
Vulnerability to Attacks: IoT devices are designed without security and thus can easily be attacked by botnets such as (Mirai), that can be employed to launch Distributed Denial of Service attacks on networks.
Privacy Concerns: As a result of the high usage of IoT devices, the privacy issue emerges because these devices track and collect information about people.

6.2 Machine Learning Solutions for Network Security

Machine learning (ML) offers powerful tools for enhancing network protection as it deals with threat detection, response, and neutralization automatically (A. Kiran et al 2023). Key ML applications in network security include:

Intrusion Detection Systems (IDS): These ML models can be employed to monitor for abnormalities in the network traffic thus indicating intrusions. Techniques such as anomaly detection, clustering, and classification are used in the identification of suspicious activities.
Network Traffic Analysis: Some of the above detectable malicious behaviors include data exfiltration, port scanning, DDoS, and other related behaviors analyzed through network traffic by the applied ML algorithms.
Behavioral Analysis: This means that by presenting users and devices to normal traffic, ML can find anomalous traffic that may be signs of compromised accounts or devices.
Automated Threat Response: ML-driven systems are capable of responding to the detected threats by containing the compromised devices, blocking the malicious traffic, and notifying the admin (Subaira, A. S et al 2017).

6.3 Applications in IoT Security

Machine learning strengthens IoT security since it offers solutions that are flexible, dynamic, and preventive (Ponmalar et al 2024). Key applications and case studies include:

Smart Home Security: IoT devices in smart homes can be observed using the help of ML algorithms to identify countless unusual patterns.
Industrial IoT (IIoT) Security: The technology in the industry examines the details from sensors and traffic in networks to identify and prevent risks.
Healthcare IoT Security: IoT devices present in the healthcare settings like patient monitors and wearable health trackers are safeguarded with the help of ML models that identify intrusive device operations or unauthorized access attempts. Medtronic uses ML to protect its connected medical devices from cyber risks.
Autonomous Vehicles: It is applied in ensuring the security of the communication lines of the self-driven cars, to ensure that the data transmitted between these cars and the infrastructure is genuine and has not been tampered with. For instance, Tesla uses ML to improve the safety of its self-driving car systems.

Through these applications, they show how it is possible to exploit the potential of ML in improving the security of the large-scale, diverse, and often resource-constrained networks and IoT systems. In other words, ML supports the safeguarding of these core structures against ever-emerging cybersecurity threats by establishing real-time, portable, and progressive security measures. Due to the constant increase in demand and availability of more interconnected devices, the continuous development of new and improved algorithms in ML will be critical in enhancing security systems.

7. MACHINE LEARNING FOR INSIDER THREAT DETECTION AND PREVENTION

7.1 Identifying Insider Threats Using Machine Learning

Insider threats are potential risks in organizations as it entails wrongful acts or even negligence on the part of an authorized personnel. ML is central to the insider threat detection process since it entails the analysis of behavioral patterns, activity logs and all forms of footprint. Key ML techniques for insider threat detection include:

Behavioral Analytics: They also look into the login times of the users, their file access patterns, and their network activity to build a baseline for each user's behaviors. Any access beyond these baselines, for instance, accessing restricted information or operations during off hours, can signal insider threats.

User Entity Behavior Analytics (UEBA): UEBA solutions employ ML techniques in analyzing different data streams originally derived from user activities, endpoints, and network traffics to identify activities that are suggestive of insider threats. These platforms use algorithms to search for correlations that may depict potential fraud or accounts under fraudsters' control.

Natural Language Processing (NLP): Analyzing written text, such as e-mails and chat histories, NLP methods look for conversations that may indicate collusion or data leakage (Pajila, P. B et al 2023).

Graph Analytics: By processing relationship and interaction between users, devices, and data in an organization, ML algorithms can detect unfamiliar links or access patterns of insiders.

7.2 Techniques for Preventing Insider Attacks

To prevent insider attacks there is need to employ technical measures, policies, and train employees. ML enhances prevention efforts by:

Continuous Monitoring: ML-driven systems are always on to track the users' activities and behaviors in real-time as a result, it is easy to notice any malicious activities and prevent them before they occur.

Privileged Access Management: This is due to the capability of the ML models in analyzing the access patterns to determine if there has been over-utilization of the privileged accounts with intent of insider abuses, thus enforcing the principle of least privilege.

Behavioral Biometrics: Thus, with the help of ML algorithms, biometric data, typing patterns, or mouse movements, to identify the user and determine impersonation or unauthorized access.

Using ML insights, organizations can enhance the protection of their systems against inside attackers, while at the same time mitigating false positives or the adverse consequences of such actions upon the firm's data and operations. Future advancements in ML prove to be effective in improving insider threat identification and prevention strategies because of constant growth in threats experienced in organizations.

8. ADVERSARIAL MACHINE LEARNING: DEFENDING AGAINST ADVERSARIAL ATTACKS

8.1 Overview of Adversarial Machine Learning

Adversarial machine learning (ML) is a set of techniques in which the actors deliberately alter the inputs so that the ML models misclassify them or act in a manner that is unpredictable. These attacks target weaknesses in the ML algorithm that stem from the model's ability to use statistical tendencies instead of understanding or being contextually aware of the situation. Adversarial attacks can take various forms, including:

Evasion Attacks: In evasion attacks, adversaries manipulate input data like images and text by introducing slight changes that are not easily noticeable but make the model misclassify the input. For instance, if you introduced some minimal noise on the image then the image classifier will classify the cat as a dog (Venketbabu et al 2024).

Poisoning Attacks: Hence poisoning attacks focus on changing the training dataset introducing adversarial examples. A part of the training data can be used to control the wrong classification or behavior during model deployment by the adversaries.

Model Inversion: This attack attempts to retrieve information on the training set or the parameters of a model by feeding the model with a particular input and observing the output.

This is especially true for such critical areas as autonomous vehicles, diagnostics, and financial management where the accuracy and reliability of the ML predictions are critical.

8.2 Strategies for Defending Against Adversarial Attacks

Guarding against adversarial attacks is a crucial one that involves applying superior solutions that enhance security from antagonistic interference with ML models. Effective defense strategies include:

Adversarial Training: This strategy involves addition of samples produced by the adversary in the training set from which the training is conducted. During training, the model is also trained with adversarial inputs in such a manner that the model will be able to identify these adversarial inputs as invalid and remove them.

Ensemble Methods: When combining models ensemble or using different models and getting their average or a combination of the outcomes then it provides better security from adversarial attacks. It becomes difficult for the adversaries to somehow influence input so that several different models that should diverge will produce the same output.

Feature Squeezing: This reduces the quality of the input data and hence challenges the adversaries to generate the correct perturbations. The quantization of input features reduces the model's sensitivity to changes that an attacker may launch.

Defensive Distillation: In defensive distillation, the model is trained on 'weaker' forms of the training data. This process smooths the decision boundaries of the model, and therefore the model's decision is less likely to be greatly affected by small changes introduced by would-be attackers.

Robust Optimization: One can also feed into the training process techniques that directly target the reduction of adversarial attacks such as the aforementioned adversarial robustness. This can be achieved by changing the objective function or certain parts of the regularization terms to prefer robustness to the precision.

The use of these defense strategies requires an appropriate evaluation of threats and the specific vulnerabilities of the certain ML model that is used. It is also important to perform periodic inspections and awareness for the adversarial attack against the steadiness and security of the ML systems in the adversarial environment.

By these means, adversarial machine learning threat is kept under control, and the dependability of the ML-based applications in critical fields is enhanced. Moreover, it becomes crucial to investigate new and better approaches for defending adversarial ML since threats are constantly evolving and pose a danger to the functioning of ML systems and models on them.

9. MACHINE LEARNING FOR CRYPTOGRAPHY AND BLOCKCHAIN SECURITY

9.1 Applications of Machine Learning in Cryptography

Machine learning (ML) algorithms are widely used in enhancing various aspects of cryptography because it aims at enhancing cryptography in terms of security, speed, and resistance to attacks. Key applications of ML in cryptography include:

Key Generation and Management: In the field of cryptography, the methods of ML assist in analyzing patterns of the cryptographic keys and the users that can enhance the methodologies of the key generation. It is proposed that ML can be helpful in offsetting the weaknesses or biases of the key generation processes and thus, make the keys more secure and random in general.

Anomaly Detection: It allows the ML models to detect and monitor any suspicious activities in the cryptographic systems and the transactions. For instance, the anomaly detection methods can identify reduction in the encryption and decryption rates suggesting an attack or weakness.

Cryptanalysis: The application of the ideas and methodology of machine learning in solving cryptanalysis problems allows automating the decryption of cryptographic algorithms and protocols. This is because the ML algorithms are capable of analyzing ciphertexts and plaintexts to determine vulnerabilities that can be exploited by attackers.

Quantum Cryptography: It is applied in creating new post quantum cryptographic algorithms and protocols. Due to the development of quantum computing, the construction and analysis of the cryptographic systems that are resistant to hacking by a quantum computer can be facilitated by ML (Yamini, B et al 2024).

9.2 Enhancing Blockchain Security with Machine Learning

Blockchain technology, known for its decentralized and tamper-resistant nature, can benefit from ML in several ways to enhance security:

Anomaly Detection in Transactions: For instance, it is possible to use the specific types of ML algorithms and analyse the patterns of the transaction activities noticing the attempts at the unauthorized actions and classifying them as fraudulent or malicious within the framework of the blockchain network. Such includes an effort to establish whether there are high or low activity levels, or any form of deviation in the transactional activity or any wallet address.

Smart Contract Security: By employing the use of ML, one is capable of analyzing the execution of smart contracts on the blockchains to identify exploitable vulnerabilities. By leveraging the data collected from ML models, it is possible to identify the specific code and paths within the smart contracts to gain the entry or manipulate the system without permission.

Network Security: Network traffic inside blockchains can be supervised and analyzed by ML techniques to identify and counter DDoS attacks, Sybil attacks and other network-borne threats. As for the typical structure of ML models, there should be easy ways to detect distorted network behaviors and prevent occurrences that could threaten the stability of the blockchain network.

Privacy-Preserving Techniques: The ML algorithms can be used to create the ways to preserve the privacy of the transactions made using blockchain while ensuring that the block chain ledger remains accurate and transparent.

These examples show the increased collaboration between machine learning and cryptography/blockchain security, how the application of the former increases the immunity of the latter against new types of threats and attacks. Thus, it can be concluded that further research and development of ML-driven solutions are critically important for the enhancement of cryptographic protocols' and blockchain-based technologies' security and scalability for the digital era.

10. PRIVACY-PRESERVING MACHINE LEARNING IN CYBERSECURITY

10.1 Importance of Privacy in Machine Learning Applications

Data privacy is an essential aspect in machine learning, especially in security related applications for purposes of analyzing and protecting personal information, financial details or business data. Preserving privacy prevents situations where people and businesses can freely incorporate machine learning technologies while safeguarding their information from being accessed or used by others maliciously. Key reasons why privacy is crucial in machine learning applications include:

Data Protection: In practice, it is common for machine learning models to process big data during the training or testing phases. Maintenance of the confidentiality about such data ensures that privacy of everyone's information is well-protected, and it cannot in one way or the other be accessed by a hacker or different other malicious use.

Legal and Compliance Requirements: Almost every country has particular rules about ML. The General Data Protection Regulation (GDPR) in Europe, or the Health Insurance Portability and Accountability Act (HIPAA) in America, that mandate data protection. These laws should be followed to the letter to ensure that the legal requirements are meet and penalties avoided.

Trust and User Confidence: This is developed based on the fact that by protecting the privacy of the individuals, people are willing to forward their data for genuine reasons such as being protected from insecurity among others or to enhance production of services.

10.2 Techniques for Privacy-Preserving Machine Learning

Several techniques and approaches are employed to preserve privacy while leveraging the power of machine learning:

Differential Privacy: This can be done through a technique known as differential privacy which determines the privacy level of a given system or algorithm. It ensures that the elimination or inclusion of the individual data does not have a huge impact on the data analysis to avoid invasion of privacy.

Homomorphic Encryption: Homomorphic encryption allows some computations to be done on the data while it is still encrypted. This technique enables the data to be encrypted while processing, and thus, the data remains unseen by unauthorized persons.

Secure Multiparty Computation (MPC): MPC enables different parties to perform a function on their input's sum without disclosing the inputs to other parties. Each party owns their data and only the outcome of the computation is shared without infringing on privacy.

Federated Learning: Federated learning ensures that it is possible for different parties to train a model in machine learning without necessarily sharing their datasets. Each party updates the model on their local data and only the model parameters, not the raw data, are transferred from one party to another.

Privacy-Preserving Data Mining: Preprocessing methods include k-anonymity, l-diversity, and t-closeness to mask datasets before analysis. Such methods make it impossible to identify individual records from a group making the results very valuable while maintaining anonymity.

10.3 Real-World Applications and Implementations

Federated Learning: google for instance applies federated learning to build predictive models from data stored on different mobile devices without sharing the data to centralized servers. This approach will increase service accuracy while at the same time providing privacy when aligning the services to an individual's preferences.

Healthcare Analytics: Privacy-preserving strategies are used in the health care industry to analyse patients' information in order to meet HIPAA requirements honestly. Differential privacy and secure computation enable medical research and treatment optimization without violating the privacy of the patients.

Financial Services: Homomorphic encryption and MPC allow banks, and other financial organizations analyse the transaction data and identify fraud while preserving customer data privacy.

Telecommunications: Telecom companies use federated learning to enhance the network and its usability without compromising the individual subscriber's privacy.

These examples demonstrate usefulness and necessity of privacy-preserving machine learning methods in security science and in other fields. In this way, one can combine the benefits of machine learning utilization with the protection of the info and compliance with the rules for the organizations. There must be continuous research and development of privacy-enhancing technologies since the privacy threats are ever-evolving in the world that is rapidly moving toward being data-driven.

11. FUTURE TRENDS AND RESEARCH DIRECTIONS IN MACHINE LEARNING FOR CYBERSECURITY

11.1 Emerging Trends in Machine Learning and Cybersecurity

Currently, new trends are emerging in the ML Cybersecurity space, which indicate the potential for new developments in the near future to enhance the ways organizations can detect, prevent, and respond to cyber threats. Key emerging trends include:

Deep Learning for Cyber Defense: Artificial intelligence approaches like convolutional neural networks and recurrent neural networks are more frequently used in cybersecurity problems involving; malware detection, intrusion detection and anomaly detection. These models are capable of learning ultra-complex patterns and behaviors from large data sets and improve the detection rate and false positive containment[Subramanian, R. S et al 2024].

Explainable AI (XAI): Indeed, as more and more models based on machine learning are in use in cybersecurity solutions, the more important is the problem of interpretability of results and decision-making. XAI techniques focus on explaining the actions of ML models, where and why a given threat was detected or classified, which builds more trust and empowers security analysts to make better decisions.

Adversarial Machine Learning Defense: Currently, adversarial attacks of the ML models are pervasive, so, there is a great need for effective defense mechanisms. The study of adversarial ML defense majorly involves providing methods including adversarial training, ensemble strategies, or adversarial detection to improve the robustness of the developed ML models against aggressive attacks.

11.2 Potential Future Applications and Innovations

Looking ahead, several promising applications and innovations are expected to shape the future of ML in cybersecurity:

Autonomous Threat Response: ML systems able to independently identify, evaluate, and counter cyber threats in real-time without external humans' interference. These systems have the potential to learn and grow with new threats and different attack vectors, thus making the defense more effective.

Privacy-Preserving Machine Learning: The further development of approaches such as federated learning, differential privacy, and secure multiparty computation will allow for the use of ML to analyse data and generate insights while still respecting participants' privacy rights and data protection legislation.

AI-Driven Security Orchestration: The integration of ML into SOAR platforms to assist in the incident response processes, eliminating redundancies in tasks and prioritizing the alerts based on risk assessment and situation analysis.

11.3 Research Opportunities and Open Challenges

Despite the rapid progress, several research opportunities and challenges remain in the field of ML for cybersecurity:

Data Poisoning and Evasion Attacks: Creating viable countermeasures to high-level attacks that target the integrity of the ML models via data poisoning or generating adversarial samples.
Scalability and Resource Efficiency: Solving for the issues of scalability of implementing the ML solutions into large networks and IoT that are associated with the proper utilization of computational resources and the avoidance of high latencies.
Interpretable and Explainable AI: Improve methods on how to explain the model results without impacting the predictive power and to increase trust and utilization of the ML models for crucial cybersecurity applications.
Integration with Human Expertise: Improving the interaction between the ML models and subject matter experts and taking advantage of business context knowledge in detection and countermeasures.

Conclusively, it is evident that machine learning in cybersecurity will shape the future of organizations' ability to deal with cyber threats effectively. Exploring those directions helps to incorporate all the potential of ML into the cybersecurity environment, meet further research questions, and protect digital assets and people's privacy from various threats.

12. CONCLUSION

In conclusion, ML has become one of the key enablers that are aiding the improvement of cybersecurity in different fields. In this survey paper, various challenges, including anomaly detection, malware analysis, insider threats and blockchain security, were discussed throughout exploring how ML solves them. Due to the great capacity of analyzing big data and the recognition of even minimal indicators that can characterize a cyber threat, the response time is greatly decreased, and the consequences of the attacks are minimized. With the help of the techniques such as deep learning, the malware detection and the intrusion detection has become more accurate and automated based on the behavioral and statistical analysis of activities. Furthermore, ML remains a vital component in enhancing privacy preservation with the aim of ensuring that privacy is protected, and data is useful for analysis. Approaches like federated learning and differential privacy suggest potential ways of achieving utility and privacy in cybersecurity. Moreover, the prospects of ML in cybersecurity will entail further development of adversarial ML defenses, autonomous threat response systems, and AI-driven security orchestration. These innovations will enable organisations to respond effectively to complex new cyber threats as and when they are being launched thus reducing risks posed by such threats and improving overall organisational security posture. Based on strategy, more focused research and development of strong models, increase integration with human decisions and optimization of explainable AI will be important. Also, the collaboration of technological organizations with universities and governmental departments can help to enhance the usage of ML-based cybersecurity while respecting legislation and ethical norms and values. To sum up, although leveraging ML results in incredible potential for enhancing cybersecurity measures, constant advancements, cooperation, and safety awareness are pivotal to outcompete threat actors amid ever-evolving threats. Through the effective use of ML, it is possible to save the assets of an organization, protect users from threats, and build a good digital environment.

REFERENCES

Anita, M., Ambhika, C., & Anish, T. P. (2024). Exploring the Landscape of Artificial Intelligence in Healthcare Applications. In AI Healthcare Applications and Security, Ethical, and Legal Considerations (pp. 29-48). IGI Global.

Anjney, P., Pandey, J. K., & Puttam, V. S. R., Ompuri, O., &. Navya, V.K. (2023). Malware detection using machine learning. *International Journal of Emerging Technologies and Innovative Research, 10*(4), 1-4, www.jetir.org

Okada, S., Fujimoto, M., Matsuda, W., & Mitsunaga, T. (2021). Malware Detection Method using Tree-based Machine Learning Algorithms. In *2021 IEEE International Conference on Computing (ICOCO)*. IEEE.

Aslan, Ö., Aktuğ, S. S., Ozkan-Okay, M., Yilmaz, A. A., & Akin, E. (2023). A comprehensive review of cyber security vulnerabilities, threats, attacks, and solutions. *Electronics (Basel)*, 12(6), 1333. DOI: 10.3390/electronics12061333

Bajpai, A., Khule, S., Sharma, V. P., Sharma, Y., & Dubey, G. (2024). Real-time Anomaly Detection in Big Data Streams: Machine Learning Approaches and Performance Evaluation. *International Journal of Intelligent Systems and Applications in Engineering*, 12(21), 915–924.

Bharadiya, J. (2023). Machine learning in cybersecurity: Techniques and challenges. *European Journal of Technology*, 7(2), 1–14. DOI: 10.47672/ejt.1486

Das, R., & Morris, T. H. (2017). Machine learning and cyber security. In *2017 International Conference on Computer, Electrical & Communication Engineering (ICCECE)* (pp. 1-7). IEEE.

Gupta, B. B., & Sheng, M. (2019). *Machine Learning for Computer and Cyber Security* (Press, C. R. C., Ed.). Preface. DOI: 10.1201/9780429504044

Khurana, S. (2017). A Review Paper on Cyber Security, *International Journal Of Engineering Research & Technology, 5*(23).

Kiran, A., Prakash, S. W., Kumar, B. A., Likhitha, T, Sameeratmaja, & Charan, U. S. S. R. (2023), Intrusion Detection System Using Machine Learning. In *2023 International Conference on Computer Communication and Informatics (ICCCI)*, Coimbatore, India.

Maithili, K., Ponmalar, A., Yamini, B., Karthikeyan, M., Anish, T. P., Maheswari, B., & Subramanian, R. S. (2024). Advances in AI and Machine Learning for Healthcare Informatics. In *Machine Learning and Generative AI in Smart Healthcare* (pp. 1-22). IGI Global. DOI: 10.4018/979-8-3693-3719-6.ch001

Nithya, T., Kumar, V. N., Gayathri, S., Deepa, S., Varun, C. M., & Subramanian, R. S. (2023). A comprehensive survey of machine learning: Advancements, applications, and challenges. In *2023 Second International Conference on Augmented Intelligence and Sustainable Systems (ICAISS)* (pp. 354-361). DOI: 10.1109/ICAISS58487.2023.10250547

Pajila, P. B., Sudha, K., Selvi, D. K., Kumar, V. N., Gayathri, S., & Subramanian, R. S. (2023). A Survey on Natural Language Processing and its Applications. In *2023 4th International Conference on Electronics and Sustainable Communication Systems* (ICESC) (pp. 996-1001).

Parikh, T. P., & Patel, A. R. (2017). Cyber security: Study on attack, threat, vulnerability. *Int. J. Res. Mod. Eng. Emerg. Technol*, 5, 1–7.

Ponmalar, A., Vijayakumar, K., Lakshmipriya, C., Karthikeyan, M., & PJ, B. P. (2024). Meta-Heuristics and Machine Learning Applications in Complex Systems. In *Metaheuristic and Machine Learning Optimization Strategies for Complex Systems* (pp. 257-275). IGI Global.

Saravanan, K., Prakash, R. B., Balakrishnan, C., Kumar, G. V. P., Subramanian, R. S., & Anita, M. (2023). Support Vector Machines: Unveiling the Power and Versatility of SVMs in Modern Machine Learning. In *2023 3rd International Conference on Innovative Mechanisms for Industry Applications(ICIMIA)* (pp. 680-687).

Sivamayil, K., Rajasekar, E., Aljafari, B., Nikolovski, S., Vairavasundaram, S., & Vairavasundaram, I. (2023). A systematic study on reinforcement learning based applications. *Energies*, 16(3), 1512. DOI: 10.3390/en16031512

Sreelakshmi, S., Babu, A. A., Lakshmipriya, C., Gracious, L. A., Nalini, M., & Subramanian, R. S. (2024). Enhancing Intrusion Detection Systems with Machine Learning. In *2024 2nd International Conference on Self Sustainable Artificial Intelligence Systems (ICSSAS)* (pp. 557-564). DOI: 10.1109/ICSSAS64001.2024.10760341

Subaira, A. S., & Anitha, P. (2014). Efficient classification mechanism for network intrusion detection system based on data mining techniques: a survey. In *2014 IEEE 8th International Conference on Intelligent Systems and Control (ISCO)* (pp. 274-280). DOI: 10.1109/ISCO.2014.7103959

Subramanian, R. S., Yamini, B., Sudha, K., & Sivakumar, S. (2024). Ensemble-based deep learning techniques for customer churn prediction model. *Kybernetes*. Advance online publication. DOI: 10.1108/K-08-2023-1516

Venketbabu, T., Aswathy, M. P., Sangeetha, J., Anish, T. P., Nalini, M., & Subramanian, R. S. (2024). Revolutionizing Image Processing: Innovations Impacts and Future Trends. In *2024 2nd International Conference on Self Sustainable Artificial Intelligence Systems (ICSSAS)* (pp. 901-907).

Yamini, B., Nithyanandhan, R., Sudha, K., Nithya, T., Vijayakumar, K., & Subramanian, R. S. (2024). Maximizing the Revolutionary Potential of Quantum Computing: Challenges, Opportunities, and Future Directions. In *2024 10th International Conference on Communication and Signal Processing (ICCSP)* (pp. 756-761).

Yavanoglu, O., & Aydos, M. (2017). A review on cyber security datasets for machine learning algorithms. In *2017 IEEE international conference on big data (big data)* (pp. 2186-2193).

Chapter 3
Intrusion Detection System:
Datasets, Threats, and Taxonomy

Prashant Pranav
https://orcid.org/0009-0009-9654-1525
Birla Institute of Technology, India

Anushkaa Prabhat
https://orcid.org/0009-0005-5115-1313
Birla Institute of Technology, India

Deepshikha Kumari
https://orcid.org/0009-0009-9654-1525
Birla Institute of Technology, India

Sandip Dutta
https://orcid.org/0000-0003-2206-2125
Birla Institute of Technology, India

ABSTRACT

This chapter provides an inclusive overview of Intrusion Detection System (IDS) and its pivotal role in modern cybersecurity frameworks. The authors explore the foundational concepts and operational mechanisms of IDS, emphasizing their importance as a critical layer of defense against cyber threats. The study investigates various types of IDS, including signature-based and anomaly-detection systems, to highlight their respective methodologies and effectiveness in network security. They examine the prevalent threats and vulnerabilities that challenge IDS, alongside effective strategies for incident handling and system resilience. The chapter also discusses advanced evasion techniques employed by attackers to bypass IDS

DOI: 10.4018/979-8-3693-7758-1.ch003

defenses and presents a taxonomy of IDS, incorporating deep learning, machine learning, and optimization algorithms. Additionally, the authors analyze datasets pertinent to IDS research and their role in enhancing system performance. With this analysis, they aim to clarify the constantly changing field of IDS and their crucial function in protecting digital networks.

INTRODUCTION

People have always been able to come up with solutions to problems through their skills, talents, and creativity. It is our ability to look at the situation, incorporate previous experience or knowledge, and come up with a solution that has always been our way of overcoming obstacles. Our views have changed over the years, but the basic concepts have always been there, from the very beginning of mankind when finding solutions meant creating tools for living to the present age of technology and science. We guess, verify, and refine our approaches until we get a reasonable answer.

We are on the threshold of a new technology revolution now, with growth like blockchain, deep learning, machine learning and quantum computing ready to revolutionize the way of life of society. These technologies appear to be aimed at some of the biggest challenges that have always confronted mankind, such as hunger, illness and climate change.

Healthcare is one of the many industries that have been remodeled by AI and ML. These technologies enhance identification in the financial therapy industry. AI accurately assists with medical fraud detection, forecasting risk, and patient management.

Imagine a crowded hospital with patient records that are accurately kept, ensuring that the medical care is both timely and accurate. Data security is not merely a custom issue at this hospital, but it is a lifeline for both patients and medical experts.

While doing standard observation, the hospital's IT department discovered odd behaviors in the patient database one day. There is an attempt to obtain private medical records by someone not allied with the hospital. The breach is quickly recognized and stopped before any data is compromised because of the strong data protection mechanisms in place. Immediately after investigating the incident, it was found out that the breach was made by a cyber-criminal who hacked into the hospital's IT systems.

This could involve revealing patient confidentiality, modifying treatment plans, or worse, altering medical records, should a malevolent insider affect an unattended electronic health system. However, despite the proximal root, damage was averted by their proactive practice in data security; this included encrypting sensitive data, devising rigorous access controls, and doing regular security assessments.

Given such instances, the most evident fact is the essence of data security in health and many other fields. Confidence of patients, legal formalities, and the general rightfulness of the healthcare system are at risk in the absence of strict security guardrails. Security measures shall not just guard against data attacks but also to protect the silence and safety of that information upon which the health and existence of human beings depend. It is for such cases as the one stated above that a company will continuously pour money into putting strong data-security measures into place in order to reduce risks.

CYBERSECURITY

Cybersecurity advocates robust measures for the safeguarding of private information, continuity of business operations, and protection of personal data. This in turn eliminates the risk of data loss, a breach of security protocols, or an aggressive online attack. There is no possibility of building a sound and durable digital society without thorough assessments of the online environment. Cyber security assessments ensure safe online practices and also promote technological advancement.

Cybersecurity Threats

There are so many types of cyber threats that exist in the cyber world today. Phishing of any kind involves deception and use of fake emails or websites in attempts to get the user's private information such as passwords or bank account details. Another big threat is malware such as viruses and worms which are designed to either disrupt networks or steal data. Attacks also included Distributed Denial of Service, or DDoS for short, where attackers send networks so much traffic that the websites and services become so busy they are nearly impossible to use. 'Insider attacks' consist of the same actions as access to leak data or violate systems but only from within. Insider threats are also very similar as they aim to breach systems or leak sensitive data with information that would normally only be known to the organization that owns such information. Strong cybersecurity management is a crucial part of dealing with any and all of these threats since it is highly useful in the managing of risks and even protecting digital assets.

Phishing is, without a doubt, one of the most common cyber threats that many people are familiar with, and for good reason – it involves the imparting of personal information such as credit card numbers and passwords. Most of the time, people who engage in these types of illegal activities use fake emails, text messages, or websites that look like they are from legitimate businesses, particularly banks or well-known online service providers, to confuse people. The main purpose here is to trick recipients into downloading malicious software attachments, clicking on evil links, or revealing confidential information directly. This abuse of trust shows why it is important to be cautious and skeptical when interacting with internet communications and websites.

Cyber Security to Protect Mental Wellness and Prevent Abuse

In the digital age, technology abuse and cyberbullying are becoming increasingly prevalent, so safeguarding one's online identity in a secure fashion is paramount. We live in an uncertain world where sharing sensitive information is vulnerable, thus cybersecurity practices are critical. Online businesses that provide psychological support to patients take the utmost care to ensure that all sensitive discussions are private. The simple yet effective practices of setting a secure password, privacy settings, and a high level of encryption had a powerful effect in thwarting misconduct and minimizing stress levels. Policing anticipates and prevents cybercrimes, which create havoc in people's minds by generating anxiety and feeling lost among noise. Secure social media is becoming a more comforting place with the growth of mental health literacy.

Here are some of the most frequent cybercrimes that can impact mental health:

- Cyber stalking
- Identity theft
- Online harassment and bullying
- Revenge porn
- Impersonation and fraud
- Doxxing
- Cyber extortion
- Malware and ransomware attack
- Social engineering

IDS: A Crucial Layer of Defense in Cybersecurity

Since most networks are not secure, it becomes very easy for fraudsters to steal data or disrupt services. Attackers always try to disable digital resources or gain access to private information. Examples of protections that serve as the first line of defense against these threats include firewalls, access control, and encryption.

Firewalls protect network entry points from a range of threats. Access control authenticates user specifications, and cryptography ensures secure communication. These methods, however, are less effective at detecting or preventing internal attacks and are mainly applied to protect against external threats. Another layer of protection is provided by intrusion detection systems, which assist in such cases by observing and detecting internal and external threats (Anwar et al., 2017 and Ahmad et al., 2021)

Imagine the computer's network as a house filled with valuable things. Now, get a security guard to protect it. It is the job of this guard to watch for any suspicious activity, like an attempted break-in. The guard will notify us immediately if they see anything suspicious. This security measure is referred to as an intrusion detection system in the computer industry. An Intrusion Detection System (IDS) functions by keeping track of all the activities on the network and flagging any unusual or potentially dangerous occurrences. In other words, it works to protect the network from hackers and cyber-attacks much like how one would employ a guard to prevent interlopers from intruding into a house.

In most cases, the service is configured in the following manner:

1. *Traffic monitoring*: An IDS observes all metrics associated with the data flowing in and out of a certain network similar to how an armed security personnel would observe an individual looking to break into a house. It searches for the atypical at all times.
2. *Pattern Matching*: Network Intrusion Detection System (NIDS) systems examine ongoing network activities against a predetermined behavior model. Other predefined rules and patterns are utilized to detect suspicious activity such as uncharacteristic login attempts or excessive data moving and unusual transfers.
3. *Anomaly Detection:* As the name implies, "anomaly detection" refers to the process of identifying undesirable activities and flagging them. A variety of threats can be identified, including malware infections, unauthorized access, and data breaches.
4. *Alert User*: Anytime an IDS detects an activity that appears to be malicious, it always informs you without delay. These include alerts, emails as well as automatic blockage of the activity.
5. *Logging Information*: The IDS maintains a log of all suspicious activities it detects. This log helps in analyzing the threats and understanding the nature of attacks, which is instrumental in improving network security over time.

Without an IDS, organizations are exposed to undetected cyber threats that can compromise private information, disrupt operations, and damage reputation. Without an IDS, potential intrusions will remain unnoticed until extensive damage has been caused, leading to longer recovery times and increased costs. Therefore, IDSs are very critical in the security of digital environments since they offer continuous monitoring and analysis of network traffic for any indication of unauthorized access or malicious activity. Also, without the abilities of prompt detection and response afforded by an IDS, companies would probably be at a loss to meet compliance grades and sustain the trust that their stakeholders and customers have bestowed upon them. Thus, in today's digitally connected world, intrusion detection systems form one of the important lines of defense in modern cybersecurity strategies—critical for proactive threat management and continuously resilient security postures.

From its very beginning as stand-alone, batch-oriented systems, IDS has evolved into the distributed networks of real-time modules. Several key functional blocks of the modern systems are the following:

- **Sensor**: These are the key modules of IDS that collect data. They either monitor system activity, log files, or network traffic in a very system-specific way. Their task is to transform raw data into events that can be processed by the IDS monitors.
- **Monitor**: Events from sensors are sent to the central processing section of an IDS, which is then analyzed against the models of behavior in the IDS itself. The updates to models may also take place together with the generation of alerts. Alerts signify security-relevant occurrences and may be escalated to higher-level monitors or resolver units.
- **Resolver:** Receives alerts or suspicion reports from monitors and determines appropriate responses. These responses may include logging incidents, adjusting the behavior of lower-level components, reconfiguring security mechanisms (e.g., updating firewall rules), and notifying system operators.
- **Controller:** Crucial in distributed IDS environments, controllers manage component configuration and coordination. They serve as a centralized point for administration and monitoring within the IDS and can also supervise operations such as restarting failed components to ensure continuous system functionality.

Effective Strategies for Handling Cybersecurity Incidents

Information technology systems are always vulnerable to compromise in the modern era. However, many firms lack the necessary tools to react to security breaches in a suitable manner. Advanced and targeted intervention tactics are required due to the growing number of occurrences. Although not all Internet users make a conscious effort to access or damage an organization's data, such actions are possible. Organizational computers are also susceptible to viruses and other types of attacks.

When external devices are connected, digital files and gadgets become even more vulnerable to potential hazards. Standard antivirus software is no longer effective due to the sophistication and automation of assaults. There are still a number of technical issues that need to be resolved, such lowering system damage and improving antivirus efficacy. IDS addresses threats by categorizing them based on the kind of attack or breach they have identified. IDS are categorized as either active or passive based on their reacting mechanisms.

Active responses involve immediate, automated actions to protect data without human intervention, but these can be limited by the system's security settings. Passive responses require human involvement and are not automated, allowing more controlled data movement by authorizing alarm events. However, this approach can lead to information leaks during security investigations and may slow network traffic as alarms are processed and reported. Some responses are automated, while others require manual intervention.

IDS often dangle or block IP addresses, block ports, send TCP resets to end connections, change access control lists, and reconfigure routers and firewalls to prevent potential attacks. IDS usually generate alarms through pop-up windows or on-screen warnings, and they can also communicate alarms to network management systems via the Simple Network Management Protocol (SNMP). Enterprises can respond appropriately to a breach with a comprehensive antivirus program in place that guards the network architecture.

An unauthorized attempt to access or modify data in a computer system or on a network is termed a cybersecurity intrusion. It includes penetration into the network, for whatever purposes from installing malicious software that steals sensitive information to creating hurdles in normal business operations. The typical perpetrators are hackers, cybercriminals, and those with insider roles who carry malicious intentions.

IDS Evasion Techniques

IDS evasion techniques are methods attackers use to bypass or elude detection by an IDS that monitors and alerts users of any mistrustful action occurring within a network. Attackers implement various techniques to avoid detection, such as fragmentation, where they break up the malicious packets into very small pieces with the goal of evading signature-based detection systems. One of the tactics employed by attackers is traffic obfuscation, where malicious content is masqueraded to appear as innocuous or normal data. The contents of a malicious payload can also be hidden from IDS inspection via encryption. Attackers can take dominance of weaknesses in the IDS itself by sending specially constructed packets or overloading it with traffic, which causes false negatives and prevents the IDS from identifying malicious activity. In addition, polymorphism is the process of repeated alteration of properties of malicious code in order to avoid signature-based detection. Such evasion strategies are seriously undermining the effectiveness of IDS, which require non-stop updates and complex detection algorithms to fight the evolving cyberthreats effectively.

Comparison of IDS with Firewalls

An IDS monitors network traffic for signatures of attacks or other types of malicious behavior or policy violations. Unlike firewalls, which refer to predefined rules in order to allow or deny traffic, IDS examine traffic patterns and behaviors for anomalies that may indicate a security breach. IDS can identify threats that might elude firewall security, such as malware infections, insider threats, and unauthorized access attempts. Host-based IDSs monitors the activities running on specific devices whereas Network-based IDS, known as NIDS, would monitor network traffic.

Firewalls proactively block unauthorized traffic at the network perimeter, while IDS are more reactive in nature; they detect suspicious activity and then send alerts to administrators after that activity has taken place. This feature, which provides information on the type and extent of security occurrences, is crucial for incident response and forensic analysis. In order to establish a multi-layered protection approach, many firms use both firewalls and IDS simultaneously. To protect against complex and always changing cyberthreats, firewalls create strong perimeter security, while intrusion detection systems (IDS) offer interior monitoring and detection. In Figure 1 types of IDS are shown below and brief descriptions of HIDS and NIDS are discussed.

Figure 1. Types of IDS

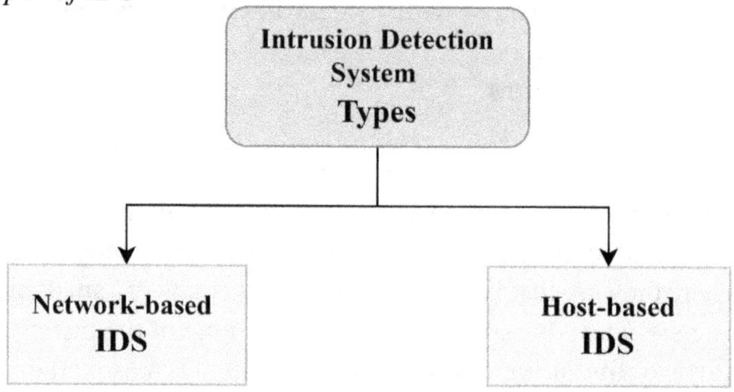

Understanding Anomaly Detection in Network IDS (NIDS)

Monitoring the information transit between hosts across networks is the area of expertise for NIDS. Often referred to as "packet sniffers," these gadgets intercept data packets as they move across TCP/IP-based network communication channels. Intercepted packets are then analyzed with great detail utilizing a wide variety of techniques. Some NIDS devices apply signature-based detection, comparing the contents of packets against a database of malicious packet "fingerprints" and known attack patterns.

One of the common approaches is signature-based detection, where packets are compared against a large database containing predetermined designs and traits of known malicious activities. In this way, NIDS could quickly identify and flag those packets matching known dangers, enabling timely mitigation measures.

The NIDS provides anomaly detection mechanisms, in addition to the signature-based ones. This approach primarily attempts to find deviations from the normal behavior of the network, such as strange traffic patterns or odd packet structure. NIDS can proactively decide on new threats and suspicious activity capable of bypassing traditional signature-based detection systems by analyzing network traffic for anomalies that may show up as security breaches.

Understanding Host-Based IDS (HIDS)

In place of NIDS, HIDS are used for monitoring specific hosts or devices in order to detect malicious activities. HIDS are built with features to monitor, detect, and respond to suspicious host device activities. They do not track network packets but focus mainly on a set of processes, system calls, dynamic link library (DLL) files, system logs, and registry keys for fast identification (Jyothsna et al., 2011), (Almaraz-Rivera et al., 2023).

There are two types of HIDS detection methods: They may be signature-based or anomaly-based. Signature-based HIDS identifies attacks by recognizing definite patterns with known attack signatures. On the other hand, anomaly-based HIDS makes use of statistical approaches or machine and deep learning methods to find anomalies. In anomaly-based HIDS, ML and DL techniques are trained using typical data samples in an effort to produce a profile that reflects usual process activities. Notifications marked as hazardous or suspicious are sent to the system administrator when behavior deviates from this profile. Therefore, compared to signature-based HIDS, anomaly-based HIDS are typically more resilient to unspecified and zero-day attacks (Satilmiş et al., 2024).

DATASETS

In this section, one of the latest dataset of IDS is discussed and pictorial representation os shown below in Figure 2.

CIC-IDS2017

This dataset is a comprehensive dataset constructed for estimating IDS and Intrusion Prevention Systems (IPSs). This dataset addresses the limitations found in previous datasets by including a wide variety of up-to-date attack types and generating realistic network traffic that closely resembles real-world data.

CIDDS

The purpose of the Coburg Intrusion Detection Data Sets (CIDDS) is to assess anomaly-based network intrusion detection systems. Beyond just rows and columns, this extensive dataset offers a multitude of information, including complete records of external server attacks. The time and duration of assaults, source and destination IP addresses, and different network metrics including packets, bytes, flows, and flags are all recorded in each entry. The dataset also assigns unique IDs, classifies each instance, and classifies the attacks by in kind.

Figure 2. Latest dataset used for IDS

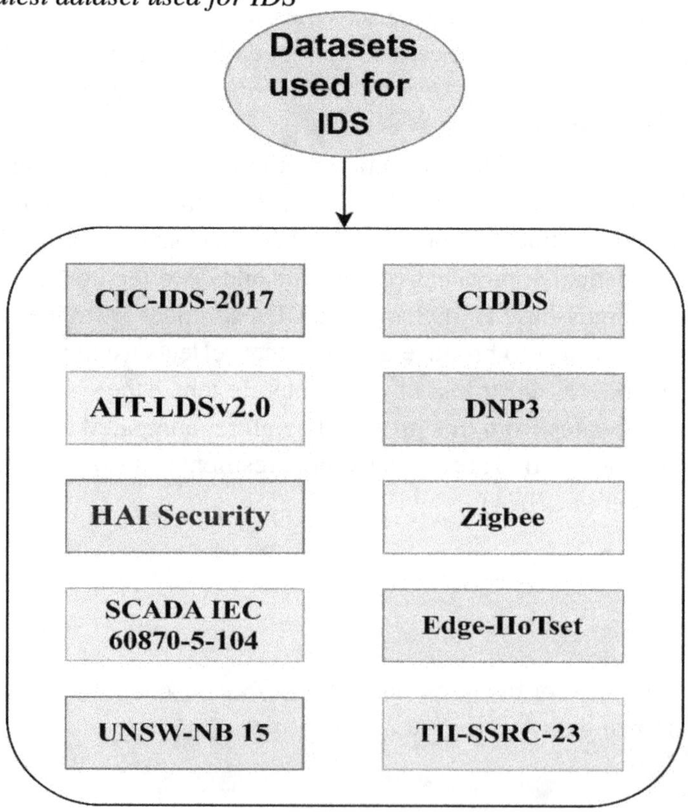

AIT-LDSv2.0 Dataset

Landauer et al. presented this dataset in their paper "Maintainable Log Datasets for Evaluation of IDS," which offers artificial log data designed for alert aggregation, federated learning, and IDS evaluation. This dataset is composed of up to eight separate datasets, each of which represents a small business network that includes firewalls, file shares, WordPress servers, mail servers, and VPNs.

Over 4-6 days, normal user behavior is simulated to create background noise, while a series of attack steps are launched against the network to simulate real-world intrusion scenarios. Log data is collected from all hosts which makes AIT-LDSv2.0 an essential resource for developing, testing, and benchmarking sophisticated intrusion detection solutions.

HAI Security Dataset

The HAI Security Dataset is a comprehensive dataset derived from an ICS testbed enhanced with a Hardware-In-the-Loop (HIL) simulator. The simulator emulates the production of power from steam turbines and pumped storage hydropower in a holistic manner to create a realistic dataset.

Its first version, HAI 1.0, was released in February 2020 and included the operational data from 38 attacks in typical and atypical scenarios. Its debugged version, HAI 20.07, was published on August 2020 for HAICON 2020 competition. HAI 21.03 was released in 2021 with a more tightly coupled HIL simulator, including more attack scenarios and pronounced attack effects to better understand the dynamic change in the system. Compared with previous versions, it became much harder to detect in HAI 22.04, which was released in 2022 with more complex and harder-to-detect attacks. More detailed data on the internal control logic of the boiler's DCS, and Python NetworkX graph data for anomaly detection analysis, are some of the new features of the latest versions, HAI/HAIEnd 23.05, designed for ICS endpoint threat detection.

IDS on SCADA IEC 60870-5-104

This dataset addresses the privacy and security challenges arising in the emerging Industrial Internet of Things (IIoT), with special focus on the obsolete and insecure IEC 60870-5-104 communication protocol, which is in wide use in critical infrastructures such as industrial health care systems and intelligent electrical grids. This dataset was generated for use in two separate H2020 projects, namely ELECTRON and SDN-micro-SENSE, used for the scientific paper "Modeling, Detecting, and

Mitigating Threats Against Industrial Healthcare Systems: A Combined Software Defined Networking and Reinforcement Learning Approach".

UNSW Dataset

The demand for strong security measures has increased due to the growing reliance on network-based systems and smart devices in many different industries. The threat environment has grown as a result of the heavy reliance on network servers, cloud computing, and remotely operated database systems for services offered by both public and commercial organizations.

DNP3 Intrusion Detection Dataset

This Dataset was released on November 23, 2022, reflects the evolving landscape of the Industrial Internet of Things (IIoT), where traditional Critical Infrastructures (CIs) are transforming into smart environments with benefits like pervasive control, self-monitoring, and self-healing. Despite these developments, this has led to exponential growth in cyber threats with the adoption of unsafe technologies. Remote communication between Supervisory Control and Data Acquisition (SCADA) and Industrial Control Systems (ICS) is made easier by DNP3, an industrial communication protocol that is widely used in the United States. Numerous topologies are supported, including multiple-server, hierarchical, multi-drop, and master-slave topologies. DNP3's design originally consisted of the Application Layer, Transport Layer, and Data Link Layer. However, as an application-layer protocol, it has now been incorporated into the TCP/IP stack. Nevertheless, DNP3 has serious security flaws since it lacks authentication and authorization procedures, just like other industrial protocols like Modbus and IEC 60870-5-104 (Fovino et al., 2010).

Zigbee Dataset

The dataset discussed addresses the increasing security challenges on the Internet of Things (IoT), particularly within smart homes dominated by Wi-Fi, Zigbee, and BLE networks. Researchers face the need for quality datasets to build and evaluate monitoring tools and IDS (IDS). However, while Wi-Fi datasets are readily available, there is a significant gap in Zigbee datasets. To fill this gap, the ZBDS2023 dataset has been introduced. It includes periods of normal activity and various labelled attack scenarios, facilitating the development and evaluation of IDS. Each emitted frame is captured by one to four demodulating passive probes, providing redundancy in MAC layer data and values of the Received Signal Strength Indicator (RSSI), which is valuable for spoofing detection systems. Additionally, the dataset includes a naive attack detection system as a baseline for future research, highlighting the challenges of exploiting RSSI time series in populated environments.

Edge-IIOT Dataset

This dataset was designed to support machine learning-based IDS in both centralized and federated learning modes, thereby enhancing flexibility and applicability. Generated from a purpose-built IoT/IIoT testbed, Edge-IIoTset encompasses a diverse array of devices, sensors, protocols, and cloud/edge configurations, making it highly representative of real-world scenarios. The dataset includes data from more than ten types of IoT devices, such as low-cost digital sensors for temperature and humidity, ultrasonic sensors, water level detection sensors, pH meters, soil moisture sensors, heart rate sensors, and flame sensors, among others. It thoroughly addresses cybersecurity by identifying and analyzing fourteen types of attacks related to IoT and IIoT connectivity protocols, which are categorized into five major threats: DoS/DDoS attacks, information gathering, man-in-the-middle attacks, injection attacks, and malware attacks. Additionally, Edge-IIoTset incorporates features derived from a variety of sources, including alerts, system resources, logs, and network traffic, ultimately proposing 61 highly correlated features from an initial set of 1176 features. This comprehensive dataset not only facilitates the detection and analysis of a wide range of cyber threats but also includes primary exploratory data analysis and performance evaluations of both traditional and deep learning approaches in centralized and federated learning contexts, offering valuable insights and benchmarks for future research and development in IoT and IIoT cybersecurity.

TII-SSRC-23 Dataset

The TII-SSRC-23 dataset is a groundbreaking contribution to the field of network intrusion detection, specifically tailored to address the limitations of existing datasets by providing a more accurate and comprehensive reflection of both benign and malicious traffic. This dataset, totaling 27.5 GB, is meticulously designed to enhance the training and effectiveness of machine learning-based IDS. It is divided into two primary categories: benign and malicious traffic, comprising eight distinct traffic types and 32 subtypes—six benign and 26 malicious (Herzalla et al. 2023).

TAXONOMY OF IDS

IDS taxonomy can be determined through a number of factors such as response strategy, deployment methodology, and detection approach. Detection techniques are generally classified as hybrid, anomaly-based, and signature-based. IDS that are signature-based compare observed behaviors to a record of known threat signatures, offering a strong defense against known assaults but having trouble identifying emerging threats. Anomaly-based IDS, however, compare current activities against a baseline of normal behavior, making them adept at spotting previously unknown threats, though they can be susceptible to false positives. Deployment methodologies categorize IDS into Network-based IDS which superintends traffic across the entire network, and Host-based IDS, which monitors activities on specific devices. Response strategies can be passive, merely alerting administrators to potential threats, or active, wherein the system automatically takes countermeasures, such as blocking suspicious traffic or isolating compromised systems. Taxonomy of IDS is shown in Figure 3.

Figure 3. Taxonomy of IDS

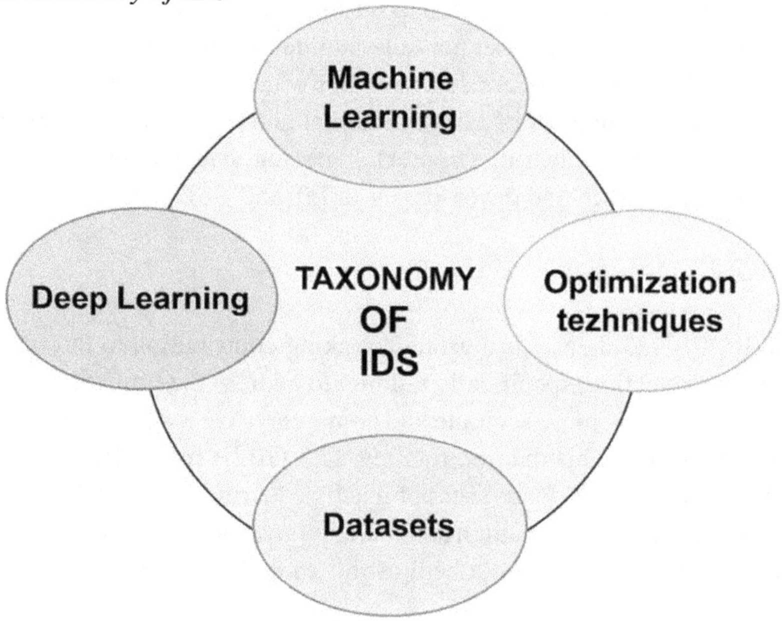

Machine Learning

Machine learning can be characterized into two main categories which are supervised and unsupervised learning. Supervised learning relies on labelled data to derive meaningful insights, with classification being one of its primary tasks. However, manually labelling data is both costly and time-consuming, limiting the availability of labelled datasets for supervised learning. Unsupervised learning, instead, can extract useful features with the use of unlabeled data, therefore facilitating the collection of training data more easily (Surakhi et al.,2022) and (Liu & Lang, 2019). While having that advantage, the performance of detection with unsupervised learning tends generally to be much lower compared with supervised schemes.

Deep Learning

More elaborately, the deep learning models to be defined represent a subclass of deep networks in an RNN: supervised models, mainly in the shape of RNNs, CNNs, and DNNs, along with DBNs; and on the unsupervised part, in shape of auto-encoders along with restricted Boltzmann machines. Deep learning models have increasingly gained popularity for IDS since 2015 because they are able to automatically learn feature representations from raw, unprocessed data be it text, images, or anything else without any human feature engineering, enabling them to achieve end-to-end processing. Compared with the shallow models, they are most especially useful for huge datasets. The main areas of study in deep learning are network architecture, hyperparameter tweaking, and optimization techniques. Autoencoders are neural networks, composed of two symmetrical parts: the encoder extracts a feature representation from the input data, while the decoder uses that representation to reconstruct the original data. In training, the model shows that the recorded characteristics are representative of the data by minimizing the difference between the original input and the reconstructed output. Notably, autoencoders do not need supervised learning and come in variants such as denoising and sparse autoencoders. Restricted Boltzmann Machines RBMs. RBMs consist of visible and hidden layers where all units are fully connected within but not between layers. Trained via the contrastive divergence algorithm, RBMs are used for feature extraction or denoising. Deep Belief Networks (DBNs) build upon RBMs by adding a SoftMax classification layer, employing unsupervised pretraining for each RBM followed by supervised fine-tuning of the SoftMax layer.

Optimization Algorithms

To minimize or maximize a function by adjusting values, optimization techniques are necessary. These methods have been most effective in intrusion detection research and are used in deep learning to optimize error functions. Among them, in feature selection and intrusion detection, Genetic Algorithm (GA), Ant Colony Optimization (ACO), and Grey Wolf Optimization (GWO) performed very well (Karatas et al., 2019).

Algorithms inspired by nature are very efficient in providing good answers to difficult questions when they are developed based on ideas and patterns in the natural world. For instance, Genetic

Algorithms (GA) employ processes like crossover, mutation and selection to evolve solutions across generations just as nature selects its creatures. The Whale Optimization Algorithm (WOA) uses the movement of humpback whales to find the best solutions, following the movements that the whales make during their hunt for food (Mohamed et al., 2022, Cerullo et al., 2018, Kim et al., 2019, and Nousiainen, 2024). In a course similar of vein, the search Aquila using Optimizer improves strategy the of balance the between exploration Aquila Rapax. and the exploitation The Slime Mould Algorithm is based on the ability of slime moulds to find their way out of complex mazes through their foraging behaviors, and so it solves a number of parameters based on this ability. The Golden Eagle Optimizer performs an efficient search by implementing both exploration and exploitation strategies to represent the hunting behavior of golden eagles.

In order to circumnavigate the solution space, Harris Hawks Optimization (HHO) uses a balance between exploration and exploitation, simulating the cooperative hunting tactics of Harris's hawks. The Spotted Hyena Algorithm uses the pack subtleties of spotted hyenas to direct the optimization process, drawing inspiration from their social and hunting behaviors. Lastly, in order to increase search methods and solutions accuracy, the Mayfly Algorithm incorporates the swarming and mating behaviors of mayflies. Each of these algorithms offers creative solutions to optimization issues, reflecting the variety of techniques present in nature. Ibrahim Hayat Hassan's approach also achieved a higher detection rate compared to conventional data mining. Among researchers using GA, (Gorzałczany & Rudziński, 2022) each reached 100% accuracy, and (Mahmood et al., 2022) attained 99.36% accuracy.

CONCLUSION

A thorough introduction to IDS and their crucial function in cybersecurity is presented in this chapter. We compared signature-based and anomaly detection techniques in NIDS and looked at the fundamental mechanisms of IDS. In addition to highlighting different IDS evasion tactics, our presentation covered practical approaches for managing cybersecurity events. A taxonomy that combines IDS datasets, machine learning, deep learning, and optimization algorithms was also provided, demonstrating the progress in IDS technology. We also inspected the importance of datasets in IDS research. IDS is still an essential part of cybersecurity and is always changing to combat more complex threats. Developing more resilient and adaptive defenses requires ongoing IDS research and innovation powered by AI and ML. This chapter lays the groundwork for future advancements in cybersecurity dealings while highlighting the significance of IDS in protecting digital infrastructure.

REFERENCES

Ahmad, Z., Shahid Khan, A., Wai Shiang, C., Abdullah, J., & Ahmad, F. (2021). Network intrusion detection system: A systematic study of machine learning and deep learning approaches. *Transactions on Emerging Telecommunications Technologies*, 32(1), e4150. DOI: 10.1002/ett.4150

Almaraz-Rivera, J. G., Cantoral-Ceballos, J. A., & Botero, J. F. (2023). Enhancing IoT Network Security: Unveiling the Power of Self-Supervised Learning against DDoS Attacks. *Sensors (Basel)*, 23(21), 8701. DOI: 10.3390/s23218701 PMID: 37960401

Anwar, S., Mohamad Zain, J., Zolkipli, M. F., Inayat, Z., Khan, S., Anthony, B., & Chang, V. (2017). From intrusion detection to an intrusion response system: fundamentals, requirements, and future directions. *Algorithms, 10*(2), 39.

Cerullo, G., Mazzeo, G., Papale, G., Ragucci, B., & Sgaglione, L. (2018). Iot and sensor networks security. In *Security and Resilience in Intelligent Data-Centric Systems and Communication Networks* (pp. 77–101). Academic Press. DOI: 10.1016/B978-0-12-811373-8.00004-5

Fovino, I. N., Carcano, A., Murel, T. D. L., Trombetta, A., & Masera, M. (2010, April). Modbus/DNP3 state-based intrusion detection system. In *2010 24th IEEE International Conference on Advanced Information Networking and Applications* (pp. 729-736). IEEE.

Gorzałczany, M. B., & Rudziński, F. (2022). Intrusion detection in Internet of Things with MQTT protocol—An accurate and interpretable genetic-fuzzy rule-based solution. *IEEE Internet of Things Journal*, 9(24), 24843–24855. DOI: 10.1109/JIOT.2022.3194837

Herzalla, D., Lunardi, W. T., & Andreoni, M. (2023). TII-SSRC-23 dataset: Typological exploration of diverse traffic patterns for intrusion detection. *IEEE Access : Practical Innovations, Open Solutions*, 11, 118577–118594. DOI: 10.1109/ACCESS.2023.3319213

Jyothsna, V. V. R. P. V., Prasad, R., & Prasad, K. M. (2011). A review of anomaly-based intrusion detection systems. *International Journal of Computer Applications*, 28(7), 26–35. DOI: 10.5120/3399-4730

Karatas, G., Demir, O., & Sahingoz, O. K. (2019, June). A deep learning-based intrusion detection system on GPUs. In *2019 11th International Conference on Electronics, Computers and Artificial Intelligence (ECAI)* (pp. 1-6). DOI: 10.1109/ECAI46879.2019.9042132

Kim, J., Shin, Y., & Choi, E. (2019). An intrusion detection model based on a convolutional neural network. *Journal of Multimedia Information System*, 6(4), 165–172. DOI: 10.33851/JMIS.2019.6.4.165

Liu, H., & Lang, B. (2019). Machine learning and deep learning methods for intrusion detection systems: A survey. *Applied Sciences, 9*(20), 4396.

Mahmood, R. A. R., Abdi, A., & Hussin, M. (2021). Performance evaluation of intrusion detection system using selected features and machine learning classifiers. *Baghdad Science Journal, 18*(2), 0884.

Mohamed, S. A., Alsaif, O. I., & Saleh, I. A. (2022). Intrusion detection network attacks based on whale optimization algorithm. *Ingénierie des Systèmes d'Information*, 27(3), 441–446. DOI: 10.18280/isi.270310

Nousiainen, A. (2024). Applying cybersecurity for IEC 60870-5-104 communication between control station and substation.

Satilmiş, H., Akleylek, S., & Tok, Z. Y. (2024). A Systematic Literature Review on Host-Based Intrusion Detection Systems. *IEEE Access : Practical Innovations, Open Solutions*, 12, 27237–27266. DOI: 10.1109/ACCESS.2024.3367004

Surakhi, O., García, A., Jamoos, M., & Alkhanafseh, M. (2022). The intrusion detection system by deep learning methods: issues and challenges.

Chapter 4
Anomaly Detection and Threat Intelligence With Machine Learning

Indira P. Joshi
https://orcid.org/0009-0009-3535-4574
Sipna COET Amaravati, India

Vijaya K. Shandilya
https://orcid.org/0009-0002-1515-4670
Sipna COET Amaravati, India

ABSTRACT

Machine learning (ML) uses multilayer neural networks to describe complex behaviours and patterns. Deep learning models on huge cybersecurity datasets can improve anomaly detection, vulnerability prediction, and real-time incident response. This chapter discusses cyber dangers and risk assessment limits. RNNs and CNNs—two deep learning models—and their cybersecurity effects are examined here. Case studies show these models can detect malware, phishing attempts, and network intrusions. The chapter also discusses deep learning cybersecurity issues. data privacy, huge tagged datasets, and computational resources as problems. The future of deep learning, including its potential to adapt to new cyberattacks and create more proactive and robust cybersecurity measures, is also highlighted. This chapter explains how deep learning may improve cyber risk analysis and digital security.

DOI: 10.4018/979-8-3693-7758-1.ch004

1. INTRODUCTION

As an increasing number of businesses adopt cloud computing, the threat landscape evolves into a more intricate and advanced domain. Conventional security methods dependent on static rule-based systems find it challenging to adjust to the dynamic characteristics of cloud networks. AI and ML are crucial methodologies for enhancing threat intelligence and identifying anomalies in cloud systems. These systems can analyse substantial data quantities, identify trends, and detect anomalies in real time, making them essential for proactive cloud security. ML and AI can automate the analysis of threat data, reducing the necessity for human involvement and enabling more rapid identification and response to potential threats. They enhance AD by analysing past data and adjusting to emerging threats, hence obviating the necessity for manual rule set modifications.

2. UNDERSTANDING ANOMALY DETECTION AND THREAT INTELLIGENCE

It is possible that the ease with which thieves can employ simple technologies like email is contributing to the recent uptick in fraud. Clicking on an email attachment that looks like it came from a family member can implant malware on your computer, leading to non-monetary losses. Resolving unpreventable problems, such as health difficulties, requires early discovery. In this context, it is critical to have computationally efficient software that can automatically recognize and alert to unusual data and behaviours. The concepts and methods for identifying outliers are the main topics of this chapter.

2.1 What is Anomaly Detection

Models and predictions based on past data are used for anomaly detection. The idea of stationarity, upon which normal conduct is predicated, states that data-generating systems have not changed much (Xu et al., 2019). Historical data will always be the most telling indicator of how a system has performed. Variable data may show cyclical patterns or long-term trends such as an increase in the average human life expectancy. In data mining and ML, anomaly analysis is a hot subject for research. The objective is to identify data points that deviate from expected trends (Chandola, V., Banerjee, A., & Kumar, 2009). When data exhibits unusual patterns that deviate substantially from the norm, it calls this an anomaly. Having said that, no formal description of this concept has yet gained widespread acceptance. In different contexts, an anomaly may have different names, such in the role of an anomaly, peculiarity, exception, aberration, or discordant item (Gupta et al., 2014). Data mining, business intelligence, and decision-making all rely on the ability to spot distinctive patterns. An earthquake or tsunami could be on the horizon if an abnormal network communication suggests a hacker or virus attack on a computer system, an unauthorized charge to a credit card, or some other natural disaster. Public health, preventing credit card fraud, cleansing data, and detecting network infiltration are just a few of the many applications of anomaly detection (Gogoi et al., 2011).

Figure 1. Attacks with Anomalies Mapping

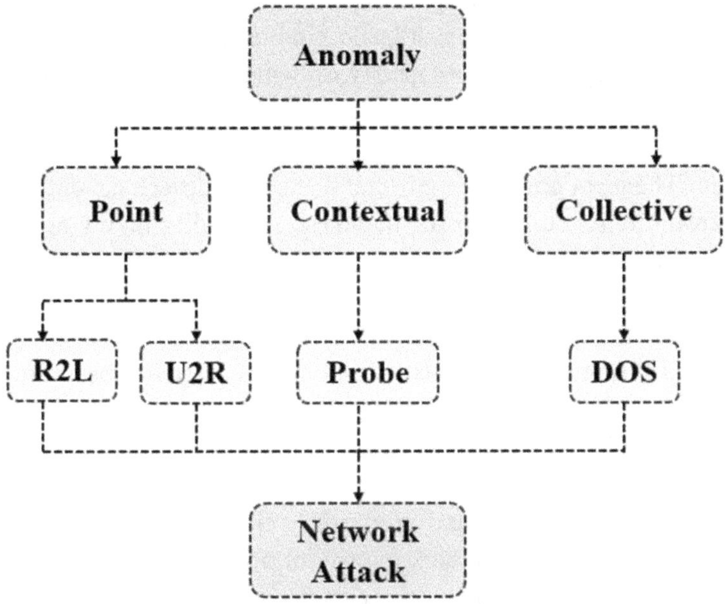

Intentionally obtaining information and reconnaissance is the basis of probe attacks. The authors of this chapter map them with contextual anomalies. U2RandR2L assaults are complex and condition specific. As comparison to others, launching sucking attacks is not straightforward. As a result, these attacks are seen as anomalies. The assault classifications are mapped out in Figure 1.

2.1.1 Types of Anomaly Detection

Anomalies can be either point, collective, or contextual in nature. As a data point, an anomaly stands out when it differs greatly from the average. When many data instances display suspicious behaviour, this is called a collective anomaly. While most anomaly detection studies concentrate on individual points of outliers, collective anomalies are less common yet provide a different classification problem. Data events that are only unusual in a certain setting are called contextual anomalies. First, the context must be established in order to detect contextual anomalies. Data clusters and feature subsets are two examples of possible contexts. An umbrella phrase that encompasses both contextual point anomalies and contextual collective abnormalities contextual anomalies, which does not restrict definition to any one kind of anomaly. In the section that follows, it will explain everything.

1. **Point Anomalies:** A single outlier observation that stands out from the rest is called a point anomaly (Zhang et al., 2020). Research on anomaly detection tends to concentrate on the most basic kind of anomaly. It displays data on a lithium-ion battery's discharge capacity, drawing attention to out-of-the-ordinary spots.

Example: The term point anomaly can be used to describe a data instance that stands out from the remainder of the database. An oddity involving points would be a person whose typical daily gasoline use is five liters but suddenly increases to fifty liters.

2. **Contextual Anomalies:** Contextual anomalies refer to observations that are aberrant in one context but not in others. Contextual abnormalities can be defined using the following attributes:
   - Contextual qualities identify the context of a given observation. For example, The contextual property of time in time-series data is that it specifies the place in the sequence of observations.
   - Behavioural traits define the non-contextual properties of an observation. Rainfall amounts can be used as a behavioural characteristic in a spatial dataset to provide global averages.

Example: using a credit card around the holidays like Christmas and New Year's typically results in higher spending than the rest of the year. This kind of unusual behavior is a contextual anomaly, sometimes called a conditional anomaly. While it might be costly, it might not be out of the ordinary because high costs are common in some contexts. However, it could be seen as a contextual oddity if the expenditure is equally high during a non-festive month.

In a certain setting, values of behavioural attributes are used to detect abnormal behaviour. Different contexts may have different standards for what constitutes normalcy; what is considered an aberration in one may be considered normal in another. Recognizing environmental and behavioural features in this quality is crucial for a contextual anomaly detection method. shows a graph of monthly temperatures for a specific location over time. A temperature of 20∘F would be seen as typical in time t1 (winter), but it could be deemed uncommon in time t2 (summer).

3. **Collective Anomalies:** By definition, a collective anomaly is an outlier in the dataset consisting of multiple anomalous observations. The presence of a set of anomalous data findings is noteworthy, even when the observations themselves may not be noteworthy. Missing values from sensor or gearbox failures are considered collective anomalies in PHM. depicts an ECG output, with the highlighted region suggesting abnormality identification. It is not normal for a human electrocardiogram to display low output for long durations. You can't call the low value an outlier. Collective anomalies can only be observed in datasets containing connected observations, but point anomalies can occur in any dataset. Whether or not data has context attributes determines the presence of contextual abnormalities. In order to uncover contextual anomalies, it is necessary to analyse a point or collective anomaly within a certain context. By including pertinent data, contextual anomaly detection can be obtained from point or collective anomaly detection. It will need a more comprehensive investigation to learn how to identify collective anomalies because these methods are so different from those used to identify point and contextual abnormalities.

Example: A group of data instances is called a collective anomaly when they behave abnormally when compared to the full dataset. As an example, in a human Electrocardiogram (ECG) reading, a single low value is not necessarily abnormal, but the persistence of low readings over an extended duration suggests an aberrant early contraction.

2.2 Threat Intelligence

Gathering information from various sources is a common practice while developing intelligent technologies. Depending on how the data impacts ongoing operations and requirements, it is common practice to release the data soon after collection. The reporting and analysis processes are necessary to rectify any mistakes in raw intelligence, which is based on incomplete data. Results are derived by comparing and weighing incomplete intelligence products. Upon completion of all steps involved in gathering intelligence, one attains perfect intelligence, sometimes called finished intelligence. Verifying information twice lessens the chances of drawing erroneous conclusions or being dishonest. Protecting oneself against both external and internal dangers is a top priority for individuals, governments, and organizations. Nobody wants critical data or money stolen by the ransomware described in this study. There has been a lot of talk about the requirements laid out by the statute for the collection of forensic material and data in high-profile cases. There are paid and free versions of network security software that may be found online and downloaded with relative ease. Organizations, individuals, and nations must comprehend threat intelligence cycles in order to propose solutions to safeguard themselves against internal and external network threats.

2.2.1 Types of Threat Intelligence

Subdivisions are a great way to consolidate data and direct efforts from many TI sources. There are subdomains within TI. In order to find and use tacit knowledge between collaborators, the authors classify TI as either formal or informal approaches (Ahrend et al., 2016). While formal intelligence primarily focuses on communicating technical indicators of compromise, informal intelligence entails exchanging knowledge, tools, and recommendations to prevent further attacks. There are two types of TI, according to the authors of. Unlike operational intelligence, which depends solely on computers for data identification, gathering, enrichment, and analysis, strategic intelligence makes use of trained human analysts to build external relationships and proprietary information sources.

Figure 2. Types of TI.

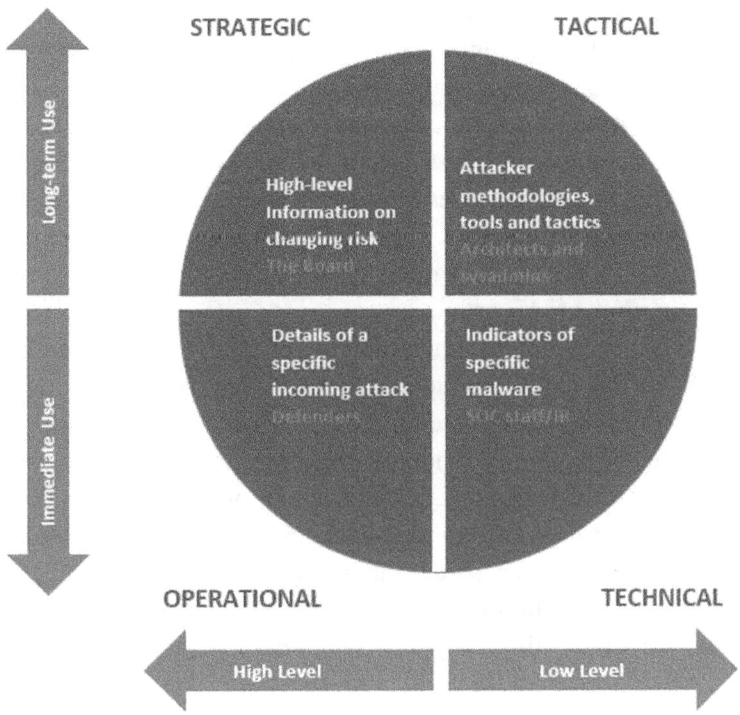

Classifies TI according to shown in Figure 2strategic and tactical intelligence. There are two levels of intelligence: high-level, used by CEOs, threat analysts, and strategic planners, and low-level, used for quantitative purposes. According to (Korstanje, 2016), there are four types of threat intelligence: strategic, operational, tactical, and technical. This subdivision is sometimes referred to as the four stages of intelligence analysis. This paradigm, initially employed in military contexts to analyse expeditionary factors, differentiates four stages (Tounsi & Rais, 2018). Subdividing the TI allows for deeper investigation and discussion of its limits. In the sequel, it examines the last subdivision.

1. **Strategic TI:** Intelligence gathered at a high level for use by decision-makers is called strategic threat intelligence. Strategists can use this guidance to better comprehend current risks and spot emerging ones. Possible items in this category include the monetary impact of cyber activity, patterns of attacks, relevant historical data, and predictions on future dangers. It is the responsibility of the board to evaluate possible attacks, rank the risks, and distribute resources ac-

cordingly. Reports, briefings, or discussions are the usual formats for strategic TI.

2. **Operational TI:** Operational threat intelligence is used by higher-level security workers like incident response team chiefs or security managers to learn about possible assaults on an organization (Li et al., 2019). Such a level of intelligence is highly rare. In order to gather useful operational intelligence, private firms cannot lawfully access attack groups or their infrastructure, including communication channels. In most cases, this power is reserved for the state. Attacks on organizations by public actors, such hacktivists, might compromise their data security. Assaults detected by open-source intelligence or closed chat forums are the main topic of this article.
3. **Tactical TI:** Threat actors' attack strategies can be uncovered by analysing tactical threat intelligence which includes tactics, techniques, and processes. First responders stay up-to-date on the latest defensive and investigative skills through tactical training. Defenders can gain tactical intelligence and influence policy changes by understanding an attacker's tooling and tactics. Reading white papers, technical press, talking to colleagues, or buying material from a source are all ways to get tactical Threat Intelligence (TI).
4. **Technical TI:** Data often retrieved through technological means is known as Technical Threat Intelligence (TTI). Technical TI frequently backs up an organization's monitoring and investigative functions, such as email filtering and firewalls, by limiting access to suspicious servers. Analytical tools, visualization, and dashboards are further potential uses for TTI. Verifying logs for previously seen connections or binaries can reveal historical attacks.

3. MACHINE LEARNING TECHNIQUES FOR ANOMALY DETECTION

ML is the study of methods for learning from data that are applied to computers. It has utilized computers to solve many different kinds of problems, but usually it's just mundane stuff or things that people with the right kind of expertise or experience have already figured out how to do perfectly. But there are plenty of very difficult tasks that can't be solved by either human experts or machines with great but basic programming skills. There are many categories into which these tasks fall. Things that don't have any human administrators. For example, in modern automated factories, it is essential to analyse sensor signals in order to predict when machines will break down (Bhattacharyya & Kalita, 2013). Interviewing human experts who can provide the data needed to build a computer system is a very challenging, if not impossible, task for programmers. By analysing recorded data and subsequent machine failures, a ML system can learn prediction rules. In contrast, ML is primarily concerned with the precision and efficiency of the end computer system. Just think about all the questions that could be asked using voice data to prove this. It is the purpose of a ML method to develop an efficient and precise system for voice recognition. A team consisting of a statistician and a psychologist could investigate potential explanations for how voice recognition works. To classify speakers according to characteristics like age, sex, or level of education, a data mining technique could sift through audio recordings for trends.

3.1 Supervised Learning for Anomaly Detection

When there are input variables and target values in the data, supervised learning is employed. An input-output mapping function is learned by the algorithm. For tasks with limited data, it could be expensive to use large-scale labelled data samples. In what follows, it will see some supervised ML model examples.

3.1.1 Convolutional Neural Network (CNN)

Images and videos are examples of two-dimensional data that CNNs, which are multi-layer neural networks, are quite good at processing. Convolutional Neural Networks (CNNs) draw inspiration from time-delay neural networks (TDNNs), which were originally developed for processing time series and voice data and alleviate the computational burden of learning by distributing weights along a temporal axis. The first effective deep learning method to train several hierarchical layers robustly was CNNs. CNN designs outperform conventional feed-forward back propagation methods by reducing the number of training parameters required by leveraging spatial and temporal correlations. Designed for little data pre-processing, CNNs are a deep learning framework (Mishra & Gupta, 2017).

Figure 3. CNN Architecture.

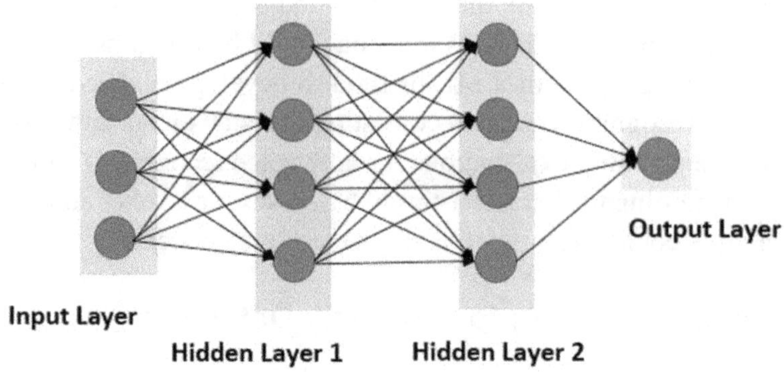

The bottom layer of a CNN's hierarchical structure receives inputs that are small portions of the image. Layers of the network use digital filtering to isolate important data points, as shown in Figure 3. Regardless of size, rotation, or shift, the method guarantees that basic properties such oriented edges or corners may be accessed by neurons or processing units.

3.1.2 Support Vector Machine

The structural risk minimisation concept, derived from statistical learning theory, serves as its foundation (Christopher J.C. Burges, 1998). Vapnik-Chervonenkis dimension (VC-dimension) regulation is required to reduce the guaranteed risk, which is defined as the sum of the empirical risk and the confidence interval, according to the concept. However, according to Zhong et al. (2013), the confidence interval expands while the minimum empirical risk decreases as the VC-dimension increases. Figure 3 shows that SVMs, or maximum margin classifiers, maximize geometric margin while minimizing empirical classification error. The process by which a SVM applies a predefined non-linear mapping to transform input vectors into a high-dimensional feature space Z.

Figure 4. An example of an SVM with linearly separable classifications.

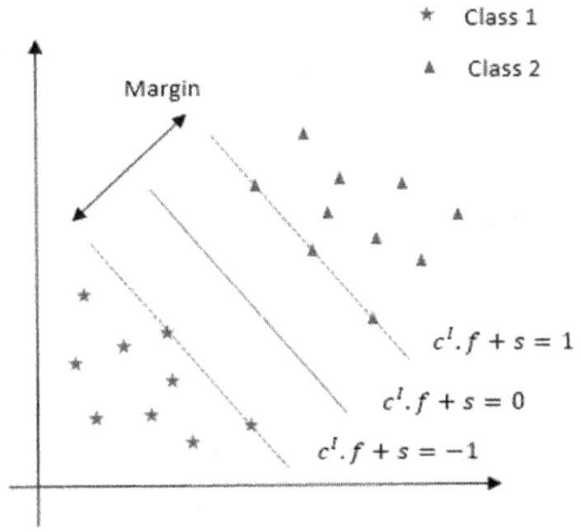

As a result, a hyperplane is formed, linking the data points while maintaining a class separation margin. If training data cannot be separated by error, the technique uses a soft margin SVM to separate the set with the fewest mistakes possible (Wang et al., 2021). SVMs typically produce a linearly separable feature space, even for non-linear features. A linear classifier uses a hyperplane with equation (3) to split the feature space, with w representing the weight vector, x representing the input vector, and b representing the bias shown in Figure 4(Ben-Hur & Weston, 2010).

$$c^l.f + s = 0 \tag{1}$$

Figure 4 depicts the geometric margin as boundary lines parallel to the hyperplane, representing the limitations shown in (4).

$$c^l.f + s \begin{cases} \geq 1 \; when \; h_t = +1 \\ \leq -1 \; when \; h_t = -1 \end{cases} \tag{2}$$

Linear Support Vector Machine (SVM) classifiers for non-linear feature spaces are constructed using kernels such as polynomial, radial basis function, or Gaussian (Cao et al., 2015). Kernels can transform non-separable input data into separable data inside a higher-dimensional space. Dividing the two groups with a hyperplane may replicate the functionality of a linear classifier.

3.1.3 Naïve Bayes (NB)

To train on non-linear feature spaces, LSVM classifiers employ kernels such radial basis functions, polynomials, or Gaussian (Sharma et al., 2011). To make data in a higher dimensional space that is separable, kernels convert non-separable input data (Amari & Wu, 1999). A hyperplane can partition the two classes, resulting in a scenario analogous to a LC.

$$A\left(W_t P_1, .., P_g\right) = A(W_t)A(P_1 W_t)\ldots\frac{A\left(P_g W_t\right)}{A(P)} \tag{3}$$

This is known as a naïve Bayes (NB) classifier. Naive Bayes models are efficient, robust, and highly accurate (Taheri & Mammadov, 2013). NB model classification accuracy reduces when attributes are not independent. NB models cannot handle non-parametric continuous attributes (Wei et al., 2011). Improvements have been made, including feature selection, to address these difficulties.

3.2 Unsupervised Learning for Anomaly Detection

There is no matching output variable in unsupervised learning; instead, it relies on input data. In order to learn more about the characteristics of data, algorithms look for patterns in it. A popular example of an unsupervised algorithm is clustering. Using intrinsic data groupings, this technique finds and predicts output for unknown inputs. Consumer spending habits can be better anticipated with this method. The section that follows gives several examples of ML models that are not supervised.

3.2.1 Local Outlier Factor (LOF)

One unsupervised technique that can spot data fraud and outliers is the Local Outlier Factor (LOF). The density score of each sample is assessed and given a weight by the Local Outlier Factor Algorithm. Anomalies with the lowest scores are identified by comparing them to other data points.

Figure 5. Local Outlier Factor (LOF).

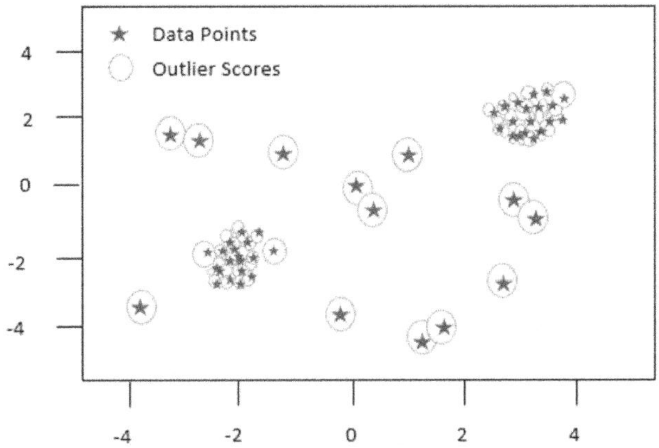

Figure 5 shown in displays data points and outlier scores. Outliers are defined as spots with lower density than their neighbours.

3.2.2 Isolation Forest (IF)

Isolation Forest belongs to the unsupervised algorithm. The Isolation Forest algorithm uses decision trees and follows the same principle as the Random Forest(Anagha et al., 2023). The isolation forest method is designed to identify irregularities, such fraudulent transactions, instead of relying on typical data points. Using the minimum and maximum values, the algorithm selects and divides features at random. The Isolation Forest Algorithm relies heavily on the contamination parameter. You have the option to set it to auto if you're not sure or to 0.1 for a 10% outlier. Outliers will be handled by the algorithm while fitting.

3.3 Semi Supervised Learning for Anomaly Detection

Combining a little amount of labelled data with a big amount of unlabelled data is common in semi-supervised learning, which is a subset of supervised learning tasks and methodologies. Unlabelled data is used for training. In contrast to supervised learning, which requires completely labelled training data, semi-supervised learning can make do with partially labelled data. Combining a small quantity of labelled data with a large amount of unlabelled data can greatly improve learning accuracy, according to many ML researchers (Matsuo et al., 2020). A trained human agent (to transcribe an audio segment, for example) or a physical experiment (to determine the 3D structure of a protein, for instance, or to determine if oil exists in a given region, for example) are common ways to get labelled data for a learning problem. Although obtaining unlabelled data is very cheap, the cost of labelling could render a completely labelled training set impractical. It is in these situations where semi-supervised learning really shines. Theoretically, semi-supervised learning is intriguing in ML as well, and it mimics the way humans learn. The following section provides examples of ML models that are semi-supervised.

3.3.1 Transudative SVM

Using unlabelled input, TSVM is an upgrade over standard support vector machines. Finding the biggest margin linear border in the Reproducing Kernel Hilbert Space is the usual goal of a standard SVM that uses just labelled data. Additionally, TSVMs make use of unlabelled data. Ideally, it like to find a way to label the unlabelled data in a way that gives a linear border the largest margin on both the labelled and unlabelled versions of the data. When it comes to unlabelled data, the decision boundary offers the best generalization error bound (Zhu, 2005). Unlabelled data appears to direct the linear boundary away from crowded places.

Figure 6. Transudative SVM (TSVM).

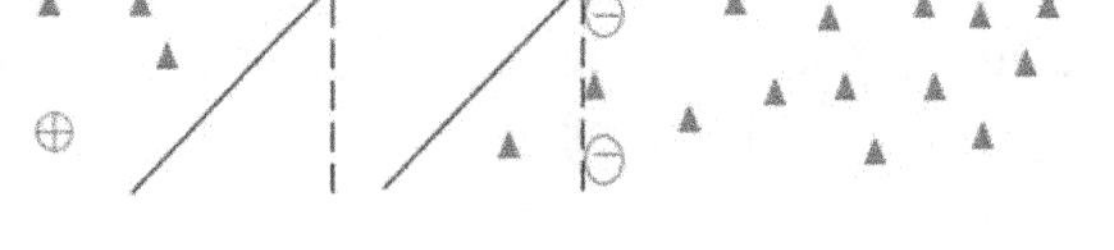

which, as illustrated in Figure 6, produces a multi-class SVM for semi-supervised learning. With the exception of SVMs, the maximum entropy discrimination approach increases the margin and is capable of handling unlabelled input. Unlike TSVM, SVMs use graph kernels. The graph kernels are specialized semi-supervised kernels that work with a regular SVM; TSVM is an optimization metric that is specific to the kernel used. However, determining the exact Transudative SVM solution is NP-hard. Several approximation algorithms have been presented and show positive results, see, (Joachims, 2000). A Semi-Definite Programming (SDP)-based training strategy that also applies to entirely unsupervised SVMs (Zhao et al., 2006). The simple binary classification scenario expresses the goal of finding a positive semi-definite matrix, M, as the process of successfully labelling unlabelled data. Using semi-definite programming on M, the support vector machine objective is stated as a continuous relaxation of the label outer product matrix yy. There are SDP solutions that work, but they are still pricey. The authors propose a multi-class SDP variation,

3.3.2 Graph-Based Methods

Graph-based methods involve drawing a network of interconnected nodes samples and edges similarities between them as measured by proximity or previous information. To facilitate their propagation along the graph, labels are presumed to be shared by linked samples. For accurate training sample labelling and consistent network outputs, a graph cut approach is the way to go. The out-of-sample problem, which occurs when labelling previously seen photographs, necessitates repeating the method. When it comes to segmentation, graph cuts are often used. The labels are passed on from one pixel or super pixel to another. In order to segment unknown images, labelled pixels are necessary. Although there is a notable distinction, atlas-based segmentation can still make use of graph-based techniques. In contrast to pixel-based segmentation, atlas-based segmentation generates an image graph. The process of test image segmentation involves propagating labels from one atlas to nearby unlabelled images in the network. It is possible to combine atlases with propagating labels in order to get a final label. Using the idea of smoothness along a graph, manifold regularization assigns labels to data that has not been discovered before. See this graph here. The Laplacian algorithm encodes node similarity. Segmentation and computer-aided diagnostics both make use of this technique. Contrary to supervised SVMs, semi-supervised SVMs assume a sparsely populated area between each class. To suit hyperplanes, semi-supervised SVM use labelled training data, whereas outside the margin, they prioritize unlabelled samples.

4. MACHINE LEARNING TECHNIQUES FOR THREAT INTELLIGENCE

One of the most common threats that contemporary institutions face is fraudulent activity that targets networked systems. Strong cybersecurity policies are essential for protecting vital data from fraudsters and hackers. It is essential to find innovative ways to prevent cyber dangers because they are growing increasingly complex. In order to improve cybersecurity strategies, this study seeks to investigate the connection between Cyber Threat Intelligence (CTI) and ML. The retail, banking, healthcare, and cybersecurity industries, among others, rely heavily on ML methods for anomaly detection, malware analysis, and risk prediction. Proactive defence relies on security teams using critical threat information CTI to better understand adversary strategies and enhance defensive measures. Data collection, processing, and classification can be mechanized by the integration of ML with CTI, enabling thorough analysis. Problems with risk assessment, obtaining accurate data, and beginning the process are all obstacles to deploying ML for BI.

4.1 NLP for Threat Intelligence

The requirements sought to identify the optimal dataset according to the use case. It is critical to identify all pertinent data sources in order to improve the accuracy and robustness of DL outcomes. A data's distribution and generalizability are affected by its description. Reduce distributional issues during Data Management by defining all data examples in the operating mode of an ML-based system. This relies on the challenging but essential premise that people can accurately recognize every conceivable circumstance when outlining needs. There has been some discussion on issues with tagged datasets pertaining to cybersecurity. It is challenging to gather high-quality, annotated data on cybersecurity events because of how sensitive and hidden they are. Considerations impacting deep learning models' capacity to generalize and perform well in situations where data is limited.

4.1.1 Applications of NLP

Sentiment Analysis: By analysing user sentiment on platforms such as Facebook, Instagram, Twitter, Google+, and Pinterest, businesses can gain significant insight into consumer issues. The goal of sentiment analysis is to deduce people's opinions on a subject from their unstructured textual data. Opinion mining and sentiment analysis are terms that describe the same thing: they both look at how people feel about certain topics, such product evaluations or cybersecurity (Fang & Zhan, 2015). Sentiment analysis has been used in various domains, including tourism, politics, marketing, and epidemiology, but its use in digital privacy and security is still in its early stages (Jurek et al., 2015). It was unable to find a study using sentiment analysis and text mining tools to analyse cybersecurity attitudes and behaviour on social media.

Entity Recognition: Metadata from CTIs typically includes logs and unstructured text. Knowledge discovery and threat association analysis rely on effectively recognizing CTI domain information, which includes domain entities. One challenge in ML is Named Entity Recognition (NER), which involves labelling sequences. Its goal is to find things in text that have a certain meaning. Recognizing entity boundaries and types is the job of the NER task. Manually created feature templates are the backbone of traditional NER models like Conditional Random Fields (CRF). Using the LSTM architecture's gate structure and cell memory state, as well as bidirectional learning of context, the BiLSTM model automatically collects context information. There is no interference between the position predictions, but the labels are related, which could provide an unlawful outcome. In order to learn label restrictions, CRF will make use of BiLSTM predictions. When it comes to entity recognition, the BiLSTM-CRF model yields combined findings. Because it uses fewer characteristics that are manually produced, this approach outperforms conventional ML algorithms when it comes to knowledge recognition and domain corpus extraction.

Topic Modelling: Discovering and identifying subjects within a corpus of documents is the goal of topic modelling. Latent topics, expressed as keywords, can be found in massive unlabelled datasets using this unsupervised learning technique. Assume, for the sake of argument, that our dataset contains newspaper articles from a number of prominent online news sources. After it feeds the algorithm the total number of topics, it will return the first k topics for each topic. Topics including politics, technology, and culture can be uncovered through keyword analysis. If it wants to get further into the major problems in each class, it might use a tagged dataset.

4.2 Anomaly Detection as a Component of Threat Intelligence

The goal of AD is to identify data patterns that deviate significantly from the norm. This method has extensive applications in fields such as medical diagnostics, industrial problem detection, fraud detection, and network intrusion detection. Finding unusual or suspicious activity within a network that could indicate a security breach is known as anomaly detection. Anomaly detection is crucial for identifying possible attacks in cloud systems due to the blurring of traditional security boundaries. Anomaly detection is an area where AI and ML algorithms really shine since they learn typical patterns of behaviour and can spot changes that could mean danger is on the horizon.

4.2.1 Use Cases

Insider Threat Detection: Former and current insiders in the intelligence establishment have sway over decision-making and access to sensitive resources. Following these steps is a typical procedure for making a decision: Certain issues require the expertise of insiders who are tasked with gathering intelligence. The next thing to do is collect and analyse data to back up your theories. Final reports submitted by insiders have direct or indirect influence on decision-making. While decisions are being made, malicious insiders might cause irreparable damage. A lot of people are focused on finding cyber insider risks (Andersen et al., 2004).

However, little effort has been made to automatically detect malicious insiders who tamper with decision-making processes.

Advanced Persistent Threat (APT) Detection: Major search engines have indexed around 1.37 billion distinct pages on the Internet. The web has progressed from a platform for serving static documents to a robust platform for delivering applications and disseminating information. Critical resources and confidential information are now shared online by businesses. Cybercrime has increased in recent years because to the prevalence and strength of the internet. The minimal likelihood of identification and prosecution makes cybercrime attractive to offenders. This has led to the growth of cybercrime as a whole and has made businesses more susceptible to assaults on their networks and services. Cyberspace is being used by governments for espionage and conflict. In order to mitigate the financial effects of cybercrime, tools such as intrusion detection systems, firewalls, and virus scanners were developed. Cybercriminals and spies have become very good at finding ways around security measures. In order to accomplish a certain goal, usually espionage, an APT employ a stealthy multistep attack. In order to accomplish their goals, APTs use multistep attacks. APTs use sophisticated techniques, like social engineering, and "zero-day exploits" to differentiate themselves from other forms of attacks. Governments and businesses are most threatened by APTs. Despite the fact that APTs frequently take advantage of unpatched security holes, existing detection methods depend on known attack signatures. Significant economic harm can be inflicted by APT assaults that are successful. In most cases, the monetary impact of such assaults is what motivates investments in security measures.

5. COMPARATIVE ANALYSIS

Cyber threats are attempts to steal information, breach integrity standards, and harm computing devices or networks. Cyber dangers include phishing, malware, IoT device attacks, denial of service, spam, network or mobile device intrusions, financial fraud, and ransomware (Jump, 2019). The study covers malware detection, intrusion detection, and spam detection. In (Virmani et al., 2022), authors examined the effectiveness of ML strategies in preventing cybercrime. Difficulties in applying ML methods were brought to light by the writers. According to the research, classifiers still require additional protection from adversarial assaults, even though ML is making cybersecurity better against cybercriminals. Cyber dangers and hostile assaults pose a significant threat to ML classifiers. The authors of (Jiang et al., 2016) provided a quick assessment of articles on implementing ML models to improve cyber security. The authors tackled common challenges in applying ML to security problems by identifying relevant datasets. In (Bhosale et al., 2020), the authors compared the performance of ML approaches for detecting anomalies. They evaluated the performance of feature selection in ML for IDS. The CNN classifier has the potential to significantly improve cyber security if fully utilised. In (Apruzzese, G., Colajanni, M., Ferretti, L., Guido, A., & Marchetti, 2018), authors examined the effectiveness of ML algorithms for detecting spam, malware, and intrusions. They argued that no ML technique is immune to cyberattacks. The authors of (Ribeiro et al., 2020) developed a statistical semi-supervised ML technique for detecting intrusions on Android mobile devices. Increased data traffic will lead to more cybercrimes. To defend Android mobile devices against advanced cybercrimes, advanced ML techniques must be developed to detect harmful activity. According to (Bouwman et al., 2020), network threat detection is a primary use of cyber threat intelligence. CTI platforms, such as the Malware Information Sharing Platform (MISP) (Wagner et al., 2016), were designed to communicate threat intelligence data. MISP is a hub-and-spoke sharing platform that provides attributes to describe network activity, including IP and MAC addresses, network ports, hostnames, domain names, email addresses, URLs, and payload hashes. It also generates rules for popular IDS like Snort (Park & Ahn, 2017), Suricata, and Bro (now Zeek). Previous studies by (Iklody et al., 2018) and (Mokaddem et al., 2019) have shown that the value of IoCs decreases with time due to their volatility. For example, an infected machine's IP address can be altered, a domain name can be exchanged for various reasons, some of which are malicious, while others are not. IoCs may become inaccurate over time and simply offer a suggestion of a cyber hazard. In an effort to improve detection accuracy, researchers have looked into both conventional and deep learning approaches. (Sarker et al., 2020) examined examples of several cyber security incidents, including unauthorised access, malware, denial of service, phishing, and zero-day assaults. Data science and ML are revolutionizing cyber security solutions, according to the authors. They demonstrated how traditional defensive strategies, including signature-based IDS, might fail in certain attacks. Using supervised and unsupervised learning, deep learning, and other techniques, the authors examined how popular data sets for cyber security research could reveal security problems. Topics such as data quality, context awareness, and prioritizing security alerts were highlighted by the writers as important topics that warrant additional investigation. There are attacks that target the data that ML models are trained om. A person's right to privacy could be violated if their adversary discovers that private data was utilized to construct a model. Typically, membership inference attacks describe these kinds of attacks. (Shokri et al., 2017) used Blackbox access to a Google and Amazon Maas model to identify if a given record was in the training data set. They generated numerous shadow models that mimicked the target model's behaviour and used training data sets they knew. They employed these models to distinguish between the target model's outputs for members and non-members of the training data. (Nasr et al., 2018) proposed a privacy technique for training ML models to prevent membership inference attacks and ensure membership privacy. The ML model's predictions on training data are indistinguishable from predictions on other data points from the same distribution in this technique. The authors created an adversarial training technique that minimises both the model's classification loss and the greatest gain from a membership inference attack.

6. ADVANTAGES AND DISADVANTAGES OF ANOMALY DETECTION

Anomaly based systems can detect misuse based on system and network behaviour, therefore it is not necessary to know the type of misuse beforehand. Because of this, abuse that a signature-based system could miss can be identified. Anomaly based systems sometimes raise numerous false alerts, even if system or network behaviour can vary greatly. Differentiating between normal and genuinely deviant behaviour is an art form in and of itself as shown in Table 1.

Table 1. Anomaly Detection Techniques Based on ML

S.NO	Techniques	Advantages/Disadvantages
1	Neural Network	1.The capacity to draw broad conclusions from sparse, noisy, or absent evidence. 2. Shows promise for spotting previously undiscovered patterns.
2	Fuzzy Logic	1.The reasoning is more of an approximation than a guarantee. 2. Very effective, particularly when dealing with probes and port scans. 3. Very demanding on resources.
3	Bayesian Network	1.First, it stores the possible connections between the relevant variables. 2. Capability to absorb both new information and existing body of knowledge.
4	Genetic Algorithm	1.Biologically inspired and employs evolutionary algorithm. 2. Selection, Crossover, and Mutation are some of the properties used. 3. Skilled in finding the best parameters and finding rules for classification.

7. EMERGING TRENDS AND CHALLENGES

In order to guarantee its efficacy and dependability in different contexts, anomaly detection a potent tool for detecting odd patterns or occurrences presents a number of obstacles that must be overcome. Here are a few of the most important obstacles:

- **Dynamic Environments of Adaptation:** Anomaly detection systems need to be flexible enough to adjust to ever-changing data distributions, settings and patterns of typical behaviour. It is crucial to construct adaptive detection of anomaly models that can dynamically alter detection thresholds and learn from fresh data continuously if we want to keep detection performance over time.
- **Reducing the Frequency of False Positives and False Negatives:** In order to make sure that anomaly detection systems work, it's important to find a happy medium between FP, where typical instances are wrongly marked as anomalies, and FN, where real anomalies not able to detect. Thoroughly adjusting detection thresholds and model parameters is necessary to maximize anomaly detection sensitivity while minimizing false alarms.
- **Explainability and Interpretability:** Building confidence, permitting interventions of human-in-the-loop and model behaviour understanding all depend on being able to interpret and explain the decisions made by anomaly detection models. Additional research and development are needed to address the ongoing difficulty of making anomaly detection technologies, like deep learning, more interpretable and explainable.
- **Imbalanced for Data Distribution:** In many anomaly detection datasets, the number of normal examples is much higher than the number of anomalous instances, indicating an imbalance in the class distributions. approaches like data resampling, ensemble approaches or cost-sensitive learning are necessary to properly handle imbalance of class, which can cause model training to be biased and detection of poor performance due to imbalanced data distributions.
- **Subtle Anomalies for Detection:** In the presence of noise or natural fluctuations in data, it is extremely difficult to spot small irregularities that differ marginally from typical behaviour. It might be challenging to distinguish subtle anomalies from normal behaviour using typical detection approaches since they may not display identifiable patterns.

To overcome these obstacles, we need to improve our ML algorithms, data pretreatment methods, model evaluation approaches, and integration of domain-specific knowledge. If anomaly detection is to fulfil its promise of facilitating data-driven decision-making across domains, increasing operational efficiency, and strengthening security, these obstacles must be overcome.

8. FUTURE DIRECTIONS

Future CTI approaches and technologies include predictive analytics and automation. CTI will integrate with other security technologies, including SIEM systems, to provide a more comprehensive view of the threat landscape(Cinar, 2023). New technologies such as blockchain and quantum computing will significantly impact CTI.

8.1 Zero Trust

According to proponents of the Zero Trust security approach, it is prudent to treat all network traffic incoming and outgoing as malicious. Prior to granting access, all necessary checks, authorizations, and confirmations must be made. This technique lessens the potential for cyberattacks and data breaches by decreasing the attack surface (Sillaber et al., 2016). The business world is rapidly adopting this strategy. Integrating CTI into a Zero Trust security strategy allows organizations to monitor emerging vulnerabilities and proactively address them. With CTI, businesses can prevent credential theft and data breaches by quickly detecting and responding to suspicious activity. For instance, in the event that a company gets a CTI alert regarding a novel malware variant that targets a particular application, it can promptly address the threat by implementing security patches or modifying existing protocols. Companies can utilize CTI to swiftly determine the severity of a data breach and proceed accordingly(Tischler et al., 2001). CTI can help organisations prioritise security initiatives based on the top threats to their assets and activities. This can help firms make better decisions about risk management and resource allocation.

8.2 Social, Governance and Environmental Issues

In modern business practises, ESG considerations environmental, social, and governance—are given top billing. Stakeholders and investors assess a company's impact on society, the environment, and governance using ESG standards. When considering ESG factors, companies place a premium on cyber security. ESG objectives can be advanced with the support of CTI, which aims to detect and lessen the impact of cyber risks on business operations (Kokulu et al., 2019). A data breach, caused by a cyberattack on an organization's infrastructure, can expose sensitive customer information and damage the company's finances and reputation. Serious societal and environmental repercussions may result from damaging customer trust and having a detrimental influence on clients. Another one here. Websites that offer fake goods or steal personal information using a company's name can be detected by CTI as phishing or brand misuse. Companies risk having their ESG goals jeopardized if cyberattacks damage their reputation and the trust of their consumers (Gascon et al., 2017). Businesses can protect their customers' data and reputation as ethical leaders by using CTI to monitor for brand misuse, phishing, and other cyber threats.

8.3 Monitoring Account Takeover

Monitoring for account takeover entails detecting online leaks of company or employee logins and passwords. Monitoring is vital as hackers often exploit stolen or leaked credentials to gain unauthorised access to corporate assets and data. Having legitimate credentials allows attackers to easily carry out cyber assaults like phishing and data theft. The recent LAPSU$ hacking event highlights the need of monitoring credential breaches. Hackers used a large database of stolen credentials to get access to sensitive and confidential information from major organisations. To reduce the risk of credential-based attacks, organisations can monitor for leaks and implement security measures such as MFA. Monitoring credential leakage is just one part of a comprehensive CSP.

8.4 Account Surface Management

ASM is another area where CTI can be useful. An organization's digital attack surface, which includes all systems, applications, and data that could be vulnerable, is monitored by ASM. Credential breaches, in-the-wild vulnerabilities found through recent instances, and vulnerabilities with a one-day or zero-day exposure can all be better understood with the help of CTI. Organizations can enhance their capacity to detect potential gaps and dangers by integrating ASM into CTI.

8.5 Use of Cyber TI

When it comes to national security and business, CTI is paramount. By shedding light on the latest trends in malware and threat actors, threat environments, vulnerabilities, attack surfaces, and data breaches, CTI can assist organizations in both preventing and responding to assaults. CTI can shed light on how cyber dangers affect people and the planet. The growth of underground marketplaces that facilitate cybercrime, such as the dark web and Telegram, can be better understood with the use of CTI. It can also aid businesses in understanding the dangers posed by these threats.

9. CONCLUSION

CTI is a domain in which ML plays a crucial role in cybersecurity. The exponential increase in CTI data is complicating the ability of security analysts to efficiently assess large datasets and respond swiftly to emerging risks. ML algorithms automate threat detection by autonomously identifying trends and anomalies that may signify cyber threats. Consequently, these hazards can be promptly recognised. This enhances both the detection speed and the capacity of security professionals to visually evaluate CTI data for valuable insights. Security professionals may utilise ML to enhance network defences, mitigate vulnerabilities, and combat cyber adversaries. It accomplishes this by facilitating comprehensive analysis from multiple perspectives and standardising the representation of threat information. The cybersecurity sector may leverage open-source CTI repositories to enhance defences, foster collaboration, and facilitate information exchange. Machine learning can enhance cybersecurity strategies to address the evolving landscape of cyber threats. It is a fundamental component of CTI. This chapter illustrates the necessity of adaptive Machine learning models to address emerging cyber threats. The significance of anomaly detection for operational resilience is underscored.

REFERENCES

Ahrend, J. M., Jirotka, M., & Jones, K. (2016). On the collaborative practices of cyber threat intelligence analysts to develop and utilize tacit Threat and Defence Knowledge. In *2016 International Conference on Cyber Situational Awareness, Data Analytics and Assessment,* CyberSA. DOI: 10.1109/CyberSA.2016.7503279

Amari, S., & Wu, S. (1999). Improving support vector machine classifiers by modifying kernel functions. *Neural Networks*, 12(6), 783–789. DOI: 10.1016/S0893-6080(99)00032-5 PMID: 12662656

Anagha, T. S., Fathima, A., Naik, A. D., Goenka, C., Devamane, S. B., & Thimmapurmath, A. R. (2023). Credit Card Fraud Detection Using Machine Learning Algorithms. In *2023 International Conference on Computational Intelligence for Information, Security and Communication Applications (CIISCA),* (pp. 419–424). DOI: 10.1109/CIISCA59740.2023.00085

Andersen, D., Moore, A. P., Stanton, J. M., Cappelli, D. M., Rich, E., & Weaver, E. a, Gonzalez, J. J., Sarriegui, J. M., Zagonel, A., Mojtahedzadeh, M., & Shimeall, T. J. (2004). Preliminary System Dynamics Maps of the Insider Cyber-threat Problem. In *Proceedings of the 22nd International Conference of the Systems Dynamics Society*, (pp. 1–36).

Apruzzese, G., Colajanni, M., Ferretti, L., Guido, A., & Marchetti, M. (2018). *On the effectiveness of machine and deep learning for cyber security.*

Ben-Hur, A., & Weston, J. (2010). A user's guide to support vector machines. *Methods in Molecular Biology (Clifton, N.J.)*, 609, 223–239. DOI: 10.1007/978-1-60327-241-4_13 PMID: 20221922

Bhattacharyya, D. K., & Kalita, J. K. (2013). Network Anomaly Detection: A Machine Learning Perspective. *Network Anomaly Detection.* Advance online publication. DOI: 10.1201/b15088-14

Bhosale, K. S., Nenova, M., & Iliev, G. (2020). Intrusion detection in communication networks using different classifiers. In *Proceedings of the 2nd International Conference on Advanced Technologies for Societal Applications,* (pp. 19–28). DOI: 10.1007/978-3-030-16962-6_3

Bouwman, X., Griffioen, H., Egbers, J., Doerr, C., Klievink, B., & van Eeten, M. (2020). A different cup of TI? The added value of commercial threat intelligence. In *Proceedings of the 29th USENIX Security Symposium*, (pp. 433–450).

Burges, C. J. C. (1998). A Tutorial on Support Vector Machines for Pattern Recognition. *Data Mining and Knowledge Discovery*, 2(2), 121–167. DOI: 10.1023/A:1009715923555

Chandola, V., Banerjee, A., & Kumar, V. (2009). Anomaly detection: A survey. *ACM Computing Surveys*, 41(3), 1–58. DOI: 10.1145/1541880.1541882

Cinar, B. (2023). Cyber Threat Intelligence: Current Trends and Future Perspectives. *Journal of Engineering Research and Reports*, 25(4), 91–105. DOI: 10.9734/jerr/2023/v25i4905

Fang, X., & Zhan, J. (2015). Sentiment analysis using product review data. *Journal of Big Data*, 2(1), 5. Advance online publication. DOI: 10.1186/s40537-015-0015-2

Gascon, H., Grobauer, B., Schreck, T., Rist, L., Arp, D., & Rieck, K. (2017). Mining attributed graphs for threat intelligence. In *Proceedings of the 7th ACM Conference on Data and Application Security and Privacy*, (pp. 15–22). DOI: 10.1145/3029806.3029811

Gogoi, P., Bhattacharyya, D. K., Borah, B., & Kalita, J. K. (2011). A survey of outlier detection methods in network anomaly identification. *The Computer Journal*, 54(4), 570–588. DOI: 10.1093/comjnl/bxr026

Gupta, M., Gao, J., Aggarwal, C. C., & Han, J. (2014). Outlier Detection for Temporal Data: A Survey. *IEEE Transactions on Knowledge and Data Engineering*, 26(9), 2250–2267. DOI: 10.1109/TKDE.2013.184

Iklody, A., Wagener, G., Dulaunoy, A., Mokaddem, S., & Wagner, C. (2018). *Decaying Indicators of Compromise*. http://arxiv.org/abs/1803.11052

Jiang, H., Nagra, J., & Ahammad, P. (2016). *SoK: Applying Machine Learning in Security - A Survey*. http://arxiv.org/abs/1611.03186

Joachims, T. (2000). Transductive inference for text classification using support vector machines. In *Proceedings of the 20th International Conference on Machine Learning*.

Jump, M. (2019). Fighting cyberthreats with technology solutions. *Biomedical Instrumentation & Technology, February*.

Jurek, A., Mulvenna, M. D., & Bi, Y. (2015). Improved lexicon-based sentiment analysis for social media analytics. *Security Informatics*, 4(1), 9. Advance online publication. DOI: 10.1186/s13388-015-0024-x

Kokulu, F. B., Shoshitaishvili, Y., Soneji, A., Zhao, Z., Ahn, G. J., Bao, T., & Doupé, A. (2019). Matched and mismatched SOCs: A qualitative study on security operations center issues. In *Proceedings of the ACM Conference on Computer and Communications Security*, (pp. 1955–1970). DOI: 10.1145/3319535.3354239

Korstanje, M. E. (Ed. (2016). Threat mitigation and detection of cyber warfare and terrorism activities. *IGI Global, January 2017*, 198–219. DOI: 10.4018/978-1-5225-1938-6.ch009

Li, V. G., Dunn, M., Pearce, P., McCoy, D., Voelker, G. M., Savage, S., & Levchenko, K. (2019). Reading the tea leaves: A comparative analysis of threat intelligence. In *Proceedings of the 28th USENIX Security Symposium*, (pp. 851–867).

Matsuo, Y., LeCun, Y., Sahani, M., Doina, P., David, S., Masashi, S., Eiji, U., & Jun, M. (2020). Machine Learning: A Review of Learning Types. *Neural Networks 152, 7*(1), 267–275. DOI: 10.20944/preprints202007.0230.v1

Mishra, C., & Gupta, D. L. (2017). Deep Machine Learning and Neural Networks: An Overview. *IAES International Journal of Artificial Intelligence (IJ-AI), 6*(2), 66. DOI: 10.11591/ijai.v6.i2.pp66-73

Mokaddem, S., Wagener, G., Dulaunoy, A., & Iklody, A. (2019). *Taxonomy driven indicator scoring in MISP threat intelligence platforms*. http://arxiv.org/abs/1902.03914

Nasr, M., Shokri, R., & Houmansadr, A. (2018). Machine learning with membership privacy using adversarial regularization. In *Proceedings of the ACM Conference on Computer and Communications Security*, (pp. 634–646). DOI: 10.1145/3243734.3243855

Park, W., & Ahn, S. (2017). Performance Comparison and Detection Analysis in Snort and Suricata Environment. *Wireless Personal Communications*, 94(2), 241–252. DOI: 10.1007/s11277-016-3209-9

Ribeiro, J., Saghezchi, F. B., Mantas, G., Rodriguez, J., Shepherd, S. J., & Abd-Alhameed, R. A. (2020). An Autonomous Host-Based Intrusion Detection System for Android Mobile Devices. *Mobile Networks and Applications*, 25(1), 164–172. DOI: 10.1007/s11036-019-01220-y

Sarker, I. H., Kayes, A. S. M., Badsha, S., Alqahtani, H., Watters, P., & Ng, A. (2020). Cybersecurity data science: An overview from machine learning perspective. *Journal of Big Data*, 7(1), 41. Advance online publication. DOI: 10.1186/s40537-020-00318-5

Shokri, R., Stronati, M., Song, C., & Shmatikov, V. (2017). Membership Inference Attacks Against Machine Learning Models. *Proceedings - IEEE Symposium on Security and Privacy*, 3–18. DOI: 10.1109/SP.2017.41

Sillaber, C., Sauerwein, C., Mussmann, A., & Breu, R. (2016). Data quality challenges and future research directions in threat intelligence sharing practice. *WISCS 2016 - Proceedings of the 2016 ACM Workshop on Information Sharing and Collaborative Security, Co-Located with CCS 2016*, 65–70. DOI: 10.1145/2994539.2994546

Taheri, S., & Mammadov, M. (2013). Learning the naive bayes classifier with optimization models. *International Journal of Applied Mathematics and Computer Science*, 23(4), 787–795. DOI: 10.2478/amcs-2013-0059

Tischler, H., Platzer, A., Vian, P., & Genetti, B. (2001). On the Design of a Cyber Security Data Sharing System. *Europa Medicophysica*, 37(1), 39–50.

Tounsi, W., & Rais, H. (2018). A survey on technical threat intelligence in the age of sophisticated cyber attacks. *Computers & Security*, 72, 212–233. DOI: 10.1016/j.cose.2017.09.001

Virmani, C., Choudhary, T., Pillai, A., & Rani, M. (2022). Applications of machine learning in cyber security. *Research Anthology on Machine Learning Techniques, Methods, and Applications*, 621–641. DOI: 10.4018/978-1-6684-6291-1.ch033

Wagner, C., Dulaunoy, A., Wagener, G., & Iklody, A. (2016). MISP - The design and implementation of a collaborative threat intelligence sharing platform. *WISCS 2016 - Proceedings of the 2016 ACM Workshop on Information Sharing and Collaborative Security, Co-Located with CCS 2016*, 49–56. DOI: 10.1145/2994539.2994542

Wang, M. W. H., Goodman, J. M., & Allen, T. E. H. (2021). Machine Learning in Predictive Toxicology: Recent Applications and Future Directions for Classification Models. *Chemical Research in Toxicology*, 34(2), 217–239. DOI: 10.1021/acs.chemrestox.0c00316 PMID: 33356168

Wei, W., Visweswaran, S., & Cooper, G. F. (2011). The application of naive Bayes model averaging to predict Alzheimer's disease from genome-wide data. *Journal of the American Medical Informatics Association : JAMIA*, 18(4), 370–375. DOI: 10.1136/amiajnl-2011-000101 PMID: 21672907

Xu, X., Liu, H., & Yao, M. (2019). Recent Progress of Anomaly Detection. *Complexity*, 2019(1), 2686378. Advance online publication. DOI: 10.1155/2019/2686378

Zhang, H., Nian, K., Coleman, T. F., & Li, Y. (2020). Spectral ranking and unsupervised feature selection for point, collective, and contextual anomaly detection. *International Journal of Data Science and Analytics*, 9(1), 57–75. DOI: 10.1007/s41060-018-0161-7

Zhao, K., Tian, Y. J., & Deng, N. Y. (2006). Unsupervised and semi-supervised two-class support vector machines. In *Proceedings - IEEE International Conference on Data Mining, ICDM*, (pp. 813–817). DOI: 10.1109/ICDMW.2006.164

Zhu, X. (2005). *Semi-Supervised Learning Literature Survey*. http://digital.library.wisc.edu/1793/60444

Chapter 5
Deep Study on Automated Adversarial Security Equipment to Machine Learning Technique

Harishchander Anandaram
https://orcid.org/0000-0003-2993-5304
Amrita Vishwa Vidyapeetham, India

Shreenidhi K. S.
https://orcid.org/0000-0002-6844-0454
Rajalakshmi Engineering College, India

R. Kiruthigha
https://orcid.org/0000-0002-4355-2548
SRM Institute of Science and Technology, India

Kapil Joshi
https://orcid.org/0000-0003-1097-8347
Uttaranchal University, India

ABSTRACT

The fundamental idea of sturdiness of machine learning (ML) is examined in this chapter, as is its crucial function in establishing the reliability of computational intelligence (CI) systems. Solidity is defined in detail at the outset of the debate, as the capacity of machine learning emulates to sustain consistent performance under a variety of unexpected and different environmental conditions. Adversary

DOI: 10.4018/979-8-3693-7758-1.ch005

neural networks (ANN) investigate how (ML) might be compromised by properly constructed input perturbations, thereby compromising their reliability as well as security. ML longevity is examined from a number of angles,

1. INTRODUCTION

Two popular study topics in information science and computing today are ML and enormous amounts of data. In the ubiquitous computing environment, ML methods and structures are playing significant roles in everything from cloud computing centres to smart Network of Things (NoT) embedded gadgets. For the field of computational research, machine learning and data mining present both significant chances and challenges. Harnessing the potential of data to make greater choices is the foundation of big data (Ofoegbu et al., 2024). A high-precision information structure can be constructed using the numerous data samples used by the machine learning system. Intelligent automation has become a crucial component of the contemporary processing system in the age of big data as pervasive computation and neural networks technologies have advanced. Nonetheless, privacy flaws concealed within the common computing and artificial intelligence systems are becoming more noticeable.

Solidity is often a premise that pertains to a single thing. In this case, a sensor may be deemed sturdy if it is resistant to perturbations from surroundings. More specifically, robust is the capacity of an arrangement, emulate, or person to exhibit flexibility and resilience in the face of unforeseen changes or concerns by maintaining consistent and dependable behaviour across a wide range of situations, variations, or obstacles. As a result, neural network emulate sturdiness is defined using the generic definition below. Associated Works Carly showed that preventive distillation approaches do not considerably increase the endurance of brain networks by putting forth three assault strategies.

The suggested approach also performs well in relation to the developed confronted sample methodology that is already in use. Nathalie suggested three attack strategies to get past the three distinct obfuscated gradients techniques, arguing that the protection measures against them are ineffective. The device ML learning's security and safety issues have drawn increasing attention. Baggie provided a timeline that highlighted the connections between the nearly ten years of predictive safety research. This piece covers a lot of ground and a lot of material. However, it excludes cross-cutting topics and merely provides an overview of the security concerns in the computerised learning space.

In contrast, this research enumerates the risks associated with learning algorithms in the environment of big data, including a number of security issues with data collection, transfer, and storing. There is a lot of data in the enormous data ecosystem. Several concurrent procedures must be used when analysing data employing machine learning. Some programs and algorithm libraries that are frequently used in artificial intelligence in the big data context also have security issues, as do these algorithms during the data mining process (Sulaiman et al., 2024).

This are complemented by an adjoined essay, which gives a solid summary of security concerns and safety measures in the two intersecting fields of data mining and machine learning. By presenting a thorough threat emulate and categorising attacks and countermeasures using an adversarial framework, the paper failed to systematise the reliability and confidentiality of machine learning techniques. The paper discusses machine learning vulnerabilities and focuses on machine learning protection however it offers no countermeasures.

2. UNIVERSALITY BOOSTED LONGEVITY

Actual risk minimisation (ARM), a concept that takes into account minimising the mean loss on observed data samples as an actual estimate of the actual risk, or the projected true risk for the full input distribution, is frequently used to calculate emulates in training under supervision. ARM makes the so-called "closed-world presumption," which holds that testing and training information are disseminated entirely and identically. The knack of an established emulate to handle new data inputs that are taken from the exact same or very similar dispersion as the test set—known as out-distribution information (OD)—is referred to as generalisation (Gongada et al., 2024). Under static ecological settings, the generalisation guarantees steady prediction performance; nevertheless, it offers no recommendations about the handling of Input-of-distribution material (IOD).

Longevity, on the other hand, is concerned with quantifying the degree of forecasting accuracy that an emulate that was trained maintains in dynamic environment situations, where input data is continuously changing. If the emulate does not generalise well, longevity might not be a major concern. We believe generalisation represents an essential but insufficient requirement for longevity. For example, not fitting (skilled with very little/biased information) or incorrect inductive bias (link learning) might cause ML emulates failing to generalise. When the distributions of the input data shifts, such emulates will probably operate badly.

The Pipeline of the ML System and Security Concerns

The full data workflow from gathering data, data preparation, selection of features, trainer training, and forecasting emulates is included in the machine learning pipeline that we define. The huge data route for a ML system. It describes every step in the process, from the first massive data collection from real-life situations to the last machine learning system test then implementation. There could be issues with safety at every level. The primary security concerns with artificial intelligence systems are highlighted, and threats are become more varied and complicated in large data environments (Lad et al., 2024). every step of a machine learning systems. Variable input tools first gather information from the actual surroundings, after which a large amount of data is obtained. Certain application scenarios necessitate data preparation in order to make the acquired data available as data to be trained and algorithms to learn from because of its complex, high-dimensional, and variable properties. During the algorithm's education phase, the system developer trains the simulation using a machine learning algorithm and makes the emulate software API available for development users to utilise. At every point of the pipeline, but there are various safety risks.

An intruder can contaminate the framework and method during the data gathering phase by inserting fraudulent information. When an artificial intelligence program structure (like the help of Tens Caffeine, or Python Torch utility functions) featuring security flaws is called during the period of training, the algorithm that uses machine learning could be exploited (Ullah et al., 2024). Furthermore, because the emulate's instruction procedure is based on a prior emulate, it is susceptible to a white-box threat, in which the target has complete knowledge of the method of training, encompassing training emulates, training sets, etc. As a result, throughout the template utilisation phase, the intruders might reuse the design. Dimensional attacks are possible utilising the deep neural networks technique. A variety of attack methods, including emulate stealing, evasion, imitation, and reverse attacks, as well as unauthorised access to APIs, are present in the pipeline's final stages (Louati et al., 2024). At several points in the process, there might be assaults based on hidden backdoors and software weaknesses. Assaults can happen throughout the inductive and model validation phases.

AI Considered Dependable Must Be Strong

Because of its remarkable reliability, computer learning—and neural network technology in particular—has been widely pushed for adoption. In between, a number of issues beyond precision standards have surfaced, including malevolent assaults on systems that rely on machine learning and potentially dangerous ML usage.

Consequently, realistic standards for existing artificial brains have been outlined in the AI dependability guidelines.

These cover six important aspects: (i) durability and protection; (ii) impartiality and non-discrimination; (iii) honesty and explanation; (iv) privacy; (v) ownership and inspection; and (vi) sustainability. Building reliable actual artificial intelligence (AI) requires the intricate interaction of these factors (Das et al., 2024).

Like that, preserving confidentiality of data may conflict with having to provide a detailed explanation of the system outcome. In this way, longevity interacts and combines with the various other elements to provide an essential component of AI dependability. Since resilient AI systems can handle unforeseen inputs and disturbances without losing the ability to function, their longevity is actually a fundamental component of safety. In applications involving safety, where incorrect actions and failures might have disastrous results, it is extremely important to guarantee the proper degree of emulate robustness. Furthermore, longevity assurance and the addition of two essential components—reliable uncertainty quantification and efficient out-of-distribution monitoring capabilities—are necessary for the safeguarding of AI systems. When the artificial intelligence technique is considered then it must be considered as AI considered dependable must be strong in Figure 1.

Figure 1. AI considered dependable must be strong

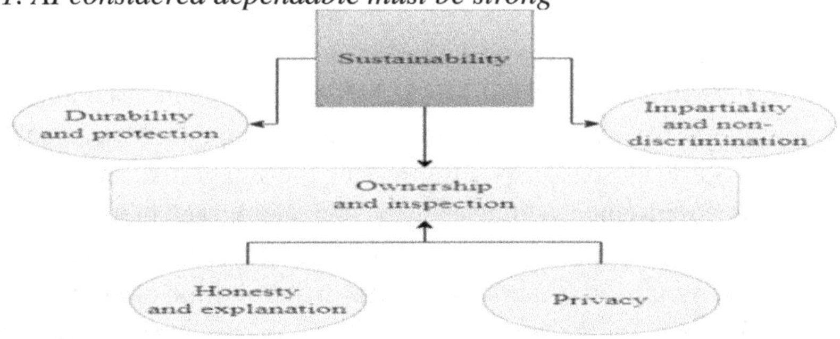

3. ML SYSTEMS CYCLE FOR COULD BE DANGEROUS

When building learning structures, many off-the-shelf programs and requirement libraries are identified upon and utilised. Because of its lengthy program chain, it has major flaws. For instance, AI engineers frequently employ Deep Flow, Coffeehouse, and Flame (Okoli et al., 2024). These building blocks do, however, contain security flaws. Attacks on the underlying software package or the system's method of learning may result in serious security issues. For instance, without compromising the algorithm's output or the emulates accuracy, an adversary may install a malware program and steal the initial data set. Artificial intelligence algorithms are more vulnerable to minor disruptions, according to research (Ghelani et al., 2024).

Jawed Su, Danilova, and Vasconcellos Vargas discovered that altering a single pixel in an image might significantly alter the algorithm's output. The dimensional gap of a deep network image (DNI) is linear, which makes it extremely sensitive to even slight changes in the input vector. As a result, the author suggests a minimal ant disturbance technique based on the inverse evolution algorithm, which can trick a variety DNI with little hostile knowledge. According to the author's paper's results findings, 66.2% of tested photos can be altered to prevent photographs on a single pixel with a typical confidence level of 96.9%. Additionally, there aren't many testing restrictions. It demonstrates how susceptible the existing DNI is to these kinds of threats.

Longevity Under Adverse and Non-Adversarial Conditions

Changes in distribution of information brought about by enemies in an attempt to trick or confuse the ML emulate are the focus of competitive longevity. Deliberate changes to the original data distribution are known as aggressive probability shifts. The changes at first concentrated on adding carefully constructed but undetectable sounds to the data. For instance, by tricking an ML system into classifying pimples as deadly skin cancers, a human-indiscernible noise can be introduced to medical photos to misrepresent the diagnosis. Subsequently, the input modifications comprise well-thought-out modifications that are noticeable and applicable in actual physical settings (Blackwood et al., 2024). When assessing the antagonistic resilience of recognition systems, for instance, adding eyewear to a photograph of a person is not the same as gently altering the picture's pixels. Consequently, improving the simulates' resistance to these minute, non-random changes in distribution of information without sacrificing its capacity to forecast real data is known as competitive longevity.

Non-adversarial longevity examines how well the model performs when data collection shifts occur due to either artificial data perturbations that mimic real-world settings or organic abnormalities. For example, photos of traffic signs taken in a region with little snowfall may naturally change to photos of an identical sign during periods of intense snowfall. A different method to simulate the influence of snow or various neutral impediments is to partially discolour the sign's photo by replacing a portion of it with white pixels (Wang et al., 2024).

Changing conditions frequently cause data-driven shifts, which cause mismatches between the classroom instruction spread and the placement. Both spatiotemporal (social standards behavioural changes in people) and non-temporal (location changes, sensing configurations) alterations are possible.

The massively parallel emulates non-adversarial longevity guarantees dependability in a variety of real-world situations, such as inherent noise or input modifications that may occur spontaneously sans malevolent intent.

Illustrations of Offensive Techniques

Development of academic work on adverse algorithms for learning. Illustrates the development of hostile neural network research. The algorithm that uses machine learning is vulnerable to delicate attacks, ranging from the notion of antagonistic attack to particular attack scenarios. At exactly the same time, several academics are dedicated on improving machine learning systems' longevity and defending against attack methods. In order to evaluate the experimental findings, we employ four distinct attack techniques: Deep Fool, Bam, which serves (Khan et al., 2024). The antagonistic image, disruptions, and examples of conflict. The example image is derived from Vision net data, while the rival images are produced using a pre-trained Resenting network. All four methods can trick an automatic neural mimic, as shown in.

4. PROTECTIVE METHODS FOR LEARNING MACHINE SYSTEMS

Categorisation of Protective Strategies

Our analysis and classification of strategies for defence is based on their qualities. The automatic learning technique's grouping of tactics for defence.

We categorise protective measures into two groups. One type of defence is reactive in nature meaning it will be used after a hack on machines that learn (Khaleel et al., 2024). The second is proactively barriers, which are implemented prior to an attack on deep learning technologies. It is often recommended to employ aggressive defence strategies. Interactive defences consist of three components: selection verification, regular retraining, and identifying attacks. In the ongoing retrain stage, new learning information and feature design are employed. To continuously implement selection identification, we must adjust what is the border across expectation and actual value. The system that uses machine learning uses the target's information to offer an array of pre-emptive defences. The perpetrator has a thorough understanding of the system. Building a strong learning algorithm and assault detection is our equivalent approach. The system is not understood by the attacker. Our equivalent approach, which includes learner groupings, randomisation, and data encryption, is to conceal both input and output from the system. By consistently applying game theory, we can create a robust safety evaluation process and enhance the safety of our system (Habeeb et al., 2024).

5. EFFICACY OF OFFENSIVE

1. Negative Instruction:
    - Results: Emulation robustness versus hostile cases is typically improved through combative instruction. When juxtaposed with simulates taught with on solid information, those trained with hostile instances frequently exhibit greater defence against comparable approaches.
    - Effects: Even though it works well, competitive training can result in higher processing costs and lower efficiency on data that is fresh. It's still difficult to balance longevity with precision, which suggests that more effective methods for training or mixed strategies are required (Katamoura et al., 2024).
2. **Process preventive**:
    - Results: Reducing the emulate sensitivity to hostile disturbances, preventive distillate might increase longevity. This approach might not prove adequate on itself, but it performs well whenever paired with various other countermeasures.
    - Effects: Investigation could look into ways to combine defending distillery with other defences to maximise its general efficacy, however the trade-off with protective condensation is the possible loss of individual capability and higher instructional sophistication.
3. **Input Pre-processing**:
    - Results: Rivalry can be lessened by using strategies like characteristic compression and data sanitisation, especially when paired with other defensive approaches.
    - Effects: Pre-processing might constitute a helpful initial line of protection, but in order to provide complete protection, it frequently needs to be combined with additional tactics. Modern pre-processing techniques and their combination with existing protections may need further investigated in investigation (Ofoegbu et al., 2024).

6. CONSTRAINTS OF EMPIRICAL TECHNIQUES

Since all of these evaluation methods rely on data fabrication or shifting data collection to verify the emulates resilience against changed inputs, their observational character is an inevitable drawback. On order to derive a statistical estimate of the confidence we have on the program when it encounters unforeseen changes in its input, they calculate longevity rankings on that information. The longevity of the emulates is not guaranteed if these techniques fail to identify failed checks (Mohammad et al., 2024).

This raises the question of whether official verification techniques, as compared to empirically-guided validation techniques, carry out a thorough investigation of a system's space given a set of attributes to check. In order to establish assurance on an emulation based on predetermined quantitative verifying criteria, scientists have suggested implementing formal methods of validation like as ReluPlex the FANNETT. The sheer number and complexity of the imitates, as well as the large dimensions of the data being used, provide problems for these approaches, such as algebraic bursting, which makes it extremely difficult to account for every potential input variable.

Because of this, its use is frequently limited to specific mimic kinds, falling beneath with the state learning the art and being less common in contemporary machine learning scenarios. The formalisation of the asset that has to be checked is a further crucial restriction; if something is not correctly defined, it must be tested. Because it is difficult to articulate and define requirements for comprehensive lifespan evaluation against physiological shifts or specific to the application constants, the majority of checking approaches concentrate on simulating lifetime versus lap norm-bounded (Alzaabi et al., 2024).

Lowering Details

For the purpose of to prevent inaccurate or unbalanced estimations, data a demeaning is the act of removing biases from samples used to train artificial intelligence imitates.

Arguably the most common data bases in machine learning applications that can be addressed computationally are that of sampling bias. To lessen ERM susceptibility to the acquisition of patterns linked to the adulthood, which leaves it open to minority stimuli like rare situations, training data examples are debased using a variety of methodologies.

To reduce variance in information, it is customary to use either more samples or down sampling. By creating fresh data points or duplicating pre-existing ones, up-sampling, also known as over sampling, raises the number of occurrences in the minority group. SMOTE (Artificial Minority Oversampling Method) and ADASYN (Innovative Hybrid Testing) are two well-liked expanding methods (Hosen et al., 2024). Security issues are concerned so all details are mentioned in Figure 2.

Figure 2. Approaches of security issue

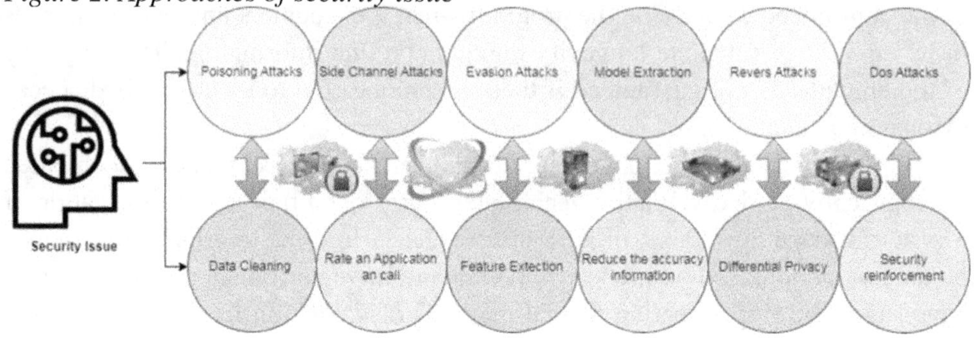

7. CONNECTION PROTECTIVE STRATEGIES AND SAFETY RISKS

Usually are several defensive strategies for every assault and a connection between each offensive and defence strategy is well-established. The machine learning system's security issue in the context of massive data is shown in the left column, and its protective measures are shown in the related right field. We will present some new countermeasures for assaults, while we won't go into much depth regarding defences for conventional security issues. For instance, the dodge attack happened during the test phase, which is when the adverse selecting features method was used (Wang et al., 2024).

The feature is chosen based on the produced classifier's generalisability and the integrity of its data handling. In addition to improving the bagging classifier's capacity for generalisation, it also strengthens its defences against evasion assaults. In order to lower the amount of information in the signal and prevent an attacker from obtaining information about the behaviour of the victim, we can restrict the rate at which an application can contact memory through the Programming Interface (MPI) or minimise the level of measurements in the case of GPU-side channel assaults. The associated defensive strategies are surveillance and protection strengthening, whereas the attackers use DoS attacks against continuous neural network techniques (Chirra et al., 2024).

Enhancing Information

Using the ERM, data enrichment seeks to increase the quantity of unique cases and diversify those used for training. By encouraging the formation of depictions of features immune to unnecessary noises or intrinsic distortions, it uses data modifications to create fresh artificial signals that promote robust generalisation. For example, fundamental picture enhancements can be physical modifications like rotational rotation, translation, and mirroring, or pixel-value modifications like contrast and hue modifications (Talukder et al., 2024).

The degree of each of these perturbations may be adjusted to guarantee a positive regularisation impact upon the results while avoiding appreciably changing the data distributed. Additional boosting methods boost the emulate's resilience to occlusions and broad knowledge loss by methodically removing data obtained from the learning inputs. Similar to dropping out, cut-out augmentation eliminates input neurone activations linked to arbitrary input picture segments. The mix-up augmenting, which uses linear mixing of previously acquired photographs and labels to promote more reliable projections on data beyond the initial distribution, is found at a greater degree of intricacy (Sanagana et al., 2024).

Technologies derived from mix-ups have helped to prolong the duration of wrongdoing. By maximising the total amount of information preserved in the original image pairs while maintaining importance characteristics during the procedure of mixing, Crossword Mix outperforms Mix Up (Olabanji et al., 2024). By randomly selecting the mask form and related shape variables (for example, a rectangle face with measured dimensions), Seamless Mix produces a uniform blurring mask that reduces harsh effects on the edges. Then, each pair of shots is blended using the comparable proportions of all of them that were obtained with the disguise (Prince et al., 2024).

Investigation on Safety Scenarios

The following part examines a particular instance: the drone deployment the business's machine learning solution. The challenging technique of producing precise reconstructions in three dimensions from 3D photos is known as photogrammetric. The first machines learning-powered photographic motor developed for commercial use is called Map Engine. With the latest version, Map Machine is analysing over 25,600 maps monthly for over 3,850 customers in 176 nations (Prince et al., 2024).

Leveraging large data, a smart drone Map Motor predictive system The Map Computer cloud computer is used by Hummed Ply's drone system to process photos smartly. It can realise how to map terrain and create high-definition maps, as well as finish the machine-learning image recognition and guidance capability.

That is the case with the Google Map Processor structure, which is the standard example of using big data-based predictive technologies (Li et al., 2024).

We examine a few potential attack points for the computer learning applications case. As far as the criminal is aware, it can be classified as a black box assault, grey panel assault or white panel assault. Attacks such as poisoning, fraud, denial of assistance, man-in-the-middle, and imitate theft may occur during imitate attacks using API authorized availability, etc (Ni et al., 2024).

Maps Photographic Map Engine uses techniques for machine learning to create the model using the data that has been downloaded to the cloud. In order to gather 2D imagery, images sensors, such as photographic equipment, are first carried by drone terminals. After then, drones will use the API gateway to connect to the web-based data centre, which offers users algorithms as a service. Numerous drone terminals submit picture data to the data centre, which uses its integrated machine learning algorithm to process and analyse the images before sending findings to the flying passengers (Schmaltz et al., 2024).

Essentially, the public cloud data centre supplies neural network replicates and computing capacity for real-time networked drone systems to enable them accomplish intelligent making of choices. Additionally, the drone includes an analytical capability known as Live Map, whose can do certain tasks related to data processing. Computer communication is done with drone map computer so detailed are described in Figure 3.

Figure 3. Intelligent drone map computer

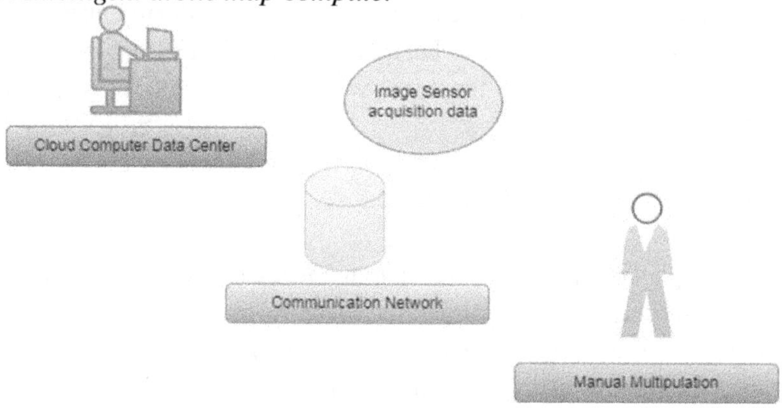

8. APPROACHES WITH EMULATE CONCENTRIC PLANNING

Knowledge Transmission

A machine learning approach called transfer learning uses the information that the system has gained from one task to enhance a related one. The idea behind transferable education is that DNI slowly acquires depictions of features that can be utilised wholly or partially moved onto a different challenge. These feature representations range from basic, task-agnostic properties (lines) to complicated, task-specific properties (forehead or ears for recognition of faces tasks) (Kolluri et al., 2024).

Retraining a DNI on a sizable and varied dataset, followed by the use of the primary n prepared layers (sometimes referred to as featured extractors) as an initialisation for another that will be subsequently prepared on another dataset, is a popular method of implementing transfer learning. There are numerous educational techniques, and the effectiveness of the understanding translation from the initially trained brain to an entirely new one depends on the method chosen. Regarding duration, it has already been shown that in some situations, both in antagonistic as well as non-adversarial ones, it can lengthen the replicates.

Although it may seem intuitive that using a limited unsupervised database using a total parameterized image network design will result in high IID performance, shortcut development and under-fitted neurones could cause the network to behave unpredictably when faced with out-of-distribution inputs. Using retrained emulates can reduce the possibility of shortcut development and under-fitted neurones. Additionally, large unlabelled target datasets can be exploited to train emulates that perform an auxiliary, pretext job to learn rich characteristic representations, such as learning to discriminate between photos, thanks to advancements on Human-supervised learning (HSL) for learning representations (Abdi et al., 2024).

Those self-learned emulates are used as prepared feature extraction algorithms in SSL learning through transfer. Unlawful use of the system's artificial intelligence methods is possible. With the help of user-uploaded 2D image data, the cloud storage centre builds the machine learning model. Data from tests and training photos is processed using deep artificial neural networks. A dimension reduction exploit on the artificial neural network is feasible if the attacker understands the basic parameters of the automated acquiring algorithm. to make it possible for the device to differentiate the photograph from other, wholly unrelated stuff. In this sense, the tailored to the system algorithms confidentially should be reinforced initially, followed by an improvement in the deeper learning dimensions correction algorithm's durability. Lastly, a procedure for filtering should be created by the system to remove the anomalous images, and the image that was edited ought to be juxtaposed to the distinctive (Joshi et al., 2024).

Putting Together

In machine learning, assembled is a potent strategy which incorporates several separate emulates that have been individually optimised on identical datasets to produce recommendations that are more accurate and improve predictive outcome in comparison to utilising only one mimic.

Since multiplicity can add durability, it has been demonstrated that ensemble resembles are more resilient than a single impersonates when examining the effect of collaboration on longevity.

Mani goes a step further by injecting a tiny subset of hostile samples into each impersonate of a symphony to make them resistant to a particular hostile approach. This benefits the entire group as a whole, even if it calls for practicing more replicates.

9. CONCLUSION

In order to thoroughly illustrate the security concerns at every stage of the machine learning model under the Big Data pipeline, this study proposes an algorithm and workflow. Each level of the machine learning workflow highlights the safety issue and preventive strategy, and security dangers and issues in AI systems are thoroughly examined and categorized. Five categories list our benefits over the linked works.

Significant findings on the weaknesses of the models it emulates and the efficacy of different defensive tactics have been gained from the study of hostile machine learning for resilient security measures.

Analysis of the experiment results and comparisons across four different attack strategies reveals that JSMA exhibits the strongest attack effect and FGSM consumes the least amount of time. The related linkages between assault and defensive tactics in an automated learning system are disclosed, and the defence techniques are categorised into reflexive protection and aggressive protection. The thorough investigation of longevity in the above section leads to the identification of replicate longevity as a crucial component in guaranteeing the credibility and dependability of artificial intelligence programs, and that drone-cloud algorithm scenario is chosen as actual.

In discussing the methods to strengthen ML longevity, this section offers a variety of gets closer each with distinct advantages and disadvantages, providing a comprehensive knowledge of their possible effects and what compromises they involve. While learning via transfer, adversarial training, and modified regularises serve as the cornerstones of robust emulation optimisation, techniques like data degrading and data enhancement are used during the data training preparation phase. Post-training techniques like imitate repairs and pruning, which work immediately on what was initially emulated to reduce its weak parts or modify them to lessen detected cracking, are last but certainly not final.

This chapter's conclusion is a call for further action for more investigation and creativity in the subject of machine learning longevity, not its end. It acknowledges that persistence is a constant endeavour rather than a fixed objective, one that necessitates constant improvement and modification regardless of ever-evolving real-world circumstances and increasingly sophisticated simulations. The methods and insights covered here not only deepen our awareness of longevity in the larger context of machine learning, but they also highlight the necessity of moving from abstract concepts to real-world applications of ML longevity. In order to effectively meet the needs of practical problems machine learning applications, particularly safety-critical ones, it promotes giving practitioners the tools they must regularly evaluate and improve the durability of their imitates on a human-in-the-loop basis.

In order to effectively confirm the resembles longevity in the absence of spontaneous distribution shifts, we then explore how DL software testing makes use of well-established methodologies to improve the search for changes in data that expose imitates flaws. Both physical and digital violent attacks are effective means of revealing mimic drawbacks, particularly when faced with carefully designed use scenarios or maliciously constructed information.

REFERENCES

Abdi, N., Albaseer, A., & Abdallah, M. (2024). The Role of Deep Learning in Advancing Proactive Cybersecurity Measures for Smart Grid Networks: A Survey. *IEEE Internet of Things Journal*, 11(9), 16398–16421. DOI: 10.1109/JIOT.2024.3354045

Alzaabi, F. R., & Mehmood, A. (2024). A review of recent advances, challenges, and opportunities in malicious insider threat detection using machine learning methods. *IEEE Access : Practical Innovations, Open Solutions*, 12, 30907–30927. DOI: 10.1109/ACCESS.2024.3369906

Blackwood, A., Carrington, J., Baryshevsky, S., & Morrison, G. (2024). The implementation of a hybrid large language emulate for adaptive cryptographic cyber defense.

Chirra, D. R. (2024). Advanced Threat Detection and Response Systems Using Federated Machine Learning in Critical Infrastructure. *International Journal of Advanced Engineering Technologies and Innovations*, 2(1), 61–81.

Das, S., Krishnamurthy, B., Das, R. R., & Shiva, S. G. (2024). State of the art: Security Testing of Machine Learning Development Systems. In *2024 IEEE 14th Annual Computing and Communication Workshop and Conference (CCWC)* (pp. 0534-0540). IEEE.

Ghelani, D. (2024). Enhancing data security: Machine learning approaches for intrusion detection in computer networks. *Journal of Environmental Science and Technology*, 3(1), 611–629.

Habeeb, M. A., Khaleel, Y. L., & Abdulnabi, A. R. (2024). Enhancing Security and Performance in Vehicular Adhoc Networks: A Machine Learning Approach to Combat Adversarial Attacks. *Mesopotamian Journal of Computer Science*, 2024, 122–133. DOI: 10.58496/MJCSC/2024/010

Hosen, M. S., Al Mamun, M. A., Khandakar, S., Hossain, K., Islam, M. M., & Alkhayyat, A. (2024). Cybersecurity Meets Data Science: A Fusion of Disciplines for Enhanced Threat Protection. *Nanotechnology Perceptions*, 236–256.

Joshi, M., Birla, S., Pal, H., Khatri, K., Kadwal, M., & Salitra, D. (2024). AI-Driven Intrusion Detection Systems: Leveraging Deep Learning for Network Security. *Nanotechnology Perceptions*, 573–585.

Katamoura, S., Aksoy, M. S., & AlKhamees, B. (2024). Privacy and Security in Artificial Intelligence and Machine Learning Systems for Renewable Energy Big Data. In *2024 21st Learning and Technology Conference (L&T)* (pp. 209-214). DOI: 10.1109/LT60077.2024.10468941

Khaleel, Y. L., Habeeb, M. A., Albahri, A. S., Al-Quraishi, T., Albahri, O. S., & Alamoodi, A. H. (2024). Network and cybersecurity applications of defense in adversarial attacks: A state-of-the-art using machine learning and deep learning methods. *Journal of Intelligent Systems*, 33(1), 20240153. DOI: 10.1515/jisys-2024-0153

Khan, M., & Ghafoor, L. (2024). Adversarial Machine Learning in the Context of Network Security: Challenges and Solutions. *Journal of Computational Intelligence and Robotics*, 4(1), 51–63.

Li, G., Wang, S., Chen, Y., Zhou, J., & Zhao, Q. (2024). A hybrid framework for ransomware detection using deep learning and monte carlo tree search.

Louati, F., Ktata, F. B., & Amous, I. (2024). Big-IDS: A decentralized multi agent reinforcement learning approach for distributed intrusion detection in big data networks. *Cluster Computing*, 27(5), 1–19. DOI: 10.1007/s10586-024-04306-9

Mohammad, N., Prabha, M., Sharmin, S., Khatoon, R., & Imran, M. A. U. (2024). Combating banking fraud with it: Integrating machine learning and data analytics. *The American Journal of Management and Economics Innovations*, 6(07), 39–56. DOI: 10.37547/tajmei/Volume06Issue07-04

Ni, C., & Li, S. C. (2024). Machine learning enabled industrial iot security: Challenges, trends and solutions. *Journal of Industrial Information Integration*, 38, 100549. DOI: 10.1016/j.jii.2023.100549

Ofoegbu, K. D. O., Osundare, O. S., Ike, C. S., Fakeyede, O. G., & Ige, A. B. (2024a). Real-Time Cybersecurity threat detection using machine learning and big data analytics: A comprehensive approach.

Ofoegbu, K. D. O., Osundare, O. S., Ike, C. S., Fakeyede, O. G., & Ige, A. B. (2024b). Data-Driven Cyber Threat Intelligence: Leveraging Behavioral Analytics for Proactive Defense Mechanisms.

Okoli, U. I., Obi, O. C., Adewusi, A. O., & Abrahams, T. O. (2024). Machine learning in cybersecurity: A review of threat detection and defense mechanisms. *World Journal of Advanced Research and Reviews*, 21(1), 2286–2295. DOI: 10.30574/wjarr.2024.21.1.0315

Olabanji, S. O., Oladoyinbo, O. B., Asonze, C. U., Oladoyinbo, T. O., Ajayi, S. A., & Olaniyi, O. O. (2024). Effect of adopting AI to explore big data on personally identifiable information (PII) for financial and economic data transformation. *Available atSSRN* 4739227.

Prince, N. U., Al Mamun, M. A., Olajide, A. O., Khan, O. U., Akeem, A. B., & Sani, A. I. (2024). IEEE Standards and Deep Learning Techniques for Securing Internet of Things (IoT) Devices Against Cyber Attacks. *Journal of Computational Analysis and Applications*, 33(7), 1270–1289.

Prince, N. U., Faheem, M. A., Khan, O. U., Hossain, K., Alkhayyat, A., Hamdache, A., & Elmouki, I. (2024). AI-Powered Data-Driven Cybersecurity Techniques: Boosting Threat Identification and Reaction. *Nanotechnology Perceptions*, 332–353.

Sanagana, D. P. R., & Tummalachervu, C. K. (2024). Securing Cloud Computing Environment via Optimal Deep Learning-based Intrusion Detection Systems. In *2024 Second International Conference on Data Science and Information System (ICDSIS)* (pp. 1-6). DOI: 10.1109/ICDSIS61070.2024.10594404

Schmaltz, K., Thompson, S., Mendes, D., & Carvalho, J. (2024). Robust defense mechanisms against adversarial ransomware attacks: Implementing a universal network-level detection filter.

Sulaiman, M., Waseem, M., Ali, A. N., Laouini, G., & Alshammari, F. S. (2024). Defense strategies for epidemic cyber security threats: emulateing and analysis by using a machine learning approach. *IEEE Access*.

[REMOVED IF= FIELD]Gongada, , T. NAgnihotri, , ASantosh, , KPonnuswamy, , VNarendran, , SSharma, , TBaker El-Ebiary, , Y. A. (2024). Leveraging Machine Learning for Enhanced Cyber Attack Detection and Defence in Big Data Management and Process Mining. *International Journal of Advanced Computer Science & Applications, 15*(2).

[REMOVED IF= FIELD]Lad, , S. (2024). Harnessing Machine Learning for Advanced Threat Detection in Cybersecurity. *Innovative Computer Sciences Journal, 10*(1).

Talukder, M. A., Islam, M. M., Uddin, M. A., Hasan, K. F., Sharmin, S., Alyami, S. A., & Moni, M. A. (2024). Machine learning-based network intrusion detection for big and imbalanced data using oversampling, stacking feature embedding and feature extraction. *Journal of Big Data*, 11(1), 33. DOI: 10.1186/s40537-024-00886-w

Ullah, F., Turab, A., Ullah, S., Cacciagrano, D., & Zhao, Y. (2024). Enhanced network intrusion detection system for internet of things security using multimodal big data representation with transfer learning and game theory. *Sensors (Basel)*, 24(13), 4152. DOI: 10.3390/s24134152 PMID: 39000931

Wang, H., Wu, J., Zhang, C., Lu, W., & Ni, C. (2024). Intelligent Security Detection and Defense in Operating Systems Based on Deep Learning. *International Journal of Computer Science and Information Technologies*, 2(1), 359–367. DOI: 10.62051/ijcsit.v2n1.37

Wang, S., Li, Y., & Chen, F. (2024). Optimizing blue team strategies with reinforcement learning for enhanced ransomware defense simulations.

Chapter 6
Deep Learning-Based Malware Detection and Classification Using Inception-ResNetv2 and DenseNet Architectures

Rasmita Kumari Mohanty
https://orcid.org/0000-0002-5828-5649
VNR Vignana Jyothi Institute of Engineering and Technology, Telangana, India

Kunda Suresh Babu
https://orcid.org/0000-0002-1533-5837
Narasaraopeta Engineering College, India

Kunda Praveen
https://orcid.org/0000-0001-7599-2356
Matrusri Engineering College, India

Gamidell Yedukondalu
https://orcid.org/0000-0001-8874-6912
CVR College of Engineering, Mangalapally, India

ABSTRACT

Malware detection and classification is a critical aspect of cybersecurity, given the increasing sophistication and prevalence of malicious software. In this chapter, the authors propose a novel approach utilizing deep learning architectures, specifically Inception-ResNet v2 and DenseNet, for the task of malware classification detection. These architectures are renowned for their ability to extract intricate features from

DOI: 10.4018/979-8-3693-7758-1.ch006

complex data, making them suitable for identifying subtle patterns indicative of malware behavior. Their methodology involves preprocessing malware samples into appropriate input formats for the deep learning models, leveraging techniques such as byte-level n-gram frequency analysis and opcode sequence extraction. The authors then fine-tune pre-trained Inception-ResNet v2 and DenseNet models on a large- scale dataset comprising various types of malware and benign software.

1. INTRODUCTION

Rising malicious software developments require strong malware detection systems and classification methods to provide digital system protection. Research work develops an innovative malware protection solution by deploying Inception-ResNet v2 and DenseNet deep learning structures to enhance security against malware assaults. Our methodology achieves its core power through deep learning models that extract complicated features from complex datasets to detect minor activity patterns signaling malicious operations.

For effective translation the research employs stringent preprocessing techniques which combine byte-level n-gram frequency analysis with opcode sequence extraction methods to convert malware samples into appropriate input data. These methods establish the basis for enhanced performance by adapting pre-trained Inception-ResNet v2 and DenseNet frameworks on datasets containing benign software alongside malware versions (Quartz, 2022). The technique stands as an accuracy improvement method for detection systems while also establishing the ability for models to adapt across multiple virus strains.

Experimental assessments show that our technique showcases excellent performance in differentiating harmful from benign samples while maintaining high detection accuracy. Our approach demonstrates resistance to adversarial attacks during real-world execution meaning it maintains operation strength when deployed. Our solution demonstrates flexible capabilities to combat diverse cybersecurity threats through its proven ability to detect malware in different families and their variants (Christiana et al., 2020).

Our research has improved cybersecurity defense capabilities through the innovative combination of state-of-the-art deep learning methods with core malware detection needs. Through our research achievements we obtained better malware detection methods yet delivered reliable scalable malware identification tools independent of cyberthreats that continue to transform. The research lays essential foundations to defend digital environments from modern attacks on rogue software (Li. et. al., 2017 & Wang et. al., 2017).

The research merges advanced deep learning frameworks such as Inception-ResNet v2 and DenseNet in order to advance the identification capabilities of malware through cybersecurity methods. The system targets high-precision models which differentiate harmful software from benign software through complex preprocessing routines and sophisticated feature decomposition methods. The proposed strategy seeks to show its superior ability to address new cyberthreats by testing with multiple datasets following extensive validation procedures. Traditional malware detection methods face multiple obstacles because they cannot identify subtle malicious behavior patterns and they struggle to adjust detection algorithms to new malware version changes which make cybersecurity challenges advanced.

A novel deep learning approach using Inception-ResNet v2 and DenseNet architectures has been proposed in this study to advance malware detection abilities. The goal is to develop models which accurately distinguish dangerous software from safe software while making use of advanced feature extraction methods for dataset training to bolster cybersecurity protection (Ghimire & Lee, 2013).

2. LITERATURE SURVEY

Traditional detection methods have fallen short under the fast-changing nature of malware therefore deep learning methods have become essential to more effectively combat this security threat. Deep learning models emerge as the superior choice compared to signature-based or heuristic approaches because they automatically find sophisticated patterns inside large datasets. Convolutional neural networks (CNNs) produce image representations by transforming malware binaries into images and exhibit outstanding accomplishment in malware classification operations. The incorporation of visual malware binary features allows for advanced detection which outperforms conventional detection technologies (Yuan et al., 2020). Sequential data analysis through opcode sequences and API call pattern monitoring gives malware models an enhanced ability to track temporal malware patterns which in turn improves detection outcomes.

Deep learning frameworks Inception-ResNet v2 and DenseNet enhance the performance of malware detection systems through recent architectural advancements. Such networks extract deep hierarchical patterns efficiently to detect subtle malware activities which standard analysis techniques miss. Scientific evidence demonstrates how these models become more accurate when linked with preprocessing approaches which analyze byte-level n-grams and extract opcodes. The hybrid structure of Inception-ResNet allows successful cybersecurity applications through its capacity to handle diverse malware datasets (Szegedy et al., 2017). The feature reuse capabilities of DenseNet have demonstrated their importance for discriminating malware families by proving effectiveness in scalable malware detection systems.

The authors present their web-based framework MLDroid in this paper for detecting malware on Android smartphones (Sahni & Nene, 2020). Because of Android smartphone popularity growth malware authors continue developing malicious programs disturbing both system security and user privacy daily. Dynamic analysis constitutes the foundation of the proposed framework for identifying malware in Android applications. Our proposed system employed feature selection approaches to choose specific parameters before conducting training experiments with actual world applications. The chosen features support model construction because they consider different machine learning approaches. Researchers performed this study analysis on more than 500 thousand Android mobile application packages. Our framework's highest detection success reached 98.8% through the combined application of four different machine learning methods (deep learning and farthest first clustering and Y-MLP and nonlinear ensemble decision tree forest approach) with rough set analysis managing feature subset selection.

Android's open-source software is made for mobile devices. When compared to other platforms, the Android platform has experienced rapid growth and acceptance. Because of its fame, malware has been growing at an exponential rate. To enable users and developers to control access to private data, system resources, and data storage needed by Android applications (apps), the Android system employed a permission mechanism (Muslim et al., 2021). An attacker could use it to their advantage to manipulate the data. A unique framework for Android malware detection is proposed in this study. We classified malware and benign using our framework's three main feature representation techniques for malware detection.

Revision of the Android app database shows fast growth despite the corresponding rise of Android malware according to Sahs & Khan (2020). Several research teams have analyzed Android malware detection but took alternative perspectives while developing their hypotheses. Research shows that machine learning presents a valid technique which successfully identifies malware attacks on Android mobile devices. Research has analyzed machine learning-based detection systems for Android malware yet diverse evaluations exist in these aspects. Our research expands upon previous examinations because it investigates multiple areas of the subject matter. The analysis in this research investigates machine learning-based techniques which detect Android malware. Our research introduces basic information regarding Android applications while discussing system architecture and security features as well as Android classifications.

Ahmad et al. (2020) used simulated and insurance datasets to evaluate Ordinary Least Squares Regression (OLSR) and Artificial Neural Networks (ANN) under conditions of multicollinearity. This research investigated which modeling technique produced the best results for highly correlated data sets while measuring performance through Root Mean Square Error (RMSE). The OLSR model received inferior performance than ANN in every scenario except when models containing nine and ten hidden layer nodes processed real-world data. The model that achieved maximum performance contained four nodes hidden within its network. Two-hidden-node ANN format delivered reduced RMSE than OLSR model alongside all other models for simulated data measurements.

Corporate financial risk management success depends on dynamic financial distress prediction efforts known as DFDP. Past research from Li et al., 2017 about ensemble FDP model construction fails to take data chronological weight into account. The paper introduces two innovative DFDP approaches built from time-based weighting mechanisms and the combined method of the Adaboost SVM ensemble. A voting ensemble under DEVE-AT structure integrates external combinations between two experts which evaluate error-based and time-based decisions using Adaboost-SVM and Timeboost-SVM algorithms. ADASVM-TW (Adaboost SVM as an integrated method with time weighting) employs a new error-time-based algorithm to update sample weights within each Adaboost execution step. The selection of these techniques benefits DFDP during financial distress concept drift events because they implement time-based weighting during Adaboost-based SVM ensemble development. An empirical experiment recreates time moving through 13 data batches containing yearly time steps using financial ratio data from 932 Chinese listed companies. The experimental results demonstrate that DEVE-AT and ADASVM-TW show better suitability for financial crisis concept drift handling and deliver enhanced DFDP outcomes versus single SVM along with batch-based ensemble with local weighted scheme, Adaboost-SVM, and Timeboost-SVM.

3. SYSTEM ANALYSIS

Their existing study outlines a novel method to control growing Android malware threats which target smartphones and tablets. The dominance of Android as the primary mobile operating system created a major security problem because its openness allows dangerous malware to hide in regular apps. This study uses deep learning capabilities to unite information from Android app background measurements with static code examination results to deliver advanced malware detection capabilities. Researchers used deep learning to build DroidDetector as an online Android malware detection system which autonomously evaluates apps to determine malware presence.

3.1 Proposed System

The proposed method uses deep learning architectures, namely Inception-ResNet v2 and DenseNet, for malware identification and categorization. We preprocess malware samples using opcode sequence extraction and byte-level n-gram frequency analysis techniques to generate suitable input formats for the models. By fine-tuning on a huge dataset, we are able to distinguish between benign and dangerous software with high accuracy. The models exhibit robustness against adversarial attacks and generalize well across various malware families and variants. Our technology uses state-of-the-art deep learning algorithms to provide a reliable and scalable solution to combat the ever-evolving threats to cyber security.

3.1.1 Advantages of Proposed System

1. Sturdy against hostile attacks, guaranteeing accurate malware identification.
2. Excellent precision in effectively differentiating between harmful and benign software.
3. Effectively generalizes to other malware families and their variations.
4. Makes use of cutting-edge deep learning methods for scalable cybersecurity.
5. To achieve the best model performance, preprocessing approaches improve input formats.

4. SYSTEM ARCHITECTURE

The system using Inception-ResNet v2 and DenseNet, the system architecture would typically involve the following key components. Our model is implemented with these following steps is shown in Fig 1.

Figure 1. System architecture

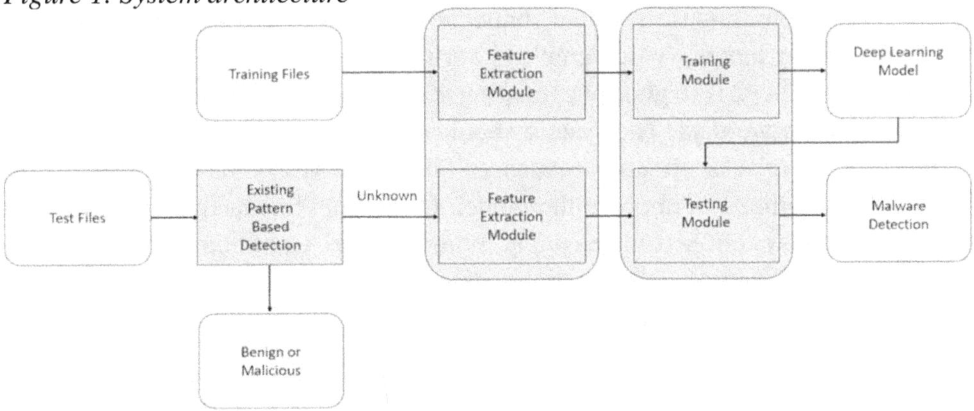

The following essential elements would normally be included in the system architecture when utilizing Inception-ResNet v2 and DenseNet. Figure 1 illustrates how our model is implemented using the subsequent methods. Gathering a diverse range of malware samples is the initial stage in the design. These samples might come from proprietary sources or publically accessible datasets like the Microsoft Malware Classification Challenge. Usually, these samples are made up of executable files, scripts, or other types of files that malware frequently uses. To build a balanced dataset needed for efficient model training, benign (non-malicious) software samples must be gathered in addition to malware samples. This guarantees that the model can differentiate between malware and legitimate software and helps avoid bias in identifying malicious files. unprocessed malware data, including

- **Data exploration:** Through this module we will perform data loading into the system.
- **Processing:** Within this module we process data after reading it for analysis.
- **Splitting data into train & test:** The module segments data into train & test portions through this process.
- **Model generation:** Project development involves two key steps that use INCEPTION RESNET V2 with DESNET.
- **User signup & login:** User registration and login entries are possible through the implementation of this module.
- **User input:** The application receives user information as input using this module to predict outcomes.
- **Prediction:** final predicted displayed

This deep learning architecture mitigates the vanishing gradient issue in deeper networks by combining the residual connections from ResNet with the advantages of the Inception model, which employs various filter sizes in parallel. Because Inception-ResNet v2 is so good at extracting features, it can be used to find complex patterns in malware data. The system should have a feedback loop in production settings where misclassifications (such as false positives or false negatives) are recorded and utilized to improve the model. Over time, this feedback mechanism makes sure the system gets increasingly more accurate. Continuous learning techniques should be supported by the architecture so that the system can adjust to new threats as they appear. Without completely retraining the model, this could entail gradual updates or online learning.

4.1 Algorithms Used

Inception ResNet V2:

Inception-ResNet v2 is an advanced convolutional neural network (CNN) architecture developed by Google researchers. By combining the concepts of the Inception architecture with residual connections, it seeks to improve the efficiency and accuracy of photo classification tasks. By integrating the multi-branch architecture of Inception networks with residual connections, which aid in reducing the vanishing gradient issue during training, Inception-ResNet v2 achieves state-of-the-art performance on a range of image recognition benchmarks.

This architecture employs multiple inception modules, each comprising multiple convolutional layers with different kernel sizes, to capture patterns and hierarchy of space at different scales within the input image (Mohanty, Sahoo, & Kabat, 2024). Additionally, it makes use of techniques like batch normalization and factorized convolutions to enhance training efficiency and model generalization.

Dense Net:

The dense connection pattern is a well-known feature of the neural network design called Dense Net, or Dense Convolutional Network. DenseNet was developed to encourage feature reuse and address the vanishing gradient problem. By physically connecting each layer within a block, it facilitates efficient information flow throughout the network (Obite, Olewuezi, Ugwuanyim, & Bartholomew, 2020). Unlike typical architectures, where each layer only receives inputs from the layer before it, DenseNet adds dense connections, where each layer receives inputs from all preceding layers within the same block. Performance and parameter efficiency are eventually enhanced by this intricately linked structure by promoting feature reuse and enhancing gradient flow.

5. MODEL REPRESENTATION

The discussion starts with an analysis of machine learning definitions before moving onto methodological examination. At first glance machine learning often appears as part of artificial intelligence but I find this classification to be misleading. Data models become the fundamental definition of machine learning when conducting data science operations using machine learning techniques.

Developing mathematical models is how machine learning helps understand database information. SqlDataAdapter involves "learning" because we can control model parameters with observed data. This enables systems to gain knowledge from examined datasets. After their application to historical data these computational models establish a foundation for forecasting along with explaining unidentified aspects of previously sampled data. The reader is free to explore connections between human brain learning and model-based mathematical training methods (Mohanty, Kumar, Padmaja, & Prashanthi, 2024).

5.1 Challenges Specific to Malware Detection in Machine Learning

Machine learning continues to advance rapidly but requirements remain in artificial intelligence development regarding additional efforts overall. Machine learning cannot solve specific hurdle factors because of its known limitations. The challenges that ML is facing currently are –

- **Imbalanced Dataset:** Malware datasets often have an uneven distribution of malicious and benign samples, leading to biased models and poor detection of minority classes.
- **Evolving Malware:** Malware constantly evolves, using obfuscation and polymorphism techniques to bypass detection, making it difficult for static models to adapt.
- **Feature Engineering Challenges:** Identifying meaningful features from malware data (e.g., API calls, opcodes, or network traffic) is complex and requires domain expertise.
- **Adversarial Attacks:** Malware authors craft adversarial samples to fool machine learning models, reducing detection accuracy.

- **High False Positive Rates:** False alarms on benign applications can erode user trust and affect system performance.
- **Scalability Issues:** Malware datasets can be large and diverse, posing challenges for training models efficiently and ensuring scalability.
- **Real-Time Detection Requirements:** Real-time malware detection requires lightweight models with fast inference times, which is challenging to achieve with complex algorithms.
- **Lack of Standardized Datasets:** There is a scarcity of publicly available, standardized datasets, leading to inconsistent benchmarks and difficulty comparing models.
- **Data Privacy Concerns:** sharing malware-related data across organizations for model training often raises privacy and security issues.
- **Dynamic vs Static Analysis:** Dynamic analysis provides more accurate insights but is computationally expensive, while static analysis is faster but vulnerable to evasion techniques.
- **Overfitting to Specific Malware:** Machine learning models may overfit to specific malware families, reducing their generalization capability to detect new or unknown threats.
- **Interpretability of Models:** Many machine learning models, especially deep learning ones, lack interpretability, making it difficult to understand why a specific detection decision was made.

5.2 Deep Learning

Proof-of-concept examinations demonstrate that the artificial neural network (ANN) functions as a basic structure for deep learning mechanisms which emerge from machine learning frameworks. This method discovers elaborate patterns in data naturally while requiring no manual programming for particular details to function. The significant rise in deep learning popularity has been enabled by parallel advancement of processing capabilities and accessible large-scale data sources. The core element within deep learning known as deep neural networks (DNNs) uses architecture that mirrors the operational structure of human brain neurons. Through their architecture these systems achieve powerful processing capabilities that enable them to effectively learn from massive data stores thereby solving complex challenges.

5.3 What is Anaconda for Python?

With its open-source foundation the Anaconda Python system provides users access to run Python programs along with other types of programs free of charge. Pursuing its goal of innovation in industry scale analytics the Python programming company continuum.io launched this creation. Nucleya provides the most common platform for Python data science and scientific and machine learning applications and usage. A global user base exceeding 30 million uses Anaconda Python which functions on operating systems including Linux, Windows and mac OS.

Anaconda Python stands out because it helps users more easily handle package installation and deployment. Your projects have access to multiple libraries along with packages through the platform. Open-source and free software accessibility permits any user to participate in Anaconda Python's development work.

How to install Anaconda for Python?

Users can download the Anaconda installer from the Anaconda Documentation website for their operating system by following provided instructions and then double clicking it during installation. Once the installer completes its download users can start the installation by double-clicking it.

Click through the terms agreement page while executing all demanded steps. When prompted to "add Anaconda to my PATH environment variable" select "yes." Addition of Anaconda to your system's PATH directory will occur when you accept this option.

The program will ask you if you want to "enable Anaconda as my default Python" following the completion of the installation process. Selecting "yes" during installation makes Anaconda operate as your default Python programming environment.

5.4 Python Language

As an interpreter the language Python functions as an object-oriented high-level programming language with dynamic semantics. The flexibility of built-in data types combined with dynamic binding and dynamic typing makes Python incredibly suitable to develop glue languages that tie pre-existing system components and for rapid application development purposes. Python's readable syntax design reduces software maintenance expenses because it's easy to understand. The language system enables code reuse through its support for modules and packages which drives software modularity.

Under the standard framework all Python interpreters and libraries exist openly under free distribution for major platforms as both source and binary materials. Developmental productivity increases become the main reason developers develop lasting interest in Python. The edit-test-debug operation remains very fast without needing a compilation phase. Programming debug in Python remains easy because a memory-size violation cannot stem from faulty code structures or invalid input. When an interpreter detects a mistake it activates an exception mechanism. A stack trace publishes during application exceptions that go beyond interpreter capture capabilities.

ISEff provides developers with a complete debugging solution that includes breakpoint configuration methods alongside arbitrary expression evaluation features along with variable view capabilities and patterned code execution. The debugger demonstrates introspection through its Python foundation. Program debugs most efficiently through simple print additions to code which profits from short edit-test-debug timelines.

As an interpreted programming language Python operates through dynamic free open-source code while maintaining high-level status. The language demonstrates dual support for procedural along with object-oriented programming paradigms. Python operates as an automatically typed language which means that we avoid declaring variable types. For instance, x = 10. Any value can serve as the variable x such as String or int and additional types.

5.5 Features in Python

There are many features in Python, some of which are discussed below as follows:

1. Open Source and Free

You can obtain Python free of charge from its official website by selecting Downloading Python then following the download link beneath. You can obtain Python through open-source licensing which permits public access to the programming language's entire programming code base. Users can download it then use it before distributing it as needed.

2. Simple coding

Programming features at the highest level exist in Python. The learning process for Python stands apart as simpler compared to C and C# and Java and Java Script alike. Learning Python basics requires only brief hours to days while programming in the language remains straightforward for everyone. Additionally, the language is developer-friendly.

3. Easy to Understand

Learning Python proves to be simple because you will notice soon enough. As previously discussed Python features an uncomplicated syntax structure. The code block definition depends on indentation instead of traditional brackets and semicolons.

4.Object-Oriented

The object-oriented programing paradigm stands as Python's essential programming feature. The Python language implements classic features of object-oriented programming such as classes alongside object encapsulation mechanisms and additional object-oriented language principles.

5.GUI based Support

SQL-, our team designed a program using the Today programming interface in conjunction with the Qt4 platform featuring medicine labeling for managing medication administration duties. The program operates with the Python language and utilizes wxPython as its framework along with the Version 4.1.2 module. Pen developers use PyQt5 as their main platform to develop graphical applications for Python.

6.High-Level Language

One high-level language is Python. Python programming allows developers to eliminate memory management while maintaining system architecture integrity and takes advantage of Python's extended capabilities as a programming language. Software developers can create Python code using either C or C++ while Boosting output by using C++ or C.

7.Easy Debugging

Errors can be located through examination of this system tool. Reading and understanding Python error tracing motifs enables developers to quickly detect and resolve operational problems within most programs. An examination of the code reveals its original design objectives.

8.Portable language

Another portable language is Python. The Python codebase requires no modifications when running between Windows systems and all variants of Linux, Unix and Mac because it operates universally across these platforms.

9.Interpreted

Python runs line-by-line code execution which turns the language into an interpreted system. Python programming undergoes no compilation process as it functions in contrast to languages like C or C++ or Java which provides better debugging opportunities. Python source code gets instant conversion into byte code format.

10.Large Standard Library

All your development tasks become easier through Python's large standard library because it provides numerous built-in modules and functions. The standard Python library includes modules that support web browsers and regular expressions together with unit testing functionalities.

11.Dynamically Typing

Python functions as a language that combines run-time determined types. Time itself resolves variable types dynamically at runtime which means we don't need to provide type specifications beforehand. Different variable types in Python include int, double, long as well as additional data types.

12. Frontend and backend development

Python code can integrate within HTML documents using the new project py script and few essential tags. Front-end Python programming becomes more accessible by implementing this method, similar to JavaScript. The core strength of using Python for this work derives from its backend operations that frameworks Django and Flask enable.

13.Dynamic Allocation of Memory

In Python programming you do not need to define variable data types. During runtime the system automatically sets memory assignments when a variable receives its value. Software developers can skip the syntax "int y=18" when declaring variable y as integer value 15 because Python automatically allocates the memory assignment. You can simply enter y=18.

5.6 Libraries/Packages

Tensor Flow

The platform Tensor Flow allows users to create differentiable programs while handling dataflows through its open-source software library framework. To support mathematical operations in symbolic form along with processing neural networks and various machine learning algorithms the library functions. TensorFlow serves Google's needs both during research development and operational tasks.

The Google Brain team developed TensorFlow to function as an internal tool at Google. The software became publicly available when it received an Apache 2.0 open-source license on November 9, 2015.

Numpy

The system package Numpy equips users with basic array handling abilities. This program enables users to work with multidimensional arrays through advanced array object performance.

Python scientific computing depends on this package as its foundational module. Among its many aspects are the following significant ones:

Running as a powerful N-dimensional array with advanced (broadcasting) features features

The system delivers effective linear algebra and Fourier transform capacities along with random number processing abilities combined with C/C++ and Fortran code generation tools.

As a fundamental multi-dimensional data-holder Numpy establishes its capability beyond its main scientific functions. Numpy enables fast and easy integration with multiple databases because it supports data type specification.

Pandas

Open-source Python library Pandas implements advanced data structures to offer top-level data handling and research tools with high performance capability. Python served as the primary tool in performing data operations along with cleaning raw data. The tool generated only minor contributions to data evaluation tasks. The resolution of this problem became possible by implementing Pandas' data library functions. No matter where the data comes from, we may use Pandas to complete the five standard processes of data processing and analysis: prepare, modify, model, and analyze. Academic fields unite with commercial sectors such as finance and economics and statistics along with analytics to perform their tasks through Python and Pandas.

Matplotlib

The Python 2D plotting package Matplotlib enables users to create figures at high quality for multiple print and interactive display options. The Python library Matplotlib serves both Jupyter Notebook and web application servers alongside Python scripts to connect with Python and IPython shells through its four interactive toolkits. The Matplotlib design enables basic applications with straightforward capabilities along with complex feature solutions. Writing a few lines of code becomes sufficient for producing plots and histograms and power spectra besides bar charts and error charts and scatter plots and various other graph visuals. Check out thumbnail images in the example graphs to view different graph output examples.

Through the use of IPython and pyplot users can produce basic plots to match MATLAB standards. Power users can access complete line style controls and axis property adjustments and font settings through Object-oriented interfaces along with familiar MATLAB method collections.

Scikit – learn

Through its standardized Python interface Scikit-learn provides different evaluation frameworks for supervised and unsupervised learning methods. The software receives distribution through different Linux distributions and operates using a simplified BSD license for commercial and academic use promotion.

There are several obstacles to overcome when integrating deep learning models such as Inception-ResNet v2 and DenseNet into practical malware detection systems. These include the need for processing resources, data availability, adversarial robustness, and interaction with pre-existing infrastructure. Notwithstanding these difficulties, these models offer a promising method for contemporary cybersecurity systems due to their capacity to increase malware detection efficiency and accuracy. It will take ongoing study, development, and innovation in deep learning methods and their use in dynamic security environments to overcome these real-world obstacles.

6. CONCLUSION

In conclusion, our study uses sophisticated deep learning architectures, notably Inception-ResNet v2 and DenseNet, to provide a novel method for malware identification and classification. We have developed a technique that successfully separates dangerous from benign software samples by utilizing the strength of these architectures, which are well-known for their feature extraction capabilities. We have transformed the malware samples into appropriate forms for deep learning model input by using preprocessing approaches such as opcode sequence extraction and byte-level n-gram frequency analysis.

The effectiveness of our suggested method is demonstrated by our testing results, which show high accuracy rates in differentiating between benign and malicious samples. Furthermore, the models show a remarkable capacity to generalize across a variety of malware families and variations, as well as resilience against adversarial attacks. This resilience is essential in battling the constantly changing cyberthreat landscape, where cybersecurity is still beset by serious difficulties due to the sophistication and widespread use of harmful software.

Our work advances malware detection methods by utilizing cutting-edge deep learning architectures, providing a dependable and expandable defense against online threats. The use of DenseNet and Inception-ResNet v2 emphasizes how crucial it is to use cutting-edge technologies in cybersecurity initiatives. Our study paves the way for future investigation and advancement in the field of deep learning-based malware detection, offering improved defenses against the ever-changing landscape of cyberattacks.

REFERENCES

Ahmad, S., Noorani, M. S., Nadarajah, S., & Mamat, M. (2020). *Multicollinearity effect in regression analysis: A feed forward artificial neural network approach. International Journal of Advanced Research in Artificial Intelligence.*

Christiana, A. O., Gyunka, B. A., & Noah, A. (2020). Android malware detection through machine learning techniques: A review. *International Journal of Online and Biomedical Engineering,* 16(2), 14–30. DOI: 10.3991/ijoe.v16i02.11549

Garg, A., & Tai, K. (2013). Comparison of statistical and machine learning methods in modelling of data with multicollinearity. *International Journal of Modelling Identification and Control*, 18(4), 295. DOI: 10.1504/IJMIC.2013.053535

Ghimire, D., & Lee, J. (2013). Geometric feature-based facial expression recognition in image sequences using multi-class AdaBoost and support vector machines. *Sensors (Basel)*, 13(6), 7714–7734. DOI: 10.3390/s130607714 PMID: 23771158

Li, X., Xie, H., Wang, R., Cai, Y., & Cao, J. (2017). Dynamic financial distress prediction with concept drift based on time weighting combined with Adaboost support vector machine ensemble. *Knowledge-Based Systems*, 120, 4–14. DOI: 10.1016/j.knosys.2017.04.005

Mohanty, R. K., Kumar, A. P., Padmaja, R., & Prashanthi, V. (2024). Deep learning for analyzing user and entity behaviors: Techniques and applications. In *Consumer and Organizational Behavior in the Age of AI* (pp. 219–250). IGI Global. DOI: 10.4018/979-8-3693-8850-1.ch008

Mohanty, R. K., Sahoo, S. P., & Kabat, M. R. (2023). Sustainable remote patient monitoring in wireless body area network with Multi-hop routing and scheduling: A four-fold objective based optimization approach. *Wireless Networks*, 29(5), 2337–2351. DOI: 10.1007/s11276-023-03276-x

Mohanty, R. K., Sahoo, S. P., & Kabat, M. R. (2024). Thermal-energy-efficient-secured-link reliable and delay-aware routing protocol (TESLDAR) for wireless body area networks. *International Journal of Computers and Applications*, 46(9), 1–13. DOI: 10.1080/1206212X.2024.2380675

Muslim, A., Mustofa, K., Widodo, S. T., & Harjoko, A. (2021). Efficient feature selection analysis for accuracy malware classification. *Journal of Physics: Conference Series*, 1918(4), 042140. DOI: 10.1088/1742-6596/1918/4/042140

Quartz. (2022). Android (GOOG) just hit a record 88% market share of all smartphones. *Quartz.*

Sahni, A., & Nene, M. J. (2020). MLDroid—Framework for Android malware detection using machine learning techniques. *Neural Computing & Applications*, 33, 12813–12825.

Sahs, J., & Khan, L. (2020). A review of Android malware detection approaches based on machine learning. *IEEE Access : Practical Innovations, Open Solutions*, 8, 124579–124607. DOI: 10.1109/ACCESS.2020.3006143

Szegedy, C., Ioffe, S., Vanhoucke, V., & Alemi, A. A. (2017). Inception-v4, Inception-ResNet and the Impact of Residual Connections on Learning. In *Proceedings of the Thirty-First AAAI Conference on Artificial Intelligence*, (pp. 4278–4284). DOI: 10.1609/aaai.v31i1.11231

Wang, W., Zhao, M., Gao, Z., Xu, G., Xian, H., Li, Y., & Zhang, X. (2019). Constructing features for detecting Android malicious applications: Issues, taxonomy and directions. *IEEE Access : Practical Innovations, Open Solutions*, 7, 67602–67631. DOI: 10.1109/ACCESS.2019.2918139

Yuan, Z., Lu, Y., & Xue, Y. (2020). DroidDet: Effective and robust detection of Android malware using static analysis along with machine learning. *Neurocomputing*, 349, 87–98. DOI: 10.1016/j.neucom.2019.01.112

Chapter 7
Malware Analysis and Classification Using Machine Learning Techniques

C. N. Manushree
https://orcid.org/0009-0001-9158-5096
Amity University, India

Girish B. C.
https://orcid.org/0009-0007-7155-3306
Amity University, India

Himanshu Khajuria
https://orcid.org/0000-0002-2438-0007
Amity Institute of Forensic Sciences, Amity University, Noida, India

Sachil Kumar
https://orcid.org/0000-0002-2681-3937
Amity University, Noida, India

ABSTRACT

The rapid evolution of malware poses a significant threat to cybersecurity, necessitating advanced techniques for effective detection and classification. Traditional methods, such as signature-based and heuristic-based detection, struggle to keep pace with the sophisticated evasion techniques employed by modern malware. This chapter explores the integration of machine learning techniques into malware analysis to address these challenges. It delves into the types and behaviors of malware, the principles of machine learning, and the processes of data collection, preprocessing,

DOI: 10.4018/979-8-3693-7758-1.ch007

and feature extraction. Through real-world case studies and comparative analyses, the chapter highlights the advantages and limitations of these models in real-time applications. Additionally, it discusses the future directions and potential of machine learning in adapting to emerging malware threats. By providing a comprehensive overview, this chapter aims to equip readers with the knowledge and tools necessary to leverage machine learning for robust malware detection and classification.

1. INTRODUCTION

Malware refers to any bad code that harms your computer or network (Ray & Nath, 2016). It is a term for very destructive and differently attributed, goal-differentiated varieties of malware. Malware analysis simply refers to the process of taking apart malicious software to understand its behaviour, functionality, and possible impact. In other words, it refers to deconstructing malware into parts while at the same time identifying techniques and targets of the malware (Dutta et al., 2022).

1.1 Importance of Malware Analysis

Malware analysis forms a key part of any cyber security strategy for the following reasons:

a. Threat Intelligence: It offers valuable insights about future threats and trends in attacks. Helps an organization become very well-versed in the latest malignant activities and create effective countermeasures accordingly.
b. Incident Response: Helps know the extent and nature of the malware attack. Helps a firm or organization act accordingly and curb further damage effectively.
c. Security Research: It contributes to the development of new security technologies and best practices. It helps the researchers to identify the vulnerabilities in software and builds countermeasures for them.
d. Attribution: It helps to find out the attackers behind the creation or circulation of malware. This information may be used in any number of ways, either to pursue legal action or to avoid further attacks.
e. Risk Assessment: This shall help organizations estimate how vulnerable they might be to a malware attack and find out where their priorities in security lie. It will help find out the weaknesses in their systems and act to forestall them (Kim et al., 2020).

1.2 Challenges in Traditional Malware Analysis

Traditional malware analysis faces several challenges, among them the following: Evolving Malware: The malware authors evolve techniques with continuous efforts to avoid detection. Obfuscation, polymorphic, and metamorphic techniques really complicate the detection and analysis of malware (Singh & Singh, 2018).

Large Scale Analysis: Usually there are numerous malware samples for analysis. It is resource and time consuming. High scale analysis is practically difficult to be performed manually.

Limitation of Dynamic Analysis: It is very resource-intensive. All types of malware behaviours may not be discovered at the time of the test. Even more, it might introduce mechanisms for self-destruction in place or avoid being detected altogether.

Virtualization challenges: In particular, virtualization environments useful to separate the malware analysis environment, in themselves could introduce some forms of limitations or artifacts impacting the analytic process (Or-Meir et al., 2019).

1.3 Introduction to Machine Learning in Cybersecurity

Machine learning has been a very powerful tool in cybersecurity, having redesigned how cyber threats are detected, prevented, and responded to today. Based on algorithms and statistical models, the ML systems analyse vast amounts of data in search of patterns, anomalies, and possible attacks (Apruzzese et al., 2023).

Some of the most important machine learning concepts for cybersecurity are: - Supervised Learning:

Trains models on labelled data to predict the outcomes.

Applied to malware classification, intrusion detection, and phishing email detection.

Unsupervised Learning:

Trains models on unlabelled data to identify patterns and structures.

Applied to anomaly detection, network traffic analysis, and user behaviour analysis.

Reinforcement Learning:

Trains models to make decisions based on rewards vs. punishment.

Applied to the development of autonomous security agents that can adapt to a situation and create of adaptive response systems.

Applications of Machine Learning in Cybersecurity: -

Malware Detection:

They can analyse file characteristics, behaviour, and network traffic to detect malicious software.

Deep learning and recurrent neural networks have been very effective techniques applied for the detection of advanced malware.

Intrusion Detection:

An ML-based approach can classify network traffic and log data for suspicious activities and potential intrusions.

Either anomaly detection approach could be implemented to solve this problem.

Phishing Detection:

ML can analyse the content of the email, sender details, and URL patterns in detecting phishing. It is able to detect even subtle linguistic clues that are there in the phishing e-mails through its application in the use of natural language processing techniques.

Network Traffic Analysis:

It can also analyse the network traffic to find anomalies, denial-of-service attacks, and botnets. Techniques that aid visualization and understanding of complex network data include clustering and dimensionality reduction.

User Behaviour Analysis:

This makes ML applicable to user behaviour patterns, thus detecting anomalies indicative of a compromise (Ford & Siraj, 2014).

These can be realized by techniques such as time series analysis, which shall identify the anomaly of activity patterns.

Following are the benefits of machine learning in cybersecurity:

Improved detection: ML can detect threats that traditional signature-based methods miss.
Automation: The majority of, if not all, the security tasks can be automated using ML, relieving much burden from human analysts.
Real-time Detection: ML can identify threats in real-time, hence fastening the response times.
Adaptability: The ML models are continuously updated with evolving threats and learn from new data.

2. FUNDAMENTALS OF MALWARE

2.1 Types of Malwares

Types of Malwares

Malware, or malicious software, comes in various forms, each with its unique characteristics and goals. Following are some common ones (Tahir, 2018).

Figure 1. Types of malwares

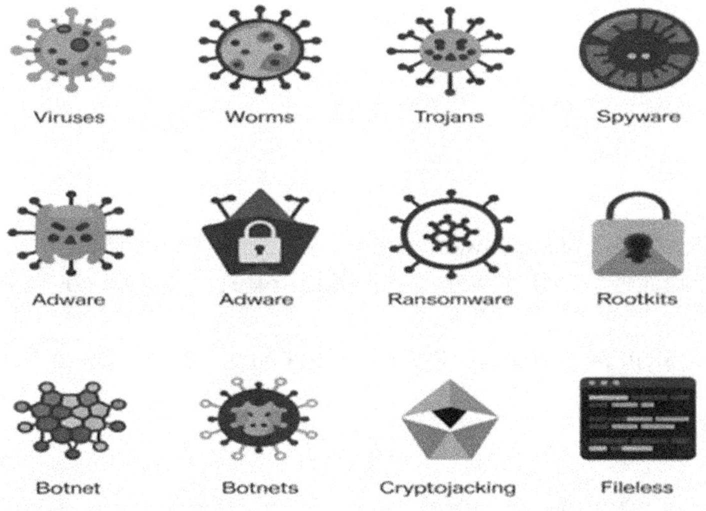

Viruses

A self-replicating program which attaches itself to other files.
Spread through infected files, emails, or removable media.
Examples: WannaCry, ILOVEYOU worm.

Worms

Self-replicating program; can spread independently and doesn't need a host file for propagation.
Mostly spread by exploiting vulnerabilities in network protocols to propagate very fast.
Examples: Code Red, Nimda.

Trojans

A malicious program posing as legitimate software.
This, however, mostly enables data theft, other malware installation, or unauthorized access.
Examples: Zeus, Emotet.

Spyware

Software that monitors secretly user's activity; it can record keystrokes, surfing history, personal data.
Keyloggers, adware are examples.

Adware

This software can place unwanted advertisements on your screen.
Software that is 'bundled' with some other software downloads or downloaded unknowingly.
It slows system performance down and, of course, tracks user behaviour.

Ransomware

This type of malware encrypts the user files and demands a ransom for decrypting procedures.
It can be spread through email attachments, links to malicious websites, and even through the exploitation of vulnerabilities.
Examples: Petya, WannaCry.

Rootkits

The malware conceals itself deep inside the OS of a system.
Can give attackers administrative access; make it very hard to detect and remove.
Examples: Blackhole Exploit Kit, LKM Rootkit.

Other Types
Botnets: These are networks of compromised computers under the control of an attacker.
Cryptojacking: This is malware that enslaves the computing power of victims to mine cryptocurrency.

Fileless malware refers to a kind of malware that survives only in memory, and does not write files on the infected system (Alenezi et al., 2020).

2.2 Malware Characteristics and Behaviour

Malware is a category of malicious software that is characterized by various features and behaviours through which it can be recognized and classified (Wagener et al., 2008). Some of the main features and behaviours are described below:

Characteristics: -
Self-Reproduction: Various forms of malware, like viruses and worms, are self-propagating and can very rapidly spread from one system to another and infect many systems.
Persistence: Malware generally uses various techniques so that it is persistent within the infected system, by scheduling tasks, changing files in the system, and remaining invisible in the process of the system.
Stealth: The malware could be designed not to show that it has been present in the system. Techniques like these include rootkits, stealthy network communications, and encryption.
Polymorphism: Some self-modify for avoiding criteria in detection. This is brought about through code alteration, encryption, or many more attributes.
Metamorphism: It is hard to distinguish based on signs as well since like polymorphic malware metamorphic malware too can remake itself wholly (Maniriho et al., 2022).
Behaviour: -
Network Activity: Malware reaches out to remote servers to get commands, updates, or exfiltrate data it has stolen. This might be unusual network traffic to unknown IP addresses or unknown protocols.

File Operations: Malware creates, modifies, or deletes files in an infected system. This includes the creation of hidden files, editing system files, and deleting sensitive data.
Registry Changes: The malware changes the system registry to achieve persistence, elevate privilege, or hide itself.
Process Creation: Malware may create new processes in the system to execute malicious functionalities or hide its activity (AlAhmadi & Martinovic, 2018)
System Resource Utilization: Malware consumes a lot of resources within the system, for instance, CPU, memory, or network bandwidth.

2.3 Malware Obfuscation Techniques

Malware obfuscation is a method that attackers use to conceal the real nature of malicious code. It creates difficulty in detection, analysis, and reverse engineering (Singh & Singh, 2018). This somehow affects security efforts on systems and makes protection from malware attacks even more challenging.

Common Obfuscation Techniques: -
Encryption:

The malware code is encrypted to appear like random data.
The decryption key is usually hidden in the malware or fetched from a remote server.

Packing:

The malware code may be compressed or packed to make it small and difficult to analyse. Special tools and techniques are needed to unpack the malware.

Polymorphism:

The malware's code changes every time it runs. This is done to prevent signature-based antivirus software from detecting it.

Metamorphism:

In this, the malware's code gets fully rewritten every time it runs, thereby appearing entirely different.

Code Obfuscation:

In a program, variables, functions, and class names are changed to make the code harder to understand.

It can also include adding unnecessary code or complex control flow structures.

Virtualization:

The malware creates a virtual environment within itself to execute its malicious code, which makes the analysis challenging.

Self-Modifying Code:

Some malware changes its own code during execution; this is hard to analyze by static analysis.

Anti-Disassembly:

Techniques are used to prevent the disassembler from properly examining the malware code.

Anti-Debugging:

These techniques hinder the use of debuggers to study and analyze malware behavior.

Dynamic Code Generation:

It does its code generation on the fly while it is in a running state, which also makes static analysis really difficult to be done.

Obfuscation Challenges:

The techniques of obfuscation have the ability to increase time and efforts made towards the malware's analysis many times. Obfuscated malware may evade detection using the traditional signature-based antivirus software. The real intentions or malicious activities performed by malware would be hard to trace due to obfuscation.

While such obfuscation techniques may make malware hard to analyse, they are not foolproof (Pomilia, 2016). Even more advanced ways of analysis can be applied, such as behaviour, dynamic, and reverse engineering analysis, to uncover obfuscated malware and enable clear understanding of how it works.

3. DATA COLLECTION AND PREPROCESSING

3.1 Sources of Malware Samples

Sources for malware samples shall be sought and understood to better gauge and mitigate cyber threats (Basu et al., 2016). These commonly include:

- Online Repositories
- Incident Response Teams
- Malware Analysis Firms
- Research Institutions and Universities
- Botnet Command and Control Servers

Figure 2. Sources of Malware samples

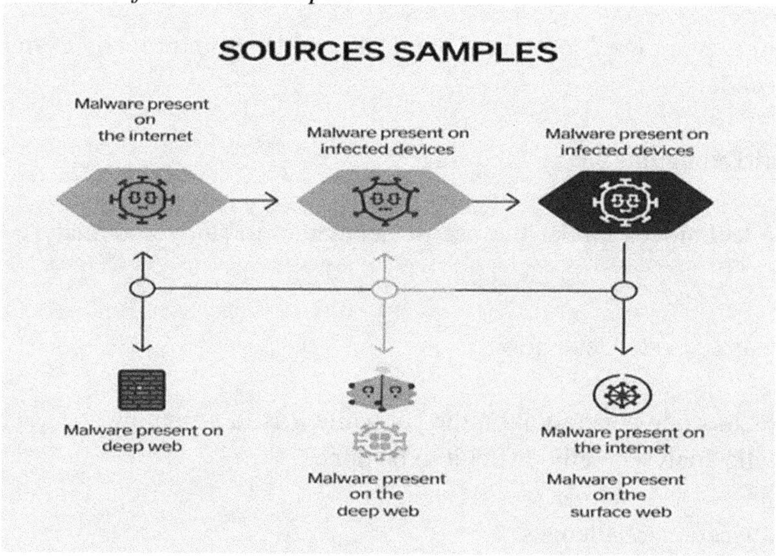

Online Repositories:
Virus Total: This would be the first place where someone would upload files to have them analysed. It provides a report of how the malware behaves, what its detection rate looks like, and many other characteristics associated with it.
Malware Bazaar: This is another repository that fuels accumulation and redistribution for malware samples.

Exif Tool: This tool allows the extraction of metadata from files; this metadata can sometimes contain information about the origin or distribution of malware.
Honeypots:
These are systems designed to attract and trap malware.
Honeypots offer a chance to collect malware samples in a controlled environment without causing any damage to the production systems.
Dark Web Markets:
Online marketplaces where malware is sold and traded.
Accessing the dark web requires special tools and precautions, but in scraping for malware samples, it can be very handy (Basu et al., 2019).
Incident Response Teams:
Those responding to cyber-attacks usually have samples of malware from real incidents.
Cooperation with incident response teams can be made to request information on current malware threats.
Malware Analysis Companies:
Companies that collect and analyse malware samples are dedicated to this work.
Such organizations often have access to considerable collections of malware samples and can provide useful intelligence
Research Organizations and Universities:
Most research institutions and universities study malware and keep malware sample repositories for research reasons.
Botnet Command and Control Servers:
Sometimes, the monitoring of botnet C&C servers may reveal new malware strains.
Key points to consider: -
Legality and Ethics: Ensure that you have necessary permission to gather the malware samples and you are working in ethical provisions of collecting and analysing the malware samples.
Risk Assessment: Identify risks that may be involved in the gathering of malware samples, such as infection and exposure to malicious code.
Security Measures: Implement appropriate security measures to the systems and data during the analysis of malware.

With the use of such sources, researchers and security experts can acquire a wide range of malware samples to be analysed and become capable of developing countermeasures for many malicious activities.

3.2 Static Analysis Data

Static analysis is the technique of understanding malware without the execution of the same. The technique gives in-depth insights into the structure, behaviour, and risks associated with malware. Data obtained during static analysis forms the base for further examination and response (Medeiros et al., 2015).

Types of Static Analysis Data: -
File Metadata:
File headers: Type and format of the file, date of its creation.
Import/export tables: List the functions and libraries imported or exported by malware. Version information: This sometimes provides information about the age or origin of malware.
Code Analysis:
Disassembly: It is a process of translating the executable code in a program to machine instructions so that it can be analysed. Control flow analysis: This involves understanding the execution flow within malware. Data flow analysis: This involves the understanding of the flow of data as it moves through the code.
String Analysis:
Textual strings: These include the identification of strings which might hold the potential for URLs, file paths, or other interesting information.
Encryption/Decryption routines: Identifying routines that are used for encrypting or decrypting data.
Signature Analysis:
Pattern matching: Malware characteristics are matched against malware signatures.
Heuristic analysis: Suspicious behaviour is identified using rules and patterns.
Structural Analysis:
Packing/Unpacking: The techniques that are used to compress or obfuscate the malware are identified.
Virtualization: The malware makes use of virtual machines or emulators for detection.
Applications of Static Analysis Data
Malware Classification: Grouping of malwares on the basis of behaviour, target, or origin.
Threat Intelligence: Gathering details on new threats and trends of attacks.
Incident Response: Details about the nature of malware attacks to apply the correct countermeasure.
Security Research: Studies on new techniques of detection and development of security tools.

Static Analysis Limitation: -

Obscuration: Hackers obfuscate or encrypt their code so that it becomes almost impossible to analyse with the help of static techniques.

Limited Behavioural Insights: Static analysis in itself cannot carry the depth of behavioral dimensions of malware if it was designed to run dynamically

False Positives: Based on structural or other resemblance, static analysis might falsely identify a clean file as a malicious one (Nagy, 2013).

3.3 Dynamic Analysis Data: A Deep Dive into Malware Behaviour

Dynamic analysis involves the execution of malware within a controlled environment, such that its behaviour may be observed. Key dynamic analysis data types are impossible to determine through static analysis (Ball, 1999).

Types of Key Dynamic Analysis Data:

a. System Calls:

API calls: These are the functions the malware is using to interface with the operating system.

Can expose the actions the malware performs, such as creating files, network connections, or changing registry settings.

b. Network Traffic:

Communication patterns: Determine how the malware is interacting with remote servers or other systems.

Data exfiltration: Identifies data being transmitted from the system.

c. File Operations:

File creation, modification, and deletion: These determine the interaction of the malware with files on the infected system.

Registry changes: Detection of system registry modifications.

d. Process creation and termination:

New process: Detection of new process generation by malware.

Process termination: Determination of which processes are terminated by malware.

e. Memory Access Pattern:

Memory usage: Identification of memory footprint and usage of malware
Data access: Identification of data access by malware.

f. Behavioural anomalies:

unusual activity: Detection of variation in system normal behaviour.
Suspicious patterns: Identification of possible malicious patterns.

Applications of Dynamic Analysis Data: -

- Malware Classification:

Categorizing malware based on its behaviour and target.

- Incident Response:

Identifying the root cause of a malware attack and taking appropriate countermeasures.

- Security Research:

Developing new detection techniques and security tools.

- Reverse Engineering:

Understanding the malware's functionality and techniques.

Challenges of Dynamic Analysis: -

- Resource Consumption:

Dynamic analysis can be resource-intensive, especially for large or complex malware samples.

- Evasion Techniques:

Malware may employ techniques to evade dynamic analysis, such as self-destruction mechanisms or anti-debugging techniques.

- Virtualization Artifacts:

Analysing malware in a virtual environment may introduce artifacts or limitations that affect the analysis results.

- Limited Visibility:

Dynamic analysis may not capture all aspects of the malware's behaviour, especially if it is designed to be stealthy (Or-Meir et al., 2019).

4. FEATURE EXTRACTION AND SELECTION

4.1 Feature Selection Methods for Static and Dynamic (Venkatesh & Anuradha, 2019)

Table 1.

Static Analysis Feature Selection	Dynamic Analysis Feature Selection
Information Gain: This quantifies the reduction in entropy uncertainty by knowing the value of a feature. High information gain thereby means that a feature is more likely to be informative.	Time Series Analysis: This is the analysis of time-series data that is obtained during dynamic analysis, such as network traffic or system calls, to detect patterns and trends.
Chi-Square Test: This test is used to determine the importance of each feature with respect to the class label, which will be malicious or benign.	Clustering: It is a process of organizing similar behaviours or patterns to identify relevant features.
Correlation Analysis: It measures the correlation of features with the class label. High correlation of features with the class label often means redundancy and can be removed.	Dimensionality reduction: Reducing the number of features but still retaining the most important information. Techniques to do this include principal component analysis and t-SNE.
Mutual Information: The dependency of a feature with a class label based on linear and nonlinear relationships.	Wrapper Methods: Test all subsets of features against a classification model. This is followed by training different models in all possible combinations and then selecting the best subset.
Filter Methods: These methods select the features based on their inherent properties and are agnostic to the classification task. Examples include frequency-based methods, variance-based methods, and correlation-based methods.	Embedded Methods: The process of feature selection is embedded within the learning algorithm itself. For example, L1 regularization, also called lasso, and L2 regularization, also called ridge regression, are capable of selecting relevant features on their own.

5. MACHINE LEARNING MODELS FOR MALWARE CLASSIFICATION

5.1 Supervised Learning

Definition: It is such a learning in which an algorithm gets a training dataset. The type of training data offered here contains at least one correct output for each input point of data. To learn the mapping function based on the new unseen data, the objective is for the model to represent how the correct output is correct.

Training: So now, suppose an algorithm is provided with labelled data. Then it gets into the habit of discovering associations between input points and their corresponding outputs.

Prediction: The algorithm is now empowered to predict an output for a new piece of data not yet encountered, based on the patterns it has learned.

Some examples are classifying an email as spam or not spam, house prices depending on its area and locality, among other features, and digit recognition in handwriting (Tchakounté & Hayata, 2017).

Figure 3. Supervised learning

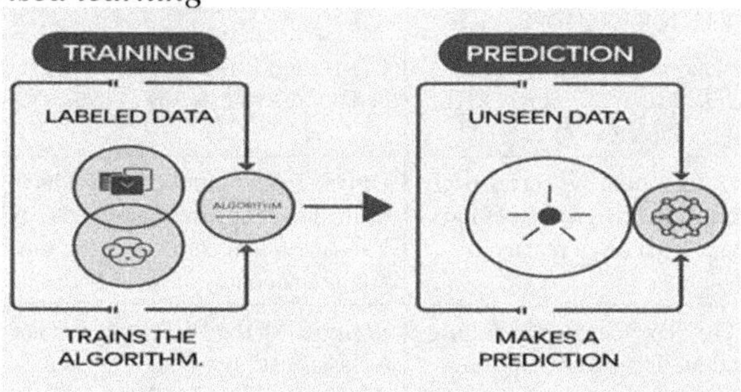

5.2 Unsupervised Learning

Definition: The algorithm learns through the input given, which is not labelled. The motive is to identify a hidden pattern or structure from the data (Smith et al., 2023).

Process:

Clustering: Divide data points into groups of similar data points.

Dimensionality reduction: It is a process to reduce the number of features so that all the important information remains retained within the data.

Association rule mining: Rules defining relationships between items in a database.

Examples:

Customer segmentation on the basis of purchasing behaviour.

Topic modelling to determine what the major topics are in a collection of documents. Anomaly detection to find unusual or suspicious data points.

5.3 Reinforcement Learning

Definition: Artificial agent which learns to interact with environment in order to maximize its rewards. The agent gets rewarded or penalized about its actions through trial and errors (Song et al., 2020).

Process:

Environment: An artificial agent interacts within an environment, takes different actions, and gets rewarded or penalized.

Rewards: An artificial agent acquires rewards and penalties based on the performed action.

Learning: An artificial agent learns how to select activities that maximize rewards over a period of time.

Examples

Training a robot to run an obstacle course, teaching a game-playing agent how to beat humans at the game, or optimizing the performance of a self-driving car.

Figure 4. Reinforcement learning

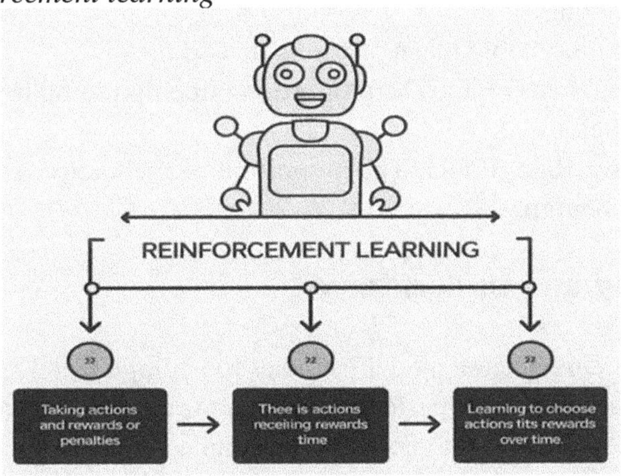

6. MODEL TRAINING AND EVALUATION

6.1 Training the Model

Model Training in malware analysis involves teaching a machine learning model to distinguish between malicious and benign software (Akhtar & Feng, 2023). This typically involves: -

a. Data Preparation: Collecting a dataset of labelled malware samples (malicious) and benign samples (benign).
b. Feature Extraction: Extracting relevant features from the malware samples, such as file metadata, code analysis results, or network traffic patterns.
c. Model Selection: Choosing a suitable machine learning algorithm, such as decision trees, random forests, support vector machines, or neural networks.
d. Training: Feeding the labelled data to the model and allowing it to learn the patterns and features associated with malicious software.

6.2 Evaluation Metrics

Evaluation Metrics for malware analysis models include: -

a. Accuracy: The overall proportion of correct predictions.
b. Precision: The proportion of correctly identified malicious samples out of all samples predicted as malicious.
c. Recall: The proportion of correctly identified malicious samples out of all actual malicious samples.
d. F1-score: The harmonic mean of precision and recall.
e. False Positive Rate (FPR): The proportion of benign samples incorrectly classified as malicious.
f. False Negative Rate (FNR): The proportion of malicious samples incorrectly classified as benign.

6.3 Overfitting and Underfitting

Overfitting occurs when a model becomes too complex and learns the training data too well, leading to poor performance on new, unseen malware.

Underfitting occurs when a model is too simple and cannot capture the underlying patterns in the data.

6.4 Model Optimization

Model Optimization involves fine-tuning the model's parameters to improve its performance. Techniques used for model optimization in malware analysis include:

a. Hyperparameter tuning: Adjusting the model's hyperparameters, such as learning rate, number of layers, or regularization strength.
b. Regularization: Penalizing complex models to prevent overfitting.

c. Ensemble methods: Combining multiple models to improve performance and reduce overfitting.
d. Data augmentation: Creating additional training data by transforming existing data.

7. CHALLENGES AND FUTURE DIRECTIONS IN MALWARE ANALYSIS

Malware analysis and classification have rapidly evolved with the power of machine learning techniques. Several challenges still exist, however, and new directions are emerging (Aboaoja et al., 2022).

Challenges:

Evolving Malware:
Malware developers do not stop inventing ways to evade detection. Other techniques, such as obfuscation, polymorphism, and metamorphism, prevent the proper categorization of malware.

Data Scarcity and Quality: Sufficient good-quality labelled malware samples are rarely procurable, especially in the case of emerging threats.

Feature Engineering: Selecting the most informative features from the samples is crucial for an efficient classification. In general, it could be very time-consuming and may demand knowledge about a certain domain.

Interpretability: Most machine learning models are complex, especially deep learning models, and hence hard to interpret. This makes it really difficult to know how the model is making decisions and exactly where biases may lie.

Computational Costs: Training and testing of machine learning models is quite time-consuming, especially when dealing with large volumes of data and complex models (Gorment et al., 2023).

Future Directions:

Advanced Machine Learning Techniques: Research in new machine learning techniques to improve malware detection and classification, such as generative adversarial networks and transfer learning.

Hybrid Approaches: Design of hybrid approaches combining machine learning with traditional signature-based techniques and behavioural analysis for the purpose of improving the detection capability.

Automated Feature Engineering: Development of automated techniques for extracting relevant features from malware samples that reduce dependence on manual feature engineering.

Interpretable Machine Learning: Interpretable machine learning models that can provide insight into the decision-making process and hence aid in understanding and addressing, if present, biases.

Federated Learning: Investigate federated learning techniques to train machine learning models on distributed data without exposing privacy.

Real-time Detection: Design real-time malware detection systems to detect and respond to emerging threats in real time.

Adversarial Machine Learning: Research techniques for defending against adversarial attacks that attempt to fool a machine learning model (Alqahtani, 2021).

DRAWBACKS:

Malware analysis is a very important process to understand malicious software, but it is not without its challenges and drawbacks:

1. Time-Consuming

Malware analysis, especially manual analysis, takes a lot of time. Complex malware can take days or weeks to fully analyse.

2. Evasion Techniques

Malware authors have often used sophisticated techniques like obfuscation, encryption, or anti-debugging to evade detection and analysis.

Polymorphic and metamorphic malware can change their code structure, making analysis even harder.

3. High Resource Intensity

Static and dynamic analysis require special tools, isolated environments, such as sandboxes, and professional analysts. All these resources can be expensive to obtain and maintain.

4. Risk of Accidental Execution

Dynamic analysis is always fraught with the risk of malware escaping the controlled environment and infecting the host system or network.

5. Lack of Complete Understanding

Static analysis might fail to capture run-time behaviour, while dynamic might not raise all the malicious functionalities therefore providing an incomplete picture.

6. Encrypted or Packed Malware

Some forms of malware use packers or runtime encryption to cloak their code, making this kind of malware difficult to be analysed unless first unpacking or decrypting it first.

7. Volume of Malware

The sheer volume of new malware variants coming in every day can be overwhelming to analysts and tools, making it hard to prioritize and analyse each sample in depth.

8. False Positives and Negatives

Automated analysis tools can generate false positives, wasting effort, or false negatives, allowing threats to go undetected.

9. Legal and Ethical Issues

Malware analysis may involve dealing with sensitive data that has been stolen, raising potential legal and ethical issues.

10. Stealth and Advanced Persistent Threats (APTs)

APTs and stealthy malware typically behave in ways that make them challenging to detect: for example, hiding inside legitimate processes or using the most sophisticated techniques, like rootkits.

11. Skill Gap

Malware analysis requires special knowledge in the areas of reverse engineering, programming, and system internals, among others, but there is a shortage of skilled professionals in this field.

12. Evolving Threat Landscape

Cybercriminals continually innovate, introducing new techniques like fileless malware, which operates entirely in memory and leaves little trace for analysis.

8. CONCLUSION

Cybersecurity is a critical aspect of malware analysis and classification using machine learning techniques (Kara, 2019). The implications of cybersecurity in this context are multifaceted:

Protecting Sensitive Data:

- Data Privacy: Malware analysis often involves handling sensitive data, such as network traffic, system logs, and potentially personal information. Cybersecurity measures are essential to protect this data from unauthorized access or disclosure.
- Data Integrity: Malware can compromise the integrity of data by modifying or deleting it. Cybersecurity practices help ensure the accuracy and reliability of data used for analysis.

Preventing False Positives and Negatives:

- Accuracy: Cybersecurity measures help improve the accuracy of malware analysis models by ensuring the quality and reliability of the training data.
- False Positives: Cybersecurity can help reduce false positives, where benign files are mistakenly classified as malicious.
- False Negatives: Cybersecurity can help prevent false negatives, where malicious files are mistakenly classified as benign.

Mitigating Adversarial Attacks:

- Adversarial Examples: Malware authors may employ adversarial attacks to deceive machine learning models. Cybersecurity measures can help detect and mitigate such attacks.
- Robustness: Cybersecurity practices can help ensure the robustness of machine learning models against adversarial attacks.

Ensuring Ethical Use:

- Ethical Considerations: Malware analysis and classification involve ethical considerations, such as privacy, bias, and accountability. Cybersecurity practices can help ensure that these ethical principles are adhered to.
- Transparency: Cybersecurity measures can help ensure transparency in the use of machine learning techniques for malware analysis, including the data used, the models employed, and the decision-making process.

Protecting Critical Infrastructure:

- Critical Systems: Malware can pose a significant threat to critical infrastructure, such as power grids, transportation systems, and healthcare facilities. Cybersecurity measures are essential to protect these systems from malware attacks.

In conclusion, cybersecurity is an integral component of malware analysis and classification using machine learning techniques. By addressing the challenges and ensuring the ethical and responsible use of these technologies, we can effectively protect our digital infrastructure and mitigate the risks posed by malware (Ray & Nath, 2016).

It is in malware analysis and classification that ML techniques have enjoyed the most success, providing automated, scalable, and more accurate methods for identification and categorization of malware. Traditional signature-based detection methods normally fail in the case of new or obfuscated malware variants since they are based on a predefined set of signatures (Dutta et al., 2022). Machine learning models learn patterns and behaviours associated with malware from large datasets and hence can generalize to detect previously unseen types of malwares.

Supervised learning techniques include decision trees, support vector machines, and deep learning models such as convolutional neural networks and recurrent neural networks, all helpful in classifying malware based on the features extracted from binary files, network traffic, or system behaviour (Tchakounté & Hayata, 2017). Unsupervised learning methods, specifically clustering, are capable of detecting new and unknown malware families by grouping similar samples according to their features (Smith et al., 2023). Challenges in the use of machine learning for malware detection include large and diverse datasets, attacks through model manipulation by adversaries, and very tricky extraction of features in dynamic and complex environments. Besides that, good balance on model accuracy and computational efficiency is important for its practical deployment in real-time systems (Sihwail et al., 2018).

Although machine learning has already offered a very powerful toolkit for malware analysis and classification, further research and development are more than required to rise up to the new challenges of evolving malware threats and improve model robustness, accuracy, and efficiency in real-world applications.

REFERENCES

Aboaoja, F. A., Zainal, A., Ghaleb, F. A., Al-Rimy, B. A. S., Eisa, T. A. E., & Elnour, A. A. H. (2022). Malware detection issues, challenges, and future directions: A survey. *Applied Sciences (Basel, Switzerland)*, 12(17), 8482. DOI: 10.3390/app12178482

Akhtar, M. S., & Feng, T. (2023). Evaluation of machine learning algorithms for malware detection. *Sensors (Basel)*, 23(2), 946. DOI: 10.3390/s23020946 PMID: 36679741

AlAhmadi, B. A., & Martinovic, I. (2018, May). MalClassifier: Malware family classification using network flow sequence behaviour. In *2018 APWG Symposium on Electronic Crime Research (eCrime)* (pp. 1-13). IEEE. DOI: 10.1109/ECRIME.2018.8376209

Alenezi, M. N., Alabdulrazzaq, H., Alshaher, A. A., & Alkharang, M. M. (2020). Evolution of malware threats and techniques: A review. *International Journal of Communication Networks and Information Security*, 12(3), 326–337.

Alqahtani, M. A. (2021). Machine learning techniques for malware detection with challenges and future directions. *International Journal of Communication Networks and Information Security*, 13(2), 258–270.

Apruzzese, G., Laskov, P., Montes de Oca, E., Mallouli, W., Brdalo Rapa, L., Grammatopoulos, A. V., & Di Franco, F. (2023). The role of machine learning in cybersecurity. *Digital Threats : Research and Practice*, 4(1), 1–38. DOI: 10.1145/3545574

Ball, T. (1999). The concept of dynamic analysis. *Software Engineering Notes*, 24(6), 216–234. DOI: 10.1145/318774.318944

Basu, I., Sinha, N., Bhagat, D., & Goswami, S. (2016). Malware detection based on source data using data mining: A survey. *Am. J. Adv. Comput*, 3(1), 18–37.

Basu, K., Krishnamurthy, P., Khorrami, F., & Karri, R. (2019). A theoretical study of hardware performance counters-based malware detection. *IEEE Transactions on Information Forensics and Security*, 15, 512–525. DOI: 10.1109/TIFS.2019.2924549

Dutta, N., Jadav, N., Tanwar, S., Sarma, H. K. D., Pricop, E., Dutta, N., ... Pricop, E. (2022). Introduction to malware analysis. *Cyber Security: Issues and Current Trends*, 129-141

Ford, V., & Siraj, A. (2014). Applications of machine learning in cyber security. *Proceedings of the 27th international conference on computer applications in industry and engineering* 118.

Gorment, N. Z., Selamat, A., Cheng, L. K., & Krejcar, O. (2023). Machine learning algorithm for malware detection: Taxonomy, current challenges, and future directions. *IEEE Access : Practical Innovations, Open Solutions*, 11, 141045–141089. DOI: 10.1109/ACCESS.2023.3256979

Kara, I. (2019). A basic malware analysis method. *Computer Fraud & Security*, 2019(6), 11–19. DOI: 10.1016/S1361-3723(19)30064-8

Kim, D. W., Shin, G. Y., & Han, M. M. (2020). Analysis of feature importance and interpretation for malware classification. *Computers, Materials & Continua*, 65(3), 1891–1904. DOI: 10.32604/cmc.2020.010933

Maniriho, P., Mahmood, A. N., & Chowdhury, M. J. M. (2022). A study on malicious software behaviour analysis and detection techniques: Taxonomy, current trends and challenges. *Future Generation Computer Systems*, 130, 1–18. DOI: 10.1016/j.future.2021.11.030

Medeiros, I., Neves, N., & Correia, M. (2015). Detecting and removing web application vulnerabilities with static analysis and data mining. *IEEE Transactions on Reliability*, 65(1), 54–69. DOI: 10.1109/TR.2015.2457411

Nagy, C. (2013). Static analysis of data-intensive applications. In *2013 17th European Conference on Software Maintenance and Reengineering* (pp. 435-438). IEEE. DOI: 10.1109/CSMR.2013.66

Or-Meir, O., Nissim, N., Elovici, Y., & Rokach, L. (2019). Dynamic malware analysis in the modern era—A state of the art survey. *ACM Computing Surveys*, 52(5), 1–48. DOI: 10.1145/3329786

Pomilia, M. (2016). A study on obfuscation techniques for android malware. *Sapienza University of Rome, 81.*

Ray, A., & Nath, A. (2016). Introduction to Malware and Malware Analysis: A brief overview. *International Journal (Toronto, Ont.)*, 4(10).

Sihwail, R., Omar, K., & Ariffin, K. Z. (2018). A survey on malware analysis techniques: Static, dynamic, hybrid and memory analysis. *Int. J. Adv. Sci. Eng. Inf. Technol, 8*(4-2), 1662-1671.

Singh, J., & Singh, J. (2018). Challenge of malware analysis: Malware obfuscation techniques. *International Journal of Information Security Science*, 7(3), 100–110.

Singh, J., & Singh, J. (2018). Challenge of malware analysis: Malware obfuscation techniques. *International Journal of Information Security Science*, 7(3), 100–110.

Smith, D., Khorsandroo, S., & Roy, K. (2023). Supervised and unsupervised learning techniques utilizing malware datasets. In *2023 IEEE 2nd International Conference on AI in Cybersecurity (ICAIC)* (pp. 1-7). IEEE. DOI: 10.1109/ICAIC57335.2023.10044169

Song, W., Li, X., Afroz, S., Garg, D., Kuznetsov, D., & Yin, H. (2020). Mab-malware: A reinforcement learning framework for attacking static malware classifiers. *arXiv preprint arXiv:2003.03100.*

Tahir, R. (2018). A study on malware and malware detection techniques. *International Journal of Education and Management Engineering*, 8(2), 20–30. DOI: 10.5815/ijeme.2018.02.03

Tchakounté, F., & Hayata, F. (2017). Supervised learning-based detection of malware on android. In *Mobile Security and Privacy* (pp. 101–154). Syngress. DOI: 10.1016/B978-0-12-804629-6.00006-7

Venkatesh, B., & Anuradha, J. (2019). A review of feature selection and its methods. *Cybernetics and Information Technologies*, 19(1), 3–26. DOI: 10.2478/cait-2019-0001

Wagener, G., State, R., & Dulaunoy, A. (2008). Malware behaviour analysis. *Journal in Computer Virology, 4*, 279-287.

Chapter 8
Integrating Machine Learning Techniques for Comprehensive Malware Classification

Sridevi
https://orcid.org/0000-0002-9768-1599
Karnatak University, Dharwad, India

T. K. Gundoor
https://orcid.org/0000-0002-6102-0094
Karnatak University, Dharwad, India

Rajeev Mulimani
https://orcid.org/0009-0008-8394-4053
Rani Channamma University, India

ABSTRACT

Malware is a global problem. Malware's impact according to studies is escalating. In the fight against malware, Malware detection and analysis techniques are the most important defense tools. That which makes a detector good, or terrible, is largely determined by its techniques of operation. Thorough understanding of the many types of malware detection procedures is essential. This chapter investigates malware detection and analysis techniques, first and second-generation malware (i.e. encrypted, metamorphic, polymorphic, oligomorphic), and the study of machine learning algorithms for malware detection techniques.

DOI: 10.4018/979-8-3693-7758-1.ch008

1. INTRODUCTION

Malware, which includes viruses, worms, and other harmful software, has long threatened the integrity and privacy of computer systems (P. Sharma & Arora, 2016). Malware has become more complex as technology has improved, allowing it to elude detection and do harm (Rieck et al., 2011). The advent of open-source technologies has also enabled the creation and distribution of malicious software, allowing for the development of new threats via hacking tools. This concerning tendency has resulted in the exponential expansion of malware, with the majority of new threats classed as variations of pre-existing dangerous code (Belaoued et al., 2019). To counteract this expanding threat, machine learning techniques have emerged as an effective malware detection method. These solutions frequently rely on training classification algorithms with datasets containing essential properties of malicious code. For example, Byte n-gram representation has been identified as an effective feature for malware detection (Malware et al., 2016). However, attackers' increased use of obfuscation techniques challenges standard signature-based detection approaches, making the task of protecting systems against malware even more difficult (Tzermias et al., 2011; Sahay and Sharma, 2016).

A program and a legal utility are usually used in non-portable executable file attacks. As a result, inherently subtype of dual tool hacks, with the host system tool being a highly strong scripting framework i.e. PowerShell, WScript, CScript. As a result, fileless attacks are not script attacks because there is a script file involved, which may be identified. These files can be easily disguised due to the nature of scripts. For some scripts, such as JavaScript and PowerShell, The essential processing tool is installed by default; others, such as Word macros, require Microsoft Word to be installed for the payload to function. Script code is typically embedded in an Office document or PDF file and is activated when the document has been seen. The document may also be including the entire as an embedded object binary and prompt double-clicking by the user. This will create a warning message in its default settings; however, the user may discover they are persuaded to ignore it through social engineering. Total 12-year malware detected by the year is shown in Figure 1.

Figure 1. 12-years total malware detected by year(av-test.org).

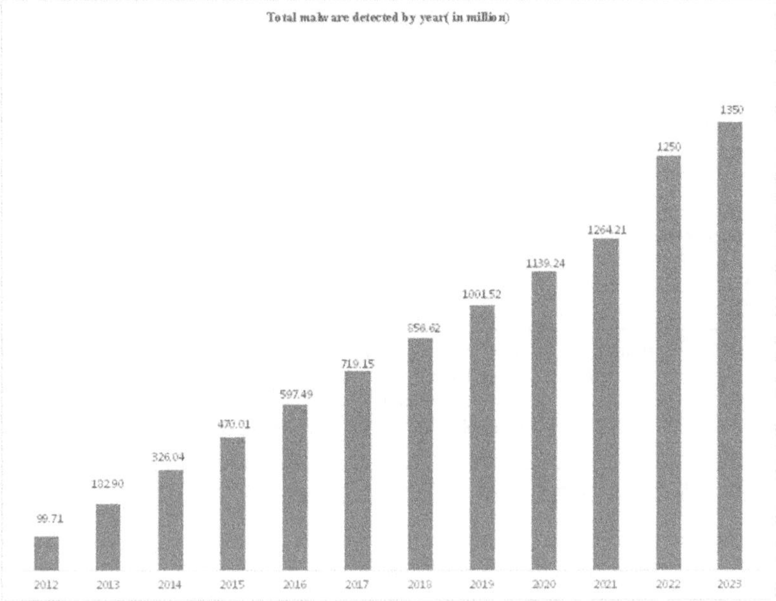

2. MALWARE CLASSIFICATION

2.1 First-Generation Malware

Most malware enters a network through methods such as a flash driver, malicious attachments, phishing, or malicious download and it can also enter via social engineering. While there are numerous malware variants, the following malware types are most likely to be encountered.

Table 1. Different types of malwares

Types	Features	Propagation Techniques	Targeted Domains
Virus	Self-replication Connect the code to a valid program. Active while the host program is in use (Cabrera & Calix, 2016; Richardson, 2009).	Introduce malicious code into trustworthy applications, which stay dormant until the malicious program such as an executable file launches and propagates to other programs.	.COM,.EXE, PDF, JPEG, boot records, scripts, and registry files are among the file formats (Cuan et al., 2018; Falah et al., 2021).
Worms	Self-replicating programs use networks to spread (Kunwar & Sharma, 2016; Zolkipli & Jantan, 2010).	Uses the network to distribute copies of itself to other systems without requesting user permission. As an example, consider Stuxnet	It primarily affects network bandwidth and trash email.
Spyware	Track user activities without their awareness	Spyware typically installs on a user's PC alongside legal software. As an example, consider the Dark Hotel. Example Dark Hotel (Prabhavathi et al., 2022; Schofield et al., 2021).	Monitor user activity, including internet visits, emails, credit card information, and passwords.
Trojan	Hide itself as a legitimate program. Allow remote hijackers to manipulate user systems.	Install on the user's computer under false pretenses and without the user's knowledge. Think about Emotet (Caspi & Herzog, 2018; Ladybird, 2021; Liu et al., 2010; Symantec, 2018; Walker, 2019).	Hackers steal user login details. Monitors system activity, including damage to files.
Rootkit	The capacity to deliberately conceal the presence of a computer while gaining privileged access. Registry keys and network connections can be hidden and masked.	These are designed to give a machine or network administrator-level access. Take Zacinlo, for instance (Prabhavathi et al., 2022; Zhang et al., 2013).	Conceals more viruses. Passwords that were stolen The Control user system was accessed by the attacker without authorization.
Botnet etc.	1. Remotely manage the user's system. 2. Both public and private network infrastructure can be centrally controlled by a zombie application (Trojan or worm). 3. Every instance of a botnet is referred to as a "bot." [57]–[59].	Botnets are commonly known as zombie networks. It is a collection of compromised systems that have joint authority over the network infrastructure. It remotely distributes spyware or spam to take over the user's computer. The central system that controls the botnet will give commands to each. Think about Echobot.	Spying on private data belonging to a user Profit from your login information.

2.2 Second-Generation Malware

This advanced malware is dangerous which can change its techniques each time to confuse the victim's access. Second-generation malware is classified into four types: oligomorphic, encrypted, polymorphic, and metamorphic.

2.2.1. Encrypted Malware

The primary goal of developing encrypted malware was to evade detection methods based on standard signatures and static code analysis. Encrypted malware consists of two sections: the encrypted body, and the decrypted code. The virus's true content is contained in the encrypted main body; The main content is converted to machine-executable code by the virus's encrypted body when it executes on the host computer. The first encrypted malware to be reported was CASCADE. (Anderson & McGrew, 2017; Li et al., 2008; You & Yim, 2010; Gavriluţ et al., 2009).

2.2.2. Oligomorphic Malware

Initially, this malware was only capable of making minor changes to the decryptor, and it could only generate a few hundreds of decryptors. By gathering the decryptors signature, to identify the presence of a signature, standard signature matching techniques are utilized. The signature method is generally not suggested for detecting this malware. Because encrypted malware can only perform on decrypted function. This malware contains a collection of various decryption patterns that are used at random on new host computers. Malware that is oligomorphic is a more sophisticated form of malware that is encrypted.

2.2.3. Polymorphic Malware

To avoid detection by signature matching, polymorphic malware can generate millions of decryptors by modifying the malware's instruction set. A variety of obfuscation techniques are used to build this malware. In 1990, Mark Washburn designed the first polymorphic malware, 1260. Polymorphic malware produces lots of alternative decryptors. It can be detected using conventional signature-based detection mechanisms. As a stealth tactic, polymorphism is employed to let malware build an infinite number of different malicious code to make analysis and detection more difficult. At any infection, their software is always changing (Cabrera & Calix, 2016; Kaur & Singh, 2014; J. Y. Xu et al., 2005).

2.2.4. Metamorphic Malware

This malware is practically impossible to identify using existing signature-based techniques, as a result, it will do massive damage to computing devices in the future. Metamorphic malware, however, is difficult to create without increasing the size. In 1995, Win95/Rewrap became the first metamorphic malware to be created. Body-polymorphic malware is the name given to this sort of malicious software. Instead of having an encrypted body, metamorphic malware has a body that is constantly changing in terms of its structure, code, and size, but its functionality has not (Bist et al., 2017; C. Choi et al., 2019; A. Sharma & K. Sahay, 2014).

3. MALWARE ANALYSIS TECHNIQUES

The analysis is the process of identifying malware to determine its behavior, origins, potential impact i.e. viruses, worms, spyware, rootkits, and backdoors, etc. The analysis technique is classified into four types: static, dynamic, memory-based and hybrid are shown in the Figure 2.

Figure 2. Malware analysis technique

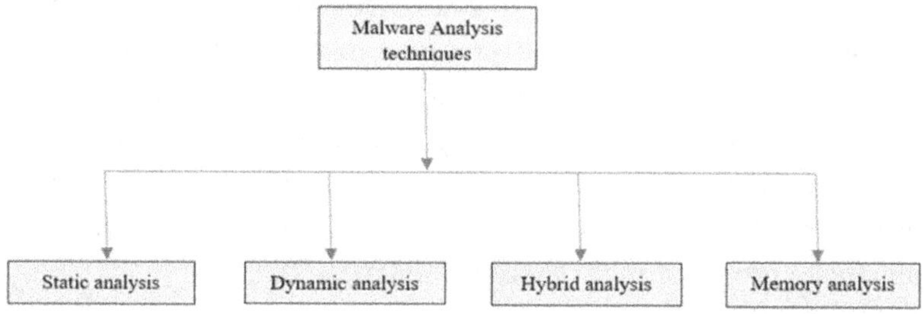

3.1 Static Analysis

In this method execution is not required for the executable file, it examines its program or structure. To detect unknown malware on the operating system, a statistical analysis approach based on opcode differences between benign and malicious executables to choose features for each group independently. Non-Portable Executable files (PE files) can be analyzed using this method, without having to run them. Binary packers like UPX and ASP Pack Shell are widely used by malware to evade being investigated. Because files do not need to be run, the static analysis could address scalability and efficiency difficulties, while dynamic analysis could potentially increase the accuracy of the features because each file can be executed and packed files will no longer be an issue. There is an advantage to static detection over dynamic detection in that it is more efficient (Damodaran et al., 2017; Djaneye-Boundjou et al., 2019; Fu et al., 2008; Ijaz et al., 2019a, 2019b; Sayal et al., 2020; Topark-ngarm, 2014).

3.2 Dynamic Analysis

This method which running the software and determines how it behaves on the system. It is typically done after static analysis has come to a halt, either due to obfuscation or all other static analysis methods have been exhausted. The interaction of malware with the computer system is tracked or noticed during dynamic analysis. To determine the flow of information from one instruction to another or from one block to another, the malware's source code is analyzed. An entire software file has hundreds of lines of code, which makes the task extremely time-consuming (Ijaz et al., 2019a; Mangialardo & Duarte, 2015; Topark-ngarm, 2014).

3.3 Hybrid Analysis

Anti-malware researchers combine static and dynamic analytic methods to gather information about malware, thereby boosting your capacity to identify and remove malware. Static analysis investigates malware's structure and properties, whereas dynamic analysis watches its activity in a controlled setting. This method provides a comprehensive picture of malware, improving detection accuracy and allowing for rapid triage and response to threats. Hybrid analysis is flexible to emerging malware methods and promotes threat intelligence exchange among cybersecurity professionals. Overall, it deepens understanding of malware behavior, enhances detection capabilities, and boosts cybersecurity defenses (Chaulagain et al., 2020; DIng et al., 2019; Düzgün et al., 2021; Lad & Adamuthe, 2020; Mirza, 2020).

3.4 Memory-Based Analysis

Recently, memory analysis has become a prominent approach for malware analysis due to its efficiency and accuracy. Researchers are drawn to memory analysis for its ability to investigate hooks and code used by malware that are outside of the function's normal scope. It analyses the running applications-related information's, and overall status in the machine using images of memory (S. Choi et al., 2020; Mimura & Tajiri, 2021; Z. Xu et al., 2017).

4. MALWARE DETECTION TECHNIQUES

Detection techniques are the methods of identifying malware on the host machine and determining whether a code is malicious or not. Signature, heuristic, behavioral, and normalization-based detection approaches are the four basic types shown in Figure 3.

Figure 3. Malware detection techniques

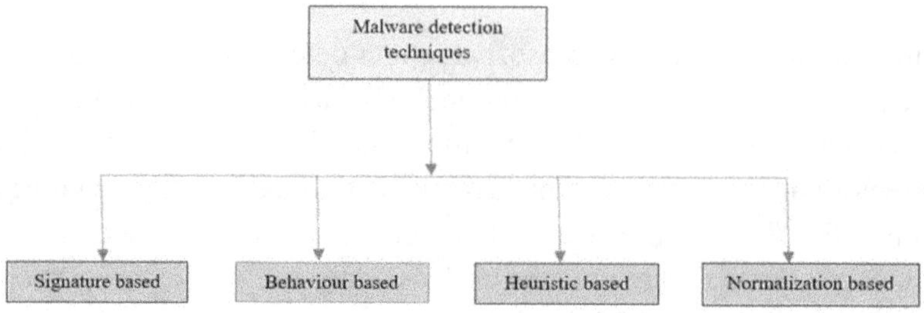

4.1 Signature-Based Detection

It is possible to identify harmful software by using patterns or signatures that have been previously identified in malware detection. As new malware threats are identified, signature-based anti-virus software must maintain a repository of known malware signatures, and this repository must be updated constantly as new threats are detected. To detect known malware, the classic signature technique strategy is a successful and easy method. A distinct short pattern of bytes is taken from the malware after it has been identified, allowing it to be distinguished from benign programs. To discover a person's identity based on their signature is an entirely reactive process. Obfuscation techniques used by malware developers pose a new challenge to signature-based approaches. Code modification is one of the techniques used in this technique. However, signature detection has a limitation in that it relies on a current signature database (Darshan et al., 2016; Limmer & Dressler, 2011; Sethi et al., 2019; Song et al., 2021).

4.2 Anomaly (Behavior)-Based Detection

It is divided into two stages: learning (training) and monitoring (detection). The object is being monitored during the phase of training. The detector is learning about the behavior of the host and process under infection (PUI) or both. Abnormality-based detection can detect zero-day attacks. To analyze the danger and determine the nature of the occurrence, anomaly-based detection uses set criteria.

4.3 Heuristic-Based Detection

A relatively recent technology, heuristic-based malware detection is more effective in detecting metamorphic malware. There was a big defense against malware between the years 2000 and 2021, and the heuristic technique of undiscovered malware was one of the possibilities for identifying new or previously undiscovered malware. Statistical methods, on the other hand, evaluate suspicious programs, looking for a particular pattern, and if the pattern is found, then a file is deemed to be infected. It is also possible to detect suspicious virtual machine actions using dynamic methods by simulating the CPU and operating system (Bist et al., 2017; Ucci et al., 2019; Vala Khushali, 2020; W & S, 2022).

4.4 Normalization-Based Detection

As part of data preparation, normalization is a process that involves converting the values of numeric columns to a common scale. Most of the time, this is done when the ranges of the characteristics that the machine learning model employs are not consistent (Mirzaei, 2019).

5. MACHINE LEARNING ALGORITHMS

Machine learning (ML) improves malware detection by allowing systems to automatically learn the patterns and behaviors associated with harmful activity. Unlike traditional signature-based solutions, ML models can detect previously unknown threats by evaluating vast datasets of files, network traffic, and system behavior. Supervised learning algorithms can distinguish between benign and dangerous files using labeled training data, whereas unsupervised learning detects irregularities in system behavior that may signal malware. Over time, ML models grow in accuracy and flexibility, reducing false positives and detecting sophisticated threats like as polymorphic and zero-day malware.

Machine learning is sometimes confused with artificial intelligence, despite being a subfield or form of artificial intelligence. Machine learning, often known as predictive analytics or modeling, is a technique for making future predictions from data. Arthur Samuel, a computer scientist, in 1959, the phrase “machine learning” was first used to characterize a computer's “ability to learn without specific programming.” Computer algorithms receive and evaluate input data to predict appropriate output values. As they acquire malware data, these algorithms learn and adapt to increase their performance.

5.1 Supervised Learning

An effective technique for identifying non-PE malware is supervised machine learning. A labeled dataset including previously identified malware characteristics and labels must be used to train a machine learning model. Based on the extracted behaviors, the model may then predict whether new, previously discovered malware is benign or malignant. The technique of gathering data by giving statistical models specific examples during the first phase, known as training, is called supervised learning. The right machine learning algorithms, such as rule-based classifiers, Bayes classifiers, Support Vector Machines (SVM), Bayesian networks, Decision Trees, Random Forest, Gradient Boosting Decision Trees, Logistic Model Trees, k-Nearest Neighbors (k-NN), Artificial Neural Networks, Multilayer Perceptron's, Multiple Kernel Learning, Prototype-based categorization, and more, must be chosen in order to guarantee the efficacy of supervised machine learning in detecting malware. Furthermore, evaluating the model's interpretability is essential. false positive rate, and ability to respond quickly to emerging threats.

5.2 Unsupervised Learning

Using algorithms to analyze the characteristics and actions of files or code to detect possible threats without depending on known signatures is known as unsupervised machine learning for malware detection in non-PE malware. There is no training phase with unsupervised methods, thus they learn straight from unlabeled data without any intermediate step. DBSCAN, K-means clustering, locality-sensitive hashing, and hierarchical clustering, distance and similarity metrics, hamming distances, Jaccard similarities other clustering methods can assist in grouping similar Non-PE malware samples together based on their features or behavior.

Semi-supervised: Instead of using labeled and unlabeled data, semi-supervised learning employs both. Unlabeled data, on the other hand, is information that lacks relevant tags so that the algorithm can make sense of the data. In this way, machine learning algorithms may be trained on unlabeled data by combining these two techniques.

5.3 Reinforcement Learning

Reinforcement learning can be used to increase the precision and effectiveness of non-portable virus detection systems. The detection models' performance may be improved over time by continually learning and updating in response to environmental feedback. In the world of cybersecurity, using reinforcement learning to detect non-portable malware can help to increase cyber defensive measures. By integrating machine learning skills, security professionals may create more robust and proactive approaches to detecting and mitigating malware attacks. The continuous learning feature of reinforcement learning is particularly suited to the dynamic nature of cybersecurity threats, allowing for real-time adaptation and reaction to emerging dangers. In addition to shielding sensitive information and systems against unauthorized attacks, this proactive approach can assist businesses in staying strong in the face of growing cyber threats. To learn via trial-and-error, reinforcement learning uses trial and error. From prior mistakes, it learns from the circumstance and adapts its strategy to reach the greatest potential result.

Highlighted a link between malware detection and machine learning algorithms by showing several machine learning strategies for threat detection. Supervised learning systems, such as decision trees and support vector machines (SVMs), use labeled datasets to categorize files as benign or dangerous. Unsupervised learning techniques, such as clustering, detect abnormal behaviors that may signal fresh malware in the absence of prior labeling. Reinforcement learning, however less often utilized, allows systems to improve malware detection by learning optimal techniques based on rewards for correct identification, which improves detection over time. The paper focuses on these various machine learning models for malware detection.

6. CHALLENGES

Signature detection technology cannot fight against the obfuscated malicious code effectively. The most prevalent sort of file that acts as a malicious attachment although, the phenomena of malicious Microsoft Office files attached to an email cannot be overlooked. Tests on new real-world attacks utilized Petya-infected Microsoft Office documents, indicating that machine learning methods may be useful when the signature method fails. Despite being restricted to the PE file format, the suggested feature engineering approach can be extended to non-portable executable files, images, PDFs, and audio files. It does not reveal the effectiveness of LSI (Large Scale Integration) in VBA macros nor evaluate the long-term effect of their methods. It is a lightweight investigates macros without requiring much time. Here real-time detection can be implemented. Not having enough samples to compare with earlier methods used by previous researchers. It was also unable to make a fair comparison with earlier results and did not have enough data.

By using new strategies and techniques to hide malicious code, malware developers are always one step ahead of computer security experts. Anti-malware solutions are a challenge in the realm of computer security since the present detection techniques and technologies are not sufficient or effective. To reduce the number of malware attacks, enhanced and sophisticated autonomous defenses are needed, according to this study. In the area of developing autonomous strategies to somewhat reduce malware problems, machine learning techniques offer a promising role, given the latest advances in malware analysis. Anti-malware solutions in the future will use machine learning approaches.

CONCLUSION

Malware remains a serious danger to computer systems, evolving in complexity and sophistication as technology advances. The exponential proliferation of dangerous software, frequently as versions of known threats, presents substantial problems to standard detection techniques. While signature-based approaches have been widely employed, the growing usage of obfuscation techniques makes them less effective. One potential solution to this problem is machine learning, with the ability to recognize and categorize malware based on key traits retrieved from malicious code. Techniques like Byte n-gram format have proven to be beneficial in increasing detection accuracy. However, the constant evolution of malware emphasizes the necessity for continued innovation in detection systems. The combination of powerful machine learning algorithms and strong feature extraction approaches can lead to more durable malware detection systems. As dangers emerge, academics and practitioners must work together to develop solutions that are flexible, efficient, and scalable. Finally, resolving the issues posed by malware involves a combination of technological innovation and proactive efforts to protect computer systems' integrity and privacy.

REFERENCES

Anderson, B., & McGrew, D. (2017). Machine learning for encrypted malware traffic classification: Accounting for noisy labels and non-stationarity. In *Proceedings of the ACM SIGKDD International Conference on Knowledge Discovery and Data Mining, Part F1296*, (pp. 1723–1732. DOI: 10.1145/3097983.3098163

Belaoued, M., Boukellal, A., Koalal, M. A., Derhab, A., Mazouzi, S., & Khan, F. A. (2019). Combined dynamic multi-feature and rule-based behavior for accurate malware detection. *International Journal of Distributed Sensor Networks*, 15(11). Advance online publication. DOI: 10.1177/1550147719889907

Bist, A. S., Patrick, A., Sharma, R., Pargein, S., & Dwivedi, S. K. (2017). Algorithms for Metamorphic Malware Detection. *International Journal of Engineering Sciences & Research Technology*, 6(6), 325–332.

Cabrera, A., & Calix, R. (2016). On the anatomy of the dynamic behavior of polymorphic viruses. In *Proceedings - 2016 International Conference on Collaboration Technologies and Systems*, (pp. 424–429). DOI: 10.1109/CTS.2016.0081

Caspi, O., & Herzog, B. (2018). *Emotet: The Tricky Trojan that 'Git Clones.'* 1–11. https://research.checkpoint.com/emotet-tricky-trojan-git-clones/

Chaulagain, D., Poudel, P., Pathak, P., Roy, S., Caragea, D., Liu, G., & Ou, X. (2020). Hybrid Analysis of Android Apps for Security Vetting using Deep Learning. *2020 IEEE Conference on Communications and Network Security*. DOI: 10.1109/CNS48642.2020.9162341

Choi, C., Esposito, C., Lee, M., & Choi, J. (2019). Metamorphic malicious code behavior detection using probabilistic inference methods. *Cognitive Systems Research*, 56, 142–150. DOI: 10.1016/j.cogsys.2019.03.007

Choi, S., Bae, J., Lee, C., Kim, Y., & Kim, J. (2020). Attention-based automated feature extraction for malware analysis. *Sensors (Basel)*, 20(10), 2893. Advance online publication. DOI: 10.3390/s20102893 PMID: 32443750

Cuan, B., Damien, A., Delaplace, C., & Valois, M. (2018). Malware detection in PDF files using machine learning. In *Proceedings of the 15th International Joint Conference on e-Business and Telecommunications, 2*, (pp. 412–419). DOI: 10.5220/0006884704120419

Damodaran, A., Di Troia, F., Visaggio, C. A., Austin, T. H., & Stamp, M. (2017). A comparison of static, dynamic, and hybrid analysis for malware detection. *Journal of Computer Virology and Hacking Techniques*, 13(1), 1–24. DOI: 10.1007/s11416-015-0261-z

Darshan, S. L. S., Kumara, M. A. A., & Jaidhar, C. D. (2016). Windows malware detection based on cuckoo sandbox generated report using machine learning algorithm. In *11th International Conference on Industrial and Information Systems,Janua*, (pp. 534–539). DOI: 10.1109/ICIINFS.2016.8262998

DIng., Y., Wang, L., Zhang, H., Yi, J., Fan, D., & Gong, B. (2019). Defending against adversarial attacks using random forest. *IEEE Computer Society Conference on Computer Vision and Pattern Recognition Workshops*, (pp. 105–114). DOI: 10.1109/CVPRW.2019.00019

Djaneye-Boundjou, O., Messay-Kebede, T., Kapp, D., Greer, J., & Ralescu, A. (2019). Static Analysis through Topic Modeling and its Application to Malware Programs Classification. In *Proceedings of the IEEE National Aerospace Electronics Conference, (pp.* 226–231). DOI: 10.1109/NAECON46414.2019.9057876

Düzgün, B., Çayır, A., Demirkıran, F., Kayha, C. N., Gençaydın, B., & Dağ, H. (2021). *New Datasets for Dynamic Malware Classification*. http://arxiv.org/abs/2111.15205

Falah, A., Pan, L., Huda, S., Pokhrel, S. R., & Anwar, A. (2021). Improving malicious PDF classifier with feature engineering: A data-driven approach. *Future Generation Computer Systems*, 115, 314–326. DOI: 10.1016/j.future.2020.09.015

Fu, W., Pang, J., Zhao, R., Zhang, Y., & Wei, B. (2008). Static detection of API-calling behavior from malicious binary executables. *Proceedings of the 2008 International Conference on Computer and Electrical Engineering, ICCEE 2008*, 388–392. DOI: 10.1109/ICCEE.2008.53

Gavriluţ, D., Cimpoeşu, M., Anton, D., & Ciortuz, L. (2009). Malware detection using machine learning. *Proceedings of the International Multiconference on Computer Science and Information Technology, IMCSIT*, 09(4), 735–741. DOI: 10.1109/IMCSIT.2009.5352759

Ijaz, M., Durad, M. H., & Ismail, M. (2019a). Static and Dynamic Malware Analysis Using Machine Learning. *Proceedings of 2019 16th International Bhurban Conference on Applied Sciences and Technology, IBCAST 2019, January*, 687–691. DOI: 10.1109/IBCAST.2019.8667136

Ijaz, M., Durad, M. H., & Ismail, M. (2019b). Static and Dynamic Malware Analysis Using Machine Learning. *Proceedings of 2019 16th International Bhurban Conference on Applied Sciences and Technology, IBCAST 2019*, 687–691. DOI: 10.1109/IBCAST.2019.8667136

Kaur, R., & Singh, M. (2014). A survey on zero-day polymorphic worm detection techniques. *IEEE Communications Surveys and Tutorials*, 16(3), 1520–1549. DOI: 10.1109/SURV.2014.022714.00160

Khushali, V. (2020). A Review on Fileless Malware Analysis Techniques. *International Journal of Engineering Research & Technology (Ahmedabad)*, 9(5), 46–49. DOI: 10.17577/IJERTV9IS050068

Kunwar, R. S., & Sharma, P. (2016). *Malware Analysis,* 1–4. DOI: 10.1145/2905055.2905361

Lab, H. S. (2021). *Emotet Botnet Takedown*. 1–7. https://www.hornetsecurity.com/en/threat-research/emotet-botnet-takedown/

Lad, S. S., & Adamuthe, A. C. (2020). Malware classification with improved convolutional neural network model. *International Journal of Computer Network and Information Security*, 12(6), 30–43. DOI: 10.5815/ijcnis.2020.06.03

Ladores, D. (2017). *EMOTET Returns, Starts Spreading via Spam Botnet*. 1–4. https://blog.trendmicro.com/trendlabs-security-intelligence/emotet-returns-starts-spreading-via-spam-botnet/

Ladybird, O. (2021). *Emotet Disruption : what it means for the cyber threat landscape The Evolution of Emotet : From Banking Trojan to Ransomware*. 1–8.

Li, Z., Wang, X. F., Liang, Z., & Reiter, M. K. (2008). AGIS: Towards automatic generation of infection signatures. *Proceedings of the International Conference on Dependable Systems and Networks*, 237–246. DOI: 10.1109/DSN.2008.4630092

Limmer, T., & Dressler, F. (2011). Improving the performance of intrusion detection using dialog-based payload aggregation. In *2011 IEEE Conference on Computer Communications Workshops, INFOCOM WKSHPS 2011*, (pp. 822–827). DOI: 10.1109/INFCOMW.2011.5928926

Liu, Y. F., Zhang, L. W., Liang, J., Qu, S., & Ni, Z. Q. (2010). Detecting Trojan horses based on system behavior using machine learning method. *2010 International Conference on Machine Learning and Cybernetics*, (pp. 855–860). DOI: 10.1109/ICMLC.2010.5580591

Mangialardo, R. J., & Duarte, J. C. (2015). Integrating Static and Dynamic Malware Analysis Using Machine Learning. *Revista IEEE América Latina*, 13(9), 3080–3087. DOI: 10.1109/TLA.2015.7350062

Mimura, M., & Tajiri, Y. (2021). Static detection of malicious PowerShell based on word embeddings. *Internet of Things : Engineering Cyber Physical Human Systems*, 15, 100404. DOI: 10.1016/j.iot.2021.100404

Mirza, N. (2020). Robotic path planning and fuzzy neural networks. *International Arab Journal of Information Technology, 17*(4 Special Issue), 615–620. DOI: 10.34028/iajit/17/4A/5

Mirzaei, O. (2019). *Techniques for Advanced Android Malware Triage.* 217.

Prabhavathi, C., Mahesh, A., Ajay, S. V., & Mythili, R. (2022). Malware Prediction Using XGBOOST and CATBOOST. *Journal of Engineering Science*, 13(5), 620–626. https://jespublication.com/upload/2022-V13I5085.pdf

Richardson, C. (2009). *Virus detection with machine learning. September.*

Rieck, K., Trinius, P., Willems, C., & Holz, T. (2011). Automatic analysis of malware behavior using machine learning. *Journal of Computer Security*, 19(4), 639–668. DOI: 10.3233/JCS-2010-0410

Sahay, S. K., & Sharma, A. (2016). Grouping the Executables to Detect Malwares with High Accuracy. *Physics Procedia, 78*(December 2015), 667–674. DOI: 10.1016/j.procs.2016.02.115

Sayal, R., Subbalakhmi, C., & Saini, H. S. (2020). *International Journal of Advanced Trends in Computer Science and Engineering Available Online at*http://www.warse.org/IJATCSE/static/pdf/file/ijatcse27912020.pdf*Mobile App Accessibility for Visually Impaired. 9*(1), 182–185.

Schofield, M., Alicioglu, G., Sun, B., Binaco, R., Turner, P., Thatcher, C., Lam, A., & Breitzman, A. (2021). Comparison of Malware Classification Methods using Convolutional Neural Network based on API Call Stream. *International Journal of Network Security & its Applications*, 13(2), 1–19. DOI: 10.5121/ijnsa.2021.13201

Sethi, K., Kumar, R., Sethi, L., Bera, P., & Patra, P. K. (2019). A novel machine learning based malware detection and classification framework. In *2019 International Conference on Cyber Security and Protection of Digital Services*, 1–4. DOI: 10.1109/CyberSecPODS.2019.8885196

Sharma, P., & Arora, J. (2016). A Review on Malware Detection Schemes Using Machine Learning Techniques. *International Journal of Engineering Development and Research*, 4(2), 2321–9939. https://www.ijedr.org/papers/IJEDR1602028.pdf

Song, J., Kim, J., Choi, S., Kim, J., & Kim, I. (2021). Evaluations of AI-based malicious PowerShell detection with feature optimizations. In *ETRI Journal43*(3), (pp. 549–560). DOI: 10.4218/etrij.2020-0215

Sharma, A., & K. Sahay, S. 2014. Evolution and Detection of Polymorphic and Metamorphic Malwares: Asurvey, . *International Journal of Computer Applications*, 90(2), 7–11. DOI: 10.5120/15544-4098

Topark-ngarm, P. (2014). *Identifying Android Malware Using Machine Learning Based Upon Both Static and Dynamic Features.*

Tzermias, Z., Sykiotakis, G., Polychronakis, M., & Markatos, E. P. (2011). Combining static and dynamic analysis for the detection of malicious documents. In *Proceedings of the 4th Workshop on European Workshop on System Security.* DOI: 10.1145/1972551.1972555

Ucci, D., Aniello, L., & Baldoni, R. (2019). Survey of machine learning techniques for malware analysis. *Computers & Security*, 81, 123–147. DOI: 10.1016/j.cose.2018.11.001

W, R. A., & S, C. (2021). *Performance Analysis of Boosting Techniques for Classificationand Detection of Malicious Websites.* DOI: 10.4108/eai.7-12-2021.2314506

Walker, J. (2019). Emotet trojan implicated in Wolverine Solutions ransomware attack. *The Daily Swig*, 1–3. https://portswigger.net/daily-swig/emotet-trojan-implicated-in-wolverine-solutions-ransomware-attack

Xu, J. Y., Sung, A. H., Chavez, P., & Mukkamala, S. (2005). Polymorphic malicious executable scanner by API sequence analysis. In *Proceedings -HIS'04: 4th International Conference on Hybrid Intelligent Systems*, (pp. 378–383). DOI: 10.1109/ICHIS.2004.75

Xu, Z., Ray, S., Subramanyan, P., & Malik, S. (2017). Malware detection using machine learning based analysis of virtual memory access patterns. *Proceedings of the 2017 Design, Automation and Test in Europe, DATE 2017*, (pp. 169–174). DOI: 10.23919/DATE.2017.7926977

You, I., & Yim, K. (2010). Malware obfuscation techniques: A brief survey. In *Proceedings - 2010 International Conference on Broadband, Wireless Computing Communication and Applications,* (pp. 297–300). DOI: 10.1109/BWCCA.2010.85

Zhang, F., Leach, K., Sun, K., & Stavrou, A. (2013). SPECTRE: A dependable introspection framework via system management mode. *Proceedings of the International Conference on Dependable Systems and Networks, Vmi*. DOI: 10.1109/DSN.2013.6575343

Zolkipli, M. F., & Jantan, A. (2010, December). Malware behavior analysis: Learning and understanding current malware threats. In *Proceedings - 2nd International Conference on Network Applications, Protocols and Services,* (pp. 218–221). DOI: 10.1109/NETAPPS.2010.46

Chapter 9
Machine Learning Algorithms and IoT Sensors for Securing the Networks

Sridevi
https://orcid.org/0000-0002-9768-1599
Karnatak University, Dharwad, India

Amrutha Kolhar
https://orcid.org/0009-0001-4940-3172
Karnatak University, Dharwad, India

ABSTRACT

As networks and Internet of Things (IoT) devices become more complex and interconnected, robust security protocols are essential. Sophisticated cyber-attacks often outpace traditional measures, necessitating the use of modern technologies like machine learning (ML). This chapter will explore how ML techniques can enhance the security of networks and IoT ecosystems. By employing ML for anomaly detection, intrusion detection, and predictive analytics, entities can proactively address security vulnerabilities. The chapter will cover various ML approaches, their application to network and IoT security, related challenges, and future directions. It aims to provide valuable insights for scholars, practitioners, and policymakers in cybersecurity and IoT deployment.

DOI: 10.4018/979-8-3693-7758-1.ch009

1. INTRODUCTION

When combining machine learning algorithm and Internet of Things sensor network security operating methods changed. The increasing numbers of IoT devices, such as medical equipment, industrial machinery, and even smart homes, require immediate network security, as they present the problem of an excessive number of devices on a network. These devices produce massive real-time data which impose both security needs and monitoring concerns. Security risks which pose dangers to complex networks made up of conjoining evolving innovative IoT architectures can be shielded in more traditional methods of security, such as encryption, firewalls may not be sufficient. Machine learning techniques enable systems to conduct autonomously in solving these problems with big dataset analysis along with trend recognition and predicting security risk. By training these ML algorithms identifying both atypical network traffic behaviour and suspicious activity that might signal a cyberattack or network breach. As they constantly learn from data they evolve autonomous capabilities that are continually improved. The consequence is a safety system that presents protection improvements continuously, dynamically, and adaptively. This is backed by a very high dependency of the protection infrastructure on the IoT sensor systems. Machine learning resolves that issue by analyzing network device data from sensors about temperature and motion and location data to detect security issues. Security systems can therefore react quickly to the real time data flow from IoT sensors to avoid high priority security breaches from becoming larger security problems. Security proactivity manifests when the machines learn and sensors together predictively respond to find and eliminate threats before they can become serious. Machine learning integrated with Internet of things sensors enables automated intelligent security task. Organizations can extract maximum value from their resource utility and marshal human judgement for complex situational decisions through the automation of security activity, such as data analysis and reaction triggering, as well as traffic monitoring. By marrying adaptive learning features from a machine learning with IoT sensory data, security continues to exact aggressive positions against future threats in a constantly evolving cyber threat environment. There are some hurdles with integrating security systems. It demands expensive physical infrastructure as well as storage capacity and computational power for integration. In addition, there are other challenges that exist. A combination of expensive hardware systems and data storage and processing capabilities becomes necessary because of machine learning algorithms' complexity and the vast IoT-produced data. The continuous need for protection exists due to the security risks from virtual attacks targeting both Internet of Things devices and machine learning models. (Canedo & Skjellum, 2016; Ismail et al., 2023; Malik & Chauhan, 2020; Mamdouh et al., 2018; Sagu* & Gill, 2020)(Al-Garadi et al., 2020; Bagaa et al., 2020)

2. BACKGROUND STUDY OF MACHINE LEARNING ALGORITHMS AND IOT SENSORS FOR SECURING THE NETWORKS

The development of present-day network security alternatives occurred through joint operations between Internet of Things sensors and machine learning algorithms. Traditional security firewalls combined with antivirus software fail to deal with the high rate of data production that happens when Internet of Things networks grow larger. IoT data undergoes advanced analysis through ML tools to detect both typical patterns and infrequent anomalies that stem from the information. Predominantly analytical programs of anomaly detection and predictive modeling process intensive IoT data outputs to uncover security breaches that manifest through irregular device actions. Machine learning implementations use traffic and user behavior data alongside sensors to identify malware threats along with unauthorized access points and appliances with communication problems. These information-driven systems acquire defensive capabilities from new data inputs during operations while maintaining existing security safeguards. The combination of industrial sensors alongside commonplace items such as webcams and smart thermostats generates real-time data which smart security systems use to track network traffic and perform device monitoring. Through coordinated action between organizations this system delivers immediate responses as well as minimizes exposure time to risks which enables real-time threat and hazard detection. To implement this system effectively we must first prevent algorithmic mistakes while solving scalability difficulties and protecting data privacy. Despite technology challenges machine learning programs exhibit strong promise to enhance IoT sensors' functionality in network protection systems. (Al-Garadi et al., 2020; Babu & Veena, 2021; Harahsheh & Chen, 2023; Mamdouh et al., 2018; Tahsien et al., 2020)

3. PRINCIPLES OF NETWORK AND IOT SECURITY

The protection of systems from the threat achieves network security's primary aim and maintains basic confidentiality and integrity in concomitance with availability. Data can only be kept safe and available for all if we follow these three foundations. For network infrastructure success in protection, encryption and strong authentication protocols must be in place to power proper access controls.

- **IoT Security Challenges:** Multiple security issues arise from managing the extensive number of IoT devices which possess different levels of protection capabilities. The combination of varied protocol standards while received minimum updates and patches creates more security risks for systems. The management of secure data interaction and upholding privacy and integrity across numerous network connections represents an essential challenge that affects both network protection technologies and Internet of Things defensive measures.

- **IoT Data Encryption:** IoT data encryption during rest periods turns valuable information into cipher texts that can't be deciphered into unrecognizable information, continuing to protect data authenticity along with trust and integrity. The sensitive information is degramed and this allows for authentic users to access the data while preventing unauthorized users from seeing the data or killing the source format of the data. By combining key management systems with resource use for encryption optimization, a convergence point for performance enhancement and security to devices with constrained power allocation is achieved.
- **Device Management and Verification:** To many people 'the internet of things' sounds suspiciously like a nightmare of the future where vast, invasive networks try to take over your house. In fact, the idea is a bit of a misnomer, and perhaps a misunderstanding: the secure Internet of things is a network, but it's a network that doesn't allow you in unless you can prove to it that you are who you say you are and you have nothing to gain by Under role-based access controls, these devices work on definitions which define the scopes and permissions to operate. The controls apply are precise operations limits that protect network integrity while preventing unauthorized entry.
- **Network Isolation and Segmentation:** The concept of network segmentation avoids spreading of security threats in the network system through dividing the network infrastructure on different parts in order to limit the damage. Firewalls combined with VLANs and isolation protocols make traffic types better isolated. The use of system segmentation and separate working areas restricts the area where an intrusion damage can occur and yields a set of limited attack zones. It guarantees protecting critical assets, without operational interruptions and secure vulnerabilities.
- **Regular Patch Management and Updates:** Scheduled software updates and patches are run to fix system deficiencies and security weaknesses that protect networks and their connected devices with modern security features. They protect their organization against future attacks by fortifying their defenses against cyberattacks by organizations following updates.
- **Threat Identification and Incident Response:** To implant IoT and network security, we need protection measures against invasion of privacy demanding protective measures against unauthorized exploitation or illicit access to private data. Data masking practices in conjunction with encryption technology

along with permission-controlled access systems give authorized personnel access to modify or view private information. The combination of behavioral compliance with privacy regulations, along with common standards, ensures user trust and protects against data breaches, and consequently demonstrates the importance of robust privacy.

- **Privacy Protection:** Iot frameworks protection controls security privacy protection of confidential data from misuse as well as unauthorized use. Since data masking encryption along with restricted access provide this capability, only authorized personnel can access or change private information. By enabling better levels of user trust from data breaches and legal compliance on one hand and following privacy regulations and standards, the benefits of robust privacy implementation are demonstrated.
- **Enhancing Security with Edge Computing:** This facilitates that the IoT systems depend less on network-based data transmission, by the way of Edge Computing security. Better real time threat analysis and compliance monitoring comes from the reduced attack surface. Edge computing at its source processes data with faster reaction speed, enhanced cyber defense capability and safeguard data quality with built-in protection features integrated in edge hardware.
- **Security-Focused Design:** The first step of security focused design in IoT systems is by making encrypted data protection using authentication methods and access rules primary developmental concerns. Early in the development of the architecture, system security is developed as a prevention of potential openings, building fortified defense mechanisms. By looking at security as an architectural pillar that allows IoT systems to operate efficiently without default protections to counterattacks, application reliability is maintained (Al-Garadi et al., 2020; Bagaa et al., 2020; Otoum et al., 2022; Tahsien et al., 2020)(Chawla et al., 2021; Otoum & Nayak, 2020; Sarker et al., 2023)

4. METHODS OF MACHINE LEARNING FOR SECURITY

Machine learning provides multiple approaches that cybersecurity businesses use to monitor risks and minimize threats. Common Machine Learning Techniques The following are typical machine learning ideas found in security applications:

- **Recognizing irregularities:** The detection of patterns in data that stand apart from standard operational behavior represents anomaly detection. Security threats identification together with system integrity protection and fraud detection requires this methodology. Data comparison to established models will deviate from normal ranges to signal system errors and infrastructures breaches alongside the arrival of new events. A set of analysis techniques working together through clustering and statistical modeling and deep learning enables the identification of peculiar behaviors within complex data sources including user actions or network traffic.

Figure 1. Anomaly detection

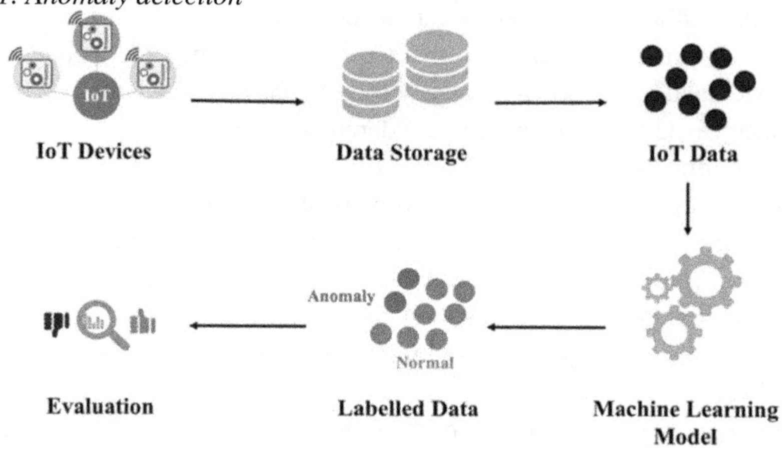

This illustration demonstrates the combination of storage systems and machine learning algorithms and IoT device telemetry for anomaly detection in IoT networks. A continuous stream of data emerges from multiple IoT device sources including sensors along with interconnected systems and cameras. A distributed and centralized data storage infrastructure accepts this dataset. The storage location and pre-processing steps which prepare the data for analysis secure facilities. Processing completes before IoT data classification occurs to provide entry for the subsequent stage. A machine learning model analyzes IoT data sets with the goal of identifying patterns to sort information between typical and uncommon groups. The training of the machine learning model depends on labeled data to differentiate regular behavior from abnormal patterns for making reliable predictions. The evaluation of IoT data by the model detects deviations that diverge from established behavioral patterns (anomalies). After evaluation the machine learning model provides labeled data output for analysis to verify its performance. To achieve robust security and dependability across IoT systems the loop demonstrates a continuous improvement process where machine learning models get better through integrated data updates and feedback acquisition.

- **Guidance-Based Learning:** Machine learning models implement guidance-based learning using labeled data as their training foundation. ARSE realizes lessons through pairs of input and output examples to establish a mapping function between them. This functional extension leads to better prediction capability for new data inputs. The two main types of problems handled by machine learning systems are classification which detects spam and regression that estimates property values.
- **Education without Guidance**: In unsupervised learning models, these models are fed with unlabeled unclassified and uncategorized data to train these algorithms, with no supervision. Usually, unsupervised learning lacks outcome predictions and looks into the fact of finding patterns and relationships from data. Organizing data points sharing identical features and dimensionality reduces union points based on their characteristic clustering functions. It provides very useful capabilities for image identification tasks and natural language processing as well as for anomaly detection and pattern exposure in large datasets for which the labelling is hard or expensive.
- **Comprehensive Education:** Multi layered artificial neural networks, called comprehensive education, use deep learning to learn how the data structures should be represented. This system has an automatic configuration method for different input data levels from basic inputs to complex patterns. Hierarchical pattern recognition using deep learning enables autonomous decision systems, audio synthesis and graphic capabilities, three key intelligent operations. This development gives rise to sharp progress on natural language processing and computer vision. Key skill is a mastery of processing high dimensional non-linear data structures.
- **Better instruction:** Here it is assumed that upon reinforced learning (by trial and error) in their environment, agents gain better training. Specifically, the agent is provided with motivational signals based on its own particular activities for which the total outcome is maximized. Supervised learning is a method of reinforcement learning which discovers valuable behaviours by trials, while reinforcement learning is a method of discovering behaviours from a sequence of trials but supervised learning needs pre labelled datasets. The model fits well when decision making under dynamic situations involving either defined unpredictable environments or environments that require either flexible or adaptable strategies responsive to sensed situations or learning outcomes.
- **NLP stands for natural language processing**: Natural language processing (NLP) is a part of artificial intelligence that teaches computers to understand how text and audio communicate between humans and just respond appropriately. It works on a wide range of processing from audio, text, collecting

the information, identifying the sentiment and processing the language intelligence. The real-time text databases are studied for concealed patterns by the NLP algorithms powered through combinations of machine learning and deep learning technologies and computational linguistics.

- **Group Techniques:** Group techniques merge individual model outputs within machine learning systems to increase both predictive accuracy and model robustness. A successful case is when the predictions from combination of multiple models such as support vector machines, decision trees and neural networks gives high predictive accuracy. Bagging is the data partitioning method that lets the machine learning models look at the segmented data segments to prevent overfitting and improves model generalization. Ensemble methods have been used in various application areas such as classification and regression techniques, anomaly detection functions, and recommendation systems for generation of enhanced prediction accuracy and reliability level in complex datasets.
- **Systems for Robotic Assault:** As a key objective of robotic assault defence, we want to be secure against malicious targeted model modification using robotic systems. An adversarial attack mimics normal human vision to produce model results that are mistaken. Training algorithms with adversarial examples, detection methods for abnormal data and adaptive safety strategies to improve resilience towards attacks, rely on protection. Effective deployment of adversarial machine learning methods for image identification and fraud detection and autonomous driving and natural language processing depend on their security and reliability. (Bagaa et al., 2020), (Roopak et al., 2019), (Uprety & Rawat, 2021)(Ge et al., 2019)(Canedo & Skjellum, 2016; Chawla et al., 2021; Ge et al., 2019; Harahsheh & Chen, 2023)(Bagaa et al., 2020; Ge et al., 2019; Moh & Raju, 2018; Tahsien et al., 2020)

5. LEARNING FROM MACHINES APPLICATIONS IN NETWORK SECURITY

Machine learning (ML) applications are essential for defending networks and linked devices against new cyber threats. Some of these uses are included in Table 1 below.

Table 1. Machine learning uses in internet of things security

Application	Description	Benefits
Anomaly detection	Through machine learning technology anomaly detection in IoT security recognizes unexpected network traffic patterns along with other nonstandard device behaviors to identify potential security threats while protecting overall system integrity.	The early identification of anomalous patterns made possible by data anomaly detection technology aids in the prevention of fraud schemes, intrusions, failure situations, and system flaws. By proactively resolving issues, the system reduces risks, improves decision-making, and fortifies security.
Systems for detecting intrusions (IDS)	Intrusion Detection Systems (IDS), which use machine learning protocols, are used by the Internet of Things to track network activities. Finding unusual patterns makes it easier to spot malicious activity and illegal access. Device protection and network security across operation domains are made possible by IDS's real-time data analysis feature.	Intrusion detection systems (IDS), which both identify and stop illegal activity on the network, are beneficial to network security. In addition to improving incident management procedures, reducing security flaws, and shielding data systems from intrusions, these solutions offer live threat surveillance capabilities, guaranteeing uninterrupted system performance and data protection.
Access Control and Authentication	User permissions are handled by access control functionalities yet authentication systems provide identity verification for restricted resource access to protect systems from unauthorized breaches.	Authentication and access control strategies ensure that only authorized workers have access to confidential data. In order to maintain system trustworthiness and comply with regulations, security activities priorities both privacy protection and the reduction of attack risk.
Intelligence on threats	Threat intelligence is the process of gathering and evaluating security threats. It helps organisations identify threats, understand attacker methods, and develop better defences and response strategies.	Through early risk identification that leads to proactive defensive measures for improved incident response capabilities, lessened attack impact, and real-time threat updates to continuously reinforce security measures, the deployment of threat intelligence technology aids organisations in securing their networks.
Device Behavior Modeling	The implementation of machine learning enables device behavior modeling to generate normal usage patterns which reveal possible security threats or unauthorized activity or equipment failures to guarantee higher protection levels and operational efficiency.	Through its capacity to identify anomalous activity patterns, device behaviour modelling improves security measures by reducing false alarm reports, enhancing proactive network defence capabilities, and identifying threats early.
Data encryption and privacy	Encryption of data through unreadable formats prevents unauthorized access during movement and storage operations so companies can preserve privacy laws and maintain confidentiality.	Encrypting data creates safe circumstances for sensitive information to be stored and transmitted, protecting personal data confidentiality, adhering to privacy laws, and preventing breaches of financial and personal information.

continued on following page

Table 1. Continued

Application	Description	Benefits
Malware Detection	Through signature-based and behavioral analysis malware detection identifies and removes harmful software which ensures both device and network integrity and security.	Systems benefit from malware detection because it guards against security threats, prevents data breaches, and preserves data integrity to fortify overall security measures and reduce downtime for improved defence against contemporary cyberattacks.
Self-Healing Systems	Autonomous self-healing technology detects problems independently to maintain an operational state while reducing downtime and improving both reliability and operational efficiency.	By automatically detecting and resolving problems, self-healing systems increase system reliability by lowering maintenance needs and downtime events. These systems provide continuous operations, increased system resilience, and increased efficiency with reduced maintenance costs.

5.1 Identifying Intruders

Network security uses machine learning algorithms to detect signals from unauthorized network access and attacks. Using machine learning algorithms, user activity used together with system records and network flow patterns, allows them to detect security breaches with anomaly detection methods. Other supervised learning techniques are leveraged by computers to teach them what is to be feared in actual time using marked benign and unsafe actions in datasets. Unsupervised learning doesn't have to classify data in advance since, in other words, it identifies the combinations of data that deviate from what it considers a norm. By improving detection precision while reducing false alarms and real time defensive actions in emerging network systems, ML based intrusion detection systems have elevated the efficacy of network security.

Figure 2. Entire internet of things intrusion detection using deep reinforcement learning

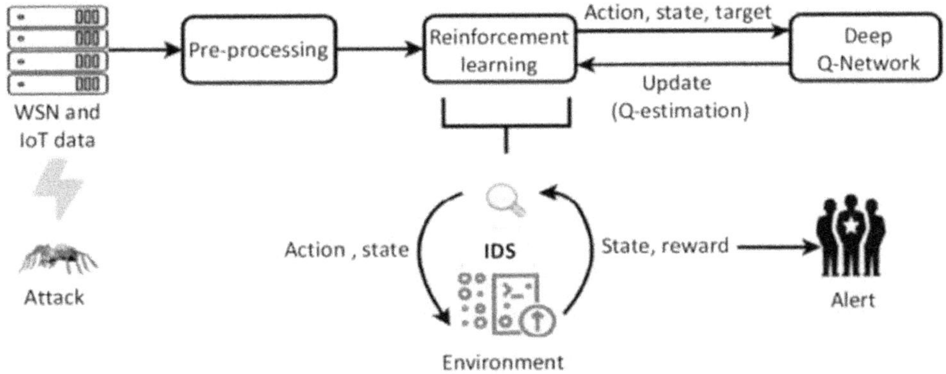

We utilise Reinforcement Learning (RL) and the Deep Q Network (DQN) to learn and detect intrusion in wireless sensor networks (WSNs) through IoT systems by detecting and preventing in the attack. Crude network data acquired from WSNs and IoTs are used as the starting point for data collection. However, data preprocessing performs data structure building, data structure establishment, and data structure extraction with regard to creating ready data structure and cleaning out noise from the data. Higher precision detection system is achieved by preparing a good set of data for analysis via preprocessing. The system acts jointly with the environment (Intrusion Detection System) in order to refine its decision capabilities, through Reinforcement Learning. The system state illustration is used for RL agent operation and then the agent evaluates this performance. However, this process is advanced even further with the Deep Q Network (DQN), which generates estimated Q values computed as expected rewards for different actions for specific conditions. Thanks to the DQN technology the model can operate well with high-dimensional complicated state action spaces. The usage of IDS environment is to continuously cheque our state and then select suspicious behaviour in order to find possible cyber threats and attacks. Detection outcomes that an intrusion raises and its severity levels are delivered to the operator in the form of alert notifications.

5.2. Malware Identification

Machine learning (ML) detects malware through its examination of file actions alongside an analysis of coding details and message patterns. Supervised learning analysis of labeled datasets couple with unsupervised anomaly detection mechanisms allow ML models to distinguish between harmful software entities and harmless ones. Security measures benefit from machine-assisted detection of new malware because such systems increase protection against endpoint and network exploits.

Figure 3. Malware detection

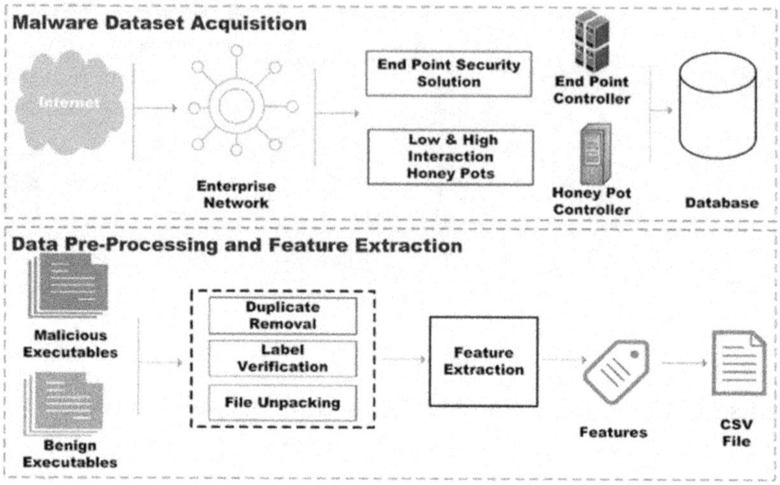

The analysis framework follows a dual approach combining malware dataset acquisition and data pre-processing with feature extraction as shown in the diagram. The first step in this framework uses an online corporate network to obtain malware dataset information. Modern networks capture and analyze threats through endpoint security solutions that protect endpoints from malware activities. The implementation includes deployment of both low and high interaction honeypots. Attackers are drawn toward these simulated vulnerable systems because the manufactured devices serve as honeypots for analyzing malware activity. Interaction levels regulate malware honeypot collaboration so researchers gain richer diagnostic data through higher engagement. The endpoint controller and the honeypot controller process and distribute data collections into storage through an associated database system. All malware samples together with their network activity logs are stored in a main database which provides the groundwork for analytical examination. Machine learning models require processed datasets that result from two operational stages that include data pre-processing and feature extraction. The data is divided into two categories: malicious executables and benign executables. The data pre-processing operations remove duplicates while verifying labels and performing file unpacking to achieve standardized data quality. Methods to prepare the field ensure the dataset doesn't have duplicate information and assigns the correct classification. It passes through a feature extraction stage that fetches out essential executable properties for extraction.(Bagaa et al., 2020; Tahsien et al., 2020)(Harahsheh & Chen, 2023)

(Ge et al., 2019; Otoum et al., 2022)(Liang et al., 2019; Malik & Chauhan, 2020) (Al-Garadi et al., 2020; Babu & Veena, 2021; Chawla et al., 2021).

6. COMBINING MACHINE LEARNING WITH THE EXISTING SECURITY STRUCTURE

With its vulnerability detection and threat enhancing capabilities, ML improves the IoT security defence mechanisms. To solve the difficulty, there exists the issue to tackle resolution of which concerns both resource and scalability limits and also privacy concerns. Once combined with machine learning, existing security frameworks reach their maximum strength since algorithms trained on huge datasets continue to enhance the system and cut the risk down, both increasing safety and reliability.

- **Threat Assessment and Prediction:** Machine learning analysis projects embedded in security systems perform real time exhaustive analysis of big datasets to improve attempts detection accuracy. Through the capability of machine learning algorithms to search for behavioural patterns and identify trends, and to identify anomalies, systems can achieve enhanced risk detection precision, and, hence, have permanent development through new intake of information to respond to complex security threats and innovative cyber-attacks. The proactive vulnerability remediation approach simplifies cybersecurity risk reduction and also improves threat awareness.
- **Examination of Behavior:** Machine learning technology used for behavioural analysis of security behaviours adds significantly to the detection and prevention capabilities of security frameworks. ML detects normal patterns based on persistent user and system behaviour analysis, and abnormal patterns such as those pointing to possible security threats. While production systems may be rife with strategic security flaws, focused on that data may reveal signs that could indicate internal security breaches or fraud attempts or, alternatively, sophisticated cyber assault techniques. This adaptive analysis ensures that security systems are adaptive to changing threats, and are able to maintain that ability of detecting changing threats, as protection strategies remain responsive.
- **Self-Acting Response:** Machine learning powers are put to use today in modern security technology to quickly and automatically execute automatic cyber threat response. Self-acting systems equipped with machine learning models enable real time security evaluation through the ability to make instant reaction choices including isolating some susceptible devices, stopping harmful behaviour or preventing the unauthorized access. Proactive threat mitigation

is the key to continued protection: it shortens response times while minimising possible threat impact. Automated replies bolster conventional security control and response activities by delivering quickly flexing countermeasures against modifications in cyber threats. By combining automation and intelligence without breaking, organisations can realign with new threats without losing resilience.

- **Enhanced Endpoint Protection:** As with any endpoint, more resilient hardware security platforms are built by continuously monitoring endpoint behaviour across existing security architectures. ML algorithms are run in real time, which see malware, unauthorized access and security vulnerabilities, and provide real time security identification of irregularities and threat detection. On the other hand, the proactive approach brings forth quick security help as well that is conditioned dynamic ability to screen new and protruding security dangers. Improved endpoint security effectiveness can be achieved from money spent on machine learning technology; increased threat detection accuracy and response time.
- **Improved Information Security:** Machine learning algorithms allow modern security systems to attain revolutionary information safety while providing new analytical capabilities. These ML algorithms detect security threats and operational loopholes with high speed and accuracy so as to provide effective response to risk due to insider threats and unauthorised access and breach of data. Securing information transmitted on open networks is strengthened by sophisticated encryption methodologies and sophisticated access control and state of art protection methodologies, and at the same time improve the integrity of the security of the overall information system.
- **Adaptive Threat Intelligence:** The combination of machine learning (ML) and adaptive threat intelligence fed into security systems allows organisations to deal better with emerging risks. Fresh threat data is then passed through complex processes which involve machine learning algorithms which autonomously shall learn new approach and techniques that accompany a new emerging attack harness. Its dynamic security system changes course against cyberattacks by adapting to ones that potentially can emerge from the changing threat landscape. In adaptive threat intelligence systems, machine learning methods enable security forces to interpret new threat information helping them secure a higher detection precision and quicker responses and better security protection.
- **Fraud Detection:** Machine learning (ML) helps with advancements in system detection of fraud experiences because behavioural analytics is actively monitoring users in real time and transaction patterns and trends. Together with the framework, powerful tools to ML algorithms are provided, enabling

them to perform accurately and fast, detecting unusual behaviour and dangerous patterns. However, the learning mechanism of algorithms adaptd to emerging fraud systems such that it derives new insight to emerging fraud systems from ongoing data acquisition and further enhance detection capabilities. These systems allow for the faster detection of significant anomalies and for the reduction of false positives through the 'programming' of these systems. Security teams have the ability to detect potential threats earlier and prevent valuable assets from being damaged or to cause a financial loss, through its proactive response features.

- **Scalability:** To address the growing system complexity and data dimensions, machine learning integration capabilities are provided to security frameworks allowing them to manage and handle both as they continue to rise. We believe that as machine learning models and datasets grow, security frameworks for encryption, as well as distributed permission systems and dynamic threat assessment capabilities, will become needed. Security measures become scalable in terms of working productively and efficiently across workplace enlargements and environmental transitions to the cloud systems.(Al-Garadi et al., 2020; Bagaa et al., 2020; Chawla et al., 2021)(Harahsheh & Chen, 2023; Santhosh Kumar et al., 2023)(Ahanger et al., 2022; Kumar et al., 2021; Urvashi Sangwan, 2024)

6.1 Incorporating Machine Learning Into Security Frameworks Requires Four Distinct Organizational Measures to be Successful

- **Data Integration:** Security frameworks based in machine learning, are dependent on the integration of data for their operational effectiveness. Security framework using machine learning draws information from various information sources consisting of system logs and user behaviour, operational metrics, and network traffic. Machine learning models find patterns, but also anomalies and potential security threats within huge datasets by performing processing operations of the entire dataset. Security frameworks based on multi source data integration are capable of discovering known attack and emerging threat more precisely. Holistic methodology provides huge security benefit by strengthening security posture while increasing detection capabilities at the same time.
- **Training and Optimizing Models**: Since machine learning is being integrated into the security world, Model Training and Optimization will improve security capabilities for threat detection and response. This procedure involves training machine learning algorithm on colossal volumes of histori-

cal security data to look for patterns, trends, and anomalies that could signal possible risk. These models are optimised for greater precision and effectiveness through continuous refinement and parameter adjustment. The security system's continued adaptability to evolving threats – and the corresponding evolution in attackers' attack methodologies – enhances our resilience and provides us with the ability to proactively thwart cyberattacks against more complex adversaries.

- **Real-time Monitoring:** Security systems based on machine learning require analysis of live data streams in a continuous mode in order to identify and fight threats evolving. In real time, machine learning algorithms analyse current system data to detect types of security threats, such as unusual events that transpire in a process. Proactive implementation organisations can take the initial security response by triggering immediate alerts that then automatically generate immediate alerts and alert security experts as well as automated protection systems. Integrating reaction speed and timely monitoring in the detection of threats in the ongoing operational environment enables successful investment of security challenge management and reduces the degree of security exposure.
- **Collaboration with Security Analysts:** In machine learning in a security context, it must be as effective as possible, and that means also relying on the cooperation from security analysts. For models to be accurate and applicable, the combination of machine learning techniques coupled with contextual knowledge and experience of security experts is a winning combo. Analysts provide real world insights and nuanced threat behaviours that help algorithms be increasingly better at identifying and addressing new risks. Therefore, machine learning models are kept adaptive to the evolving threat landscape through this collaborative approach and aid faster and more accurate threat detection and response.
- **Privacy and Compliance Considerations:** A privacy and compliance considerations thing is really important inside security framework machine learning. In particular, privacy is what the opposite side is, which, in other words, is restricting outside access to user data and the other opposite one is the compliance when data handling is not complying the rules or legislation that is now in place. For these needs to be met, strong security protocols are needed, such as frequent audits, complex encryption techniques and guarding at entry. Transparent data practices, user permission, don't expose data while you use it. Data anonymization is used to make it both safe and responsible for using machine learning. Thus, they prioritized privacy and regulatory compliance while organisations keep users believing and ethical standards.

(Malik & Chauhan, 2020)(Islam et al., 2021)(Waheed et al., 2021)(Bagaa et al., 2020; Tahsien et al., 2020)(Roopak et al., 2019; Tahsien et al., 2020)

7. CHALLENGES AND LIMITATIONS

There are several challenges and limitations when implementing machine learning (ML) in cybersecurity, including:

- **Adversarial Attacks:** The purpose is to help in security machine learning models from adversarial input data in threat detection operations and classification functionalities. Malicious actors and their affiliated counterpart, modify samples along with network traffic, to deceive artificial intelligence into offering wrong solution to make it easy for them to elude detection tools. It is known that many detection methods were created to fight such attacks, and yet they do not offer absolute prediction of the appropriate behaviour of machine learning models when detecting fraud, malware, and intrusion. In order to eliminate these security obstacles successfully, rigorous model validation philosophies must be combined with anomaly detection techniques, as well as adversarial training philosophies.

Figure 4. Adversarial attacks

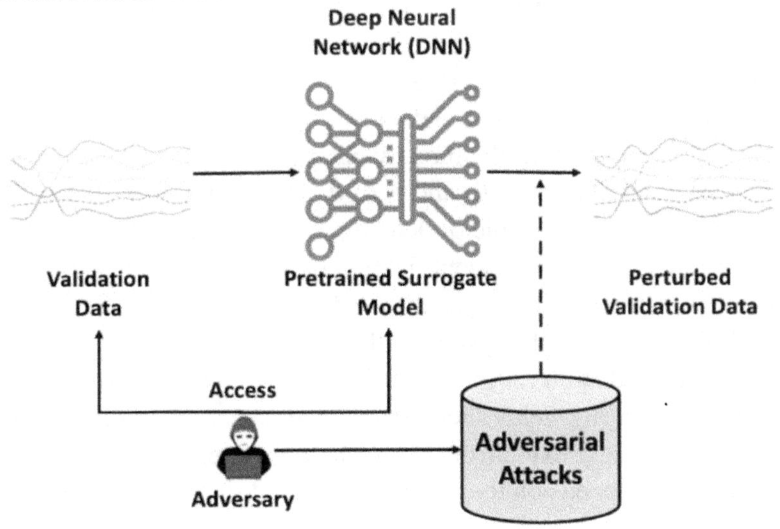

Deliberate adversaries modify input data with the intent of exploiting security machine learning models in threat detection operations and classification functionalities. A sampling of malware attackers and their counterparts encode their malware samples, along with all the network traffic, in such a way as to deceive artificial intelligence into thinking that the answers it is receiving are, in fact, wrong solutions. Yet many detection methods have been created against these attacks, but none offers an absolute assurance of the machine learning models' correct performance in spotting fraud and malware as well as intrusion. The successful elimination of these security obstacles requires philosophies of rigorous model validation and adversarial training merged with anomaly detection techniques. Resilient ML methodology powered advanced security systems that provide key defence against active security threats that are constantly changing.

- **Data Quality and Quantity:** And machine learning models require high quality data and plenty of it to be successful in security tasks. To learn effectively, machine learning models require large datasets — and excellent data quality. As such, dependable datasets are necessary for modelling accuracy, since systems can then detect and respond, safely, to security alert models. Unexplored threats coupled with many false alarm alerts is the result of poor or incomplete data quality leading to improper generalizations. Existing machine learning models must be updated and analyzed over vast ranges in the dataset continuously due to the constant adaptation of security threats.
- **Concept Drift:** Concept Drift is characterized by changes in statistical data properties through time and alters the effectiveness of machine learning models. The more attacks invent modern patterns, and threats evolve, the riskier it becomes to rely on traditional security models as they lose their ability to see new patterns through their defence approach. Adaptive learning becomes increasingly important as the threat landscape continues to evolve, as models must be able to automatically increase their effectiveness. Because machine learning systems are capable of detecting when there is concept drift in their system, which leads to the identification of a complete set of attack methods and emergent threats, their systems' detection capabilities greatly strengthen their ability to protect the system with comprehensive security.
- **Model Interpretability:** An essential challenge for applications of machine learning for security fields such as malware detection and intrusion prevention are the power to explain decision making processes. Credibility to the security analyst depends on the information about the decision-making process that triggers the threat flagging. Security analysts must be able to verify data accuracy and accept the information for effective solutions, and the system relies on total transparency.

- **Overfitting:** If a model has too much detail in a given data set, it loses the ability to recognize general patterns because it keeps information that predicts future predictions but doesn't generalize to the next datasets. The model showed this behaviour with poor performance on unfamiliar data, leading to poorly performing threat detection accuracy and generating false positive results. Regularized models trained on diverse data sets, such that cross validation against them corresponds to future operational environments are needed in order to provide proper defence against overfitting.
- **Scalability:** Security systems need to balance an expanding quantity of data with keeping operational efficiency. Since organisations need to process big data sets in order to effectively recognize threats, it is significantly important to have the correct system sizing. careful optimization is required to be able to deploy hardware that will allow machine learning operations to succeed and hardware to function within the security system while also optimizing security team performance.
- **Privacy Concerns:** Privacy problems caused by privacy violation triggering machine learning algorithms using private information they should protect. At present inadequate protective measures and anonymization techniques in these models may cause these models to leak personal information.
- **Privacy protecting methods are necessary:** Federated learning and differential privacy. Data analysis methods during data analysis protect users by preserving sensitive information to provide the valuable business insights.
- **Human Expertise:** Human professional involvement will be necessary for the successful implementation of machine learning for security applications. Machine learning models produce the valuable insights, but those insights need suitably skilled human analysts to understand and control what information is generated. These models are among the most potential but domain expertise, statistical analysis, and security know how combine to unlock that potential. Threat detection accuracy and effective security operations are achieved by combining correct implementation of the machine learning system with security analyst attention to issues.
- **Bias and Fairness:** Machine learning models make security results less dependable and less accurate. Fair decisions made using faulty selection processes are made from data that deviates from true representation and from models that provide predictive data that is in error. Fairness is the number one priority when building these models because it ensures very precise output, especially when you're working with data from various sources.
- **Implementation Costs:** Machine learning based security systems suffer from high implementation costs, including acquiring the data and building the infrastructure and making organization wide changes. A proper combi-

nation between machine learning methods and existing security practices is required to make use of it the effective management of financial costs and logistical requirements. Combining regulatory standards with human oversight will drive the development of security methods that efficiently use modern technological capabilities and traditional protection methods. (Ge et al., 2019)(Ahmad & Alsmadi, 2021; Santhosh Kumar et al., 2023)(Ahanger et al., 2022)(Al-Garadi et al., 2020; Tahsien et al., 2020)(Al-Garadi et al., 2020; Bagaa et al., 2020; Roopak et al., 2019)

8. FUTURE DEVELOPMENTS IN NETWORK AND INTERNET OF THINGS SECURITY

- **Enhanced Anomaly Detection:** Tools of machine learning are actively helping organizations in real time monitoring of network traffic behavior to detect anomalies that may point to indications of upcoming security threats. The incredible data processing capabilities of these models enable them to provide the necessary base to detect security threats at an earlier stage than had otherwise been possible by identifying abnormal behaviours that deviate from usual operation. Organizations can improve their security profile by being able to detect threats faster.
- **AI and Blockchain Collaboration:** Information security needs are being changed and consequently, the systems involving blockchain technology and artificial intelligence systems are taking huge popularity. Blockchain provides data management decentralization to very large systems such as IoT networks and artificial intelligence while providing guarantee of data integrity since blockchain is limited to modifications in the system. These technologies are merged IoT security infrastructure that connect these technologies and maintain data integrity through powerful defenses for unauthorized tampering and illegal access and having the best possible protection of sensitive IoT data.
- **Federated Learning:** Federated learning provides a mechanism for training models across multiple sites with data localization and thus no data movement required. This framework guarantees stored data stays in local storage thereby reducing vulnerabilities and providing crucial user privacy requirements as a constraint in Internet of Things security. Data stays decentralized and central storage of data is no longer needed – in cases where breaches are less likely – improving the security and privacy protection provided through federated learning machine learning applications.
- **Zero Trust Architecture (ZTA):** Popular solution for organizations want to improve the security beyond what traditional perimeter-based system pro-

vides is Zero Trust Architecture (ZTA). The verification system checks every device and software traveling through network connections, regardless of their source, thus making it different than the traditional zero trust security model. This access control method provides Internet of Things systems with IoT trust assurance of the authorized trusted entity; therefore, cyberattacks or illegal access are prevented.

- **Advanced Threat Detection (ATS):** Artificial intelligence is an indispensable technology that criticality depends on to enhance its capabilities to provide threat intelligence. AI solutions for risk assessment process through data analytics to discover potential threat with many sets of data and developing new capabilities to detect upcoming threat. Unlike this reactive method, risk detection and mitigation happen faster through one of the vital means of protecting rapidly growing IoT ecosystems that must manage the rising numbers and data volumes.
- **5G Security:** Recently the IoT devices have been facing novel security challenges owing to the rising adoption of 5G technology. Quantum encryption techniques are implemented to communicate and develop various encryption methods under post quantum cryptography for data protection from quantum computing threats. Even in the 5G era data integrity protection and the security of IoT device continues to require updated encryptions, with the corresponding need for continuous observation, and for the protection of complex data.
- **Predictive Maintenance:** In predictive maintenance of machine learning in IoT, machine learning is applied frequently. It uses machine learning models that analyze device performance data to alert users to potential equipment issues through data from the Internet of Things. The system can provide solution for immediate repairs as well as the pre-planned activities of maintenance. IoT networks sustainability as presented in this approach guarantees extended device lifespan as well as the appropriate security effectiveness and operational integrity of IoT systems.(Hussain et al., 2020; Malik & Chauhan, 2020)(Ismail et al., 2023; Vargas et al., 2021)(Ali & Montenegro, 2016; Bagaa et al., 2020).

9. PRIVACY AND ETHICAL CONCERN

Unlike traditional network security approaches the expanding adoption of ML and IoT technologies raises increasing ethical concerns alongside privacy debates. The usage of these technologies requires personal data storage while creating privacy concerns regarding the collection and ownership and protection of personal data.

The discussion becomes harder to follow because of matters like surveillance and unauthorized access and user consent issues. Protection of privacy rights becomes essential in achieving robust security as these technologies advance requiring better regulations and transparent practices to build user trust.

9.1 Privacy Concerns

- **Predictive Maintenance:** Within IoT ecosystems implementation of predictive maintenance in delaying and fixing expensive outages and security anomalies triggered by aging and failing devices.
- **Monitoring and Tracking:** Continuous IoT device surveillance combined with tracking activities creates major ethical problems that respect individual privacy. Smart home devices use tracking technology to collect detailed information about personal daily activities through monitoring personal behaviors. planet-wide data loss and public disclosure of information have the potential to create undesirable consequences. The prevention of exploitation and protection from privacy violations require strong data security protocols alongside open-channel data management practices and clear ethical boundaries for monitoring IoT technology usage. (Moh & Raju, 2018; Waheed et al., 2021)(Ahmad & Alsmadi, 2021; Harahsheh & Chen, 2023; Liang et al., 2019)

9.2 Ethical Concerns

- **Biased Machine Learning Algorithms**: Slow machine learning algorithms tend to reproduce training dataset biases hence creating unfair results which do not represent true societal nature and fairness. Security analytics that receive skewed training data will learn to recognize dangerous behaviors among specific population groups even when these behaviors are non-existent. The integrity of automated decision systems alongside their potential to spread negative stereotypes and unfairly practice patterns represent major ethical dilemmas. The reduction of training data biases remains essential for developing machine learning systems which demonstrate accountable equitable behavior.
- **Need for Responsibility and Accountability**: AI and machine learning systems gain crucial security decision-making responsibilities but the identification of responsible parties for system failures and misleading output remains essential for current times. When security AI fails at threat detection or causes false security alarms someone needs to accept legal responsibility for these mistakes between the developers and those implementing the sys-

tem and AI systems themselves. Identifying clear organizational responsibility becomes essential for holding stakeholders responsible regarding AI system outcomes. Demonstrating clear accountability can preserve public confidence in advanced technologies while promoting their appropriate employment. Sridevi, and Gundoor, T.K. (2024), Tukkappa K Gundoor, Dr. Sridevi. (2024), Gundoor, T. K., Sridevi, & Mulimani, R. (2025), Kolhar, A. & Sridevi. (2025).

- **Transparency and User Trust**: Building and protecting user trust depends exclusively on complete transparency about data collection methods and usage practices and security measures. The complete user awareness about the processes which gather their data goes alongside explanations regarding data usage objectives and data security methods that protect their personal information. Organizations that present these details with clarity both boost user comfort and execute technology deployment ethically. Formal disclosure practices reduce technology resistance by demonstrating data protection integrity while easing user concerns about data security to motivate new technology adoption. Even the most technically advanced systems will generate public doubts when transparency concerning usage or data collection is not established from the start (Gundoor, T. K., & Sridevi, 2022).
- **Adherence to Regulations** Organizations need to develop and apply detailed data accumulation and handling procedures which follow privacy standards found in the General Data Protection Regulation (GDPR) and the Digital Services Act (DSA). The exact guidelines that show business how to deal with personal data exist while preserving individual rights. Established data governance protocols address all security concerns alongside privacy policy and user consent violations which explains why ethical standards strongly benefit from appropriate data governance structures. (Ahanger et al., 2022; Ali & Montenegro, 2016)

Machine learning security improvements result in privacy and ethical problems because of the massive amount of personal data processed while automated decisions contain potential biases. A solution to these matters requires an upfront method based on clear communications, human oversight accountability and user protections standards. Users need transparent data usage communication alongside rights education and developers must be responsible along with their AI systems for their actions. Protecting user data requires a combination of privacy-preserving methods including data anonymization practices, encryption protocols and federated learning approaches for both successful security implementation and user privacy protection (Al-Garadi et al., 2020; Hussain et al., 2020; Sarker et al., 2023)(Bagaa et al., 2020; Harahsheh & Chen, 2023)(Bagaa et al., 2020).

REFERENCES

Ahanger, T. A., Tariq, U., Ibrahim, A., Ullah, I., Bouteraa, Y., & Gebali, F. (2022). Securing IoT-Empowered Fog Computing Systems: Machine Learning Perspective. *Mathematics*, 10(8), 1–20. DOI: 10.3390/math10081298

Ahmad, R., & Alsmadi, I. (2021). Machine learning approaches to IoT security: A systematic literature review [Formula presented]. *Internet of Things : Engineering Cyber Physical Human Systems*, 14, 100365. Advance online publication. DOI: 10.1016/j.iot.2021.100365

Al-Garadi, M. A., Mohamed, A., Al-Ali, A. K., Du, X., Ali, I., & Guizani, M. (2020). A Survey of Machine and Deep Learning Methods for Internet of Things (IoT) Security. *IEEE Communications Surveys and Tutorials*, 22(3), 1646–1685. DOI: 10.1109/COMST.2020.2988293

Ali, Q., & Montenegro, S. (2016). Explicit Model Following Distributed Control Scheme for Formation Flying of Mini UAVs. *IEEE Access : Practical Innovations, Open Solutions*, 4, 397–406. DOI: 10.1109/ACCESS.2016.2517203

Babu, M. R., & Veena, K. N. (2021). A survey on attack detection methods for IOT using machine learning and deep learning. In *2021 3rd International Conference on Signal Processing and Communication, May*, (pp. 625–630). DOI: 10.1109/ICSPC51351.2021.9451740

Bagaa, M., Taleb, T., Bernabe, J. B., & Skarmeta, A. (2020). A Machine Learning Security Framework for Iot Systems. *IEEE Access: Practical Innovations, Open Solutions*, 8, 114066–114077. DOI: 10.1109/ACCESS.2020.2996214

Canedo, J., & Skjellum, A. (2016). Using machine learning to secure IoT systems. In *2016 14th Annual Conference on Privacy, Security and Trust, (pp.* 219–222). DOI: 10.1109/PST.2016.7906930

Chawla, N., Singh, A., Kumar, H., Kar, M., & Mukhopadhyay, S. (2021). Securing IoT Devices Using Dynamic Power Management: Machine Learning Approach. *IEEE Internet of Things Journal*, 8(22), 16379–16394. DOI: 10.1109/JIOT.2020.3021594

Ge, M., Fu, X., Syed, N., Baig, Z., Teo, G., & Robles-Kelly, A. (2019, December). Deep learning-based intrusion detection for IoT networks. In *Proceedings of IEEE Pacific Rim International Symposium on Dependable Computing,* (pp. 256–265). DOI: 10.1109/PRDC47002.2019.00056

Gundoor, T. K. (2022). IoT-Enabled 5G Networks for Secure Communication. In *Information Security Practices for the Internet of Things, 5G, and Next-Generation Wireless Networks* (pp. 1-29). IGI Global.

Gundoor, T.K., & Sridevi (2022). "Identification Of Dominant Features in Non-Portable Executable Malicious File," In 2022 Second International Conference on Computer Science, Engineering and Applications, Gunupur, India, (pp. 1-6), .DOI: 10.1109/ICCSEA54677.2022.9936451

Gundoor, T. K. Sridevi, & Mulimani, R. (2025). AI-Based Solutions for Malware Detection and Prevention. In M. Almaiah & Y. Maleh (Eds.), *Machine Intelligence Applications in Cyber-Risk Management* (pp. 107-134). IGI Global Scientific Publishing. DOI: 10.4018/979-8-3693-7540-2.ch006

Harahsheh, K., & Chen, C. H. (2023). A Survey of Using Machine Learning in IoT Security and the Challenges Faced by Researchers. *Informatica (Slovenia)*, 47(6), 1–54. DOI: 10.31449/inf.v47i6.4635

Hussain, F., Hussain, R., Hassan, S. A., & Hossain, E. (2020). Machine Learning in IoT Security: Current Solutions and Future Challenges. *IEEE Communications Surveys and Tutorials*, 22(3), 1686–1721. DOI: 10.1109/COMST.2020.2986444

Islam, N., Altamimi, M., Haseeb, K., & Siraj, M. (2021). Secure and sustainable predictive framework for iot-based multimedia services using machine learning. *Sustainability (Basel)*, 13(23), 1–15. DOI: 10.3390/su132313128

Ismail, S., Dawoud, D. W., & Reza, H. (2023). Securing Wireless Sensor Networks Using Machine Learning and Blockchain: A Review. *Future Internet*, 15(6), 1–45. DOI: 10.3390/fi15060200

Kolhar, A. & Sridevi. (2025). Future Trends and Innovation in Machine Intelligence for Cyber Risk Management. In M. Almaiah & Y. Maleh (Eds.), *Machine Intelligence Applications in Cyber-Risk Management* (pp. 415-438). IGI Global Scientific Publishing. DOI: 10.4018/979-8-3693-7540-2.ch018

Kumar, P., Kumar, R., Srivastava, G., Gupta, G. P., Tripathi, R., Gadekallu, T. R., & Xiong, N. N. (2021). PPSF: A Privacy-Preserving and Secure Framework Using Blockchain-Based Machine-Learning for IoT-Driven Smart Cities. *IEEE Transactions on Network Science and Engineering*, 8(3), 2326–2341. DOI: 10.1109/TNSE.2021.3089435

Liang, F., Hatcher, W. G., Liao, W., Gao, W., & Yu, W. (2019). Machine Learning for Security and the Internet of Things: The Good, the Bad, and the Ugly. *IEEE Access : Practical Innovations, Open Solutions*, 7, 158126–158147. DOI: 10.1109/ACCESS.2019.2948912

Malik, S., & Chauhan, R. (2020). Securing the internet of things using machine learning: A review. In *2020 International Conference on Convergence to Digital World - Quo Vadis*, (pp. 9–12). DOI: 10.1109/ICCDW45521.2020.9318666

Mamdouh, M., Elrukhsi, M. A. I., & Khattab, A. (2018). Securing the Internet of Things and Wireless Sensor Networks via Machine Learning: A Survey. In *2018 International Conference on Computer and Applications, ICCA 2018, Section II*, (pp. 215–218). DOI: 10.1109/COMAPP.2018.8460440

Moh, M., & Raju, R. (2018). Machine learning techniques for security of internet of things (IoT) and fog computing systems. In *Proceedings - 2018 International Conference on High Performance Computing and Simulation* (pp. 709–715). DOI: 10.1109/HPCS.2018.00116

Otoum, Y., Liu, D., & Nayak, A. (2022). DL-IDS: A deep learning–based intrusion detection framework for securing IoT. *Transactions on Emerging Telecommunications Technologies*, 33(3), 1–14. DOI: 10.1002/ett.3803

Otoum, Y., & Nayak, A. (2020, July). On securing IoT from Deep Learning perspective. In *Proceedings - IEEE Symposium on Computers and Communications*. DOI: 10.1109/ISCC50000.2020.9219671

Roopak, M., & Tian, Y. G., & Chambers, J. (2019). Deep learning models for cyber security in IoT networks. *2019 IEEE 9th Annual Computing and Communication Workshop and Conference,* (pp. 452–457). DOI: 10.1109/CCWC.2019.8666588

Sagu*, A., & Gill, N. S. (2020). Machine Learning Techniques for Securing IoT Environment. *International Journal of Innovative Technology and Exploring Engineering, 9*(4), 977–982. DOI: 10.35940/ijitee.D1209.029420

Sangwan, U. (2024). Efficient Cyber Security Framework for IoT Using Machine Learning Algorithms. *Journal of Electrical Systems*, 20(6s), 2444–2451. DOI: 10.52783/jes.3233

Santhosh Kumar, S. V. N., Selvi, M., & Kannan, A. (2023). A Comprehensive Survey on Machine Learning-Based Intrusion Detection Systems for Secure Communication in Internet of Things. *Computational Intelligence and Neuroscience*, 2023(1), 1–24. DOI: 10.1155/2023/8981988

Sarker, I. H., Khan, A. I., Abushark, Y. B., & Alsolami, F. (2023). Internet of Things (IoT) Security Intelligence: A Comprehensive Overview, Machine Learning Solutions and Research Directions. *Mobile Networks and Applications*, 28(1), 296–312. DOI: 10.1007/s11036-022-01937-3

Sridevi, and Tukkappa K Gundoor. (2025). "Identifying Nobel Features in Non-Portable Executable Malware Files," IAENG International Journal of Computer Science, *52*(1), 121-129.

Sridevi, and Gundoor, T.K. (2024). Artificial Intelligence on Knowledge Management and Industry Revolution 4.0. In R. Kumar, V. Jain, V.C. Ibarra, C.A. Talib and V. Kukreja (Eds.), Knowledge Management and Industry Revolution 4.0. DOI: 10.1002/9781394242641.ch6

Tahsien, S. M., Karimipour, H., & Spachos, P. (2020). Machine learning based solutions for security of Internet of Things (IoT): A survey. *Journal of Network and Computer Applications*, 161(February), 102630. Advance online publication. DOI: 10.1016/j.jnca.2020.102630

Tukkappa, K. Gundoor, Dr. Sridevi. (2024). Optimized Feature Selection and classification for Non-Portable Executable Malware. *International Journal of Communication Networks and Information Security (IJCNIS), 16*(4), 546–552. Retrieved from https://ijcnis.org/index.php/ijcnis/article/view/7107

Uprety, A., & Rawat, D. B. (2021). Reinforcement Learning for IoT Security: A Comprehensive Survey. *IEEE Internet of Things Journal*, 8(11), 8693–8706. DOI: 10.1109/JIOT.2020.3040957

Vargas, H., Lozano-Garzon, C., Montoya, G. A., & Donoso, Y. (2021). Detection of security attacks in industrial iot networks: A blockchain and machine learning approach. *Electronics (Basel)*, 10(21), 2662. Advance online publication. DOI: 10.3390/electronics10212662

Waheed, N., He, X., Ikram, M., Usman, M., Hashmi, S. S., & Usman, M. (2021). Security and Privacy in IoT Using Machine Learning and Blockchain. *ACM Computing Surveys*, 53(6), 1–37. DOI: 10.1145/3417987

Chapter 10
Cybersecurity for Preserving Mental Wellness and Preventing Abuse

Arvindhan Muthusamy
Amity University, Greater Noida, India

Tarun Kumar
https://orcid.org/0000-0002-8507-8522
Galgotias University, India

Minakshi
https://orcid.org/0000-0001-7586-6309
King Khalid University, Saudi Arabia

ABSTRACT

The rapid surge in cybercrime during the COVID-19 pandemic has become a pressing concern for mental health professionals. The increased reliance on digital technologies for work, education, and healthcare has led to a rise in cyber-attacks, with perpetrators exploiting vulnerable individuals through methods like phishing scams and online harassment. These incidents can have severe psychological consequences, such as heightened anxiety, depression, and post-traumatic stress. To address this challenge, the text explores the dynamic interplay between cybersecurity practices and the preservation of mental health and well-being. It examines various cyber threats, including cyberbullying, doxing, and revenge porn, and their emotional and mental impacts on victims, such as anxiety, depression, and social withdrawal.

DOI: 10.4018/979-8-3693-7758-1.ch010

1. INTRODUCTION

Cyber security is crucial to mental health and abuse prevention as we utilize technology more. The COVID-19 epidemic has made this problem worse because more individuals use online platforms for business, education, and mental health. Computers and cybercrime can harm patients' mental health. Thus, psychiatrists, as well as other mental health practitioners, must be aware of them. Mental health doctors should first educate their patients on reputable cyber security resources to assist them in negotiating the online realm responsibly. Telemedicine and virtual treatment have helped during the pandemic, but privacy and security concerns have arisen. Healthcare organizations must apply standards of excellence to reduce cyber incidents and protect patient data (Kumar et al., 2024b).

Telemedicine platforms are essential to healthcare delivery; hence, their robustness is critical. Balancing privacy and security issues with online treatment advantages will be a constant struggle, but it is necessary to protect mental health. Cybercrime can cause vulnerability, anxiety, and post-traumatic stress. Mental health providers must be cautious in identifying and fixing these issues to reduce patient online assault risk (Krishnan et al., 2023).

1.1 Cybercrime and Mental Health Implications

There has been a surge in cybercrime since the pandemic. Malicious individuals have been attacking people in many ways, including phishing scams, ransomware attacks and online harassment, causing severe mental conditions such as anxiety, depression and post-traumatic stress disorder. Those who are already suffering from mental illness and in need of treatment may be particularly vulnerable to the consequences of cybercrime. Their symptoms only get worse while their ability to recover is being held back.

1.2 Protecting the Vulnerable

Groups such as the elderly and those with cognitive impairments are especially vulnerable to these kinds of attacks due both to their limited technological literacy and the ease with which manipulation can be applied to them. Healthcare workers and caretakers have a vital role to play in arming this part of the population with information and support to help temper the mental health consequences should something go wrong (Zhou et al., 2024).

1.3 Strengthening Cyber Resilience

During the pandemic, cyber-attacks have found some of the healthcare institutions' prime targets: cases reporting ransomware, phishing, and denial-of-service attacks disrupt critical services and threaten this all-important patient information. As such, these institutions must prioritize robust cybersecurity measures in order to protect mental health while also preventing abuse. Best practices include keeping systems updated on an ongoing basis, training employees, and doing drills and exercises with your incident response team.

Cyber-attacks have a detrimental effect on the individual victims of the crime and all other service users who cannot obtain the necessary support from the company they use. Access to assistance is particularly crucial for vulnerable individuals during crises and times of need, such as when there is a high risk of suicide, when there are interruptions in medication supply, and when medication adherence requirements are being monitored. These concerns prompt inquiries on the appropriate approach to support persons before, during, and following such occurrences(Arslan et al., 2024). What is the potential impact of data breaches and service outages on psychological and other clinical outcomes? What activities should a mental health professional undertake after becoming aware of such intrusions or interruptions to the system?

Furthermore, cyber-attacks, such as the WannaCry attack, caused concern and overwhelming powerlessness among many individuals. Upon experiencing identity theft, what is the impact on the socioeconomic level of the victims? Figure 1 illustrates that a data breach can undermine or even eradicate the confidence between service consumers and providers. Inadequately planned reactions to cybersecurity breaches could further contribute to the negative perception surrounding the approach and acceptance of mental health treatments. For instance, users may begin to either avoid or postpone getting therapy or intentionally withhold or provide inaccurate information during evaluations, therefore compromising their standard of care.

Figure 1. Types of cybersecurity attack

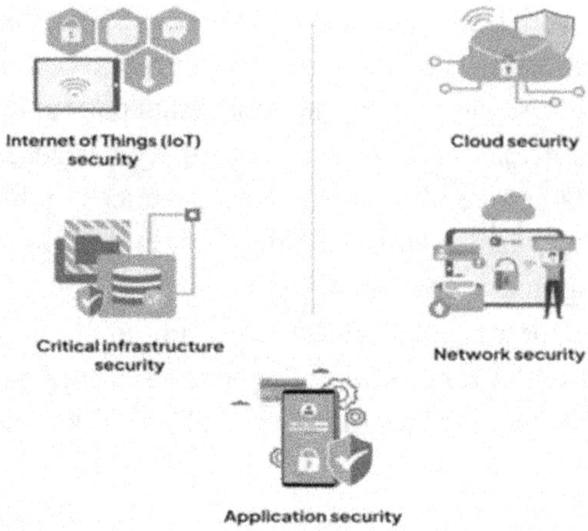

The interplay between cybersecurity practices and preserving mental health and wellbeing. The role of mental health professionals in addressing the cyber security challenges faced by their patients.

The adverse effects of cybercrime on mental health, such as increased feelings of vulnerability, anxiety, and post-traumatic stress.

2. LITERATURE REVIEW

The rapid growth of cybercrime during the COVID-19 pandemic has become a significant concern for psychiatry. The increased reliance on digital technologies for work, education, and healthcare has led to a surge in cyber-attacks, with perpetrators targeting vulnerable individuals through various means, such as phishing scams and online harassment (Awadallah et al., 2024).

2.1 Types of Cyber Threats Affecting Mental Wellness

The phenomenon of cyberbullying is a grave and escalating issue in the era of digital technology, carrying extensive implications for mental health and overall welfare. Effectively managing this issue necessitates integrating education, assistance, technology resources, and legislative structures to safeguard persons against harassment and foster a more secure digital milieu.

2.2 How Cyberbullying Occurs

There are several ways in which cyberbullying can appear, such as:

Sending the same nasty, insulting, or otherwise objectionable message or content to the same person repeatedly is harassment. Using public forums or comment sections to post angry and provocative comments to generate a response from the victim is known as flaming. Masquerading, or impersonation, is the practice of pretending to be another person in order to submit degrading or embarrassing material online or to deceive people into divulging sensitive information about the victim.

Figure 2. Different cyber threats affecting social media

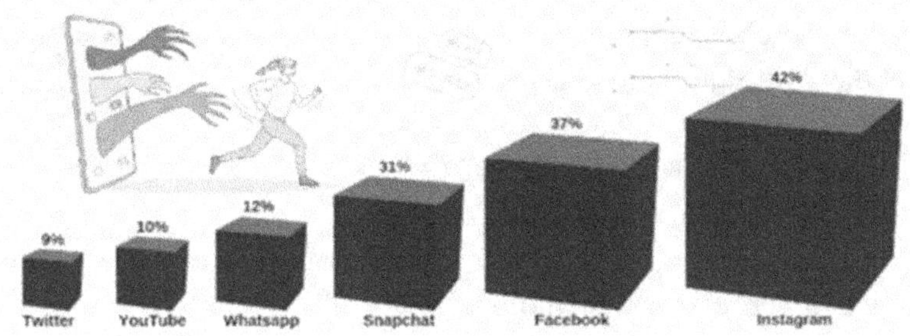

Doxycycline: Making someone's private information (such as their address or phone number) available to the public. It is the practice of tricking or outing someone into divulging private or embarrassing information to have it shared online in a public forum. Leaving someone out of a group, discussion, or social activity on purpose might cause them to feel rejected and alone. Figure 2 explains the cyber threats affecting social media and how victims experience fear and discomfort due to cyberstalking, defined as persistent and unwelcome attention through online platforms, frequently accompanied by threats.

2.3 Sites Where Online Harassment Occurs

Cyberbullying can occur on a wide variety of online sites, such as:

Bullies frequently use social media platforms such as Instagram, Facebook, Twitter, TikTok, and Snapchat to harass, threaten, or otherwise harm their targets.

Harassing or abusive text messages, including insults and threats, is a typical kind of cyberbullying that occurs over cell phones.

Online Forums and Chat Rooms: Bullies frequently resort to publicly viewable comment sections, discussion forums, or chat rooms to shame and abuse those they harass. Multiplayer online games provide a platform for bullying, whether via voice chat, in-game communications, or the public humiliation of a player's performance(Alsoubai et al., 2024).

2.4 Maintaining One's Disguise

One distinct and potentially harmful feature of cyberbullying is the bully's seeming anonymity. In cyberbullying, the bully can hide underneath a false identity, unlike in conventional bullying, when the bully's identity is generally known(Buheji & Buheji, 2024). Bullies are more likely to say and do something they would never dream of doing in person when they are anonymous.

On top of that, the persistent and ever-present quality of the harassment is due to its digital origin. As the attacks can happen at any time of day or Night and follow the victim across every one of their digital platforms, victims of cyberbullying frequently discover that there is no haven.

2.5 Emotional and Mental Effects

Victims of cyberbullying may suffer from a variety of severe and long-lasting psychological repercussions, including:

2.6 Anxiety and Depression

Feelings of profound melancholy, loneliness, and despair can result from persistent online abuse. It might exacerbate depression in extreme instances.

Victims of cyberbullying frequently suffer from low self-esteem, particularly when their intellect, looks, or talents are criticized or diminished(Aggarwal & Gaur, 2024).

Stress: Victims of persistent online harassment may feel trapped in a toxic online community and unable to find a way out.

Anxieties: Because they think they could be assaulted at any second, victims may start to be highly cautious about their online presence. If they are the target of cyberstalking or a boxer, they may also feel threatened and worried about their safety.

A common symptom of cyberbullying is a victim's isolation, whether it be from other people online or in person. Isolation, the deletion of social media accounts, and the avoidance of once-enjoyed connections are all possibilities.

Academic and Work Performance: Victims of cyberbullying may experience a decrease in motivation and performance because of anxiety and stress that makes it difficult for them to concentrate on their work or study. Regarding cyber dangers and mental health, technology serves a dual purpose. Even while there are a lot of helpful digital resources for mental health, there are also a lot of cyber hazards that people use that can make their mental health problems worse.

3. THE ROLE OF TECHNOLOGY IN MENTAL HEALTH TOWARD CYBER THREAT

3.1 Improving Mental Health with the Use of Technology

When it comes to improving mental health treatment, technology is now indispensable, especially in the following ways:

a) Services for Counselling and Therapy OfflineOffline

Because of the rise of online rehabilitation platforms, users can now speak with licensed mental health professionals by chat, phone, or text. People who, for whatever reason, cannot pay or access more traditional behavioural health treatment will find this quite helpful.

Individuals' mental health benefits from the availability of online therapy since it is efficient, flexible, and, in many cases, cheaper than traditional treatment methods. A person's mental health can be tracked and managed in real time, which can alleviate feelings of stress, anxiety, and depression(Kumar et al., 2024a).

b) Psychological Health Implications

Mood Fit, Headspace, and Calm are useful apps for managing stress, anxiety, and emotional wellbeing wellbeing. These apps provide guided meditation, mood tracking, sleep support, and mindfulness activities.

These applications are good for mental health because they help one control one's emotions and provide easy ways to cope with everyday pressures.

c) Supportive group settings and online networks

A Place to Talk: Online forums and groups provide a supportive environment where people can confidently discuss mental health difficulties. Reddit, Facebook, other social media platforms, and online support groups for mental health, such as 7 Cups, provide a secure space for people to discuss their struggles. For anyone struggling with mental health issues like loneliness, these groups could be an absolute lifesaver. The advantages of these groups include a feeling of belonging, psychological assistance, and the chance to learn coping skills from others.

Figure 3. Psychological health implications

Thanks to technological advancements, text lines, chat services, and suicide prevention hotlines provide instantaneous crisis care (R. F. Bellini, 2024). The National Suicide Prevention Lifeline and Crisis Text Line are two resources that provide round-the-clock support.

Figure 3 describes the psychological health implications and effects on Emotional Wellbeing: Real-time crisis intervention technologies have spared innumerable lives by offering prompt psychological assistance and practical direction in times of acute crisis.

d) Implementing AI for Mental Health

Artificial intelligence (AI) in mental health evaluations can improve the accuracy of diagnosis and the development of individualized treatment programs for various mental health issues. Chatbots like Wombat offer Conversational AI treatment, which provides real-time mental health help.

Effects on Mental Health: Artificial intelligence aids in the early diagnosis of mental health problems and permits prompt treatment. It also assists people who do not consistently contact therapists.

e) Anxieties through social media

Presenting an idealized version of oneself on social media is standard practice. Most people only share the most positive aspects of their lives on social media, boasting about their accomplishments and most significant features (Kumar et al., 2023). This tendency toward comparison and competitiveness may cause users to experience feelings of inferiority complexes and poor self-esteem. Feelings of FOMO (fear of missing out) can also develop when people are constantly bombarded with photos and updates from other people's lives.

Figure 4. Anxieties through social media

f) Be Aware of the Psychological Effects of Social Media

Experiencing cyberbullying or being constantly compared to others on social media can amplify emotions of feeling inadequate, worry, and despair, which can lead to excessive use of these platforms. Figure 4 describes the anxieties and the psychological effects of social media.

a) Minimize Contact with Depressing Material: Watch what you click on online. Stop “doom-scrolling,” constantly viewing unpleasant news and unfollowing accounts that bring you down.
b) Manage Your Social Media Accounts with Care: Unfollow or mute negative accounts. Instead, surround yourself with people who encourage growth and wellbeing.
c) Establish usage boundaries to limit your time on social media. Many applications and devices have built-in functions that can help you keep track of your time online.

d) Take a digital detox: Taking a vacation from social media every so often might help you relax, recharge, and feel better physically and mentally. Make the most of this time to reconnect with real-life friends and pursuits.

Figure 5. Psychological effects of social media

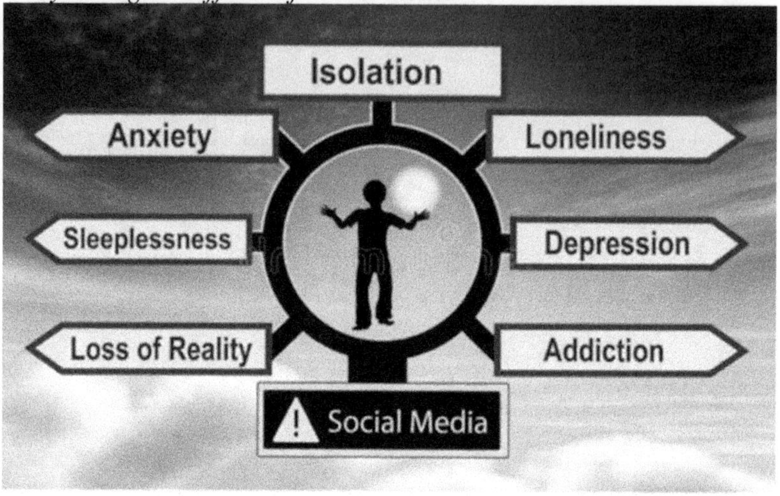

4. MENTAL HEALTH SUPPORT FOR VICTIMS OF CYBER THREATS

It is essential to seek mental and psychological help in order to recover after being impacted by a cyber threat (Mohamed & Abuobied, 2024).

One way to cope with the psychological impact that cybercrime has had on you is to talk to someone about it. This could be a trusted friend, family member, or therapist.

Figure 5 implies the effect of social media and talking to a psychological expert if you are having trouble coping with cyber-related stress, sadness, or another kind of mental illness. Treatment platforms that are available online might be a great help.

Cyberbullying, identity theft, and victims of misconduct might find a haven in online discussions and discussion boards where they can join assistance groups to talk about their incidents and get help.

4.1 Stay Informed about New Cyber Threats

Staying informed about the latest cyber risks and how to safeguard yourself is crucial, as they change quickly.

- **Get Security Updates Through Subscription:** To stay informed about cybersecurity news, subscribe to publications or follow trustworthy sources that cover new risks and how to protect yourself.
- **Educate Yourself on Digital Safety:** Countless groups provide access to free cybersecurity courses and materials. By familiarizing yourself with these issues, you can take greater responsibility for your online safety.

4.2 Monitoring and Regulatory Security Measures

If you have been a victim of cybercrime, it is crucial to be aware of your rights and how to report cybercriminals.

Cyberbullying and harassment should be reported. Several nations have passed legislation to prevent them. If the problem gets worse, notify the proper authorities.

a) **Proof from Documents:** Remember to keep any messages, screenshots, or other evidence that can be helpful in reporting or legal action if you experience online harassment or threats. One of the most significant risks to people's mental health in the modern digital age is cyberbullying and abuse (Saxena et al., 2024). Cyberbullying, bullying, and mocking are just a few examples of abusive behaviours made easier by the web's privacy and reach. Suicidal thoughts, despair, and worry are some of the serious mental health issues that victims may experience as a result of these acts. It will take a combination of technological solutions, legislative changes, and educational initiatives to solve these problems.

b) Different Types of Cyberbullying

   1. Cyberbullying: This refers to the practice of using online platforms to harass, threaten, or embarrass someone. Cyberbullying has the potential to influence more people than traditional bullying because it can happen at any time and reach a large audience.
   2. The practice of doxing is the public disclosure of sensitive data about a person without their agreement. Concerns for one's safety are among the real-world repercussions that could result from this.
   3. "Trolling" refers to intentionally causing trouble or stirring up emotions in online groups. Although often disregarded as innocuous, trolling has the potential to develop into extreme harassment (Tseng et al., 2024).

4. "Revenge Porn" refers to the distribution of explicit photos or films without the victim's consent, typically to make the victim feel ashamed.
5. Online and physical eavesdropping: The targeted individual experiences fear and discomfort due to prolonged and unwelcome scrutiny.

c) Effects on Mental Health

Cyberbullying has the potential to cause severe and long-lasting psychological harm. Constant exposure to harassment can cause victims to feel hopeless and depressed, which can lead to the following symptoms:

- Anxiety and Depression.
- Deterioration of Self-Respect: Being the target of bullying can erode a person's sense of value and self-assurance.
- Social Withdrawal: To escape additional harassment, victims could withdraw socially and professionally.

Extreme instances of trauma caused by online harassment might result in Post-Traumatic Stress Disorder (PTSD).

d) Technology-Based Remedy

1. Machine learning and artificial intelligence (AI): These technologies can instantly identify and remove harmful information. Algorithms can detect threats by analyzing language patterns and user behaviour.
2. Platforms may enhance privacy settings to give users greater control over their data and who can contact them.
3. Systems for Registration and Support: Victims can seek treatment and take action against abusers with accessible mental health support and easy-to-use reporting tools. Fourth, end-to-end encryption: stopping communications from being intercepted and used for personal gain is a big deal (Kaur et al., 2024).

Rules and Policies

1. Governments have the power to pass laws that address online bullying and harassment, giving individuals a clear path to seek legal redress.
2. Accountability of Established Platforms: According to Foreign policy, Platforms might be more prepared for future security incidents if they are responsible for the content they host. Ultimately, though, this means all kinds of small websites will die due to a lack of visitors, and anyone wishing to make money online can only do so through unethical means
3. International Cooperation: There needs to be a closer international, combined response to online harassment, which often transcends national boundaries perfectly in implementation (George, 2024).

5. EDUCATION AND AWARENESS

1. **Education about Online Safety:** To safeguard people against bullying outside of the schoolyard online, this awareness should gradually start from pre-school age up to middle school and beyond. People have to be made acutely aware that they can now be instantly contacted by others even without knowing the other party's identity.
2. **Awareness Campaigns**: A public information campaign might bring home the seriousness of online attacks and clarify that those who stand by could also become targets.
3. **Support Networks:** Providing a place where victims can share their experiences and offer each other support may help to reduce the psychological impact.

5.1 Future Directions

As the intersection of technology, policy and instruction develop, how to curb online harassment and abuse in the future At this moment, with an increasingly global heft on this continent, we are setting down grounds that will help shape tomorrow's Internet In the digital age, online harassment and abuse have grown to constitute serious threats not only for humanity That the web was able to democratize communication and make the world a smaller place also lets such things as cyberbullying, doxing or trolling find new sources of abuse and depravity much to everyone's chagrin It is possible now for a person to anonymously publish so-called news, which is largely opinion given out digitally while remaining completely unknown to others (R. Bellini et al., 2024). From cyberbullying and doxing, it's not a long step to identity theft and swindles within the web. In just this way, the consequences of these activities are devastating. Victims frequently end up tortured by intractable patterns of anger; enormous anxiety leads to cramps that tax both brain power and physical endurance; men who feel there's no other way out choose suicide's green light on account of unbearable stress.

5.2 Forms of Online Harassment and Abuse

1. **Cyberbullying:** This refers to the Internet's use of electronic devices to bully, intimidate, and disgrace individuals. Unlike traditional forms of harassment, cyberbullying is always on Night, and the audience is often broad, which has a greater effect.
2. **Doxing:** Making someone's private information public without their consent. This can have profound real-world implications for the personal security or practical circumstances of those spied on.

3. **Trolling** is the act of intentionally upsetting and harassing others on the Internet, typically in online forums. While it's sometimes dismissed as harmless, trolling can escalate to multiple extreme forms of harassment.
4. **Revenge Porn:** Sharing intimate images or videos without the victim's consent--often meant to humiliate and shame them.
5. **Stalking:** The persistent and unwanted attention, which can appear both online or offline, and life-threatening traumas to victims.

5.3 Psychological Impact

Severe and long-lasting psychological trauma can be caused by cyberbullying. Every possible ordeal that victims may face

After being the object of constant harassment, one may begin to feel depressed and hopeless.

Victims of bullying often report a decline in self-esteem and confidence as a result of the trauma they have endured.

Social Withdrawal: People may isolate themselves professionally and socially to avoid further harassment.

Post-Traumatic Stress Disorder (PTSD) can develop in extreme cases of trauma brought on by cyberbullying.

5.4 Solution Based on Technology

The first is machine learning and AI: these systems can detect and delete malicious content immediately. Algorithms may analyze user actions and language patterns to identify potential threats.

Adjusting the privacy settings on platforms may give users more control over their data and the people who can contact them.

Registration and Support Systems: Utilizing easily accessible mental health resources and notification methods, victims can get treatment and act against abusers (Shandilya et al., 2024).

Finally, end-to-end encryption is a huge concern since it prevents the interception and misuse of information.

5.5 Policy and Procedures

Legislation addressing cyberbullying and harassment and providing victims with a means to seek justice can be enacted by governments.

Second, we can push for more stringent security measures from internet platforms if we hold them accountable for the content they host.

Since cyber abuse often crosses international borders, combating it through international cooperation is essential.

5.6 Understanding and Integrity

Initiatives to Enhance Digital Literacy: It is of the utmost importance to educate individuals on how to be secure while utilizing the World Wide Web and evade harassment.

By drawing attention to the problem of cyberbullying and encouraging bystanders to take action, outreach efforts can help end this epidemic.

5.7 Protecting Data Online

Several cybersecurity precautions can be put in place to reduce the likelihood of exposure to hazardous content:

First is content filtering, which implements content filtering technologies on both the network and the devices to prevent users from accessing malicious websites.

By bringing more people onto the side of cyberbullying and asking bystanders for help-back strategies, we can look forward to the dawn of this epidemic ending.

a) Efficient Age Verification Systems: Research and create new ways to ensure that only adults can get at pornographic materials.
b) Content Moderation Enabled by AI: When AI can quickly and accurately identify dangerous posts or pictures on social media, it can delete them immediately.
c) The fourth feature of secure browsing is improved safe browsing, with the emulation-based and virtualization-based security scheme also having the function to automatically detect and delete malicious code.
d) The fifth system is this user reporting system, which allows users to easily report unwanted information.

8. FUTURE PROJECTIONS

In a rapidly evolving digital world, safeguarding one's mental health and trying to stop online abuse are the top two priority tasks. The impact of mental health cyber hazards is enormous, and accompanying new technology to protect these people from becoming victims makes it more challenging than ever. Governments, institutions and IT companies increasingly recognize the imperative for comprehensive policies and regulations to address all these problems.

a) Policy and Regulation Are Necessary

Users are vulnerable to various online threats due to the ubiquitous aspect of the Internet and the growing dependence on digital platforms for communication, employment, and entertainment. Some examples of these dangers include being a victim of cyberbullying or harassment, having your personal information stolen, or becoming addicted to playing games or social media. Figure.6. implies the mental health training reaction to Serious mental health problems, such as anxiety, despair, and, in the worst instances, self-harm or suicide, can result from these problems if appropriate rules and regulations are not in place.

b) Support for Mental Health

Needing digital hubs to disseminate information about mental health and putting measures in place to support victims of internet abuse in the early stages. Moderators and support employees are required to undergo mental health training.

Figure 6. Mental health training reactions

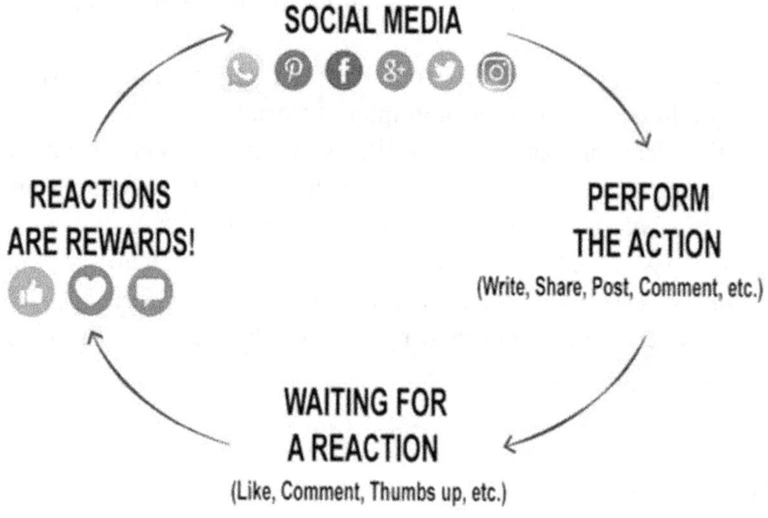

9. CHALLENGES IN POLICY AND REGULATION

1. Ensuring a Balance Between Free Expression and Protection Finding a balance between user protection and free speech takes much work for policymakers. However, it is essential to find this middle ground to keep the Internet accessible while protecting vulnerable people.

   Section 2: Technological Progress It is not uncommon for policy development to lag behind the quick rate of technical change. Rules need to be malleable enough to accommodate developing technology and new dangers.

3. Enforcing Laws Between Nations Due to the Internet's global nature, implementing legislation across multiple jurisdictions is challenging. International cooperation is important for policies to be effectively implemented.
4. Discretion Issues Policies should safeguard users while simultaneously honouring their right to privacy. Overly intrusive procedures result in privacy breaches and a loss of faith in online services.
5. Businesses' Reluctance Some tech companies may resist restrictions that force them to adapt their platforms or alter their business models. It is a continuing issue to balance corporate interests with user protection.

9.1 Efficiently Enforcing Rules and Regulations

1. Engagement of Multiple Stakeholders Authorities, digital firms, mental health experts, teachers, and user advocacy organizations must collaborate to develop policies effectively. This inclusive approach considers all viewpoints.

Scientific studies on the effects of digital technology on psychological wellbeing should form the basis of any policy decisions. To make educated decisions, research and data collection must continue.

2. Regulating on the Go Implementing adaptable regulatory frameworks is crucial to keeping up with technological developments and risks. Policy reviews and revisions may be part of this process.

9.2 Future Trends in Policy and Regulation

1. As AI becomes more widespread in moderated content and user engagement, more rules may be needed to guarantee ethical use and eliminate bias.

2. Risk Assessment for Psychological Health Mandates in tomorrow's legal environment could force internet companies to often look into how their respective platforms affect mental wellbeing and adjust as necessary.
3. Digital Wellness Scores App and platform customers could make more informed decisions about their online behaviour if standardized digital wellness scores were in place.
4. Personalized Governance Technological progress may result in regulatory strategies that take opposite directions from those with more general rulemaking, targeting security measures according to individual user needs and tastes.

10. CONCLUSION

Only when policymakers and regulators join forces to create a healthier place online for mental health can we eliminate bullying and abuse? How we supervise and protect people in cyberspace lies in the syncretic "our side" of things. When comprehensive policies that are flexible and responsive to the user's needs are established, technology gets neatly wrapped with mental health risks. Still in the definitive stage of development but already widely accepted as essential are regulations that are tough enough to hold users back from the increasingly rapid technological development, Me and Man. The digital era demands that devotion to mental health and equal still a great deal of investment be enlarged Pursue. Having got it right in the first place, the next generation may be able to grow up with a pretty new type of digital experience. Today's problem of children coming into contact with harmful online content requires a holistic approach encompassing cybersecurity, education initiatives, new legislation and technological advances. A more supportive and safe online space for mental health can be achieved by raising digital literacy, establishing robust content regulation systems and allocating adequate Mental Health resources when this triple-crown approach is successful. Bringing people into face-to-face contact with each other is the inevitable consequence of inevitable progress. It policies at the present age when the digital world is constantly changing. Cyberbullying and harassment are widespread problems that require comprehensive responses. Nowadays, we can guard people against cyberbullying-related damage to health and protect their mental wellbeing by bringing new technologies, new policies, and new education together in concert.

REFERENCES

Aggarwal, A., & Gaur, S. (2024). Applying Artificial Intelligence to Explore Online Harassment and Cyberbullying Prevention. In *Impact of AI on Advancing Women's Safety* (pp. 104–120). IGI Global.

Alsoubai, A., Razi, A., Agha, Z., Ali, S., Stringhini, G., De Choudhury, M., & Wisniewski, P. J. (2024). Profiling youth's offline and online risk experiences to develop targeted interventions for online safety. *Proceedings of the ACM on Human-Computer Interaction, 8*(CSCW1), 1–37.

Arslan, G., Kabasakal, Z., & Taş, B. (2024). Childhood Psychological Maltreatment, Mindful Awareness, Self-Transcendence, and Mental WellbeingWellbeing in Emerging Adults. *Emerging Adulthood*, 12(1), 18–28. DOI: 10.1177/21676968231208246

Awadallah, A., Eledlebi, K., Zemerly, J., Puthal, D., Damiani, E., Taha, K., Kim, T.-Y., Yoo, P. D., Choo, K.-K. R., Yim, M.-S., & Yeun, C. Y. (2024). Artificial intelligence-based cybersecurity for the metaverse: Research challenges and opportunities. *IEEE Communications Surveys and Tutorials*, 1. DOI: 10.1109/COMST.2024.3442475

Bellini, R., Tseng, E., Warford, N., Daffalla, A., Matthews, T., Consolvo, S., Woelfer, J. P., Kelley, P. G., Mazurek, M. L., & Cuomo, D. (2024). Sok: Safer digital safety research involving at-risk users. In *2024 IEEE Symposium on Security and Privacy (SP)* (pp. 635–654). DOI: 10.1109/SP54263.2024.00071

Bellini, R. F. (2024). Abusive Partner Perspectives on Technology Abuse: Implications for Community-based Violence Prevention. *Proceedings of the ACM on Human-Computer Interaction, 8*(CSCW1), 1–25. DOI: 10.1145/3637292

Buheji, M., & Buheji, B. (2024). Mitigating risks of slow children development due to war on Gaza 2023. *International Journal of Psychology and Behavioral Sciences*, 14(1), 11–21.

George, A. S. (2024). Virtual Violence: Legal and Psychological Ramifications of Sexual Assault in Virtual Reality Environments. *Partners Universal International Innovation Journal*, 2(1), 96–114.

Kaur, G., Mukherjee, D., Moza, B., Pahwa, V., Kaur, K., & Kaur, K. (2024). The dark web: A hidden menace or a tool for privacy protection. *IP International Journal of Forensic Medicine and Toxicological Sciences*, 8(4), 160–167. DOI: 10.18231/j.ijfmts.2023.034

Krishnan, S. D., Pelusi, D., Daniel, A., Suresh, V., & Balusamy, B. (2023). Improved graph neural network-based green anaconda optimization for segmenting and classifying lung cancer. *Mathematical Biosciences and Engineering*, 20(9), 17138–17157. DOI: 10.3934/mbe.2023764 PMID: 37920050

Kumar, T., Kumar, P., & Namasudra, S. (2024a). A DNA-based Authentication System for Securing Cloud Data Storage and Transactions. In *2024 11th International Conference on Computing for Sustainable Global Development* (pp. 1692–1698).

Kumar, T., Namasudra, S., & Kumar, P. (2023). Providing data security using DNA computing in the cloud computing environment. *International Journal of Web and Grid Services*, 19(4), 463–486. DOI: 10.1504/IJWGS.2023.135587

Kumar, T., Kumar, P., & Namasudra, S. (2024b). *User Revocation-Enabled Access Control Model Using Identity-Based Signature in the Cloud Computing Environment.*

Mohamed, N. N., & Abuobied, B. H. H. (2024). Cybersecurity challenges across sustainable development goals: A comprehensive review. *Sustainable Engineering and Innovation*, 6(1), 57–86. DOI: 10.37868/sei.v6i1.id207

Saxena, R., Saxena, S., & Singh, A. P. (2024). Mindful Approaches to Sustainable Healthcare: Nurturing Mental Health and Wellbeing. In *Preserving Health, Preserving Earth: The Path to Sustainable Healthcare* (pp. 231–237). Springer.

Shandilya, S. K., Datta, A., Kartik, Y., & Nagar, A. (2024). *Digital Resilience: Navigating Disruption and Safeguarding Data Privacy*. Springer. DOI: 10.1007/978-3-031-53290-0

Tseng, E., Bellini, R., Lee, Y.-Y., Ramjit, A., Ristenpart, T., & Dell, N. (2024). Data Stewardship in Clinical Computer Security: Balancing Benefit and Burden in Participatory Systems. *Proceedings of the ACM on Human-Computer Interaction (pp.* 1–29). DOI: 10.1145/3637316

Zhou, F., Ma, Z., Rashwan, A. K., Khaskheli, M. B., Abdelrady, W. A., Abdelaty, N. S., Hassan Askri, S. M., Zhao, P., Chen, W., & Shamsi, I. H. (2024). Exploring the Interplay of Food Security, Safety, and Psychological Wellness in the COVID-19 Era: Managing Strategies for Resilience and Adaptation. *Foods*, 13(11), 1610. DOI: 10.3390/foods13111610 PMID: 38890839

Chapter 11
Cybersecurity Measures for Protecting Mental Health in the Digital Age

Dankan Gowda V.
https://orcid.org/0000-0003-0724-0333
Department of Electronics and Communication Engineering, B.M.S. Institute of Technology and Management, Karnataka, India

Anjali Sandeep Gaikwad
https://orcid.org/0000-0001-7786-9925
Department of Computer Application, Institute of Management, Bharati Vidyapeeth University, Kolhapur, India

Renu
https://orcid.org/0009-0001-8592-6771
TMIMT, Teerthanker Mahaveer University, Moradabad, India

H. G. Govardhana Reddy
https://orcid.org/0000-0001-6340-4975
Alliance School of Applied Mathematics, Alliance University, Bengaluru, India

Sunil Saini
https://orcid.org/0009-0000-6288-2297
Department of Computer Science and Engineering, University College of Engineering, Punjabi University Campus, India

ABSTRACT

As the world advances towards the integration of technology, more emphasis is placed on the relationship between cybersecurity and mental health. In this chap-

DOI: 10.4018/979-8-3693-7758-1.ch011

ter, the authors discuss the impact of cybersecurity on the preservation of mental health, as well as the processes of safeguarding the related rights upon pointing out the directions of protection against the use of the internet as a weapon, cyber bullying, and harassment. In this chapter, they explore the effects of cybersecurity threats on mental health and the topic of safe online space. In order to illustrate the best current practices and new technologies protecting users from mental health information leakage, they present the most effective cybersecurity measures. Proof of the successful application of these measures is provided through relevant case studies and examples from practice. In that context, this chapter offers practical advice and directions for organisational policymakers, mental health experts, and tech gurus in the creation and deployment of efficiency cybersecurity structures that embrace and support mental health.

INTRODUCTION

Overview of the Digital Age and Mental Health

The increase and the complexity of the new technologies which dominate people's lives have been changed with the emerging of digital age. The use of the Internet and social networks, as well as other types of modern means of communication, has made possible the greatest level of connection, availability of information and convenience. But the world that has become digitalised over the recent years was also followed with new problems especially psychosomatic ones (A. Brown, S. Green, and P. Black, 2024). The impact of social networking means becomes so invasive that threats, teasing, and stalking are nearly normal; all these are detrimental to the well-being of people.

Figure 1. Graph showing the rise of digital platforms over time and its impact on mental health incidents.

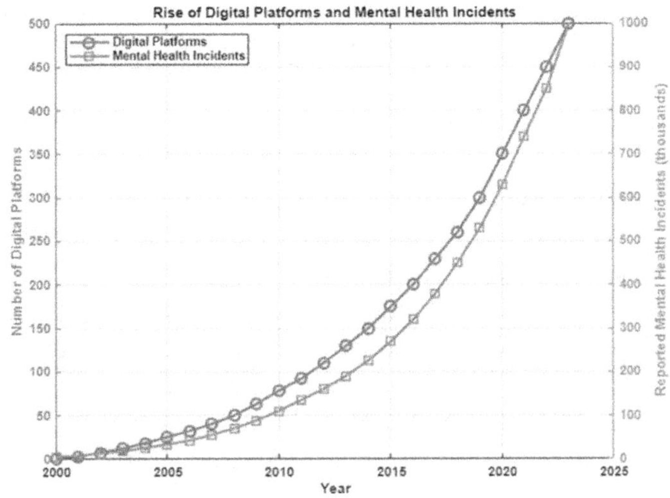

Today there is so much connectivity out there because of the digital media, but still people are lonely, stressed and even clinically depressed. In as much as social networks create room for social interactions, they are one of the main causes for low self-esteem, social comparison (A. Evans et al., 2024). Cyber bullying is another form of bullying whereby a person harasses another through the use of computers and internet with adverse repercussion on the psychological wellbeing and efficiency and worth of an individual (B. Nguyen and J. Hernandez, 2024). Besides, due to the relative anonymity afforded by online spaces, such people may not be easily restrained much less punished

The digital platform is evidenced in Figure 1 that shows a two axis graph, mapping the progressive upward motion of the digital platforms and the corresponding increase of mental health incidents in the years between 2000 and 2023. The left y-axis is for the digital platforms and the right y-axis is for the reported mental health incident in thousands (C. Murphy et al., 2024). The circles focus on the days of evolution of the digital sites while the squares represent the occurrences of mental health crisis. more specifically, the number of digital platforms has increased in a direct proportional to the instances of Mental Health Issues (D. Harris and L. Phillips, 2024).

In terms of this, the superiority of cybersecurity in the conservation of mental health is well illustrated. Encryption is not only the key to preventing hacking attacks and protecting individual and special data but also is the key to help create secure online environments which will also help or promote good wellbeing (F. Garcia et al., 2023). Examples of such chances are vices like cyber abuse, cyber bullying and digital harassment, measures taken by cybersecurity can also save on mental health. Because the nature of these digital platforms is always evolving at a technological level, there is increasing concern over adequate protection in terms of cybersecurity supplemented by psychological well-being (H. Lee and J. Kim, 2024).

Purpose and Scope of the Chapter

In this chapter's KSAOs, the first aim is to discuss the relationship between both the factors, that is cybersecurity and mental health both of which are compounded by the growing usage of the internet. Since this chapter surveys the state of cyber threats to mental wellness, and highlights the most successful protective measures, readers should gain a detailed appreciation of how to safeguard mental health in cyberspace. Here, psychological impacts of cyber threats are researched, current practices in cybersecurity are examined, and features of new technologies that can contribute to mental health protection are discussed (J. Foster and S. Brown, 2023).

That is why the subject of the present chapter is the range of cyber threats, including online abuse, cyberbullying, and digital harassment and their psychological consequences. It also takes stock of existing security strategies and explores their relevance and adequacy of protecting mental health (J. Wang et al., 2024). To this end, using the principles of exposition, the chapter will provide lessons from different case scenarios and examples of actual experiences regarding the effectiveness of cybersecurity measures protecting mental health.

In addition, the chapter looks at the impact of newer technologies in strengthening up the means of cyber security (K. Anderson and P. Martinez, 2024). For instance, artificial intelligence (AI) and machine learning are proposed as a solution to anticipate the cyber threats in order (K. Prasad, S. R, and A. K. N, 2024). Another potential future trend which is also discussed to include mental health monitoring systems in cybersecurity frameworks is also offered as a topic that can offer fully protection.

The concept of ethical consideration is interlinked within this particular chapter, emphasizing on the compromisable between security and the users (K. Taylor and G. Wilson, 2024). Concisely, informed by the various ethical principles guiding research, this chapter explores particularly the aspects of informed consent, reporting of research, and utilisation of vulnerable population (L. White et al., 2024). This can only come about through multi stakeholder input that involves policymakers, mental health care practitioners, and technocrats to develop workable cybersecurity framework that consider mental health (M. Lewis et al., 2023).

In conclusion, this chapter will give operational appreciations and recommendations to the various stakeholders. As such, the chapter commences with the critical discussion of major challenges and concludes with the pragmatic measures for strengthening cybersecurity that will, in turn, help policymakers, mental health practitioners, and technologists design protective frameworks that uphold the mental health of citizens in the digital space. The aim is the creation of secure societies and individuals that help them develop their talents and achievements without being affected by cyber threats to their psychological stability. Therefore, this chapter addresses the existing publications gap related to cybersecurity and mental health and will help to protect psychological well-being in the age of technology.

THE IMPACT OF CYBER THREATS ON MENTAL HEALTH

Types of Cyber Threats

The new types of risks that are tied to technology have consequences which have disastrous effects on mental health. Other types of abuses include cyber bullying and cyber stalking and there are people who are harassed based on their color, sex or opinion. This kind of abuse can as simple as making nasty remarks or calling names, all the way to threats of physical harm. Victims experience lack of power, and fear that leads to the degradation of their psychological wellbeing.

Figure 2. Bar chart showing types of cyber threats and their psychological effects.

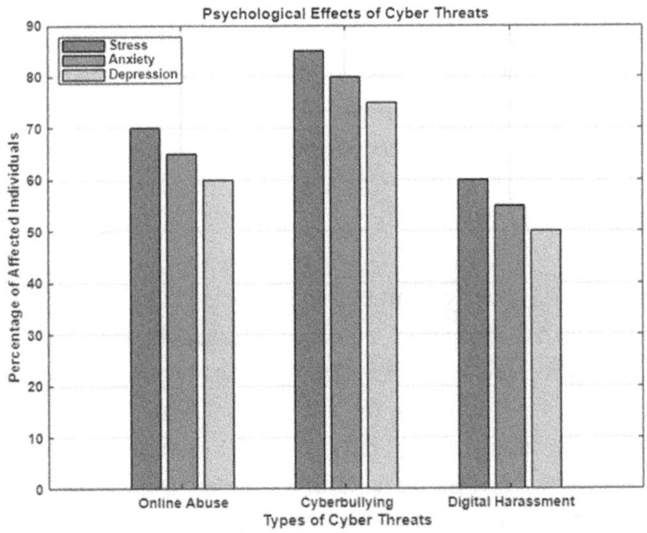

Figure 2 illustrates the impact of the other categories of cyber threats through the help of a grouped bar chart. The x-axis lists the types of cyber threats: cyberstalking, cyberbullying, and cyber harassment. The figure on y-axis reflects the proportion of population that is at the backpack of these threats. The bars are grouped into three categories: stress," anxiety," and "depression." This figure tries to illustrate how each of the types of cyber threats affects the mental health of the victim, where cyberbullying causes the highest levels of stress and anxiety (M. Smith and R. Jones, 2024). Another form of cyber threat includes; cyber bullying which is rife among adolescents and young people (N. Hall and J. Lee, 2023). While physical bullying is violent and personalised, 'cyber bullying' is more liberal as it remains with the bully and the target all seasons of the day, even invading the privacy of their homes (P. Allen and L. Mitchell, 2023). It sometimes encompasses a section of engaging in 'cyber bullying,' that is, spreading rumors, circulating other people's information without their permission, and opening accounts with the intention of bringing down that particular person. The Read Tryner also established that internet bully is facilitated by the anonymous nature that is likely to hard the perpetrators understand the impression of their actions has on the recipients (P. Miller et al., 2023). The longer it takes, the worse the position is with a child who is being a victim of cyberbullying – the consequence of such actions as bullying is emotional suffering and loneliness and attempts at suicide.

Cyberbullying is defined as behavior that is within a wide continuum of cybertalking and aims at disturbing or threatening individuals online. This covers stalking, doxing which is sharing peoples' information without their permission and swatting which is calling in a fake emergency to get the police to a particular person's house (R. Adams, M. Baker, and N. Clark, 2024). Cyber bullying leads to high level of psychological distress and trauma; the targeted feels like he or she is being followed by the harasser. Feeling chased or threatened hinders normal performance and can cause a number of psychological disturbances.

Psychological Effects

A cyber threat is not strictly limited to causing physical injury as we shall enact but any damage to the psychological aspect of a person as well. Targeted individuals and groups become stressed, anxious and potentially depressed because of cyberbullying, harassment, and intimidation (S. Chandrasekaran, V. Dutt, N. Vyas, and A. Anand, 2023). The previous attacks put the Jewish people in a vulnerable position where they never feel safe from the next attack according to Moshe Halbertal. This kind of stress can be highly damaging, causing negative consequences for both mental and physical wellbeing, such as sleep disruptions, regular head aches and constantly weakened immune systems.

The next adverse effect is anxiety which is defined by excessive worrying, fearing and suspense of a dangerous event. They become socially withdrawn, due to the fact they dread persona rapprochement contacts in the parks as well as online.

Consequently there might be severe issues regarding social interactions, including isolation, and troubles in private and working life spheres (S. Davis and L. Thomas, 2023). Another emotion is also observed in recipients of threats with indications of depression that gives depressive signs such as hopelessness, feelings of sadness and had found themselves losing interest in activities previously enjoyed. It's impossible to sink into hopelessness and despair and believe that the harassment will never stop; such feelings put individuals with severe depressive disorders at the risk of experiencing complete mental breakdowns.

The results of cyber threats on human mental health show sustained neuropsychiatric consequences. Online abuse trauma can cause PTSD where the abused have to constantly relive the bad incidents through flashes of images, or nightmares. Stress and fear all the time can also cause new episodes of other anxiety disorders and a major depressive disorder (S. R. Kawale, 2023). They can even turn to how to hurt themselves or even kill themselves by coy self- harming behaviors due to emotional pain and feeling of loneliness. For this reason, people who become victims of cyber threats cannot seek help, and this makes their mental health worst.

Case Studies and Real-World Examples

As for the consequences that the presence of cyber threats has on the mental condition of a person, cases can be mentioned and discussed by several people. A good example of this is the Amanda Todd story, a teenager from Canada who was both bullied through electronic media and harassed online. A young lady named Amanda whose character I watched as cheerful received several harassing messages and people shared with her several graphic images before she developed depression and anxiety and killed herself. What her case demonstrates is just how lethal cyber bullying is and why all the right precautions must be taken.

Another one is the story of Tyler Clementi — an American university student who has become a victim of digital harassment when his roommate secretly videotaped him during sex and posted the video on the Web. Tyler, a pronounced figure of the online bullying due to his constant antics and overall trolling he presented to Internet, was driven to suicide, and with the help of this action of reporting and mocking him, as well as violating his privacy, it is possible to come to conclusion that cyberbullying has catastrophic impacts concerning one's mental health (S. Turner et al., 2024). These examples demonstrate that threats in the cyber sphere can have an opportunity to lead to irreversible consequences which proves the importance of adequate protection of the individual's psychological states.

In a different setting, doxxing has also been the source of much psychological harm. For example, when a news journalist, who reports sensitive stories, received threats, her identity was exposed by publishing her home address and phone number. This led to many threatening phone calls as well as barrage of threats to stake her house and therefore; anxiety/panic/AOR [Anxiety, Oral pointers, Rating scale]. Such examples reveal that there is clear evidence of the harm caused by digital harassment; and people's right to privacy should be protected.

These cases, and other real life examples clearly point at the need to start addressing the mental aspect of cyber threat. These findings briefly relate to the previous literature detailing the psychological impact of cyber threats on patient and stakeholder populations to inform the design and adoption of cybersecurity strategies designed to mitigate negative mental health outcomes.

CURRENT PRACTICES IN CYBERSECURITY FOR MENTAL HEALTH PROTECTION

Overview of Existing Cybersecurity Measures

A current focus on cybersecurity measures has seen an expansion of the goals of efforts to counter the increased threats within the digital environment, especially those that endanger mental health. Encryption, firewalls, and antivirus are general cybersecurity processes that act as the primary barrier of digital security. They have functions like data storage, data retrieval, protection of systems from virus and hackers and so on. Both encryption and firewalls with anti-viruses make sure that data is safeguarded from the wrong hands, while the rest detects and gets rid of the threat. However, several of these may play a vital role in everyday cybersecurity, they can be inadequate to deal with the issues given with online abuse, and harassment. An exploded pie chart in Figure 3 shows the utilization of various cybersecurity measures. The chart breaks down various components into segments such as encryption, firewalls, antivirus, AI detection for threats, users' reporting, and education (T. Robinson and E. Walker, 2023). The presented exploded slices for 'Firewalls' and 'User Reporting' demonstrate how much attention is paid to these actions (V. Kalpana and V. Hariram, 2023). This figure highlights the fact that it is not only possible but also necessary to use different approaches in terms of cybersecurity methods and tools along with the user's effort. For beating cyber bullying and harassment in particular, other measures have been added up. Online communities have therefore integrated aspects that can be used to filter abusive content and also adopted machine learning solutions to deal with the content.

Figure 3. Pie chart showing the distribution of different cybersecurity measures.

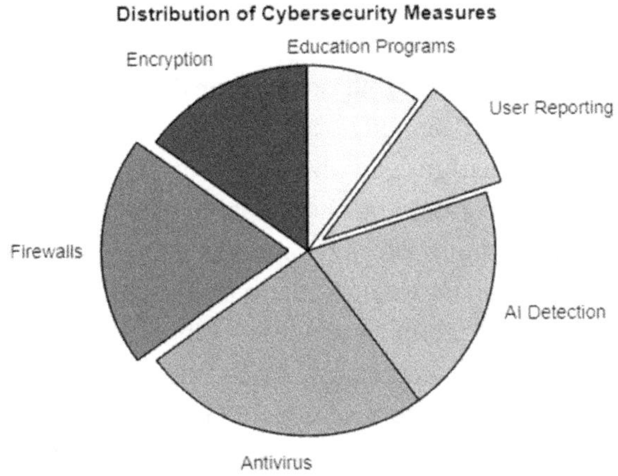

These technologies can accurately scan through text, images and videos to pick out such negative behaviors as hate speeches, bullying among others in addition to threats of violence. For example, Twitter and Facebook have bot systems through which users report abuse, where after they ban or suspend the particular account. These measures are in turn aimed at helping put into practice the usage of the respective services in a safer way by reducing incidence and threat of danger to the potential victims.

Furthermore, user reporting has to be considered as an essential attribute of cybersecurity against cyber abuse. Most of the forums allow users to flag any instance of abuse for moderation, and the moderators can access the site (R. Agrawal, V. Dutt, and N. Vyas, 2023). This user-based approach helps users fight harassment cases and foster the security of the social site. Besides, educational work and focus on increasing users' concern with safety and politeness during interaction on the Internet are being conducted. These programs seek to cultivate acceptable acceptable behavior in cyberspace and to persuade people to act appropriately in cyberspace.

Analysis of Effectiveness

The current cybersecurity practices in the protection of mental health is as follows: These basic precautionary measures that include encryption and or setting up of firewalls are considered very effective methods of putting data in a position whereby it will not undergo insecurity. These are important steps to safeguard personal information and personal data which form the core ingredient for mental health protection. When users have such perception of the data, there is little tension and health risks of a data leak and identity theft.

However, the specific measures are not quite so effective when it comes to combating abuse and harassment that occur over the internet. Most of the abusive comments are subsequently detected by the automated detection systems every day, and machine learning algorithms can also filter out most of them (S. Suneetha and S. R. Patil, 2023). These technologies are capable of dealing with large amount of data, every platform can immediately respond to a threat. However, these systems are not foolproof all the time. Pertinently, there is always high likelihood of either the tool flagging non-abusive content as abusive – false positives or vice versa – false negatives. It is hard for the automated system to filter the abuse due to the language subtleties and changes in the pattern of abusive behavior.

User reporting, however, has its shortcomings which are discussed below. Using the reported user cases makes it possible to miss instances of abusive demeanor as it takes time to review the reports by the users. They do not report abuse also because they are afraid of what might happen to them or that their report will not be affecting anything. Moreover, the outcomes of the educational programmes and the efficiency of awareness raising are difficult to evaluate. However, these programs are useful in fostering civility of cyberspace users although the benefits of using them in eradicating abuse as well as harassment may hardly be seen.

Case Studies and Real-World Examples

Some real-life examples and few case studies depict that how cybersecurity measures can successfully be employed for safeguarding the mental health. The UK government's partnership with social media is a good example, where social media is used in fighting online abuse. Due to high cases of cyber bullying, the government has provided regulatory measures with the Social Network Sites Code of Practice falling under the Internet Safety Strategy. This initiative helped to create appropriate reporting tools, enhance the policies on content controlling, and provide main support for all the victims of cybercriminals. This strategy has been effective since they have recorded less incidence of cyber bullying and more safer users.

One of them is the successes of the Australian eSafety Commissioner, an office created specifically for this purpose. The eSafety Commissioner has therefore put in place different programs and resources … to protect users from abuse and harassment in cyberspace. One of them is the "Cyberbullying Complaint Scheme", an individual can report specific severe cases of cyberbullying. This has been efficient in addressing extreme cases of cyber bullying whose support to the victims where necessary is essential is addressed efficiently.

The social media platform Instagram has also done a lot to improve cybersecurity to safeguard mental health. The features launched included comments, which can be automatically hidden depending on the user's preference, and controls which let the users prevent particular users from interacting with them. For instance, an option such as "kindness prompting" is incorporated in Instagram where users are required to opt-out of helpful comments instead of defaulting at helping or not helping. A positive effect of these measures is the reduction in the amount of abuse people take from other users; thus improving the general internet etiquette.

Also, the employment of artificial intelligence to prevent cases of cyberbullying and identification of the cases has proved useful. Popular sites such as Youtube have programmed their platform to use artificial intelligence in rooting out evil speech such as hate speech and acts of violence. In the sphere of enhancing these algorithms as well as human oversight, the advancement has enhanced the ability of the platform in protection of its user base from potential unique abuse.

In conclusion, protection of mental health through cybersecurity today is characterized by its relative strength and weakness; constant improvement is being made today, so that the effectiveness of different present practices can be further advanced. By utilizing the existing technology, promoting the independence of users and employing multi-faced strategies, organizations help develop safer environment for user's psyche. Coordinated with the institutionalized preventive measures and community involvement, the mentioned steps form a positive trajectory for decreasing the tribune of cyber threats on the mentality of a society in the age of informatization.

EMERGING TECHNOLOGIES AND INNOVATIONS

Advanced Cybersecurity Tools

New technologies in the field of cybersecurity are becoming instrumental in defending mental health in a new environment. Of all these, artificial intelligence (AI) and machine learning are noteworthy for their high ability to find and prevent cyber threats. Basically, AI is able to detect various indices of potentially malicious activities from large amounts of data within a few seconds. The machine learning algorithms are developed on the basis of previous cyber threats in form of large data sets and thus become more efficient with time. These technologies assist in outlining fresh stereotype models of cyber bullying and abuse that cannot be easily described by the conventional method. For instance, deep understanding is the ability of AI to look into the context and other less conspicuous aspects of other online interactions in order to identify cyber bullying, hate speech and other forms of harassment. Through use of Artificial Intelligence and machine learning, detection can be performed in real time and immediate action taken to eliminate the posts and their effects, on the victims' psychological well-being.

Self-sustaining technical systems are also noteworthy improvements for Blockchain in building safe virtual spaces. In a way that blockchain is a distributed ledger it is rather transparent and far from fraudulent since records of any given transaction cannot easily be altered without being noticed. This technology can also improve the details that are tight in security and also offer protection to data that is important in an organization or business. For example, blockchain can protect personal information and ID to avoid cases when personal data leak results in harassment or other forms of cyberbullying. In addition, decentralization inherent in blockchain may assist people to take control over their information and minimize potential misuse of this data by different actors. If blockchain technology is introduced into cybersecurity policies, it is possible to create safer and more stable conditions for user interaction while they themselves understand how valuable their mental health is. Here, the worth of adoption rates of both AI and blockchain technology over the year 2010 to 2023 are represented in a line plot format as illustrated in Figure 4. On the X axis, the number of years is marked, whereas on the Y axis, the extent of adoption measured in the percentage level is marked. It presents circles for the AI adoption and squares for blockchain adoption of the plot. Analyzing the data, a progressive growth in both technology adoption is visible and although the graph is close to being parallel, AI adoption is marginally an inch higher than blockchain. This figure shows just how much these more sophisticated technologies will be crucial to improving cyberspace security in the future.

Figure 4. Line plot showing the adoption of AI and blockchain technologies over time.

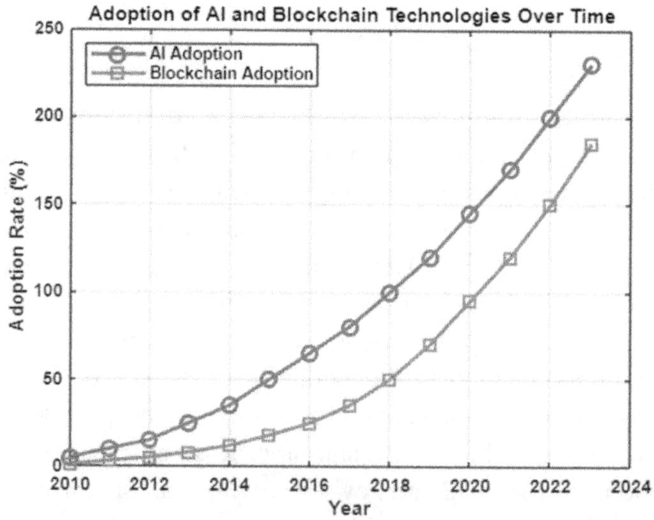

Future Trends

Future trends in the present context reveal predictive analytics as a promising driver toward proactive mental health protections within cybersecurity context. Business intelligence is the extraction of useful information from structured data or other forms predictive analytics refer to the application of statistical models and learning to come up with forecasts and trends analysis. Again, when discussing cybersecurity, predictive analytics can help to estimate risks which could occur in future preventing them from happening. For example, basing on the stats about people's behavior, machine learning algorithms can estimate potential examples of cyberbullying or stalking. Such foresight allows strategizing to prevent incidents and arm users with notifications, reinforce monitoring, and build automated safeguards. The questions designed help to identify possible threats and respond to them before they cause harm to mental health, and build safer environments for online communication.

Another new trend is the use of cybersecurity measures to add monitoring of mental health as well. As the reality of the effects that cyber threats have on mental health emerged, companies began shifting most of their focus towards including mental health as a factor in cybersecurity approaches. A goal can also be more innovative, specific techniques are capable of monitoring specific aspects of psychological alteration, including alterations in speech, use of the computer or the internet and social reputation. For instance, based on NLP techniques, a signal of an opposite polarity such as depression, anxiety, or suicide will be detected from social media posts and other online communications. Thus, the effectiveness of these monitoring systems in security terms can be complemented by an identification of the need to give timely interventions and assistance to potential victims of such behaviors. Such an approach does not only improve the efficiency of cybersecurity technologies but also address mental health as an important aspect in the developments of the digital world.

Moreover, an individual approach in cybersecurity innovations is the promising to protect mental health. The dynamic cybersecurity model implemented models the use of artificial intelligence and machine learning for the customization of security risks based on the user's habits. These systems are capable of monitoring user data and choose which protections to forge based on the user's preferences including content filtering, privation settings, and menace notifications. It also makes the security practices more user friendly and effective for the users while making them compliant to better security measures against cyber attacks. In addition, the specific recommendations are more effective than general ones since they can be continually updated in response to new users' behavior and threats. This approach is beneficial for the users as it protects them from the negative impact of concentrating on worsening symptoms and it also puts the users as the once in charge of their online security.

Therefore, enhancing the protection of mental health the integration of emerging technologies and innovations in cybersecurity is imperative. Advancement in future technology like Artificial intelligence, Machine learning, blockchain is some of the right technologies when it comes to preventing cyber risks. Possible future developments are the trend of prediction based on analytics and further enlargement of cybersecurity by including mental health evaluation. That way, stakeholders dispose themselves to award the aforementioned benefits and foster a protective online culture that strongly focuses on emotional stability. Thus, positive changes in cybersecurity technologies carry on signaling that the prospect for better mental health remains a possibility based on improved safety for individuals in the virtual environment.

CREATING SAFE DIGITAL ENVIRONMENTS

Strategies for Prevention

Designing safe online spaces needs strategies for the prevention of unwanted use of the digital platform, online bullying, and digital harassment. The most promising strategy is to provide people with extensive educational and awareness raising campaigns. They are meant to help inform the general population to instill in them understanding to do's and don'ts with regard to cyber threats and impacts on one's mental state and equip those people with knowledge as to how they can protect themselves in a virtual world. From improving the comprehension of acceptable Netiquette, personalized settings, and knowing that one can always report an abuser, education programs can help people feel they are in charge of their experiences. School going children, college going students, working population and other communities in society are all targeted with the educational interventions through schools, workplaces and community agencies. Figure 5 illustrates the efficiency of the preventive measures that entail constructing safe cyber space. The x-axis lists the strategies: Courses, computer skills, psychological and social support methods and measures, and legislation. The y-axis is labelled the 'Effectiveness Percentage.' It is for this reason that the bars are segmented by immediate benefits, short-term and long-term benefits. This figure displays the individual summarized advantages of each intensity and policy interventions exert the strongest positive impact on Digital Safety.

Figure 5. Stacked bar chart showing the effectiveness of different preventive strategies.

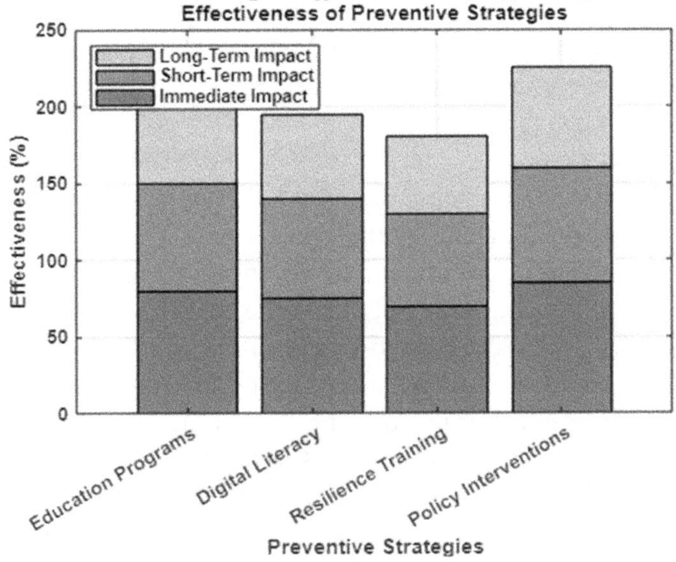

Digital literacy and resilience training should be assumed as fundamental aspects when designing preventions' approaches. Another is the concept of digital literacy which goes beyond instrumental use of computers or navigation skills in the web page and involves the ability of sifting through the content, evaluating risk and threats, and or thinking about the consequences of one's digital persona. Technical solutions in training programs include teaching users the general principles of using security passwords, methods of identifying and avoiding phishing scams, as well as the use of privacy control settings. Whereas resilience training is more particular to building up psychological coping assets to handle adversity while on the web. This includes skills in handling negative and abusive posts in social networking sites and blogging, managing impression online, and building up a positive community in blogging sites. When citizens do not get knowledge about cyber threats, the impact of cyber events on mental health is severe; otherwise, by improving the skills of digital literacy, one won't experience serious mental health concerns due to cyber threats.

Community and Policy Approaches

Government has a special responsibility of protection of its users through legislation that may govern the areas of the Internet most conducive to malicious behavior. Legal and government institutions may govern the permissible conduct of the citizens of SNSs by insisting from the digital corporations to design such capabilities to enhance their application's ability to prevent abuse and harassment.

These can vary from report on measures, actions responding to complaints of users, measures of sanctions against platforms that do not provide sufficient protection for their users. Also, they can support investigations and projects targeting cyber harassment and abuse, which, in turn, contributes to the invention of acceptable cybersecurity instruments and strategies.

It also important for mental health practitioners and technologists to work together in developing holistic approaches to digital safety. The Psychologists might supply data on the effects brought about by the cyber threats whereby after offering this information, they will be in a position to advise on how the impacts can be managed suitably. Technologists can, however, create the tools and interfaces needed for these interventions' successful execution. For instance, adding features of mental health support in social applications like, offering directories for help seeking by victims of cyber harassment or incorporating mood-identifying technological elements where the platform monitors the user's psychological state would add a lot of value to safety features. Aligning the interests of MH specialists and IT specialists, the development of secure environments that help users maintain their MH can be successfully launched.

Case Studies and Real-World Examples

A few successful community and policy interventions show that it is feasible and productive to fashion more secure virtual settings. Needless to say, there are legal undertakings which are fairly famous, for instance, the New Zealand's Harmful Digital Communications Act which aims to regulate the handling of cyber bullies and cyber harassers. This also ensures that when a certain group of people is being bullied in cyberspace they are also given an opportunity to report the matter and get justice while it also makes the digitization platforms to remove the content as soon as it is reported. The act also created independent Netsafe that provides help and advice for victims of cyber harassment. Through education, Netsafe has achieved its goal of increasing awareness levels about emerging dangers within the digital world, and offering specifics on how threats can be dealt with effectively.

One more successful case can be distinguished, namely the General Data Protection Regulation within the European Union that embraces personal data protection with respective provision for digital identity security. Under GDPR users are given a chance to have control over their data and to ensure that company implements strict protocols to protect the users' data. By means of this legal instrument, the GDPR has shifted more accountability to organisations for the breaches and misuse of people's data and guarding against identity theft, and online bullying. That is why the regulation also raises the level of transparency and confidence that helps users to interact more with the digital environment.

In the expanse of community interventionist model, it is worth to look at the "Be Strong Online" campaign in United Kingdom. This is an online programme by The Diana Award that involves youth themselves to teach other young people digital resilience. The program enables students to become misconstrued messengers on cybersafety, cyberspace etiquette, and friendship tactics with peers being bullied online.

Innovative measures by the tech companies have also helped them contribute to the creation of better environments in cyberspace. For instance, Facebook is using AI technologies to prevent posting and identification of damaging content and the company boasts of impressive success. They can easily detect such things as hate speech, threats and any other form of abusive content, thus making such interaction with users minimal. Moreover the useful information sources accessible relating to mental health problems which Facebook provided in cooperation with mental health organizations helps to address the effects of online abuse.

These two case studies and other examples demonstrate how stakeholders and professionals require a complex solution to work towards the development of safer digital therapy experiences. Attention raising, enhanced understanding, cyber literacy, and preparedness; policies; and partnerships between caregivers in the field of mental health and the authors of advancements in information technology are also important assets. Through identifying what has worked as well as continuing to extend entrepreneurship, it is possible to design for well-being online to make portions of the digital world safe for everyone and out of harm's way without forfeiting the gains the new technological age is bringing.

ETHICAL CONSIDERATIONS

Balancing Security with Privacy

The two areas of cybersecurity and protection of mental health present many ethical issues, and one of them is security and privacy. When it comes to protecting individuals from cyber risks in the digital world there is sometimes the need for associated oversight and observation. But this approach may clash with the right to be let alone enshrined in Article 26 of the Constitutional right to privacy. This is the main conundrum of the book: how responsive to the threat of cyber–attack can and should the protection of citizens' personal lives be allowed to become? Although the existence of other people's online activities can make a person aware of cyber bullying, digital harassment and all the other threats it poses, it also creates scenarios for excess control and abuse of an individual's information.

Figure 6. Dual-axis plot showing the balance between security measures and user privacy concerns over time.

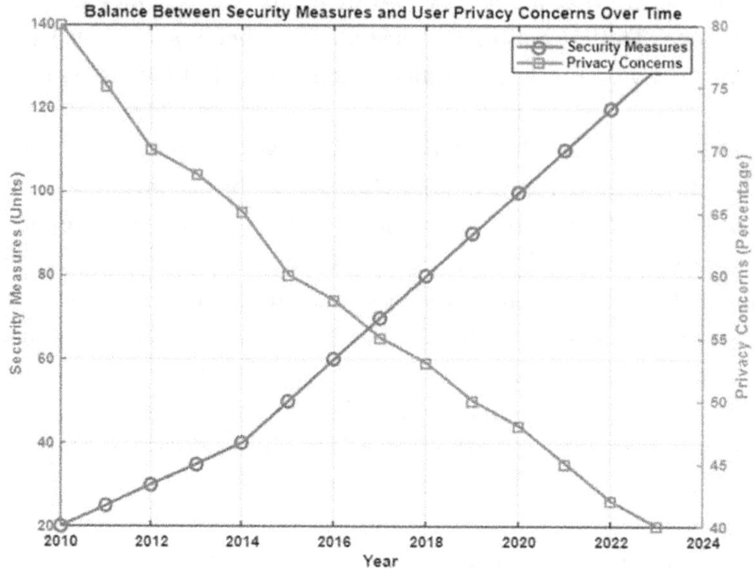

The dual-axis plot of Figure 6 allows the balancing of security measures with the user privacy concern from 2010 to 2023. On the left of the graph, on the vertical axis, it is represented by the units of security measures that are 862799; on the right of the graph, the value on the vertical axis is represented in percentage as the privacy concern is 1. In the plot, circles are used for indicating security and squares for privacy. This figure graphically represents this relationship, hence making it easy to decipher why it is difficult to balance security and users' privacy. The difficulty is that they need to be secured while at the same time not being invasive to privacy. This needs some measures that firstly, the collection of data is limited to the essential one and secondly, the possible use through ill-faith manner or intrusion is prohibited. Regarding such issue as transparency concerning data collecting and its goals, it is imperative to point out that users have to be trusted. For example, one can provide users with information regarding how their information is being watched and all the threats being addressed to reduce privacy fears. Besides, the preprocessing of data when it is appropriate to do is a helpful way since it can cover up data that can be a potential threat when it comes to privacy, while at the same time not compromising a lot on security.

Informed Consent and Transparency

Basically, the tenants informing ethical cybersecurity are patient and informed consent along with transparency. Mandatory pre-vendor-vetting disclosure of current cybersecurity obligations, and post-vendor-vetting notification of how they collect and use the user's personal information are critical for trustworthiness and corporate ethicality. Informed consent requires that clear and accessible information should be laid down regarding such aspects as: Which data is being collected? How is it going to be used? What are the risks? And the benefits? Users should be allowed to switch off or enable certain data gather procedures to enable them to make educated decisions on their online safety.

Transparency is closely connected with the idea of informed consent, since the latter implies the user being clearly informed on the measures, policies and technologies applied in the course of protection. That entails frequent dissemination of any shift in the cybersecurity measures, incidence of hacking or other violations of IT security. Transparent practices also mean admitting that present day technologies are not perfect, and the possibility of some threat being flagged as false positive or false negative exists. Organisations must ensure that the two talk to each other through promoting transparency to ensure that the implementation of cybersecurity measures are met.

Several practical steps to increase the role of informed consent and transparency are connected with the creation of easily understandable privacy policies and consent forms. These documents should not be construed to contain complicated corporate language and hence should be easy to comprehend by all users. Other useful interface features for users may include features like privacy dashboards, where users can easily change ther personal privacy settings. Therefore, when organizing cybersecurity processes, as well as taking clear actions toward users' rights, the consent approach can actually decrease the presence of ethical issues which may appear when improving security.

Addressing Vulnerable Populations

Specific steps need to be taken for the people that fall in the vulnerable category when addressing cybersecurity issues. These are the groups of people that will be highly affected by cyber threats that affects their mental health in a way that they need to be protected. The new generation is probably unaware of virtual dangers and such children can easily be exploited, psychologically and physiologically in this social realm. Peer to peer bullying, online grooming, and exposure to any unsuitable material is dangerous and potentially very harmful to their psychological well-being.

Closing the protection of children and adolescents presupposes the development of the adequate cybersecurity infrastructure which will take into consideration a specific age of a child or teenager, but it will not infringe upon individual rights and freedoms. For instance, filters and surveillance equipment installed in the house to monitor children interaction can help the parents to supervise their children and act appropriately. But these tools should also protect the child's rights to privacy and also encourage the child to share with someone about internet safety. Education programs aimed at young users will allow them to understand real scenarios and how to counter them. What this means is that it will always lie on schools and other community-based organization to provide such programme and ensure that youths are safe while using internet.

Other special groups, for example, those with mental illness, the elderly and the disadvantaged also needs special consideration. Such groups could have specific risks regarding the new universe – for example, they could be more often exposed to the cyber threats, or the subject of the given work could be somehow linked to difficulties in finding support service. This approach should envision that cybersecurity should be safeguarding all users with cybersecurity measures regardless of their age, gender, race, physical challenges or disability. This may encompass the development of web applications for those with disabilities, to offer of specific grants and services and involving caregivers to hear their concerns first-hand.

As for the effect of cybersecurity on the society. IF policymakers and technologists do not pay careful attention to the possible reinforcement of existing inequalities, it is equally important that any protective measures that are implemented are done in earners– and receivers–fairness. This also involves handling the digital divide where possibly some groups in society cannot get what will enable their security to be handled by cybersecurity. Technological development should therefore be directed in such a manner that it can be made available to all by providing a chance to those of all classes to use such technologies safely.

Therefore, ethical dilemmas encountered into cybersecurity for the protection of mental health are as follows not so clear cut: security versus privacy, consent versus openness and arguably most critical how of the dealing with the vulnerable. Facing the threats noted above and with the goal to create both effective cybersecurity measures and the appropriate ethical environment for all users, stakeholders should act thoughtfully. All these aspects are crucial for building trust and creating environments for people's mental well-being and technology inclusion for everyone.

CHALLENGES AND RECOMMENDATIONS

Identifying Key Challenges

As the attempts to maintain mental health through cybersecurity in the post-modern technological age are defined, the theoretical, practical, and philosophical problems have been outlined. Technically, the threat situation in cyberspace is becoming increasingly dynamic, and the parties putting up protective shields cannot cope with this rate of threat development. This has to do with the fact that hackers are always coming up with new ways to breach security systems because doing otherwise would be fairly easy. Also, it remains challenging to incorporate advanced technologies such as AI and machine learning into frameworks for cybersecurity. Som of the technology are data receptive requiring optimum algorithms for them to run and these could prove very expensive and time consuming to implement. To visually illustrate how the identified barriers affect cybersecurity effectiveness, a radar chart is used in Figure 7. The chart plots three key barriers: line 127 technical social ethical among technical social and ethical impacts the degree of percentage effects. Multidimensionality and complexity of challenges are depicted in the radar plot, where technical barriers were found to have the highest impact. This figure suggests that addressing these diverse barriers requires an integrated model to improve cybersecurity.

Figure 7. Radar chart showing different types of barriers and their impact on cybersecurity effectiveness.

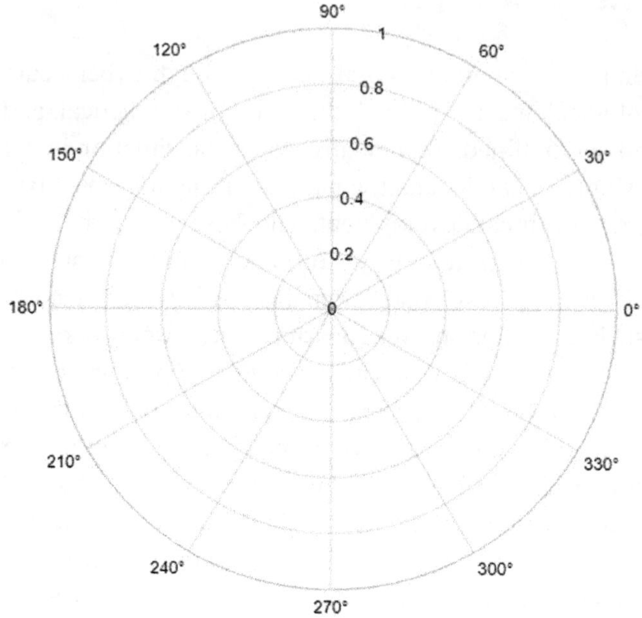

Figure 8. Line plot showing future directions in cybersecurity research and development areas.

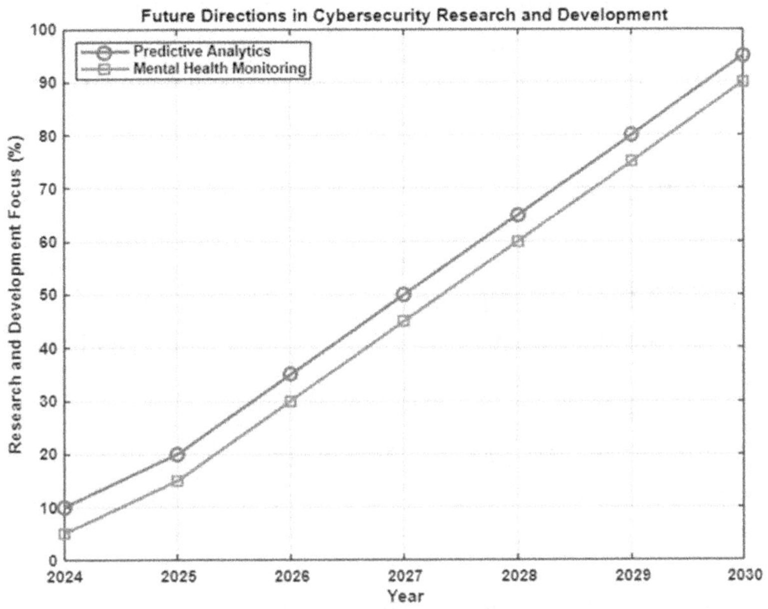

There is a line plot enumerating future prospects of further research and development in this domain from 2024 to 2030 in Figure 8. The horizontal axis is the years and vertical axis is the focus percentage. The plot employs circles for the performance of the predictive model and squares for the stats of the mental health. Mental health services show a slightly higher trend in terms of focus and demand in comparison to substance misuse services. It points to the significance of the emerging fields in availing transformation of cybersecurity to protect mental health. Social barriers also pose some of the biggest problems that may be faced in the process of implementing lean thinking. Although people have been sensitized towards the reality of cyber threats, awareness varies from actual practice. Users fail to operate on the principles of safe computing since they lack necessary knowledge, they are careless, or in some cases, security measures are just too cumbersome. Also the victim might fall prey to embarrassment and has the feeling that he/she cannot report the incident and or seek help if the incident was cyber bullying or online harassment. While this underreporting may be for a good reason, it distorts statistics and can hamper efforts to design and implement useful cybersecurity measures. Ethical considerations are not any less important as such. This paper looks at the tension that has arisen between such a need for surveillance in order to counter and or identify threats posed by cyber threats and the right to privacy. If it is possible to overdue with surveillance it becomes a dangerous thing to practice as it will compromise peoples rights and main ten, on the other hand, if there is no supervision often there will be negative effects to the users. First of all, prescriptive cybersecurity has to be both necessary and sufficient for protection while being sensitive to differences. Higher risk populations such as children, elders and excluded populations are at a higher risk online, but may have limited protection mechanisms available to them.

Actionable Insights

These challenges cannot be solved only through application of technology, education and policies, but need a combination of all. On this ground, a practical measure toward the improvement of cybersecurity is the unending innovation, adoption of artificial intelligence, and machine learning. Such technologies can be used to increase the speed of identification of such threats and responses, and, therefore, increase the level of security of cyberspace. For instance, new algorithms could be created through which models can identify patterns of abuse and had them banned or marked automatically. To tackle technical challenges, it is necessary to use technology collaborations between universities, businesses, and private entities, so that cybersecurity measures are innovative and affordable.

One of the most important functions of education is that knowledge should guide behavior. Comprehensive programs of educating 'net-savvy' citizens should be adopted for the users of different age, which would spread the information about the significance of cyberspace security and the way to ensure it. These programs should include simple principles such as password creation, identifying phishing scams, and utility of privacy settings. Also, the institutions are able to adapt the principles of resilience training on the psychological impacts of the cyber threats and therefore integrate organizational culture that supports the staff.

From this policy perspective, governments should ensure and enforce that any organization operating in this digital realm, should be bound by standard cybersecurity policies. This entails issues to do with reporting procedures including provision of check and balances, regimen on handling consumers' complaints and sanctions in case of violation. There should also be mechanisms for legal utilization of surveillance, especially in the processes of accruing insignificant information while the data collected should not be taken or used without the subject's permission, and the use of this technology should only be done in moderation. Moreover, such specific programs to address the needs of special individuals and groups should be developed. Using popular strategies may mean the financing of cybersecurity awareness campaigns by communal organizations and agencies or subsidies for protective technologies for the needy.

Recommendations for Stakeholders

The prevention and tackling of mental health issues through cybersecurity needs the combined effort of policy, practitioners and engineers. This paper claims that the authorities concerned should focus on the formulation of holistically well-coordinated cybersecurity policies that respect the confidentiality of information. It also includes in passing laws to guard users' rights when using the internet, to supporting research into possible threats and strategies; and to promoting collaboration between developed nations in the fight against cybercrime. They should also support funded comprehensive education that would include cybersecurity in schools, and the communities to ensure a digitally equipped and safe society.

Psychologists and other mental health care workers can play an important part of the response to the psychological consequences of cyber threats. They should expect their inclusion in cybersecurity policies agendas and talk to engineers on how to foster programs to support individuals with mental health concerns. A range of principles for mental health should be implemented such that any case involving someone who has been a victim of cyberbullying or online harassment deserves special attention. They can also participate by undertaking projects that seek to establish the effect of cyber threats on mental health to inform on policy and practice development.

Cybersecurity technologists and software developers must continue to consider how to design more effective yet usable technology. This includes creating easy to use security controls that could present the user with no challenge, but at the same time making sure the security measures are flexible enough to warrant security for different users and settings. Coordination with mental health services is therefore imperative so as to ensure that the technologies work around the requirements of the vulnerable cyber victims. Technologists should also be the ones calling for ethically sound practices in surveillance technologies creation and use.

Therefore, it is possible to formulate the conclusion that the problem-solving scenario such as the preservation of mental health within the framework of cybersecurity seems quite difficult. Such critical issues and understanding some effective strategies and enhancing roles of all the related actors make it possible to set up safer information technologies for mental health. By constant advancements, improvement on existing structures on knowledge and formulation of relevant and effective policies we can ensure that the advancements in the digital front are realized safely and in parity.

CONCLUSION

Technology and cybersecurity have become significantly correlated with the emotional well-being of the citizens of the present advanced society. This accompanied by new levels of greatness hence connectivity and convenience due to enhanced digital platform has also given rise to new forms of risk that may affect mental health. Consequently, such cyber threats as online abuse, cyberbullying, and digital harassment can cause psychological consequences, stress, anxiety, depression, as well as chronic mental disorders. While present day security technologies are quite sophisticated, they need to constantly adapt to these threats to safeguard the people's mental well-being. The studies demonstrate how technologies such as AI, machine learning and blockchain can help to identify and mitigate cyber threats and hence make cyberspace safer. It is about education, about awareness and finally about policymakers, mental health professionals, and technologists working together towards providing a safe environment to citizens of the New World Wide Web.

More specifically, more research and development are required to improve the prospects of cybersecurity that underlines mental health. As the future work it is suggested to develop the approach for predictive risk analysis for cyber threats to prevent them, as well as initiatives to implement the system of monitoring mental state of employees within the system of cybersecurity. Individualized approaches that will involve creating unique cybersecurity solutions that can change with the customer's behavior is also going to be vital. In addition, there is always the future research to develop the correct ethical behavior with regards to surveillance on security and privacy and freedom. This is why policymakers need to keep on creating the right conducive laws and enforcing them to enhance the culture of safety in the digital platforms.

This can be translated only as the fact that since technology has encroached upon all spheres of human life, it is necessary to address the issues arising with the use of digital technology. From the events occurring in the modern cyberspace it has emerged that threats active in cyberspace can adversely influence an individual's psychological state, therefore a need to create an effective security system to protect the users from these vices. Working collectively with educators, implementing new technologies, and designing policies to support mentally safe virtual spaces we can guarantee people would willingly stay and interact in cyberspace. By using cybersecurity to protect mental health, its constant use will ensure that technology in the advanced areas is pursued and adopted without having adverse repercussions on the health of individuals. In this venture, all individuals have a part they need to play in the creation of a safer and psychologically sound internet.

REFERENCES

Adams, R., Baker, M., & Clark, N. (2024, September). "Resilience Training for Digital Literacy and Cybersecurity," IEEE Trans. Human-Mach. *Syst.*, 35(4), 550–559.

Agrawal, R., Dutt, V., & Vyas, N. (2023) "Improved Healthcare System with Quantum Computing," In *2023 International Conference on Artificial Intelligence and Smart Communication (AISC)*, Greater Noida, India, (pp. 99-103).

Allen, P., & Mitchell, L. (2023, December). "User-Centric Cybersecurity Solutions for Mental Health," IEEE Trans. Human-Comput. *Interact.*, 11(4), 450–461.

Anderson, K., & Martinez, P. (2024, July). Technologists' Role in Mental Health Protection. *IEEE Transactions on Computers*, 60(2), 102–111.

Brown, A., Green, S., & Black, P. (2024, April). The Role of Cybersecurity in Mental Health Protection: An Overview. *IEEE Security and Privacy*, 21(2), 14–22.

Chandrasekaran, S., Dutt, V., Vyas, N., & Anand, A. (2023) "Fuzzy KNN Implementation for Early Parkinson's Disease Prediction," 2023 7th International Conference on Computing Methodologies and Communication (ICCMC), Erode, India, 2023, pp. 896-901. DOI: 10.1109/ICCMC56507.2023.10083522

Davis, S., & Thomas, L. (2023, October). Community Approaches to Fostering Safe Digital Spaces. *IEEE Transactions on Communications*, 22(1), 66–77.

Evans, A.. (2024, February). Protecting Vulnerable Populations in Cyberspace. *IEEE Trans. Soc. Comput.*, 10(3), 123–132.

Foster, J., & Brown, S. (2023, September). Predictive Analytics for Cybersecurity and Mental Health. *IEEE Transactions on Knowledge and Data Engineering*, 22(5), 556–567.

Garcia, F.. (2023, November). Ethical Considerations in AI-Driven Cybersecurity. *IEEE Comput.*, 56(9), 94–103.

Hall, N., & Lee, J. (2023, November). Integrating Cybersecurity and Mental Health Protection. *IEEE Trans. Syst. Sci. Cybern.*, 17(1), 23–34.

Harris, D., & Phillips, L. (2024, June). Role of Mental Health Professionals in Cybersecurity. *IEEE Trans. Med. Informatics*, 23(4), 420–429.

Kalpana, V., & Hariram, V. (2023) "Artificial Intelligence based Health Monitoring System on IoTH platform," In *2023 Second International Conference on Augmented Intelligence and Sustainable Systems (ICAISS)*, Trichy, India, (pp. 1458-1463).

Kawale, S. R. (2023) "Cloud-Based Multi-Layer Security Framework for Protecting E-Health Records," In *2023 International Conference on Artificial Intelligence for Innovations in Healthcare Industries (ICAIIHI)*, Raipur, India, (pp. 1-7).

Lee, H., & Kim, J. (2024, July). Impact of Cyber Threats on Mental Health: A Case Study. *IEEE Transactions on Cybernetics*, 24(5), 1018–1027.

Lewis, M., (2023, August). Future Directions in Cybersecurity Research. *IEEE Transactions on Emerging Topics in Computing*, 8(3), 212–223.

Miller, P., (2023, August). Education Programs for Cybersecurity Awareness and Mental Health. *IEEE Transactions on Learning Technologies*, 15(2), 220–230.

Murphy, C. (2024, March). Challenges in Implementing Cybersecurity for Mental Health Protection. *IEEE Transactions on Systems, Man, and Cybernetics*, 28(2), 230–241.

Nguyen, B., & Hernandez, J. (2024, April). Actionable Insights for Enhancing Cybersecurity. *IEEE Transactions on Information Forensics and Security*, 19(3), 342–353.

Patel, M., & Shah, R. (2024) "Informed Consent and Transparency in Cybersecurity Measures," IEEE Trans. Dependable Secur. Comput., *11*(1), pp. 89-98.

Prasad, K., S. R, and A. K. N, (2024) "Design and Implementation of an AI and IoT-Enabled Smart Safety Helmet for Real-Time Environmental and Health Monitoring," In *2024 IEEE International Conference on Information Technology, Electronics and Intelligent Communication Systems (ICITEICS)*, Bangalore, India, (pp. 1-7).

Robinson, T., & Walker, E. (2023, December). Balancing Security and Privacy in Digital Environments. *IEEE Transactions on Information Technology in Biomedicine*, 12(2), 150–160.

Smith, M., & Jones, R. (2024, February). Blockchain Technology for Enhancing Digital Privacy and Security. *IEEE Access : Practical Innovations, Open Solutions*, 11, 9456–9472.

Suneetha, S., & Patil, S. R. (2023) "Advancements in Multi-Cloud Applications for Enhanced E-Healthcare Services," In *2023 International Conference on Artificial Intelligence for Innovations in Healthcare Industries (ICAIIHI)*, Raipur, India, (pp. 1-7).

Taylor, K., & Wilson, G. (2024, June). Cybersecurity Protocols for Preventing Online Abuse. *IEEE Network*, 36(4), 42–49.

Turner, S. (2024, May). Guidelines for Policymakers on Cybersecurity and Mental Health. *IEEE Trans. Cyber Secur.*, 12(1), 56–67.

Wang, J. (2024, March). Machine Learning Techniques in Cyberbullying Detection: A Survey. *IEEE Communications Surveys and Tutorials*, 26(1), 78–96.

White, L. (2024, May). Digital Harassment: Detection and Mitigation Strategies. *IEEE Internet of Things Journal*, 8(3), 1204–1215.

Chapter 12
Examining How Safety Technologies Affect in Mental Wellness Healthcare Web of Device

Harishchander Anandaram
https://orcid.org/0000-0003-2993-5304
Amrita Vishwa Vidyapeetham, India

K. S. Shreenidhi
https://orcid.org/0000-0002-6844-0454
Rajalakshmi Engineering College, India

Kapil Joshi
https://orcid.org/0000-0003-1097-8347
Uttaranchal University, India

J. Ghayathri
Presidency University, India

ABSTRACT

A major advancement in the incorporation of medical care is Web of Device (WOD) for monitoring psychological wellness and health. WOD is a network of connected products that gather and share data in real-time, offering an ever-present, discrete, and data-driven method for wellness tracking. WOD has the potential to revolutionize mental wellness by facilitating the early identification, evaluation, and treatment of disorders of the mind, hence enhancing patient results and standard of living. This review examines the complex interplay between security technologies and mental wellness. Safety at work, information security, and surveillance technologies are

DOI: 10.4018/979-8-3693-7758-1.ch012

examples of safety innovations that are essential to our contemporary world and are meant to shield people, businesses, and society from various dangers.

1. INTRODUCTION

The quickly changing world of technology in order security technologies are now an essential component of our everyday existence. These tools are essential for protecting both our digital and physical lives, from routers protecting our identities on the web to CCTV cameras for checking public spaces (Brown et al., 2020). An urgent and significant wellness concern that has to be addressed urgently is a worldwide rise in mental wellness. Economic and social forces and swift local address population have made things tougher in the nation of India. A survey in 2021 discovered that 201 million Indians faced anxiety and despair, among other mental wellness (Conley et al., 2022). Young professionals and individuals are living in a stressful and depressing feeling due to the prejudice associated with mental wellness, expectation to perform well academically, and unstable employment.

Security technology has developed dramatically in the last few years, partly because of worries about online attacks, violence, safety for everyone, and data breaches (Dutta et al., 2024). The widespread incorporation of safety features into our environment has led to an increasing curiosity about the wider effects of such innovations on people's mental wellness. This alarming trend highlights the need for all-encompassing policies relating to mental health, such as stigmatization initiatives, accessible mental wellness services, and awareness efforts.

Having the right to privacy, and safety at all times and striking a balance between security and freedom are only a few of the essential components of human existence that are impacted by security technology's effects on mental health (Moghimi et al., 2022). Corona outbreak has brought attention to how fragile mental health is on a global scale. Continued solitude, financial stress, and a fear of illness have significantly increased the prevalence of mental wellness issues in societies like America. The Agency for the Control of Diseases (COD) stated in 2021 March that approximately 50% of adults had a mental wellness or substance use problem (Saxena et al., 2025). Similarly, during the pandemic, contacts and requests for assistance increased by 35%, according to mental health groups in the UK.

In addition, this review seeks to identify possible approaches and tools to mitigate the negative consequences and encourage responsible use of technology for safety (Lo et al., 2021). Lastly, that hopes to offer detailed evaluations and helpful suggestions that might guide subsequent investigations, the creation of laws and regulations, and general debate about the important connection between mental wellness and security (Asad et al., 2023).

Here's an in-depth examination of how safety technologies can impact mental wellness in the context of healthcare Web of Devices in healthcare as WoD.

1. Wearable Devices: Wearable devices like fitness trackers, smartwatches, and health monitors may be tracking physical activity, sleep patterns, and vital signs etc.
2. Environmental Sensors: Environmental sensors can monitor temperature, humidity, lighting, and air quality, creating a safe and comfortable environment.
3. Fall Detection Systems: Fall detection systems can alert caregivers and emergency services in case of a fall, ensuring prompt assistance.
4. Medication Management Systems: Medication management systems can track medication adherence, sending reminders and alerts to patients and caregivers.

2. SAFETY TECHNOLOGY FOR MENTAL WELLNESS AND WOD COMPONENTS

Physical safety: Keeping real, actual possessions and environments safe requires the implementation of security protocols. They cover a wide range of device and frameworks designed to stop unwanted entry, breaches, and incursions in actual-life environments (Leitão et al., 2018). For example, authorisation device control admission to buildings or particular sections inside them, making sure that only people with permission can enter. Security systems are intended to identify and report any illegal activity or violations, setting off countermeasures to lessen possible risks.

It is connecting and sharing information through different systems and devices over the web by means of a web of tangible items integrated with applications, sensors, and additional devices (Elavsky et al., 2022). Important WOD parts of the Web of Things consist of:

Sensing and actuators are devices that can both conduct operations (like altering the environment's lights) and receive results (like pulse trackers) (Sorkin et al., 2021).

- **Access:** the systems that transfer data between devices, like Wireless LAN, and other Smartphone lines (Odgers et al., 2020).
- **Information computation:** Machine learning (ML) along with the Web of Contents is frequently used in the evaluation of information tools (Raj et al., 2024).
- **User Interface:** Systems (which include smart phone software) that let people connect using Internet of Things (IoT) devices to keep an eye on and control their health wellness (Kaaria et al., 2023).

Information Retrieval (IR) with User Interface refers to the process of designing and developing systems that enable users to effectively search, retrieve, and interact with information from various sources, such as databases, libraries, or the internet.

Information Retrieval involves indexing: Organizing and structuring data to facilitate efficient searching. Querying: Allowing users to submit queries or search requests. Ranking: Returning relevant results, often in a ranked order, based on their relevance to the query and User Interface (UI) plays a crucial role in IR systems, as it enables users to formulate queries: Enter search terms, phrases, or questions. Interact with results: Browse, filter, and refine search results. Provide feedback: Indicate relevance, usefulness, or satisfaction with the results.

It is the actual structure defined as the ration of factor and information retrieval is explained in Figure 1 that shows the access from information computation to user interface.

Figure 1. Information retrieval with user interface

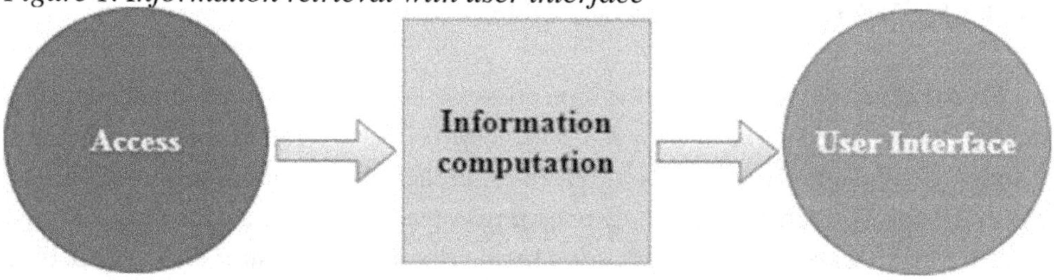

Safety online: Protecting online possessions, information, or network connectivity is the main focus of safety reasons, as opposed to physical safety. Given our growing TATA on Croma digital, security measures are essential for fending off a wide range of online dangers. Firewalls in particular which act as virtual obstacles that hinder unwanted internet access and defend against digital assaults, are essential parts of safety (Yadav et al., 2024). Evil software, sometimes known as infection, is intended to be found and eliminated by software called antivirus to protect digital safety.

Observation device: comprises a range of instruments and frameworks that are employed to keep an eye on and record actions, frequently in private as well as public domains. Video recording devices are a common system for monitoring found in homes, businesses, and neighbourhoods (Verma et al., 2023). Cameras collect video that may be watched in actual time or stored for examination at another moment. However, because they possess the ability to gather and examine enormous volumes of information pertaining to individuals, they additionally open up important privacy and moral dilemmas. Safety technology for mental wellness and WOD Components are explained in Figure 2.

Figure 2. Safety technology for mental wellness and WOD components

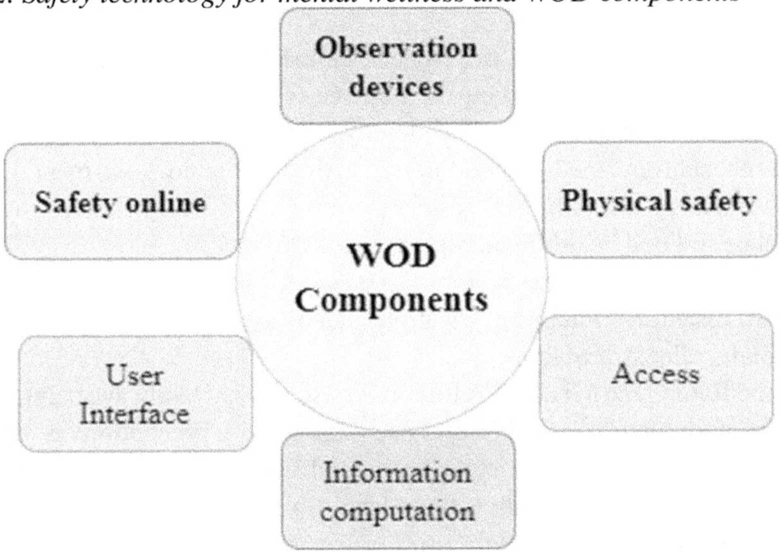

3. CONCEPT OF MENTAL HEALTH MONITORING

While mental wellness is crucial for general health, it gets overlooked or condemned. Can have a negative impact on human relationships, productivity, or quality being (Hegde et al., 2023). Melancholy frequently results shortage of drive and enthusiasm for routine tasks, having a major negative impact on mental wellness. These mental wellness issues can interfere with one's life at all levels, which stresses the need for supportive reliable assistance.

The emergences of the Web of Drives (WOD) and associated ideas such as computing everywhere have worked notably to increase more frequency of mental wellness problems. The relationship between physical and mental wellness is strongly linked, and the link between the two is accepted by all (Saleh et al., 2023). Depression, emotional strain, and mental wellness problems can all negatively impact one's physical health.

4. MEASURING MENTAL WELLNESS

State to somebody's mental or physical wellness has significant harm on their total physiological working, making them an essential component. Chronic pressure, for instance, has been linked to reduced body immunity, issues with digestion, and heart and other chronic medical conditions. On the other hand, good mental wellness can inspire healthy habits like consistent exercise and a well-balanced diet, which support general good health (Natarajan et al., 2023).

Avoid disasters- Major ramifications can be avoided with early diagnosis of mental wellness problems.

Immediate Care Mental Wellness: Assistance led to always being available wake of an attack or danger because taking many precautions is seamlessly integrated with rescue safety with mental wellness (Dadkhah et al., 2024). These systems can quickly sound alarms in the event of a violation, inform investigators, and notify authorities or law enforcement agencies.

General protection: Improved when safety precautions are installed in areas where people congregate, like avenues, ground, and bus stops. Specifically, recording devices provide round-the-clock monitoring, documenting activities visually, and discourage illegal activity.

WOD keeps developing and our knowledge of mental wellness expands, intelligent WOD solutions for tracking mental wellness and well-being have the ability to completely change the way that provides mental wellness care by encouraging prompt treatment, individualized support, and ultimately raising people's quality of life everywhere (Renugadevi et al., 2023).

Violence Prohibition: Residents of the local population are encouraged to participate better in public life by going to assemblies, taking public transit, and engaging in leisure activities without worrying about being a victim of fraud because they feel safe. As a result, safety devices encourage communal harmony and systematic utilization of common areas.

5. UPCOMING PATH

Identification verification: Recognising faces and scans of fingers are two examples of physical identification techniques that provide peace of mind. They have yet to also bring up issues with monitoring and safety. Further research should examine how widely used digital fingerprints may affect people's mental wellness (Subhan et al., 2023).

In an environment during which mental wellness is not more an inner conflict but rather an ongoing path towards completeness and growth, we may unlock the positive effects of Smart WOD solutions through an ensemble effort involving researchers, mental wellness providers, technological professionals, and ultimately, the people whose happiness is at dangers (Suleski et al., 2023). It's critical to comprehend the psychological effects of biological adoption and to assess if it causes sensations of intrusiveness or uneasiness in people.

Fingerprint scanners with connected devices: Numerous sensors found inside electronic watches and fitness bands can track physiological signals such as wellness, they are provided with body fever and other time sleep patterns. Still also brings up issues with snooping and safety. Additional ought (Bendowska et al., 2023) to examine how widely used electronic fingerprints may affect people's mental wellness.

For instance, higher body fever and greater wellness plus rate variability might indicate signs of higher stress levels or nervousness. Sleep and DND may (SOTIRE et al., 2025) indicate sadness or other mental wellness problems. WOD have the ability to identify possible mental wellness issues and (Das et al., 2020) notify patients or medical professionals in order to arrange for additional testing or treatment alerts by electronic tracking device. Benefits of security are shown in Figure 3.

Figure 3. Benefits of security technology for psychological well-being

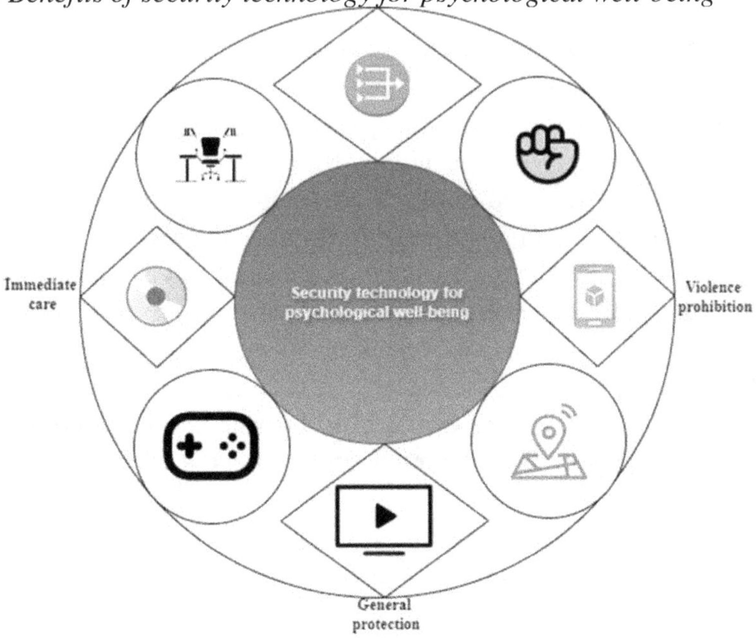

Web of Device Safety: The "Web of Devices" refers to the interconnected network of physical devices, vehicles, home appliances (Yogi et al., 2018), and other items embedded with sensors, software, and connectivity, allowing them to collect and exchange data. This concept is also known as the Internet of Things (IoT). The Web of Devices is growing quickly, which means that linked devices have a number of security flaws (Kim et al., 2025). These flaws may result in invasions of privacy, illegal access, and even damage to individuals. In addition, people need to give their express consent (Oberhuber et al., 2025) for their data to be collected and used for wellness monitoring. The Web of Devices enables these connected devices to communicate with each other, share data, and perform various tasks, creating a more integrated, automated, and efficient system (Hecker et al., 2025). Here are the strengths and weaknesses of Wellness Healthcare Web of Devices where the overall strengths are to improve patient engagement and wellness healthcare Web of Devices enables patients to take a more active role in their healthcare, encouraging them to monitor their vital signs, track their progress, and make informed decisions. It also enhances remote monitoring. where some weaknesses are as data security and privacy concerns in which the Web of Devices relies on the collection and transmission of sensitive patient data, creating concerns about data security, privacy, and potential cyber threats and interoperability challenges that connects the integration of diverse devices, systems, and data formats can be complex, leading to interoperability challenges and potential data silos.

6. CONCLUSIONS AND FUTURE SCOPE

A fundamental change in how we approach wellness healthcare has occurred with the merger of Clever WOD technology with mental wellness monitoring. This thorough analysis has revealed both the advantages and disadvantages of these technologies, highlighting their potential to improve the security of wellness that may obtain unparalleled comprehension of our mental and emotional state by utilizing a system of linked devices and powerful statistical analysis. This will allow for timely treatment, individualized encouragement, and eventually, a better way of life. Morally and practically necessary to strike an agreement amongst the need for secure and maintaining one's own health. Prioritizing moral norms, cantered on user responses, scientific cooperation, and awareness campaigns is crucial to achieving this balance.

The utilization of a networked device, we may obtain a significant understanding of a person's psychological condition and offer tailored assistance and solutions. To fully utilize Smart WOD in behavioural inspection, it is as important to concentrate on the issues around privacy, interpreting data, and moral issues.

It is morally and practically necessary to strike the right equilibrium between the need for security and maintaining one's personal health. Prioritizing standards of ethics, cantered on responses, academic cooperation, and education campaigns is crucial to achieving this balance. In our linked society, promoting peaceful coexistence between encryption and behavioural depends critically on continuing study findings, legal issues, and user responsibility as technological progress.

Future directions involve integrating mental health support where safety technologies should incorporate mental health support features, such as counseling services and stress management tools. Addressing equity and accessibility which involves the safety technologies should prioritize equity and accessibility, ensuring that all individuals can benefit from these technologies. Developing cybersecurity protocols provides robust cybersecurity protocols that should be developed and implemented to protect patient data and safety and further fostering human centered design where safety technologies should be designed with human-centered approaches, prioritizing user needs, and promoting intuitive and user-friendly interfaces.

REFERENCES

Asad, M. M., Erum, D., Churi, P., & Guerrero, A. J. M. (2023). Effect of technostress on Psychological well-being of post-graduate students: A perspective and correlational study of Higher Education Management. *International Journal of Information Management Data Insights*, 3(1), 100149. DOI: 10.1016/j.jjimei.2022.100149

Brown, S. D., Dahill, D., Karakilic, E., King, D., Misha, P., Pirrioni, S., & Vedi, P. (2020). Psychological wellbeing and safety in a global context: a rapid evidence assessment.

Conley, C. S., Raposa, E. B., Bartolotta, K., Broner, S. E., Hareli, M., Forbes, N., Christensen, K. M., & Assink, M. (2022). The impact of mobile technology-delivered interventions on youth well-being: Systematic review and 3-level meta-analysis. *JMIR Mental Health*, 9(7), e34254. DOI: 10.2196/34254 PMID: 35904845

Dadkhah, S., Neto, E. C. P., Ferreira, R., Molokwu, R. C., Sadeghi, S., & Ghorbani, A. (2024). Ciciomt2024: Attack vectors in healthcare device-a multi-protocol dataset for assessing iomt device security.

Elavsky, S., Blahošová, J., Lebedíková, M., Tkaczyk, M., Tancos, M., Plhák, J., Sotolář, O., & Smahel, D. (2022). Researching the links between smartphone behavior and adolescent well-being with the FUTURE-WP4 (modeling the future: understanding the impact of technology on adolescent's well-being work package 4) project: protocol for an ecological momentary assessment study. *JMIR Research Protocols*, 11(3), e35984. DOI: 10.2196/35984 PMID: 35258467

Hecker, C., Hufnagl, C., Oellerer, A., Griessenauer, C. J., & Killer-Oberpfalzer, M. (2025). The Artisse intrasaccular device: A new intrasaccular flow diverter for the treatment of cerebral aneurysms. *AJNR. American Journal of Neuroradiology*, 46(1), 84–89. DOI: 10.3174/ajnr.A8478 PMID: 39779289

Kim, A., Lee, H., & Lee, S. (2025). In Touch with Those in Need: How Touchscreen Devices Lead Consumers to Support Social Causes. *Journal of the Association for Consumer Research, 10*(1), 000-000.

Leitão, S., Mc Carthy, V. J., & Greiner, B. A. (2018). Health and safety practitioners' health and wellbeing—The link with safety climate and job demand-control-support. *Accident; Analysis and Prevention*, 119, 131–137. DOI: 10.1016/j.aap.2018.06.017 PMID: 30025354

Lo, C., Yu, J., Görges, M., & Matava, C. (2021). Anesthesia in the modern world of apps and technology: Implications and impact on wellness. *Paediatric Anaesthesia*, 31(1), 31–38. DOI: 10.1111/pan.14051 PMID: 33119935

Moghimi, E., Knyahnytska, Y., Omrani, M., Nikjoo, N., Stephenson, C., Layzell, G., Frederic Simpson, A. I., & Alavi, N. (2022). Benefits of digital mental health care interventions for correctional workers and other public safety personnel: A narrative review. *Frontiers in Psychiatry*, 13, 921527. DOI: 10.3389/fpsyt.2022.921527 PMID: 35873240

Natarajan, R., Lokesh, G. H., Flammini, F., Premkumar, A., Venkatesan, V. K., & Gupta, S. K. (2023). A novel framework on security and energy enhancement based on internet of medical things for healthcare 5.0. *Infrastructures*, 8(2), 22. DOI: 10.3390/infrastructures8020022

Oberhuber, M., Unterguggenberger, M., Maar, L., Kogler, A., & Mangard, S. (2025). Power-Related Side-Channel Attacks using the Android Sensor Framework. In Network and Distributed System Security Symposium 2025.

Raj, G., Sharma, A. K., & Arora, Y. (2024). Analyzing the Effect of Digital Technology on Mental Health. In *Strategies for E-Commerce Data Security: Cloud, Blockchain, AI, and Machine Learning* (pp. 54-82). IGI Global. DOI: 10.4018/979-8-3693-6557-1.ch003

Renugadevi, N., Saravanan, S., & Sudha, C. N. (2023). Revolution of smart healthcare materials in big data analytics. *Materials Today: Proceedings*, 81, 834–841. DOI: 10.1016/j.matpr.2021.04.256

Saleh, S., Cherradi, B., El Gannour, O., Gouiza, N., & Bouattane, O. (2023). Healthcare monitoring system for automatic database management using mobile application in IoT environment. *Bulletin of Electrical Engineering and Informatics*, 12(2), 1055–1068. DOI: 10.11591/eei.v12i2.4282

Saxena, M., Avanesh, N. M., Niranjan, L. R., & Mohanty, P. (2025). Wearable Technologies Leading to Employee Performance and Productivity: Exploring the Mediating Role of Mental Health and Wellbeing. In *Technological Enhancements for Improving Employee Performance, Safety, and Well-Being* (pp. 111-130). IGI Global.

Sorkin, D. H., Janio, E. A., Eikey, E. V., Schneider, M., Davis, K., Schueller, S. M., Stadnick, N. A., Zheng, K., Neary, M., Safani, D., & Mukamel, D. B. (2021). Rise in use of digital mental health tools and technologies in the United States during the COVID-19 pandemic: Survey study. *Journal of Medical Internet Research*, 23(4), e26994. DOI: 10.2196/26994 PMID: 33822737

Subhan, F., Mirza, A., Su'ud, M. B. M., Alam, M. M., Nisar, S., Habib, U., & Iqbal, M. Z. (2023). AI-enabled wearable medical internet of things in healthcare system: A survey. *Applied Sciences (Basel, Switzerland)*, 13(3), 1394. DOI: 10.3390/app13031394

Suleski, T., Ahmed, M., Yang, W., & Wang, E. (2023). A review of multi-factor authentication in the Internet of Healthcare Things. *Digital Health*, 9, 20552076231177144. DOI: 10.1177/20552076231177144 PMID: 37252257

Verma, H., Chauhan, N., & Awasthi, L. K. (2023). A Comprehensive review of 'Internet of Healthcare Things': Networking aspects, technologies, services, applications, challenges, and security concerns. *Computer Science Review, 50*, 100591. Hegde, P., & Maddikunta, P. K. R. (2023). Amalgamation of Blockchain with resource-constrained IoT device for Healthcare applications–State of Art, Challenges and Future Directions. *International Journal of Cognitive Computing in Engineering*.

Yogi, M. K., & Bhavani, K. G. D. (2018). A Propulsive Roadmap for IoT Beyond 2025. *International Journal of Advanced Networking and Applications*, 10(2), 3808–3815. DOI: 10.35444/IJANA.2018.100210

Chapter 13
Cyber Security for Preserving Mental Wellness and Preventing Abuse:
An Insight Into Online Child Abuse Detection and Prevention

Kanya J. Katkar
https://orcid.org/0009-0006-4178-7948
Narayan Shastri Institute of Technology, India

Monica Anna Fernandes
https://orcid.org/0009-0005-1224-0188
Narayan Shastri Institute of Technology, India

Falak Prajapati
https://orcid.org/0009-0004-6117-9582
Narayan Shastri Institute of Technology, India

Kiran R. Dodiya
https://orcid.org/0009-0001-9409-7303
Gujarat University, India

Akash Khunt
https://orcid.org/0000-0001-5117-0040
Narayan Shastri Institute of Technology, India

Divya Patel
https://orcid.org/0009-0006-7630-1485
Narayan Shastri Institute of Technology, India

ABSTRACT

This chapter examines the crucial intersection of cybersecurity and mental wellness in today's digital world. It explores how cybersecurity practices can protect cognitive health and prevent abuse, addressing issues like cyberbullying, harassment, stalking, identity theft, and data breaches—all of which affect mental health. Through research and case studies, it stresses the importance of digital literacy, mental health

DOI: 10.4018/979-8-3693-7758-1.ch013

awareness, and safe online behavior. A collaborative model is proposed, involving mental health professionals, technologists, educators, and cybersecurity experts, to create secure, supportive digital spaces. The chapter also highlights "Cyber Guardians" and the role of technology, law enforcement, and human intervention in protecting children online. Social media and machine learning are discussed as tools for identifying abuse and improving content moderation. Strategies for prevention, community partnerships, and future technologies are explored to foster a safer digital environment, offering hope for a secure online world for all.

1. INTRODUCTION

1.1. Overview of Cybersecurity and Mental Wellness

In this digital age, two of the main concerns are online safety and mental wellbeing. Causes for concern have extended to include a new risk of threats such as social engineering as which was traditionally focused on protecting networks, systems, and data from cyberattacks and hackers. There has been a surge in risks like cyber threats, data breaches, cyber bullying, and online abuse which raises serious questions as to the impact these factors have on mental wellbeing. The overview does discuss the interplay between cyber security and mental wellbeing and emphasis is placed on both in regard to the need to protect them (Waterworth et al., 2023).

Cybersecurity encompasses control measures, systems and measures for protecting networks, computers and information from damage or legal intrusions. Although it emphasizes the technical aspect, the human dimension of the cyber security also has to be addressed. Cyberattacks like identity theft and ransom attacks are often cited as having a direct impact on the victims' psychology (Admass et al., 2024). Moreover, these violations are likely to entail a collective sense of discomfort, worrying and fear. To illustrate, people whose confidential information has been compromised tend to experience the feeling that their identity can be stolen. Studies indicate that individuals who are victims of crimes on the internet tend to exhibit higher levels of stress and anxiety and lowered feelings of general security. Sometimes as a result of deep psychological stress, illnesses such as depression or post-traumatic stress disorder do occur (DeLiema et al., 2021). There are two other categories of cyber harassment that come under the umbrella of cybersecurity harms, which are cyberbullying and online harassment. With the rapid rise in the usage of social media, cyberbullying has emerged as a huge challenge primarily among the younger population (Nixon, 2014). Victims of cyberbullying tend to have low self-esteem, have anxiety and depression, and in some extreme cases, develop suicidal ideations. There is evidence supporting that cyberbullying victims are more prone to emotional disturbance and suicidal tendencies when controlled for other variables which was published in JAMA network open 2020. The internet makes things easier for perpetrators as it grants them anonymity lacking in ordinary life, which aggravates vulnerability. Thus, the degree of the mental effects of cyberbullying may be more severe and prolonged than that of ordinary bullying (Maurya et al., 2022).

As the concern for mental health issues have increased, organizations have begun to adopt mental health policies as part of their safety strategies for the reason that there is correlation between cybersecurity and mental health. It is now becoming a norm to incorporate stress management strategies into cybersecurity training programs which indicates the importance of mental fortitude when dealing with the various forms of threats in cyberspace (Iwaya et al., 2022). Personal digital cleanliness and mindfulness techniques are essential to all individuals. Attending to cyberthreats incessantly can result in stress, however, practicing mindfulness techniques will help alleviate that distress. Relief from a fear of exposure may be achieved by instilling safe practices such as reducing the time one spends on social media, updating their applications regularly, and avoiding unprotected communication (*The Theory and Practice of Cyber-Mindfulness*, n.d.).

1.2. Objectives of the Chapter

1. Understanding the Relationship Between Cyber Security and Mental Health
2. Confronting the Threat of Cyberbullying and Online Harassers
3. Concern about the Sexual Abuse of Children on the Internet
4. Encouraging Child-Friendly and Responsible Digital Practices
5. Law and Ethics Pertaining to Protection of Children
6. Courses on Cybersecurity and Its Importance in Mental Toughness
7. Innovation in Cyber Tools and Tech Used in Protecting Children

2. THE IMPACT OF CYBER THREATS ON MENTAL HEALTH

2.1. Cyberbullying

Cyberbullying has been identified as an important problem amongst youth in the last decade. Bullying' is usually defined as being an aggressive, intentional act or behaviour that is carried out by a group or an individual repeatedly and over time against a victim who cannot easily defend him or herself. Several main types – physical, verbal, relational (e.g., social exclusion) and indirect (e.g., rumour spreading) – may be referred to as 'traditional' forms of bullying (Watts et al., 2017). In recent years bullying through electronic means, specifically mobile phones or the internet, has emerged, often collectively labelled 'cyberbullying'. A corresponding definition of Cyberbullying is the use of technology to harass, threaten, embarrass, or target another person (Peebles, 2014). Online threats and mean, aggressive, or rude texts, tweets, posts, or messages all count. So does posting personal information, pictures, or videos designed to hurt or embarrass someone else. Intimidation or mean comments that focus on things like a person's gender, religion, sexual orientation, race, or physical differences count as discrimination, which is against the law in many states. That means the police could get involved, and bullies may face serious penalties (*Dealing with Bullying: Strategies to Fight Teen Bullying*, n.d.).

Online bullying can be particularly damaging and upsetting because it's usually anonymous or hard to trace. It's also difficult to contain, and the victim doesn't know how many people (or hundreds of people) have read the messages or posts. People are able to be tortured continuously every time they check their phone or computers (*Cyberbullying - National Bullying Prevention Center*, n.d.).

2.1.1 Consequences of Cyberbullying

Cyberbullying can have a serious impact on people, especially children. The emotional and psychological impact on victims can be profound, left with anxiety, depression, or blow to their self-esteem. These emotions may result in isolation from peers, a decline in academic performance, and extreme thoughts of self-harm or suicide. Moreover, the omnipresent nature of online harassment forces the victims to use the medium on which they are harassed, and which adds to their distress threaten the use of this medium which threatens to use this medium without anymore escape. Structural alienation and fear have effects on both bystanders and perpetrators, creating a hostile culture that can poison communal relations. In conclusion, overcoming cyberbullying is essential for the mental health and well-being of both individuals and communities (Albikawi, 2023).

Detecting cyberbullying is greatly essential for creating a safe environment on the web. These cutting-edge technologies like machine learning, and natural language processing, allow us to detect malicious behaviour more accurately and quickly. Detecting such violations early enables not only to address deeply human suffering and the fallout of its impacts on victims, but it's also a key to a future solution and prevention. Through collaboration, platforms, educators, and policymakers can help implement stronger detection systems, raise more awareness, and foster better online behavior. So, an initiative for detecting cyberbullying can be a proactive step towards making individuals more empowered and a workplace more respectful of everyone (Alabdulwahab et al., 2023).

2.2. Harassment and Stalking

'Cyber stalking', this is one of the crimes of a man that he uses the internet and other technologies to harass or stalk another person online. Cyber stalking can include defamation, false accusations, teasing, and even extreme threats. Often these connections will not end despite the receiver requesting the person to stop. The content is usually inappropriate; it can be distressing and, therefore, is frightening for the individual who just starts. Cyber Harassment refers to repeated, unsolicited harassment from a single person through cyberspace Web or mobile technologies with an intent of causing harm as threaten, terrify, humiliate or stalk someone. For example, social media: stealing passwords, impersonating, sharing information without permission, posting embarrassing information or threatens of violence through social network sites., getting others in on the harassment act (*Here's How You Can Take Action against Stalking in India*, n.d.). To prevent yourself from being the victim of cyberstalking, you should follow these habits:

1. **Education:** This should make safer cyberspace, by conducting workshops and disseminating other resources especially targeting young person regarding signs of internet harassment and stalking, and its impact on young people's lives.
2. **Adjust privacy settings:** One of the first things you can do to change your privacy settings. Most social media networks and other online accounts allow you to decide who can see and contact you.
3. **Low profile:** Some people find it difficult to maintain a low profile online. However, you should always avoid posting your phone number and address and think twice before posting real-time information about where you are and who you're with.
4. **Digital Literacy:** The general development of digital literacy informs better cybersecurity practices. Developing a cybersecurity mindset, in turn, improves the digital literacy. Educating digital literacy to students and teachers/staff promotes awareness of the consequences of their online activity (Alismaiel, 2023).

2.3. Identity Theft and Data Breaches

Identity theft occurs when criminals steal a victim's personal information to carry out criminal acts. Taking on the victim's identity by utilizing such stolen information, the criminal executes a variety of fraud transactions in the victim's name. Cyber criminals commit identity theft by using sophisticated cyberattack tactics, including social engineering, phishing, and malware. Identity theft can also come from very basic moves of criminals stealing mail, going through dumpsters, and listening in on phone conversations in public places. The point of most cyberattacks is to obtain enough information on the victim to take his or her identity to perform some fraudulent activity. The breaching of an event wherein confidential or private protected or sensitive information is leaked to any unauthorized person is termed as a data breach, which could be due to an accidental mistake or an intentional source of stealing information from an individual or an organization (*What Is Identity Theft? Types and Examples*, n.d.).

This cybersecurity incidents like identity theft and data breaches can impacts on mental health. The feeling of violation, stress, anxiety, and fear characterizes the victims normally when they find out that their personal data is being compromised. Handling financial consequences, regaining their identity, and then dealing with the complexity of legal and administrative procedures stress a victim to the point where he or she feels hopeless and depressed. In addition, the worry about future breaches and lack of privacy creates an extended period of vigilance and interferes with daily activities and relationships. Overall, the psychological burden of such events would necessitate urgent cybersecurity actions as well as support systems for victims (Budimir et al., 2021).

2.4. Emotional Ramifications for Victims

Some of the emotive implications on victims include the following:

1. **Fear and Anxiety:** Victims may have fear over their safety with personal information exposed, expecting possible identity thefts or harassment.
2. **Loss of Trust:** The victim then begins to lose confidence in the technology and, most times, institutions in place to safeguard information and computer networks. Loss of trust may even extend to becoming mistrustful of online interaction and services with which one must deal both privately and professionally.
3. **Shame and Embarrassment:** The greater proportion of cyber victims will suffer feelings of shame and embarrassment because of the victimization. This is often more prevalent in attacks when such attack was caused by an individual's mistakes that trigger them, for instance falling a victim of phishing fraud.
4. **Isolation:** Victims move to the periphery of society. There is a natural desire for solitude, which grows more and more because of humiliation or fear. Isolation increases if they feel that others do not understand what happened to them.
5. **Anger and Frustration:** There may be burning anger directed at the perpetrators, but equally frustration with the healing process itself, particularly in systems where there are complex bureaucratic interventions.
6. **Depression:** The emotional cost of such an incident can result in depression and hopelessness, especially if the event has a far-reaching effect, i.e., if you have lost your job or sustained financial losses.

7. **Post-Traumatic Stress:** The most severe cases tend to resemble what might be called PTSD symptoms, including obsessive thoughts about the event and heightened sensitivity to reminders of the attack.
8. **Reputational Damage:** Later on, the breach could also cause reputational damage as it relates to a spoiler of public perception and aspects of self-esteem which still causes long-term emotional trauma for the individuals and other entities involved.
9. **Loss of Economic resources by Psychogenic stress:** Above point also includes that people got psych from potential lost economic resources which can be result by attack such as loss of job, settlement of liabilities and gaining of goods and services.
10. **Resiliency at the time of attack:** Resiliency is not always intuitive, but the lessons learned and maintaining personal boundaries will take even greater strength in general resilience as far as cyber security are concerned. Emotional effects, when and if they occur, tend to linger long after the initial trauma, and, perhaps, become chronic, reverberating into almost every area of a victim's life. Support systems, education and awareness, all are crucial considerations on which victims base the solutions they get to solve over problems (Short et al., 2015).

3. THE ROLE OF CYBERSECURITY IN PROMOTING MENTAL HEALTH

3.2. Importance of Computer Literacy

In today it is crucial in digital environment as we are discussing mental health through cybersecurity, and one should have knowledge of the basic computer literacy. Learning computing, the internet and digital literacy enables people to have a safer and more confident experience during their online journey. Computer Literacy empowers users to effectively secure their personal information, recognize potential threats online and become more responsible for digital pursuits; underpinned by Computer Literacy (*Importance of Digital Literacy Skills for Students | Learning. Com*, n.d.).

First and foremost, computer literacy allows you to inform yourself as a user on what the threats are such as phishing scams, malware types, identity theft among many other things. If people know what those threats are, we can become better at protecting ourselves. For instance, one with computer knowledge is more likely to be able to identify a possible harmful email or link and thus lessen the chances of falling into traps that put their identities at risk. This is one of the means to stay healthy as mental wellness also requires online safety. Also, computer literacy allows people to use the privacy settings effectively and safety features. A lot of online platforms do provide those options in their settings to allow users dictate who sees what and how it is shared. Computer literate people are able to go into these settings and tailor their privacy preferences very simply. This power return over personal information is necessary, especially for those in the vulnerable position of seeking help with mental health problems. Knowing that their data is secure plays a role in whether users use online mental health resources, to educate themselves about your own suffering or symptoms of someone else's — as well with the community and also professionally (Li & Liu, 2021).

In addition, being computer literate also means understanding how to behave responsibly online and as such keeps the digital world a more pleasant place for us all. Those who recognize the value of being polite and compassionate—even online —will retaliate against aggression less often (and therefore be bullied so-to-speak) The awareness of another, nurtured in computer literacy contributes to these safe spaces where they engage with work-family-colleagues and can openly discuss mental health issues without risking victimisation or discrimination. Finally, computer literacy enables people to exploit the plethora of mental health and other well-being/informational resources available online. There are any number of apps that allow you to track your mood and practice mindfulness, as well websites with resources and support for anyone who knows their way around a computer. This in particular is an important factor for those that may not have a support system around them or would rather quietly seek help. It could inform people where to get help, so they receive the professional support that keeps their mental health from deteriorating even further (Jæger, 2021).

3.3. Understanding Safe Online Behaviour

Understanding cybersecurity is essential in a digital world and forms the basis of mental health to some extent starting from computer literacy today. Computer Literacy is the knowledge and ability to use computers and the Internet effectively. Several factors in relation to mental wellness play into this. Computer literacy also allows them to avoid common online threats like phishing scams, malware and identity theft. If people learn what these threats are and how they operate, because when that happens, they become more solvable. Someone who can identify a strange email or link is less likely to be scammed and thus, their personal information be released. This sort of awareness helps to provide security in online spaces and these are important aspects when dealing with good mental health. It can help you access privacy measures and security settings in social media, as well in other online platforms. Almost every online service or app includes privacy settings that grant users some say over who can see their information and how it can be passed along. This familiarizes the user with these tools and allows them to customize their privacy settings in a way that make sense for them. With the control in possession of personal data, people feel secure on sharing such kind of records especially when they are suffering from mental health issues. Making the online space safe for sharing experiences is important in allowing individuals to become actively engaged with resources and community support related to their mental health (*Understand the Importance of Cyber Security: Guardian Against Threats!*, n.d.).

In addition, computer literacy develops responsibility to resources on the Internet. Those online go through their days in a mad rush to ensure that cyberspace is an endless array of respectful communication; by doing so, these people shall be saved from either bullying or being bullied. With computer literacy, we make safe online spaces for discussions of mental health that do not become judgmental or persecuted by promoting a culture of kindness and support. Finally, when people are computer literate, they usually have access to numerous mental resources that can be accessed online. There are loads of different apps and websites available for info as well as support to manage your mental health, also offering mood trackers or mindfulness exercises. The resources are easy for people with experience using computers to access and use, which may be helpful when an individual lacks a local support system or does not wish to disclose having the need of help from others (*Cyberbullying: What Is It and How to Stop It | UNICEF*, n.d.).

This means that computer literacy is crucial to keeping humans sane — literally; Being able to function in the online world puts practically every resource needed for mental well-being at our fingertips. Those with a familiarity of computers can help keep themselves safe online, and they provide an example to others as they fully utilize privacy settings encouraging positive behaviour while seeking support for mental health. Computer literacy will continue to be among the most important skills for everyone as technology continues to advance, so remember that especially if you want a higher quality of life in this digital age (*The Importance of Digital Literacy in the Modern World | by Gary A. Fowler | Medium*, n.d.).

4. COLLABORATIVE MODELS OF CARE

4.1. Involvement of Mental Health Providers

Collaborative efforts for identifying and preventing online child abuse should include the mental health providers due to psychosocial consequences of such trauma in children. Some collaborative models, such as I described in my previous Psychology Today blog (here), spread the work among a variety of professionals—

educators, social workers and law enforcement officers even mental health specialists. This is a multi-disciplinary process which helps to consider all of the things that we know are important in relation child development and therefore due respect for the multiple dimensions associated with online abuse. Behavioural changes, anxiety, depression or social isolation are all signs mental health providers can identify as displaying early development of emotional distress in children that needs to be treated promptly if observed. Individuals with mental health expertise can provide important intervention and tools needed for assisting children who have been exposed to online abuse, particularly if they are able to embed within current frameworks. This can help to support healing through work on the child's self-esteem and teaching of coping strategies, while providing a safe environment for expression of their feelings with someone who is not directly involved (Yu et al., 2023).They advocate for evidence-based, strategic approaches to mental health in child protection by partnering with policy makers and community based-groups. That's not only responsive to the psychological states of the affected children, but also preventative and proactive, trend sparking protection against such related incidents on online platforms (Walsh et al., 2022).To add relevance for the higher levels of intervention, particularly for detection and prevention around online child abuse, the involvement of mental health services in collaboration enables greater effectiveness of care models across an extensive locus of outcomes. And by strengthening the mental health emphasis in these models, they weave together holistic models that comprehend the multifaceted intersection between emotional well-being and trauma recovery, which in themselves set the standard for child-friendly online platforms (Leo et al., 2024; Walsh et al., 2022).

4.2. Role of Technologists and Educators

It takes a coalition across regions and sectors to combat online child abuse — from technologists to educators and beyond it. Technologists have a huge role to play both in building new tools, and new strategies, and implementing them in meaningful ways to make children safer online. In particular, through the development of smart technologies which deploy advanced algorithms to signal flashing signs of abusive content (chat monitoring systems and/or filtering technologies) or excessive predatory behaviour in unhealthy interactions. AI (artificial intelligence) and machine learning is a boon, giving technologists the ability to make systems that can learn over time as well, improving their detection rates for new trends in online abuse, lending effectiveness to an outlet for paranoia. More importantly, they must also make sure that these tools are easy to use and user-friendly enabling them at educational settings as well as home-based applications (*Tech Industry and Researchers Come Together to Tackle Online Child Sexual Exploitation and*

Abuse – Safe Online, n.d.). With the help of technologists, educators make use of technology-driven platforms and educational apps to interact children via multimedia ways and teach them about safety in a very creative manner according to every age group(*The Role of Schools in Promoting Online Safety | Learning.Com*, n.d.).In addition, joint initiatives between technologists and educators can result in the creation of an all-encompassing training program for teachers — as well as staff too. This training, in turn can teach educators how to spot the signs of online abuse and educate them about potential technological solutions. This is the status of a culture that, exercising awareness and vigilance with every level in educational institutions can come to significantly decrease it (*The Importance ofTeacher Training Programs in Transforming Education - EdIndia*, n.d.).

The collaboration of technologists with educators can also be expanded to build safer online learning spaces. The need for securing children in their educational activities comes as more and more learning events are held digitally. Educators also need to ensure they lead by example whilst teaching students how technology can be used responsibly in an educational context and where threats may occur from some external influences that might put the children at risk.

The model of technology-developers working with teachers, is successful in alerting and helping to prevent online child abuse as well as educating kids on how they can operate safely. Such a holistic approach is necessary to build community resilience and engagement around protecting kids online (Lee & Hancock, 2023).

3.1. Cybersecurity Measures for Mental Wellness

Cybersecurity supports psychological warmth by ensuring the protection and private access to various corners of internet. That alone is a major point in protecting personal stuff, particularly when it comes to private medical data (psycho-social related). Examples of this include data encryption, which obfuscates information so only the intended people can read it; secure databases where your personal health data is stored and all privacy settings that make sure none but not healthcare providers get to have access. People will feel comfortable using online resources for their mental health if they know that their details are safe and secure, not leaking out in the ether (*The Role of Cybersecurity in Mental Well-Being*, n.d.).

. Providing mental health space within cybersecurity education means individuals are even less likely to panic when it comes to saving face (*Cyber Security in Action: Safeguarding the Youth from Cyberbullying*, n.d.).

4.3. Partnership with Cybersecurity Professionals

In creating security protocols for online services children use, from social media to educational tools and gaming environments. Cybersecurity experts can detect vulnerabilities in these platforms by performing risk assessments and penetration testing, leading to the enhancement of safety functions. To give another example, they might build next generation monitoring systems that identify harmful actions or speech as it occurs and intervene to prevent harm. Cybersecurity professionals can also help with the development of reporting functions which will allow children and their parents to report anything they think is wrong in an efficient manner without unnecessary obstacles. You will also work with cyber security professionals on training and awareness engagements. Conducting workshops and providing resources to educate educators, parents, and children on online safety signals & dangers as well cybersecurity hygiene will have a broad impact. The startup is on a mission to educate, encouraging conversation online and in the real-world so that every kid can grow up healthy with digital (*Why Collaboration Is Essential for Cybersecurity Teams*, n.d.).

Secondly, these partnerships are extremely important in influencing policy and best practices within organizations. Collaborative online safety policy Involving cybersecurity professionals will help in creating a wider and more all-inclusive perspective on digital interactions that would mean the standards and understanding of response, intervention can be much clearer. In collaboration with law enforcement, educators and mental health practitioners, they can develop strategies to stop kids from being harmed online while also safeguarding their rights.

So, key take away will be with in partnership cybersecurity expert to make digital world safer for children. A multi-faceted strategy for the detection and prevention of online child abuse thanks to their identification, protective technology development, and awareness raising powers. In order to create a structure that can both respond and prepare, we have to bring together the best aspects of tech companies — their creative minds who never stop pushing for tools that better themselves — with educators, mental health providers and all those within a community (whether school or otherwise) whose heart is in reducing abuse (Rawindaran et al., 2023).

5. CYBER GUARDIANS AND CHILD PROTECTION

5.1. Definition and Importance of Cyber Guardians

Cyber guardians are also called protectors or overseers before guarding virtual spaces while helping protect the use of and preventing dangerous online exchanges for kids. These are the users or organizations who protect young people from exploitation bullying etc. That is, cyber guardians using tools including parental control software, filtering and digital literacy education are an integral part of the ecosystem that provides for a safe cyberspace for children. Cyber guardians are described as those who tend to be more in the fray and protect children within digital landscapes. This could include parents, teachers, cops, tech companies and cyber safety experts...that is, those responsible in keeping an eye out for kids about to step into what is arguably the most dangerous place beneath today's sun (*Cyberbullying (for Teens)*, n.d.).

5.1.1 Importance of Cyber Guardians in Child Protection

1.Protecting Children from Cyberbullying and Harassment: By acting as cyber guardians for children, parents can keep an eye on their online activity to make sure they have never take the fall over missed opportunities that could potentially cause emotional or psychological damage. A recent study revealed that children being cyberbullied were more likely to suffer from anxiety, depression and other forms of mental health distress.

2.Preventing Exploitation and Grooming: Cyber predators might try to groom the children as their peers or trusted adults. Cyber guardians can be used to supervise as well as counsel children on how to recognize online predators for what they are, report suspicious behaviour and also reminding them the importance of cyber boundaries thus minimizing chances of grooming.

3.Promotion of Digital Literacy and Safety Practices: Educating all the children regarding digital literacy enables cyber guardians to train children on how to identify and avoid online risks, understand privacy concerns, and navigate the online world more safely. Educating a child through safe online practices, strong passwords, and avoiding phishing spells real empowerment for him or her in cyberspace.

4.Facilitation of Mental Health and Emotional Support: The cyber guardian is more able to identify behaviour that may provoke apprehension regarding the behaviour of certain children, such as withdrawal or unusual interactions, and may offer more concrete help in the matter. Cyber guardians are effectively intervening before problems spiral out of control, establishing themselves as critical players in securing children's mental health at the present digital age (*How to Prevent Cyberbullying (for Parents),* n.d.).

5.2. Identifying and Preventing Online Child Exploitation

Sexual exploitation of children online is a broad category that covers a wide range of behaviours and situations. This broadly includes grooming, live streaming, child sexual abuse material consumption, and coerced and blackmailed children. These will include:

The child involved into conversations about sexual acts by an adult Sending nude or pornographic images to children or exposing themselves via live streaming, asking a child to view pornographic images/videos. Asking a child to perform sexual acts, expose themselves or share a sexual image. Taking or making and sharing or showing indecent images of children. Online child sexual exploitation is considered something that occurs generally with adults abusing children; however, increasingly there has been research that demonstrates that the child exploitation material which is shared is one that emerges through social media-irrespective of the fact that it is actually child-produced. Sometimes these are called self-generated sexual content, and they are mostly in the form of 'sexting,' which is requesting, capturing some bits or series of explicit material from each other. A child may be or feel pressured, forced or coerced into taking and sharing these explicit images with their peers or friends(*What Is Online Child Sexual Exploitation?,* n.d.).

5.2.1 Preventing Online Child Exploitation

UNICEF, the Child Fund and other groups lead the charge on community-based approaches and digital literacy to tackle online abuse. First is the strengthening of regional child protection systems and internet safety messaging for children to include emerging threats online to child exploition, such as deep-fake technologies and online grooming that would make children more vulnerable to exploitation. Additionally, this creates a space for children on the internet, wherein, UNICEF promotes the advancement of child protection online for children through advocacy for accountability within the government and collaboration with tech businesses focused around the same theme on the platform. Legal reform and global advocacy go hand in hand with global initiatives working together to eliminate exploitation. Nonprofit organizations advocate for safe online practices while putting corporate responsibility in the limelight with the 2023 initiative of Child Fund's #TakeItDown campaign. In the U.S., the push from the Kids Online Safety Act aims to set up the safer internet norms for the younger audience. Go through these resourceful campaigns and educational resources for ways to stay informed (Nations, n.d.).

5.3. The Role of Technology and Law Enforcement

India and the United States faced high rates of cybercrime last year. More than 3.13 million cyber incidents occurred in India in 2019. After the pandemic, online activities increased leading to a rise in cyber crimes. Indian laws identify four main types of cybercrime targeting children: child trafficking, cyberbullying, pornography, & identity theft. The government has implemented laws to tackle cybercrime. These include the Information Technology Act of 2000 and the Indian Penal Code of 1860. In 2008 the law related to information technology was updated. Several parts of the Information Technology (Amendment) Act of 2008 were revised to address new challenges arising from the increasing digital information and rise of cybercrime. The Information Technology Act of 2000 outlines penalties for knowingly allowing a computer virus to compromise a system or network under Section 43. Section 43A deals with compensation for data breaches.

6. UNDERSTANDING ONLINE CHILD ABUSE

6.1. Forms of Online Child Abuse

1. Child Sexual Exploitation (CSE) and Abuse Material

Involves sharing, production, and consumption of sexual images or videos involving children, typically referred to as child sexual abuse material (CSAM).

2. Online Grooming

Online grooming refers to the act of an adult rapport-building with a child for sexual exploitation, e.g., coaxing the child into production of pornographic material.

3. Trafficking and Online Recruitment for Exploitation

There are many forms of exploitation for which many children, mostly in developing nations, are groomed and recruited online-these include labour, sex, and other kinds of exploitation trafficking.

4. Cyberbullying and Harassment

Cyberbullying includes making nasty or threatening comments, igniting rumours, or engaging in any other conduct that might trigger psychological damage to children.

6.2. Innovative Detection Approaches

1.Artificial Intelligence/ Machine Learning

Approach: AI algorithms-which include machine learning, natural language processing, and computer vision-are used to detect behaviours in online data that might signal child exploitation. AI is able to recognize grooming language, abusive images, and suspicious behaviour all in real-time

2.Facial Recognition and Age Estimation

Approach: Facial recognition algorithms in combination with age estimation allow platforms to know if a user in an image or video is a child, helping in identifying illegal content.

3.Behavioral Analysis and Sentiment Analysis

Approach: Patterns of online behaviour and sentiment analysis algorithms can identify grooming, coercion, or predatory patterns therein. These have come to rely on features involving language in use, relationship dynamics, and mood shifts.

4.Internet of Things (IoT) and Wearable Tech Monitoring

Approach: The ethical, secure integration of IoT devices and wearable technology provides deep behavioural insights into children's digital circumstances, thereby alerting parents or guardians to potential dangers.

6.3. Tools and Technologies for Protection

1.Qustodio

Highly ranked on several platforms, this software is pricier than some but delivers when it comes to controls and safety. With the ability to block and limit inappropriate content, games, and apps, monitor social media, manage screen time, and track location, your bases are covered.

2.Kaspersky

In addition to block contents, this online safety tool also blocks harmful YouTube search queries, screen time, games, and apps. It is worth noticing that it reviews only the activities carried out on Facebook with several expert recommendations from child psychologists on various online issues.

3.Net Nanny

While it does not monitor activity on social media, there is certainly a plethora of support given in parental controls and basic stuff, like the ability to set screen-time limitations, an internet filter, and the ability to block apps and websites on a pornographic basis and thus very efficient. Alerts and such activity are reported in a daily feed which can be viewed on any browser.

4.Mobicip

With Mobicip, you can monitor all devices from one app, block and lock devices at a moment's notice, analyse one month of Internet browsing history, block websites by category, permit or block the use of social media apps, games, video-streaming apps, and sites. However, it doesn't permit monitoring of social media.

5.Circle

The Circle Home Plus is a one-of-a-kind cube-sized device which works with your Wi-Fi connection to control each and every device on your home network. The control takes place through an app and comes with a subscription plan-a monthly subscription for three months, one year, or for a lifetime. Choose filters for each device according to the age, track history or pause internet access. Circle also offers a reward-setting to allow for more screen time. It also enables location tracking.

6.WebSafety

This uni-dimensional software monitors rather than blocks web content. Parents receive real-time alerts on their phones whenever their children visit an inappropriate website, or when new apps are downloaded or concerning topics or words are mentioned in an SMS. If a photo is uploaded on an active social network, the parent is alerted with perspectives on the posting and the comments track. Screen time curfew and lock-the-device capability are available with very instantaneous, location-tracking devices and geo-fencing.

7. THE POWER OF SOCIAL MEDIA IN ADDRESSING ABUSE

7.1. Social Media as a Monitoring Tool

Social media platforms are an essential mechanism to detect, monitor and respond towards online child abuse. Social networks are now home to millions of kids, interacting on a daily basis and these platforms have started to deploy sophisticated detection technologies designed not only for detecting abuse such as adult content or grooming behaviours but also devices that can look at micro-contextualized messaging suggesting exploitation attitudes.

7.1.1 Reporting Mechanisms and Support

With the development of modern technology, social media platforms are becoming increasingly aware and attempting to take responsibility in reducing potential impacts on children by providing reporting mechanisms and advice lines. This is why reporting mechanisms are important; they enable users, including kids and their parents or guardians, to flag inappropriate content which may contain abusive behaviour for review by teams of moderators that work around the clock reviewing this type of harmful material. Several social media networks have also made the reporting process simpler, allowing to quickly and anonymously report inappropriate concerns by children or those who care for them. These streamlined pathways are vital for minimizing harms, where rapid action e.g. removal of content, suspension or escalation to law enforcement as appropriate can prevent continued deleterious effects on victims within the platform environment.

8. INNOVATIONS FOR A SAFER ONLINE ENVIRONMENT

8.1. The Role of Machine Learning in Content Moderation

Machine learning (ML) has tremendously transformed content moderation using technology to identify and manage harmful content in online channels, enabling safer environments for general internet users, especially the younger ones. More and more social media sites are using machine learning (ML) algorithms specifically developed to identify, classify and in some cases automatically censor or flag abusive content–and particularly content that exploits children. These systems use sophisticated tools in natural language processing (NLP), pattern recognition, and computer vision to analyze huge volumes of data quicker and more accurately than human moderation ever could.

Computer Vision algorithms help identify images/videos and are essential to detect this harmful text (images). Such algorithms are trained to analyse images and visuals according to some set of visual hints which hint at explicit or abusive material. For example, computer vision models can check for scenes or actions known to correlate in child abuse content even with poor lighting and low-resolution images. They also classify content by how offensive it is, which differentiates between explicit materials and sexually suggestive ones that can separate nudity from pornography — important factors for deciding the priority of a case to be considered by a team member. ML also aids in content moderation by learning from new forms of abuse being conducted on the platform. Machine learning systems can be re-trained on new data as the attackers find ways to bypass previous filters, and keep catching them despite emerging threats. The capacity of ML models to bend and move, tuning their strategies on-the-fly is — especially in the context of online child abuse detection where we can never truly appreciate what our age will be tomorrow or denounce definitively a trend past or present1— crucial advantage for staying out ahead. In general, ML in content moderation is enhancing the power of protection against online child abuse and dangerous contents. By leveraging automation, these tools move some of the burden away from manual review so that human moderators remain more sane and can intervene faster. Due to this capability, ML tools also become a handy tool in flagging and even blocking harmful content before it disseminates across the audience making online environment safe for users especially people like children (*Parents, Caregivers, Teachers — FBI*, n.d.).

8.2. Mobile Applications for Immediate Support

Mobile applications offer important functionalities to find and end online child abuse quickly by affording instant access to resources, support and options for victims alongside immediate reporting channels for parents/caregivers. These apps do so many great things like giving direct reporting avenues a place online abuse, and the ability for people to anonymously report inappropriate content, harassment or exploitation. In this way, children are able to combat abuse without the fear of repercussions. In addition, several applications offer educational information (articles/writing resources), some of which are in the form videos or interactive content to educate viewers about what online abuse is; how best practices for using the internet work; when signs of abuse can be recognised and practical coercion understood. Mobile apps allow users to report and to educate themselves with access of support services (counselling) for immediate assistance. It could include chat support, video calls with counsellors or simply a panic button to dial emergency services immediately. Moreover, in-app safety features like privacy settings, content filters and parental controls can work to change the parenting landscape too by providing an opportunity for parents to supervise their children's online activities thus helping them mitigate exposure of unsolicited materials. Others also include a community component to provide that additional bit of prodding from peer support groups or online forums, where users have similar experiences and offer advice. But current implementation of mobile applications is not trouble free as well. Data Privacy is at the heart of everything what we are doing; whenever, you collate any information from user side, it become very risky during child and vulnerable age group. They must account for regulations such as COPPA and implement strong data protection. Even the owners of these applications have only basic skills in information technologies and donations or have governmental funding for building and maintaining.

8.3 Technologies for Data Protection and Security

With the rise of social platforms, online predators and cyber threats have become a growing concern for children, a matter that can only be resolved by prioritizing concerns about data privacy and security as technology evolves. Centres key recommendations include for the tech industry to adopt end-to-end encryption in all forthcoming messaging as well as social media platforms so that future communications are kept secure. This tech ensures that only the intended receivers have access to these messages and in this way it protects children on their manner of conversation. Moreover, recent privacy laws and technologies favouring data minimization seek to constrain third-party platforms access only the personal information essential to deliver their services. This approach provides higher privacy for minors and reduces the risk of your data being manipulated, creating a safer cyber world (*Enhancing Online Platforms Safety*, n.d.).

9. STRATEGIES FOR PREVENTION AND PROTECTION

9.1. Cyber Awareness Programs

Cybersecurity awareness is education and training of employees on dangers in cyberspace, what might prevent them, and how they would react when they experience a security threat. It in stills sense in them about proactive responsibilities concerning the company and the safekeeping of its assets and resources. In simple terms, it means knowing what type of security threats exist and responding responsibly to avoid possible risks. Cybersecurity awareness refers to the knowledge about the latest security threats, the best practices of cybersecurity, and This keeps them informed concerning cyber-risks your business is exposed to daily; how these risks impact on your business; and individual and collective roles and responsibilities as regards the safety and security of digital assets. A cyber awareness program aims to educate the individual and organizations on cyber threats and promote best practices for online safety. The application is intended to familiarize the non-technical people with areas like phishing and malware, just so they are aware of what some common threats look like and can respond appropriately. They reduce opportunities for a breach and protect information from sensitive to confidential, while cultivating security awareness in an organization or community. Moreover, they endorse behaviour and remained constant in the ever growing digital space(*7 Reasons Why Security Awareness Training Is Important*, n.d.).

9.2. Parental Control and Education

Parental control software will help a parent track what their child can see and do online. Some of the ways this would help a parents to secure children:

1. **Block access:** block some particular web sites or apps and also functionality
2. **Filtering content:** filter out a particular type of content or material from the list to include adult material, social media content, suicidal related content, violent, alcohol, etc.
3. **Limited communication:** Parents can limit whom they can communicate with their child and manage the application on which they use to communicate. Tracking their child's usage on those connected devices, say parents. This includes all sites, apps used, frequency and time spent.
4. **Setting time limits:** Parents can set time limits and block access after some time.
5. **Geolocation:** Parents may check the geolocation feature where they can trace a device location.
6. **Configuration protection:** The parent can enable the configuration protection that disables all unwanted changes to the parental control settings.

That in effect, proactively protecting their children from cyberthreats like cyberbullying as well as harmful content that eventually fosters open conversation and more confidence on kids while trying to explore the Internet with security. This at long last boils down to encouraging healthy, secure and sensible internet use by responsible means of parental controls. But this is not enough; education is essential. Parents should continue discussing online safety issues with their children and how to avoid phishing scams, cyberbullying, and respect for privacy. Having a discussion like this will lead children to the right decisions and good online behaviour. When used hand in hand, this creates a web of strengthening forms of parental guidance and education that would keep kids safe in this digital world while also giving them the knowledge and tools to deal with this new world responsibly and safely(*Parental Controls | How to Keep Your Child Safe*, n.d.).

9.3. Community Engagement and NGO Collaborations

In cybersecurity, working with communities and NGOs is essential to generate awareness, resilience, and professionalism against the digital threats. As cyber threats become more sophisticated, far too many communities are vulnerable because they lack the awareness and resources. Such challenges need to be tackled by NGOs actively campaigning and mobilizing community efforts to create programs and projects that empower citizens and organizations to protect their digital domains.

1. **Raising Awareness:** Perhaps one of the more important roles NGOs can play in the space of cybersecurity is to raise awareness of potential threats. Workshops, seminars, and community events are some ways to educate people about common cyber-risks such as phishing, ransomware, and social engineering attacks. By making clear these threats, NGOs can encourage members of the community to better understand the importance of cybersecurity, as well as the measures they can take to protect themselves.
2. **Training and Skill Development:** In addition to awareness programs,NGOs can also provide training programs that help community members gain cybersecurity skills. These can span everything from basic digital hygiene to training in what it takes to build careers in cybersecurity for those who aspire to. Basic cybersecurity training like how to secure their personal devices or identify phishing is important in giving participants hands-on skills they can apply in daily life. Providing tools such as checklists as well as best practice guides can supplement what they have learned and help people put that knowledge to use.
3. **Collaboration with Local Organizations:** NGOs can work with local organisations such as schools, libraries and community centres, in order to increase their impact. It is by forming joint activities that they can promote digital literacy among certain audiences that may be more at risk to these threats. For instance, interventions focused on older individuals can address their specific challenges, while interventions that are youth-based can focus on responsible online behaviour and the importance of privacy.
4. **Incident Response and Community Resilience:** Another essential field of engagement for NGOs is enhancing community resilience to cyber events. Community response teams can provide on call help during events of cybersecurity incident, enabling victims and organizations to better deal with aftereffects

of cybercrime. Such teams can also facilitate the sharing of information about current threats and proven prevention measures." NGOs can also create a synergy between local organizations by being part of a network where non-profits share knowledge and experiences that lead to a global picture of cyber security issues.

In conclusion, Engagement with communities and partnership with NGOs working in cybersecurity are key to creating a resilient digital ecosystem. Through awareness, training, partnerships and policy advocacy, NGOs can empower communities to protect themselves from cyber threats. Such collaborations not only address pressing cybersecurity challenges but also help establish long-term resilience, making both people and institutions better prepared to navigate an evolving digital frontier. By continuing to have a hand in it, communities can create safer online transactions that build trust and safety (*Increased Cybersecurity Essential For NGOs: Help Available*, n.d.).

10. FUTURE DIRECTIONS AND INNOVATIONS

10.1. Emerging Technologies for Child Safety

A frequency and complexity are on the higher end of the spectrum for cyber threat occurrence in modern times. This implies the need for people and their various organizations to be very sophisticated with the advanced technologies associated with Cybersecurity; with this, they would defeat many of these threats effectively to protect sensitive data. This is because there always surfacing new threats day to day.

Some of the Advanced Cybersecurity Technologies Include:

1. **Artificial Intelligence and Machine Learning:** The most significant contributors to this revolution in cybersecurity are Artificial Intelligence and Machine Learning. The technologies analyse a great deal of data, learn from patterns, and create predictions about the threats that might arise. With such technologies, the experts in cyber security will be able to identify and respond to threats much faster and accurately.
2. **Internet of Things Security:** Internet-connected devices that are being employed in more and more domestic and commercial households are highly exposed to various cyberattacks, which might be the beginning of significant calamities. Their security features include encryption access controls, and monitoring devices for secure IoT data as well.

3. **Blockchain:** Even though most people associate this term with cryptocurrencies, it also has a lot of potential to revolutionize cybersecurity. It allows for safe storage for sensitive information by designing a decentralized database. Hackers will find it very hard to get unauthorized access because they have no authority in the control of data in such databases.

10.2. Revolutionizing Prevention Methods

Zero Trust Architecture: A model where "never trusts, always verifies." In this case are the organizations admitting that there can be outside threats, (and god forbid), inside threats as well, and organizations are moving towards more stringent access control and continuous verification to address the risks.

1. **AI and Machine Learning:** It refers to using advanced algorithms at the back end examining copious amounts of data such that certain patterns or unusual behaviours in the analysis can recognize possible cyber threats. This also allows for proactive detection and response mechanisms, as well as leverage with detecting an attack before it has already happened.
2. **Behavioural Analytics:** This allows tracking of user behaviour and definition of baselines of normal activity, therefore helping them spot patterns that would indicate security breaches. This improves the ability to identify threats and reduce false positives.
3. **Automated Threat Intelligence:** Automation makes the collection and analysis of threat intelligence easier, keeping organizations ahead of emerging threats. Real-time data sharing among platforms allows teams to act promptly on new vulnerabilities.
4. **Endpoint Detection and Response (EDR):** Solutions in the EDR domain provide continuous monitoring and endpoint response capabilities to help an organization identify and remediate threats as quickly as possible at the device level.
5. **Extended Detection and Response (XDR):** This is an integrated approach in which multiple security products are combined into one system for the provision of full visibility and response capabilities throughout the entire IT environment.

Cloud Security Posture Management As organizations continue to increasingly migrate to the cloud, CSPM tools will come in handy in managing and securing cloud environments through a continuous assessment of configurations, compliance, and vulnerabilities.

10.3. Building Safer Digital Spaces

Cyber security can be basic in designing a better space by protecting the system, network, and data that constitute our digital worlds. This will include stronger measures such as firewalls, encryption, and multi-factor authentications. User education should form an integral part of any cybersecurity initiative because it educates the personnel with all the information they need to spot phishing attempts and stick to best practices, thus making them protectors of the organization. Clearly stated cybersecurity policies define users' responsibilities and augment a security-aware culture.

11. CONCLUSION

11.1 Summary of Key Points

The chapter continues to draw existential connections between cyber security and mental wellbeing; it then elaborates its specific focus of online CSA in this context. This highlights how cyber threats — be they bullying and harassment, identity theft or data breaches — help lead to mental health problems such as depression for so many of their victims, and particularly for children. The emotional consequences of these threats only underscore the relevance of solutions like this awareness campaign. It comes in terms of effective cybersecurity measures and a strong digital education as to how we can safely navigate cyberspace — all of which as professionals and people we need to bring to the table to create a safer cyberspace. Additionally, collaborative care models are emphasized which would pave the way for mental health providers to work with other stakeholders such as- technologists, educators, and cybersecurity professionals to work on designing more secure deeper online spaces. They also explore the idea of cyber guardians and how these protectors can join up to battle child abuse on the internet. Having addressed social media in the previous chapter, we look at its potential for developing innovative detection methods, threat measures in combating online abuse or harassment, before considering its dual role as a monitoring mechanism and platform reporting units as discussed in some scholarly papers. Ultimately, it advocates for future innovations — the use of machine learning and mobile apps, for example — that could be optimized to make the digital landscape for children safer.

REFERENCES

Admass, W. S., Munaye, Y. Y., & Diro, A. A. (2024). Cyber security: State of the art, challenges and future directions. *Cyber Security and Applications*, 2, 100031. DOI: 10.1016/j.csa.2023.100031

Alabdulwahab, A., Haq, M. A., & Alshehri, M. (2023). Cyberbullying Detection using Machine Learning and Deep Learning. *International Journal of Advanced Computer Science and Applications*, 14(10), 424–432. DOI: 10.14569/IJACSA.2023.0141045

Albikawi, Z. F. (2023). Anxiety, Depression, Self-Esteem, Internet Addiction and Predictors of Cyberbullying and Cybervictimization among Female Nursing University Students: A Cross Sectional Study. *International Journal of Environmental Research and Public Health*, 20(5), 4293. DOI: 10.3390/ijerph20054293 PMID: 36901301

Alismaiel, O. A. (2023). Digital Media Used in Education: The Influence on Cyberbullying Behaviors among Youth Students. *International Journal of Environmental Research and Public Health*, 20(2), 1370. DOI: 10.3390/ijerph20021370 PMID: 36674128

Budimir, S., Fontaine, J. R. J., Huijts, N. M. A., Haans, A., Loukas, G., & Roesch, E. B. (2021). Emotional Reactions to Cybersecurity Breach Situations: Scenario-Based Survey Study. *Journal of Medical Internet Research*, 23(5), e24879. DOI: 10.2196/24879 PMID: 33978591

Cyber security in Action: Safeguarding the Youth from Cyberbullying. (n.d.). Retrieved December 31, 2024, from https://cxotoday.com/press-release/cyber-security-in-action-safeguarding-the-youth-from-cyberbullying/

Cyberbullying (for Teens) | Nemours KidsHealth. (n.d.). Retrieved December 31, 2024, from https://kidshealth.org/en/teens/cyberbullying.html

Cyberbullying - National Bullying Prevention Center. (n.d.). Retrieved December 31, 2024, from https://www.pacer.org/bullying/info/cyberbullying/

Cyberbullying: What is it and how to stop it | UNICEF. (n.d.). Retrieved December 31, 2024, from https://www.unicef.org/end-violence/how-to-stop-cyberbullying

Dealing with Bullying: Strategies to fight Teen Bullying. (n.d.). Retrieved December 31, 2024, from https://tooshytoask.org/help/personal-safety/cyber-bullying/

DeLiema, M., Burnes, D., & Langton, L. (2021). The Financial and Psychological Impact of Identity Theft Among Older Adults. *Innovation in Aging*, 5(4), igab043. Advance online publication. DOI: 10.1093/geroni/igab043 PMID: 34988295

Here's How You Can Take Action against Stalking in India. (n.d.). Retrieved December 31, 2024, from https://thebetterindia.com/45671/stalking-india-women-complaint-online/

How to Prevent Cyberbullying (for Parents) (for Parents) | Nemours KidsHealth. (n.d.). Retrieved December 31, 2024, from https://kidshealth.org/en/parents/cyberbullying.html

Importance of Digital Literacy Skills for Students | Learning.com. (n.d.). Retrieved December 31, 2024, from https://www.learning.com/blog/reasons-digital-literacy-is-important-for-students/

Increased Cybersecurity Essential For NGOs: Help Available. (n.d.). Retrieved December 31, 2024, from https://www.forbes.com/sites/davidhessekiel/2024/09/19/increased-cybersecurity-essential-for-ngos-help-available/

INHOPE - Association of Internet Hotline Providers | Enhancing Online Platforms Safety Tools for a Child-centred Digital Future. (n.d.). Retrieved December 31, 2024, from https://inhope.org/EN/articles/enhancing-online-platforms-safety-tools-for-a-child-centred-digital-future

Iwaya, L. H., Babar, M. A., Rashid, A., & Wijayarathna, C. (2022). On the privacy of mental health apps: An empirical investigation and its implications for app development. *Empirical Software Engineering*, 28(1), 2. DOI: 10.1007/s10664-022-10236-0 PMID: 36407814

Jæger, B. (2021). Digital Citizenship – A Review of the Academic Literature. *Der Moderne Staat – Zeitschrift Für Public Policy, Recht Und Management, 14*(1), 24–42. DOI: 10.3224/dms.v14i1.09

Lee, A. Y., & Hancock, J. T. (2023). Developing digital resilience: An educational intervention improves elementary students' response to digital challenges. *Computers and Education Open*, 5, 100144. DOI: 10.1016/j.caeo.2023.100144

Leo, M., Bourke-Taylor, H., Odgers, S., & Tirlea, L. (2024). Online interventions for the mental health and well-being of parents of children with additional needs: Systematic review and meta-analysis. *Australian Occupational Therapy Journal*, 1440-1630.13004. Advance online publication. DOI: 10.1111/1440-1630.13004 PMID: 39482259

Li, Y., & Liu, Q. (2021). A comprehensive review study of cyber-attacks and cyber security; Emerging trends and recent developments. *Energy Reports*, 7, 8176–8186. DOI: 10.1016/j.egyr.2021.08.126

Maurya, C., Muhammad, T., Dhillon, P., & Maurya, P. (2022). The effects of cyberbullying victimization on depression and suicidal ideation among adolescents and young adults: A three year cohort study from India. *BMC Psychiatry*, 22(1), 599. DOI: 10.1186/s12888-022-04238-x PMID: 36085004

Nations, U. (n.d.). *Child and Youth Safety Online | United Nations*. Retrieved December 31, 2024, from https://www.un.org/en/global-issues/child-and-youth-safety-online

Nixon, C. L. (2014). Current perspectives: The impact of cyberbullying on adolescent health. *Adolescent Health, Medicine and Therapeutics*, 5, 143. DOI: 10.2147/AHMT.S36456 PMID: 25177157

Parental controls | How to keep your child safe. (n.d.). Retrieved December 31, 2024, from https://www.esafety.gov.au/parents/issues-and-advice/parental-controls

Parents, Caregivers, Teachers — FBI. (n.d.). Retrieved December 31, 2024, from https://www.fbi.gov/how-we-can-help-you/parents-and-caregivers-protecting-your-kids

Peebles, E. (2014). Cyberbullying: Hiding behind the screen. *Paediatrics & Child Health*, 19(10), 527–528. DOI: 10.1093/pch/19.10.527 PMID: 25587229

Rawindaran, N., Jayal, A., Prakash, E., & Hewage, C. (2023). Perspective of small and medium enterprise (SME's) and their relationship with government in overcoming cybersecurity challenges and barriers in Wales. *International Journal of Information Management Data Insights*, 3(2), 100191. DOI: 10.1016/j.jjimei.2023.100191

7. *reasons why security awareness training is important*. (n.d.). Retrieved December 31, 2024, from https://www.cybsafe.com/blog/7-reasons-why-security-awareness-training-is-important/

Short, E., Guppy, A., Hart, J. A., & Barnes, J. (2015). The Impact of Cyberstalking. *Studies in Media and Communication*, 3(2). Advance online publication. DOI: 10.11114/smc.v3i2.970

Tech Industry and Researchers come together to tackle online child sexual exploitation and abuse – Safe Online. (n.d.). Retrieved December 31, 2024, from https://safeonline.global/tech-industry-and-researchers-come-together-to-tackle-online-child-sexual-exploitation-and-abuse

The Importance of Digital Literacy in the Modern World | by Gary A. Fowler | Medium. (n.d.). Retrieved December 31, 2024, from https://gafowler.medium.com/the-importance-of-digital-literacy-in-the-modern-world-e6913c09a2f8

The Importance of Teacher Training Programs in Transforming Education - EdIndia. (n.d.). Retrieved December 31, 2024, from https://edindia.org/the-importance-of-teacher-training-programs-in-transforming-education/

The Role of Cybersecurity in Mental Well-being. (n.d.). Retrieved December 31, 2024, from https://www.psychologs.com/the-role-of-cybersecurity-in-mental-well-being/?srsltid=AfmBOorkmzM1137wXVce3OowRoD2PPgtt6_HvUrc3vLDBAD2KAe-MCNt

The Role of Schools in Promoting Online Safety | Learning.com. (n.d.). Retrieved December 31, 2024, from https://www.learning.com/blog/role-of-schools-online-safety/

The Theory and Practice of Cyber-Mindfulness. (n.d.). Retrieved December 31, 2024, from https://www.annacollard.com/post/the-theory-and-practice-of-cyber-mindfulness

Understand the Importance of Cyber Security: Guardian Against Threats! (n.d.). Retrieved December 31, 2024, from https://www.simplilearn.com/tutorials/cyber-security-tutorial/what-is-cyber-security

Walsh, K., Eggins, E., Hine, L., Mathews, B., Kenny, M. C., Howard, S., Ayling, N., Dallaston, E., Pink, E., & Vagenas, D. (2022). Child protection training for professionals to improve reporting of child abuse and neglect. *Cochrane Database of Systematic Reviews*, 2022(7), CD011775. Advance online publication. DOI: 10.1002/14651858.CD011775.pub2 PMID: 35788913

Waterworth, J. A., Salamanca-Sanabria, A., Inkster, B., Knibbs, C., & Bada, M. (2023). Cybersecurity: A critical priority for digital mental health. *Frontiers in Digital Health*, 5, 1242264. DOI: 10.3389/fdgth.2023.1242264 PMID: 37781452

Watts, L. K., Wagner, J., Velasquez, B., & Behrens, P. I. (2017). Cyberbullying in higher education: A literature review. *Computers in Human Behavior*, 69, 268–274. DOI: 10.1016/j.chb.2016.12.038

What Is Identity Theft? Types and Examples. (n.d.). Retrieved December 31, 2024, from https://www.investopedia.com/terms/i/identitytheft.asp

What is online child sexual exploitation? | ACCCE. (n.d.). Retrieved December 31, 2024, from https://www.accce.gov.au/help-and-support/what-is-online-child-exploitation

Why Collaboration Is Essential for Cybersecurity Teams. (n.d.). Retrieved December 31, 2024, from https://gca.isa.org/blog/why-collaboration-is-essential-for-cybersecurity-teams

Yu, R., Perera, C., Sharma, M., Ipince, A., Bakrania, S., Shokraneh, F., Sepulveda, J. S. M., & Anthony, D. (2023). Child and adolescent mental health and psychosocial support interventions: An evidence and gap map of low- and middle-income countries. *Campbell Systematic Reviews*, 19(3), e1349. DOI: 10.1002/cl2.1349 PMID: 37621301

Zeanah, C. H., & Humphreys, K. L. (2018). Child Abuse and Neglect. *Journal of the American Academy of Child and Adolescent Psychiatry*, 57(9), 637–644. DOI: 10.1016/j.jaac.2018.06.007 PMID: 30196867

Chapter 14
Cyber Guardians:
An Insight Into Online Child Abuse Detection and Prevention in India

B. C. M. Patnaik
https://orcid.org/0000-0002-5979-0989
KIIT University, India

Ipseeta Satpathy
https://orcid.org/0000-0002-0155-5548
KIIT University, India

Vishal Jain
https://orcid.org/0000-0003-1126-7424
Sharda Unuiversity, India

ABSTRACT

The digital era has ushered in significant progress and conveniences for society, yet it has also paved the way for new avenues of criminal activities, such as online child abuse. India, with its extensive and expanding internet user base, encounters notable challenges in tackling online child abuse. For the purpose of this study, various parts of Odisha is considered for data collection. The respondents include the selected children, parents, and cyber experts (NGO personnel who are working to control this). As far as variables are concerned, core group discussion being done constituting various stake holders along with variables that are identified from the review of literature. The sample size is around 193 respondents and perception method is used, and data is calculated under five-point Likert type scale. The objectives of the current study are to study the awareness level of various child abuse dynamics associated with and to contribute in the in the existing literature.

DOI: 10.4018/979-8-3693-7758-1.ch014

INTRODUCTION

The phenomenon of cybercrime underscores the imperative to safeguard individual privacy and data integrity. This encompasses a range of issues, including hacking, malware distribution, identity theft, financial and medical fraud, as well as offenses targeting individuals through the misuse of personal information. The act of sharing messages, images, and recordings necessitates the explicit consent of the individuals involved. Cybercrime presents considerable threats to diverse populations, including the perpetrators themselves. Protecting children from the dangers of cybercrime is an urgent priority that warrants significant attention. Researchers engaged in the study of cybercrime encounter obstacles that extend beyond mere statistical analysis. Recent dialogues among scholars have indicated that conventional criminal justice publications are often reluctant to feature their research, frequently asserting that cybercrime lacks legitimacy as a crime and fails to engage a wide readership. In response, academics have started to incorporate references to federal and state legislation in their manuscripts to emphasize that the behaviors examined in their research are indeed unlawful and subject to legal repercussions. Nevertheless, many scholars continue to perceive their work as insufficiently recognized within traditional crime discourse, indicating a potential shift towards a greater emphasis on cybersecurity. Cybercrime represents a contemporary and intricate challenge within the broader context of cybersecurity.

The issue of violence against children is a significant global challenge that poses serious threats to their health and overall development. This violence can take multiple forms, including physical, sexual, and emotional abuse, as well as neglect. (WHO Global report, 2020) The repercussions of such violence are extensive, leading to a range of immediate and long-term health consequences, including increased mortality rates, cognitive impairments, and difficulties affecting both physical and mental health.(Norman et. al) In recent years, the rise of online child sexual exploitation and abuse (OCSEA) has emerged as a particularly alarming concern, driven by the growing prevalence of technological devices and Internet accessibility. (Ali.S et.al, 2023, Riberas-Gutiérrez, M et.al, 2023)

It is crucial to emphasize that the Internet itself is not the origin of these crimes; rather, the misuse of technological advancements has broadened the scope and capabilities of child sexual abuse on a larger scale (Henry, N et. Al, 2018) Young children and adolescents who engage with the Internet at an early age, possess personal devices such as smartphones and tablets, and exhibit increased online activity are particularly vulnerable to elevated online risks.(Açar, K.V, 2017). A recent study involving a nationally representative sample of 2,639 young adults found that 15.6% of participants reported experiencing historical incidents of online child sexual exploitation and abuse (OCSEA). This included various forms of abuse such as image-based sexual abuse (11.0%), self-generated child sexual abuse images (7.2%), non-consensual sexting (7.2%), online grooming by adults (5.4%), revenge pornography (3.1%), sextortion (3.5%), and online commercial sexual exploitation (1.7%) (Finkelhor, D et.al, 2022).

The reports a staggering 87% increase in the volume of child sexual abuse materials since 2019, as indicated by data from the National Center for Missing and Exploited Children (NCMEC). Concurrently, in certain nations, one in five children has fallen victim to online child sexual exploitation and abuse (OCSEA).(Kloess, J.A et.al, 2019) As new technologies emerge, offering innovative communication avenues, offenders adapt their strategies to perpetrate OCSEA. Various digital environments, such as social media platforms, peer-to-peer networks, online gaming sites, and the dark web, provide extensive venues for the distribution of harmful content, enabling perpetrators to identify and exploit their victims (Açar, K.V, 2017). A study analyzing transcripts of interactions between five offenders and their victims revealed that some perpetrators utilized subtle and complex tactics to establish relationships with minors, including the practice of online grooming (Fang, Z et.al, 2022).

REVIEW OF LITERATURE

Ruth Lewis articulated that due to instances of abuse, women who are both visible and audible highlight that cybercrime, which initially emerged as a new and democratic public sphere, now reflects the same gender disparities found in the offline realm. This observation is supported by the UK National Study on Experiences of Online Abuse among Women (Lewis, 2017).

Charu Nangia has conducted an analysis of the interplay between the constructed environment and crimes targeting children and women. The intelligent grid system is employed to enhance the management of various services associated with the built environment, including the operation of CCTV cameras, sensors, lighting, alarms, locks, and other database-related facilities (Nangia, 2019).

The research examines the past two years, during which the proliferation of the internet, the swift advancement of digital technologies, and the extensive use of social media have contributed to a notable rise in new forms of violence against children and women. This phenomenon is referred to as violence (Mamunur, 2019).

The paper has examined the evolution of information and communication technology, noting a global increase in the participation of both men and women in this emerging field, including in developing nations. This investigation provides a comprehensive analysis of "cyber violence against women and children." The findings aim to enhance public understanding of cyberbullying and explore potential strategies for its prevention. Nadeesha Adikari, (2016).

The study highlights the cyber-crimes that women face, revealing deficiencies in the current legal frameworks and policies within the Indian judicial system, as well as proposing measures to enhance safety against online harassment. Children often become vulnerable targets for various forms of cyber abuse, including online grooming, privacy violations, bullying, pornography, sexual harassment, morphing, and spoofing. The authors address several critical issues within the country, focusing on strategies to safeguard children from cybercrime, emphasizing the importance of legal support and the implementation of effective cyber laws. Debarati Halder, K Jaishankar, (2016).

The author examines how advancements in information technology and social networking platforms have facilitated new avenues for violence, particularly targeting children. Forms of this violence include cyberbullying, online harassment, cyber dating abuse, revenge porn, and cyberstalking. The concept of violence has been extensively explored in academic literature, and the initial research landscape concerning cyber violence has been evaluated, with recommendations for future inquiry provided. Existing studies indicate a plethora of definitions regarding the methods employed to visualize and quantify cybercrime-related violence (Emma Louise Backealter, 2018).

The research focused on the prevailing patterns of cybercrime, which predominantly involve offenses against individuals. Findings revealed that numerous underage girls and other child victims have tragically taken their own lives following the unauthorized dissemination of their private images and videos online. This raises the question of who constitutes the most vulnerable. Advocating against cybercrime and enhancing protective measures, alongside fostering global awareness of this issue, is crucial in addressing the persistent nature of cybercrime that impacts the state, individuals, and collective societal, mental, social, cultural, and economic stability, particularly for affected women (Natasha Kabir, 2018).

The overarching aim of this research is to enhance the formulation of cybersecurity legislation and regulatory frameworks in Kenya, thereby enabling women and children to exercise their right to freedom of expression without the threat of exploitation, harassment, or violence. This initiative seeks to foster a safe and secure societal environment. Specific objectives have been established to achieve this significant aim (Alice Munyua alter, 2010).

The paper reveals that cybercrimes are offenses that can only be perpetrated through computers, computer networks, or various forms of information technology. It aims to mitigate the proliferation of viruses, malware, hacking, and distribution attacks. The definition of these crimes is provided below. While they primarily target computer or network resources, such attacks can lead to numerous secondary repercussions (Mike McGuire and Samantha Dowling, 2013).

Furthermore, the study indicates that cyber violence associated with male pornography is closely correlated with attitudes that condone violence against women and children. A considerable number of researchers, practitioners, and policymakers contend that pornography constitutes a form of violence against women and children, rather than merely being a subject of academic inquiry or popular literature, particularly among students engaged in human sexuality and media studies. This calls for critical reflection on adult pornography and encourages individual actions to halt the production and consumption of harmful sexual media, including the darker aspects of the Internet (Walter DeKeseredy, 2015).

The research examines the existing literature on the influence of online forums within the context of cybercrime economics, highlighting a notable gap in the investigation of gender dynamics within these communities. This study focuses on the role of gender in cybercrime forums, employing a novel research methodology that integrates qualitative analysis with data science techniques to scrutinize a substantial dataset of forum posts. The results indicate that a specific segment of cybercriminal behavior is linked to these forums, where participants often express gender-related ideologies. The use of identity and misconceptions serves to rationalize one's standing within this subculture, with a tendency to internalize hacking as a masculine endeavor. These insights are considered in relation to their implications for policy development and intervention strategies aimed at lower-tier cybercrime communities. Mara Bada, (2009).

Researchers have made significant progress in elucidating the characteristics, prevalence, and dynamics of violence against women and children (VAWC), emphasizing the necessity for data to inform scientific inquiry and policy formulation. It is imperative to establish precise metrics to effectively quantify VAWC incidents and their repercussions. An interdisciplinary research consortium is essential to deepen the understanding of the intricate nature of VAWC. Beyond intervention and prevention strategies, there is a pressing need for a comprehensive agenda to rectify existing gaps and propel VAWC research forward. Catherine Kaukinen, (2018).

The research examined contemporary crimes against women and children, which have emerged as a significant issue affecting nations globally. Numerous countries are actively seeking to mitigate this challenge. Efforts are being made to implement measures aimed at curbing the increasing incidence of cyber crimes targeting women. Each year, a substantial volume of data is collected through crime reporting, which proves invaluable for crime analysis and contributes to preventive strategies. Analyzing crime statistics can reveal patterns, interconnected clues, and critical covert relationships among various offenses. Additionally, data mining methodologies can enhance our comprehension of these crime trends. Vivek Jaglan, (2007).

The paper highlighted that violence against women constitutes a breach of human rights and is not a recent occurrence. Throughout Indian history, this issue has manifested in various forms. Numerous feminists have advocated against such violence and sought to secure women's and children, rights within society; however, the plight of vulnerable women and their exploitation persists. The advent of the World Wide Web, mobile devices, and tablets has transformed women's lives significantly. While these technological advancements have brought considerable advantages, they have also introduced negative repercussions, notably the rise of cyber crime. Pooja Sangwan, (2019).

The study highlighted the overarching challenges encountered by individuals involved in cybercrime, as well as the awareness levels among the youth regarding these issues. This examination is characterized as a systematic distribution, encompassing a broad spectrum of concerns. The present paper utilizes both primary and secondary data sources. As digital citizens within the cyber realm, individuals inherently possess statistical information pertaining to their locations and activities, resulting in a compromise of privacy. This situation presents direct security challenges. At a macro level, the article conceptualizes the phenomenon of cybercrime among young people (Sanjesh Hamsa, 2018).

The author noted that women frequently serve as subjects in surveys concerning cyber victimization. The work titled Cybercrime and the Victimisation - Love, Rights and Regulations represents a significant contribution to the literature on cybercrime. It highlights various dimensions such as cybercrime, hacking, defamation, morphing, and electronic blackmail. These elements are intended to instill fear, exert control, and inflict harm, often perpetrated by criminals who evade identification or punishment for numerous reasons (Debarati Halder, 2012).

The research has examined the impact of advancing information and communication technologies, highlighting that these developments have significantly facilitated and accelerated our ability to communicate and exchange ideas and information. In the context of women's support services, it has been observed that the proliferation of these technologies has also led to their misuse as tools of oppression against women. Furthermore, the internet and social media platforms have increasingly become spaces where women experience feelings of insecurity and vulnerability, as noted by Jessica West (2014).

The paper focused on the application of data mining technology for fraud detection, aiming to establish a model for identifying scams and elucidating the mechanisms behind their creation. This challenge extends beyond merely curtailing fraudulent activities; it also encompasses the imperative of apprehending such activities promptly. Data mining techniques are distinct from traditional learning methods and are specifically tailored to identify ambiguous claims. This approach is predominantly employed in various sectors, including healthcare, insurance, and e-commerce, as discussed by K. Chithra Lekha and S. Prakasam (2018).

This research has conducted a systematic literature review focusing on the factors contributing to cybercrime. The objective of this study was to assess the extent of cybercrime, revealing that adolescents are particularly vulnerable to such offenses. Key factors identified as contributing to cyberbullying include negative attitudes, diminished self-control, psychological issues, bystander behavior, social disparities, excessive use of mobile devices and the Internet, as well as corruption within educational institutions. Notably, older individuals in society have been identified as perpetrators of online fraud (Israt Jahan, 2015).

Furthermore, the investigation has examined instances of copycat crimes, highlighting the significant influence of popular culture on specific criminal behaviors and incidents. Despite this, there remains a limited understanding of how copyright issues intersect with criminal conduct. The study emphasizes the importance of popular culture as a catalyst for criminal behavior and its connection to copycat incidents, which may contribute to the normalization of offending behavior (Jacqueline Helfgott, 2015).

Objectives of the Study

To study the awareness level of various Child abuse dynamics associated with.
To contribute in the existing literature.

Scope of the Study

The current study is restricted to three major districts of the state such are Khordha, Cuttack and Ganjam areas of Odisha, India. The respondents mostly include children, parents and cyber experts, NGO personal who are working to control this. For the accuracy of data children between 13 to 17 age group only considered. The focus was basically on cyberbullying, cyber teasing, cyber stalking, cyber defamation, cyber trolling and preventive measures

METHODOLOGY

For the current study 8 focus group discussion were conducted consisting of 5 people in each group. Initially 44 attributes identified and after the discussions the number of attributes restricted to 38 only. This includes 8 attributes related to cyber bullying, 4 attributes under cyber teasing and 9 attributes under cyber stalking, 3 attributes related to cyber defamation, 4 attributes related to cyber trolling and 10 attributes related to cyber abuse preventions. The study employed a straightforward approach to calculate the scores for various child cyber abuses. This was done using a weighted mean method for the different sub-variables. To measure each perception attribute, a 5-point Rensis Likert type scale was utilized. The scoring system assigned a weight of 4 to responses indicating completely agree, a weight of 3 to responses indicating agree, a weight of 2 to neutral responses, a weight of 1 to do not agree, and a weight of 0 to responses indicating completely not agree. The mean score was calculated by summing the assigned weights (4+3+2+1+0) and dividing it by 5, resulting in a mean score of 2.

Sample Size Determination

According to Rummel's 1970 study and Schwab's 1980 research, a reasonable ratio for measuring sample size is between 1:4 and 1:10. The recommended approach suggests using a minimum sample size of four items and a maximum sample size of ten items. Applying this method to our study, since we have taken 28 items, the minimum and maximum sample sizes should be 152 and 380 respectively. Following the aforementioned guideline, we gathered 293 observations after eliminating the common outlier. Therefore, for this study, a sample size of 193 aligns with Rummel and Schwab's rule from 1970 and 1980.

Table 1. Sampling frame

Children	Parents	Cyber experts	NGOs
47	61	32	53

Cyberbullying

Cyberbullying refers to the act of disseminating negative, harmful, misleading, or derogatory information about individuals. This behavior also encompasses the sharing of personal or private details that may lead to embarrassment or humiliation for the affected parties. Such actions occur through various digital devices, including smartphones, computers, and tablets, utilizing platforms such as SMS, text messaging, applications, social media networks, online forums, and gaming environments where individuals can observe, engage with, or distribute content.

Cyber Teasing

Cyber teasing refers to a specific attitude, mindset, and behavioral pattern characterized by actions that are perceived as insulting and humiliating to the victim. Typically, this phenomenon manifests as the harassment of women by unknown individuals in public settings, such as streets and public transportation. However, when such acts are perpetrated through information and communication technologies (ICT), they are classified as Cyber Teasing.

Cyber Stalking

Cyberstalking refers to the utilization of Information and Communications Technology (ICT) to pursue, dominate, manipulate, or consistently intimidate individuals, whether they are minors, adults, or business entities. It represents both a method employed by online aggressors and a classification of individuals exhibiting psychopathological behaviors in their use of ICT. This phenomenon encompasses explicit or implicit threats of physical violence, ongoing monitoring, and the collection of information aimed at exerting influence and control over a victim.

Cyber Defamation

Cyber defamation refers to the dissemination of harmful or false statements about an individual through electronic means and the internet. When an individual shares defamatory remarks or transmits emails that contain such damaging content to others with the intent to harm the reputation of the victim, this behavior qualifies as cyber defamation.

Cyber Trolling

Cyber trolling refers to the intentional act of posting unsolicited and often contentious remarks across diverse online platforms, aimed at eliciting an emotional reaction from the audience. This engagement often leads to disputes or arguments, which may serve merely for entertainment purposes or for other particular advantages. In an era where virtually anyone can comment on social media updates, respond to tweets, participate in community discussions, or pose anonymous inquiries, the phenomenon of trolling has become ubiquitous in online interactions.

Table 2. Analysis of data

Weighted Average mean of various category of respondents					
Attributes	**Code**	**Children**	**Parents**	**Cyber experts**	**NGOs**
Cyberbullying					
Engaging in the dissemination of derogatory or demeaning content regarding an individual on digital platforms	CA1	3.34	3.54	3.59	3.47
Sharing a compromising or humiliating image or video of someone.	CA2	3.55	3.34	3.38	3.25
Fabricating a false online identity that impersonates another person	CA3	3.64	3.34	3.41	3.25
Issuing online threats that incite an individual to inflict self-harm or harm others.	CA4	3.38	3.48	3.16	3.40
Inciting animosity based on religious, racial, regional, ethnic, or political grounds through the publication of hateful remarks or materials	CA5	3.19	3.51	3.31	3.43
Exploiting another person's identity online to solicit or distribute personal, fabricated, or degrading information about them.	CA6	3.38	3.46	3.13	3.38
Continuously undermining a player's reputation, demanding financial compensation, colluding against a player, or leveraging personal information to issue direct threats.	CA7	3.17	3.40	3.56	3.30
Circulating narratives, images, jokes, or cartoons online that are designed to cause embarrassment or humiliation to others.	CA8	3.38	3.28	3.22	3.17
Cyber Teasing					
Social Media Platforms (such as Facebook, Instagram, Snapchat, Twitter, etc.)	CA9	3.34	3.34	3.38	3.43
SMS (text messages transmitted via cellular networks)	CA10	3.32	3.23	3.34	3.11
Instant Messaging Services (including WhatsApp, Facebook Messenger, and other similar platforms)	CA11	3.26	3.18	3.25	3.06
Electronic Mail (E-mail)	CA12	3.40	3.43	3.25	3.34
Cyberstalking					
Engaging in the act of leaving menacing or intimidating remarks in the guestbook, on the victim's website, social media accounts, or blog.	CA13	3.55	3.28	3.22	3.17
Dispatching inappropriate electronic greeting cards directed at the victim.	CA14	3.17	3.30	3.31	3.19
Publishing personal advertisements under the victim's name.	CA15	3.68	3.38	3.31	3.28

continued on following page

Table 2. Continued

Weighted Average mean of various category of respondents					
Attributes	**Code**	**Children**	**Parents**	**Cyber experts**	**NGOs**
Establishing websites, profiles, or other accounts that convey messages intended to threaten or harass the victim, or creating scenarios that suggest the victim is responsible for a particular website featuring provocative or pornographic content.	CA16	3.53	3.21	3.38	3.09
Utilizing hate speech, which encompasses language that belittles, insults, threatens, or targets an individual based on their identity and various characteristics, including sexual orientation, disability, or religion.	CA17	3.26	3.31	3.41	3.21
Gaining unauthorized access to the victim's email or social media accounts to obtain personal information, read communications, or alter passwords.	CA18	3.17	3.43	3.34	3.24
Assuming the victim's online identity with the intent to damage their reputation or interpersonal relationships.	CA19	3.23	3.30	3.47	3.19
Tracking the victim's movements through GPS, tracking applications, or spyware.	CA20	3.19	3.23	3.25	3.11
Placing orders for goods or services in the victim's name, which frequently includes subscriptions to adult content or the purchase of sex toys, with deliveries sent to the victim's workplace.	CA21	3.36	3.36	3.22	3.26
Cyber Defamation					
Disseminating disparaging comments about individuals or organizations on online platforms.	CA22	3.40	3.39	3.16	3.30
Sharing negative statements regarding individuals or organizations on social media and networking sites	CA23	3.38	3.46	3.44	3.23
Circulating misleading information about individuals or organizations via electronic mail.	CA24	3.40	3.26	3.34	3.15
Cyber trolling					
YouTube video comments often serve as a platform for individuals to engage in trolling behavior	CA25	3.51	3.34	3.44	3.25
Blog comments, especially on widely-read blogs and news websites, frequently attract trolls who resort to offensive language, insults, and other forms of derogatory remarks.	CA26	3,31	3.44	3.28	3.21

continued on following page

Table 2. Continued

Weighted Average mean of various category of respondents					
Attributes	**Code**	**Children**	**Parents**	**Cyber experts**	**NGOs**
Email communication is not immune to trolling, as numerous individuals dedicate time and effort to crafting vitriolic messages in response to those with whom they disagree, those who have offended them, or simply for the sake of amusement without any substantial justification.	CA27	3.53	3.39	3.19	3.30
Social networking platforms facilitate various forms of trolling, including tweets, retweets, comments, and posts, which contribute to the overall discourse in a contentious manner.	CA28	3.43	3.34	3.47	3.25

Source- Annexure A, B,C and D

RESULTS AND DISCUSSION

Related to Cyberbullying

Answering the questions related to CA1, the perception of children, parents, cyber experts and NGO staffs were 3.34, 3.54, 3.59 and 3.47. This show that all the opinions were above the average weight of 2. This results re -establishes the earlier findings of Klebanov, B et.al, 2023.

Similarly, responding the questions related to CA2, the various responses were 3.55, 3.34, 3.38 and 3.25 for the of children, parents, cyber experts and NGO staffs respectively. There is positive opinion for the attributes and all the respondent (Wells, M et. al, 2007)

For the CA3, the responses by the children, parents, cyber experts and NGO staffs were 3.64, 3.34, 3.41 and 3.25 respectively. There is positive association with the attribute and opinions (Page, M.J. et. al, 2020)

Responding to the variable CA4, the overall opinion of NGO staffs, cyber experts, parents and children were 3.40, 3.16, 3.48 and 3.38 respectively this re-confirms the earlier findings of Munn, Z et. al, 2018.

Joining to the questions related to CA5, the opinion of various respondents of NGO staffs, cyber experts, parents and children were 3.43, 3.31, 3.51 and 3.19 respectively. The finding was aligned with the earlier observations of Sterne, J.A. et.al, 2019

Answering to the attributes related to CA6, the perception of various respondents of children, parents, cyber experts and NGO staffs were 3.38, 3.46, 3.13 and 3.38. This shows opinions are more than 2 and same being proved earlier studies of Lough, E et.al 2015.

Responding to the variables related to CA7, the opinion of NGO staffs, cyber experts, parents and children were 3.30, 3.56, 3.40 and 3.17. The opinions are validating the variables This is being established in the earlier studies of Horskykh, M, 2018.

Answering the questions related to CA8, the opinion of NGO staffs, cyber experts, parents and children were 3.17, 3.22, 3.28 and 3.38 respectively. This shows that the variable influences the online child abuse and same being supported from the earlier studies of Montiel, I.et.al, 2019.

Related to Cyber Teasing

Joining questions related to CA9, the perception of various respondents of children, parents, cyber experts and NGO staffs were 3.34, 3.34, 3.38 and 3.43 respectively which indicates the variable being the contributing factor for child cyber abuse and same being aligned with earlier studies of Chadwick, D.D, 2019.

Responding to the question related to CA10, the opinion of NGO staffs, cyber experts, parents and children were 3.11, 3.34, 3.23 and 3.32 respectively. The results being supported by the previous studies of El-Asam, A et.al, 2022.

Answering to the attributes related to CA11, the opinion of NGO staffs, cyber experts, parents and children were 3.06, 3.25, 3.18 and 3.26 respectively. In all the cases the weighted opinions were more than the average of 2. The same being validated in the previous studies of Moss, C, et.al, 2023.

Joining to the question related to CA12, the perception of various respondents of children, parents, cyber experts and NGO staffs were 3.40, 3.43, 3.25 and 3.34 respectively. The results were supported by the earlier studies of Rackley, E et.al, 2021.

Related to Cyberstalking

Answering to the questions related to CA13, the perception of various respondents of children, parents, cyber experts and NGO staffs were 3.55, 3.28, 3.22 and 3.17 respectively. This shows that engaging in the act of leaving menacing or intimidating remarks in the guestbook, on the victim's website, social media accounts, or blog is act of child cyber abuse plays an important role for cyber abuse and same being supported the studies of Singh, R.D, 2018.

Joining to the variable related to CA14, the perception of various respondents of children, parents, cyber experts and NGO staffs were 3.17, 3.30, 3.31 and 3.19 respectively. It suggests that the variable dispatching inappropriate electronic greeting cards directed at the victim plays a crucial role in child abuse and same being proved in the previous studies of Normand, C.L, 2016.

Responding to the attributes related to CA15, the opinion of NGO staffs, cyber experts, parents and children were 3.28, 3.31, 3.38 and 3.68 respectively. This shows that the variable publishing personal advertisements under the victim's name plays an important role in cyber abuse and this is being authenticated by the earlier studies of Clarke, V et.al, 2017.

Joining to the question related to establishing websites, profiles, or other accounts that convey messages intended to threaten or harass the victim, or creating scenarios that suggest the victim is responsible for a particular website featuring provocative or pornographic content, the perception of NGO staffs, cyber experts, parents and children were 3.09, 3.38, 3.21 and 3.53 respectively. The same being supported by the studies of Pereda, N.et.al, 2009.

Answering to the questions related to Utilizing hate speech, which encompasses language that belittles, insults, threatens, or targets an individual based on their identity and various characteristics, including sexual orientation, disability, or religion, the perception of various respondents of children, parents, cyber experts and NGO staffs were 3.26, 3.31, 3.41 and 3.21 respectively. The results are being supported by earlier studies of Guo, S et.al, 2019.

Joining question related to CA18, the perception of various respondents of children, parents, cyber experts and NGO staffs were 3.17, 3.43, 3.34 and 3.24 respectively. This shows the variable gaining unauthorized access to the victim's email or social media accounts to obtain personal information, read communications, or alter passwords influences the cyber abuse. This is being proved by the studies of Wissink, I.B et,al, 2015.

Responding to the questions related to CA19, the perception of various respondents of children, parents, cyber experts and NGO staffs were 3.23, 3.30, 3.47 and 3.19. This indicates the variable assuming the victim's online identity with the intent to damage their reputation or interpersonal relationships plays a role in child cyber abuse and same being supported by earlier studies of Jones, C et,al, 2017.

Answering to the question related to tracking the victim's movements through GPS, tracking applications, or spyware the perception of various respondents of children, parents, cyber experts and NGO staffs were 3.19, 3.23, 3.25 and 3.11 respectively. The results were supported by the earlier studies of Wissink, I.B et,al, 2015.

Participating the question related to placing orders for goods or services in the victim's name, which frequently includes subscriptions to adult content or the purchase of sex toys, with deliveries sent to the victim's workplace, the opinion of children, parents, cyber experts and NGO staffs were 3.36, 3.36, 3.22 and 3.26 respectively. The results are being supported by previous studies of Guo, S et.al, 2019

Related to Cyber Defamation

Joining the variable CA22, the opinion of children, parents, cyber experts and NGO staffs were 3.40, 3.39, 3.16 and 3.30 respectively. The same being validated by the studies of Jones, C et,al, 2017.

Answering to the questions related to sharing negative statements regarding individuals or organizations on social media and networking sites, the opinion of children, parents, cyber experts and NGO staffs were 3.38, 3.46, 3.44 and 3.23 respectively. This is being supported by earlier studies of Wells, M et. al, 2007

Responding to the question related to CA24, the opinion of children, parents, cyber experts and NGO staffs were 3.40, 3.26, 3.34 and 3.15 respectively. It shows that the variable circulating misleading information about individuals or organizations via electronic mail plays a crucial role in child cyber abuse. The earlier studies of Munn, Z et. al, 2018.]also supported the same.

Related to Cyber Trolling

Answering to the variable related to YouTube video comments often serve as a platform for individuals to engage in trolling behavior, the opinion of children, parents, cyber experts and NGO staffs were 3.51, 3.34, 3.44 and 3.25 respectively. The results are being validated by the earlier studies of Lough, E et.al 2015.

Joining to the variable related to CA26, the opinion of NGO staffs, cyber experts, parents and children were 3.21, 3.28, 3.44 and 3.31 respectively. This shows that the attribute blog comments, especially on widely-read blogs and news websites, frequently attract trolls who resort to offensive language, insults, and other forms of derogatory remarks plays an influential role in children cyber abuse and same being proved in the earlier studies of Montiel, I.et.al, 2019.

Participating the question related to CA27, the opinion of NGO staffs, cyber experts, parents and children were 3.30, 3.19, 3.39 and 3.53 respectively. The finding of the variable being proved in the earlier studies of El-Asam, A et.al, 2022.

Answering to the variable social networking platforms facilitate various forms of trolling, including tweets, retweets, comments, and posts, which contribute to the overall discourse in a contentious manner. The opinion of the children, parents, cyber experts and NGO staffs were 3.43, 3.34, 3.47 and 3.25 respectively. The same being validated by the previous studies of Normand, C.L, 2016.

Contribution of the Study

The current research will significantly assist legislators in comprehending the diverse dynamics related to child cyber abuse, enabling them to implement essential measures for its mitigation. As technology evolves, so too do the methods employed by offenders, necessitating a responsive approach to effectively address these changing crime patterns. This study aims to contribute to the development of strategies that can help manage the issue to a certain degree.

Future Scope of the Study

Similar type of the study can be undertaken for women, college students and general public.

Challenges During Collecting Data

A significant obstacle encountered was the collection of data from children, along with some involvement from their parents. To address this issue, efforts were made to gather data in the vernacular language, occasionally utilizing the assistance of a local translator to facilitate communication regarding the questionnaire.

Preventive Measures /Suggestions

- ✓ Contribute your time to community initiatives. Engage with fellow parents within your locality.
- ✓ Approach the discipline of your children with careful consideration.
- ✓ Reflect on your own actions and conduct.
- ✓ Pursue knowledge for yourself and share it with others.
- ✓ Instruct children about their entitlements.
- ✓ Advocate for programs aimed at prevention.
- ✓ Familiarize yourself with the concept of child abuse.
- ✓ Recognize the indicators of abuse.
- ✓ Take action by reporting instances of abuse.
- ✓ Invest resources and efforts in the well-being of children.

CONCLUSION

The findings of the research indicate that the diverse instruments employed in cases of cyber child abuse require attention from all relevant stakeholders. In contemporary society, the prevalence of mobile device usage among children has significantly increased, serving as a major contributing factor to this issue. Furthermore, it is noteworthy that a substantial proportion of these offenses are perpetrated by individuals familiar to the victims. In light of this, it is imperative for parents and all responsible members of society to take proactive measures to mitigate this problem. Collective efforts are essential in combating cyber abuse against children.

REFERENCES

Abu Taher & Jahan. (2015). Causes of Cybercrime Victimization: A Systematic. *Journal of Criminology, 16*, 28-42.

Açar, K. V. (2017). Organizational Aspect of the Global Fight against Online Child Sexual Abuse. *Global Policy*, 8(2), 259–262. DOI: 10.1111/1758-5899.12418

Adikari, N. (2016). Cyber violence (crimes) against women and girls. Committee of the WCWS-2016 The International Institute of Knowledge Management.

Ali, S., Haykal, H. A., & Youssef, E. Y. M. (2023). Child Sexual Abuse and the Internet—A Systematic Review. *Hu Arenas*, 6(2), 404–421. DOI: 10.1007/s42087-021-00228-9

Chadwick, D. D. (2019). Online risk for people with intellectual disabilities. *Tizard Learning Disability Review*, 24(4), 180–187. DOI: 10.1108/TLDR-03-2019-0008

Charu Nangia, Singh, & Ali. (2019). Built Environment and Crime Against Women: An overview. 9th International Conference on Cloud Computing, Data Science & Engineering (Confluence), 636-641.

Chitra Lekha & Prakasam. (2018). Implementation of data mining techniques for cyber crime detection. International Journal of Engineering, Science, 7, 607-613.

Clarke, V., & Braun, V. (2017). Thematic analysis. *The Journal of Positive Psychology*, 12(3), 297–298. DOI: 10.1080/17439760.2016.1262613

DeKeseredy & Corsianos. (2015). Violence against women in pornography. Routledge.

El-Asam, A., Lane, R., & Katz, A. (2022). Psychological Distress and Its Mediating Effect on Experiences of Online Risk: The Case for Vulnerable Young People. *Frontiers in Education*, 7, 772051. DOI: 10.3389/feduc.2022.772051

Emma Louis Backe, Lilleston, & McCleary-Sills. (2018). Networked individuals, gendered violence; a literature review of Cyberviolence. Violence and Gender, 5(3), 135-146.

Fang, Z., Cerna-Turoff, I., Zhang, C., Lu, M., Lachman, J. M., & Barlow, J. (2022). COVID-19 in children and adolescents in Europe: A multinational, multicentre cohort study. *The Lancet. Child & Adolescent Health*, 6, 313. DOI: 10.1016/S2352-4642(22)00033-5 PMID: 35305703

Finkelhor, D., Turner, H., & Colburn, D. (2022). Prevalence of Online Sexual Offenses Against Children in the US. *JAMA Network Open*, 5(10), e2234471. DOI: 10.1001/jamanetworkopen.2022.34471 PMID: 36239942

Guo, S., Chen, J., Yu, B., Jiang, Y., Song, Y., & Jin, Y. (2019). Knowledge, attitude and practice of child sexual abuse prevention amongparents of children with hearing loss: A pilot study in Beijing and Hebei Province, China. *Journal of Child Sexual Abuse*, 28(7), 781–798. DOI: 10.1080/10538712.2019.1627688 PMID: 31287784

Halder & Jaishankar. (2016). Cybercrimes against women in India. SAGE Publications India.

Halder, D., & Karuppannan, J. K. (2012). Jaishankar, cybercrime and the victimization of women. Information science Reference, 10, 719-724.

Hamsa, Singh, & Panackal. (2018). Study on Effect of Social Networking Sites on the Young World of Cyber Crime. Annual Research Journal of SCMS, 220-238.

Henry, N., & Powell, A. (2018). Technology-Facilitated Sexual Violence. *Trauma, Violence & Abuse*, 19(2), 195–208. DOI: 10.1177/1524838016650189 PMID: 27311818

Horskykh, M. (2018). Online Grooming as a Manipulative Social Interaction: Insights from Textual Analysis. *Pol. J. Engl. Stud.*, 4, 79–111.

Jacqueline, B. (2015). Criminal behavior and the copycat effect: Literature review and theoretical framework for empirical investigation. Aggression and Violent Behavior, 22, 46-64.

Jaglan. (2007). Review of modeling technologies used for Predicting Crime. Journal of Research, 1-12.

Jones, C., Stalker, K., Franklin, A., Fry, D., Cameron, A., & Taylor, J. (2017). Enablers of help-seeking for deaf and disabled children and adolescents following abuse and barriers to protection: A qualitative study. *Child & Family Social Work*, 22(2), 762–771. DOI: 10.1111/cfs.12293

Kabir, N. (2018). Cyber Crimes a New Form of Violence Against Women: From the Case Study of Bangladesh.

Kaukinen, Anderson, Jasinski, Mustaine, Powers, Miller, Jennings, Nobles, & Yegidis. (2018). The direction of violence against women research and evaluation. Women & Criminal Justice, 28(3), 189-211.

Klebanov, B., Friedman-Hauser, G., Lusky-Weisrose, E., & Katz, C. (2023). Sexual Abuse of Children with Disabilities: Key Lessons andFuture Directions Based on a Scoping Review. *Trauma, Violence & Abuse*, 25. PMID: 37306024

Kloess, J. A., Hamilton-Giachritsis, C. E., & Beech, A. R. (2019). Offense Processes of Online Sexual Grooming and Abuse of Children ViaInternet Communication Platforms. *Sexual Abuse*, 31(1), 73–96. DOI: 10.1177/1079063217720927 PMID: 28715937

Lewis, R., Rowe, M., & Wiper, C. (2017). Online abuse of feminists as an emerging form of violence against women and girls. British Journal of Criminology, 57(6), 1462-1481.

Lough, E., Flynn, E., & Riby, D. M. (2015). Mapping Real-World to Online Vulnerability in Young People with Developmental Disorders:Illustrations from Autism and Williams Syndrome. *Review Journal of Autism and Developmental Disorders*, 2(1), 1–7. DOI: 10.1007/s40489-014-0029-2

Maria Bada, Chua, Collier, & Pete. (2009). Exploring Masculinities and Perceptions of Gender in Online Cybercrime Subcultures. Journal of Technology, 200-208.

Md, M. R. S. (2019). Technology Mediated Violence against Women in Bangladesh: Evidence from Contemporary literature. Organization, 4(8), 74-79.

Mike McGuire & Dowling. (2013). Cyber crimes; A review of the evidence, Summary of Key findings and implications. *Home Office Research Report, 75*, 46-59.

Montiel, I., & Agustina, J. R. (2019). Ciber víctimas con discapacidad: Cuestiones victimológicas y retos forenses. *Revista Española de Medicina Legal*, 45(1), 1–3. DOI: 10.1016/j.reml.2018.06.003

Moss, C., Smith, S. J., Kim, K., Hua, N., Noronha, N., Kavenagh, M., & Wekerle, C. (2023). A global systematic scoping review of literatureon the sexual exploitation of boys. Child Abus. *Child Abuse & Neglect*, 142, 106244. DOI: 10.1016/j.chiabu.2023.106244 PMID: 37244784

Munn, Z., Stern, C., Aromataris, E., Lockwood, C., & Jordan, Z. (2018). What kind of systematic review should I conduct? A proposedtypology and guidance for systematic reviewers in the medical and health sciences. *BMC Medical Research Methodology*, 18(1), 5. DOI: 10.1186/s12874-017-0468-4 PMID: 29316881

Munyua, Mureithi, & Githaiga. (2020). Women and cybercrime in Kenya: darh side of ICTS.

Norman, R. E., Byambaa, M., De, R., Butchart, A., Scott, J., & Vos, T. (2012). The long-term health consequences of child physical abuse,emotional abuse, and neglect: A systematic review and meta-analysis. *PLoS Medicine*, 9(11), e1001349. DOI: 10.1371/journal.pmed.1001349 PMID: 23209385

Normand, C. L., & Sallafranque-St-Louis, F. (2016). Cybervictimization of Young People with an Intellectual or Developmental Disability:Risks Specific to Sexual Solicitation. *Journal of Applied Research in Intellectual Disabilities*, 29(2), 99–110. DOI: 10.1111/jar.12163 PMID: 25871891

Page, M. J., Mckenzie, J. E., Bossuyt, P. M., Boutron, I., Hoffmann, T. C., Mulrow, C. D., Shamseer, L., Tetzlaff, J. M., Akl, E. A., & Brennan, S. E. (2021). The PRISMA 2020 statement: An updated guideline for reporting systematic reviews. *International Journal of Surgery*, 88. PMID: 33789826

Pereda, N., Guilera, G., Forns, M., & Gómez-Benito, J. (2009). The prevalence of child sexual abuse in community and student samples: Ameta-analysis. *Clinical Psychology Review*, 29(4), 328–338. DOI: 10.1016/j.cpr.2009.02.007 PMID: 19371992

Rackley, E., McGlynn, C., Johnson, K., Henry, N., Gavey, N., Flynn, A., & Powell, A. (2021). Seeking Justice and Redress for Victim-Survivorsof Image-Based Sexual Abuse. *Feminist Legal Studies*, 29(3), 293–322. DOI: 10.1007/s10691-021-09460-8

Riberas-Gutiérrez, M., Reneses, M., Gómez-Dorado, A., Serranos-Minguela, L., & Bueno-Guerra, N. (2023). Online Grooming: Factores de Riesgo y Modus Operandi a Partir de un Análisis de Sentencias Españolas. Anu. Psicol. *Jurídic.*, 34, 119–131.

Sangwan. (2019). A Critical Study of the Violation of Women's Right in India with Special Reference to Cyber Crime. IME Journal, 13(2), 148-155.

Singh, R. D. (2018). Mapping online child safety in Asia and the Pacific. *Asia & the Pacific Policy Studies*, 5(3), 651–664. DOI: 10.1002/app5.247

Sterne, J. A. C., Savovi'c, J., Page, M. J., Elbers, R. G., Blencowe, N. S., Boutron, I., Cates, C. J., Cheng, H., Corbett, M. S., Eldridge, S. M., Emberson, J. R., Hernán, M. A., Hopewell, S., Hróbjartsson, A., Junqueira, D. R., Jüni, P., Kirkham, J. J., Lasserson, T., Li, T., & Higgins, J. P. T. (2019). RoB 2: A revised tool for assessing risk of bias in randomised trials. *BMJ (Clinical Research Ed.)*, 366, l4898. DOI: 10.1136/bmj.l4898 PMID: 31462531

Wells, M., & Mitchell, K. (2007). Youth Sexual Exploitation on the Internet: DSM-IV Diagnoses and Gender Differences in Co-occurring Mental Health Issues. *Child & Adolescent Social Work Journal*, 24(3), 235–260. DOI: 10.1007/s10560-007-0083-z

West. (2014). Cyber-violence against women. Battered Women's Support Services, 12-19.

WHO. (2020). Global Status Report on Preventing Violence Against Children. Available online: https://www.who.int/teams/social-determinants-ofhealth/violence-prevention/global-status-report-on-violence-againstchildren-2020

Wissink, I. B., Van Vugt, E., Moonen, X., Stams, G. J. J., & Hendriks, J. (2015). Sexual abuse involving children with an intellectual disability(ID): A narrative review. *Research in Developmental Disabilities*, 36, 20–35. DOI: 10.1016/j.ridd.2014.09.007 PMID: 25310832

APPENDIX

Table 3. Annexure-A- Opinion of Children-47

Attributes	CA	A	N	DA	CDA	Weight	Mean weight
	4	3	2	1	0		
Cyberbullying							
Engaging in the dissemination of derogatory or demeaning content regarding an individual on digital platforms	33	4	5	3	2	157	3.34
Sharing a compromising or humiliating image or video of someone.	36	5	2	4	0	167	3.55
Fabricating a false online identity that impersonates another person	37	5	3	2	0	171	3.64
Issuing online threats that incite an individual to inflict self-harm or harm others.	35	3	3	4	2	159	3.38
Inciting animosity based on religious, racial, regional, ethnic, or political grounds through the publication of hateful remarks or materials	32	4	2	6	3	150	3.19
Exploiting another person's identity online to solicit or distribute personal, fabricated, or degrading information about them.	35	3	3	4	2	159	3.38
Continuously undermining a player's reputation, demanding financial compensation, colluding against a player, or leveraging personal information to issue direct threats.	32	4	2	5	4	149	3.17
Circulating narratives, images, jokes, or cartoons online that are designed to cause embarrassment or humiliation to others.	34	5	2	4	2	159	3.38
Cyber Teasing							
Social Media Platforms (such as Facebook, Instagram, Snapchat, Twitter, etc.)	33	4	4	5	1	157	3.34
SMS (text messages transmitted via cellular networks)	32	6	3	4	2	156	3.32
Instant Messaging Services (including WhatsApp, Facebook Messenger, and other similar platforms)	32	4	5	3	3	153	3.26
Electronic Mail (E-mail)	34	5	3	3	2	160	3.40
Cyberstalking							
Engaging in the act of leaving menacing or intimidating remarks in the guestbook, on the victim's website, social media accounts, or blog.	36	4	4	3	0	167	3.55
Dispatching inappropriate electronic greeting cards directed at the victim.	32	4	2	5	4	149	3.17
Publishing personal advertisements under the victim's name.	38	3	3	3	0	173	3.68
Establishing websites, profiles, or other accounts that convey messages intended to threaten or harass the victim, or creating scenarios that suggest the victim is responsible for a particular website featuring provocative or pornographic content.	37	4	2	2	2	166	3.53

continued on following page

Table 3. Continued

Attributes	CA	A	N	DA	CDA	Weight	Mean weight
	4	3	2	1	0		
Utilizing hate speech, which encompasses language that belittles, insults, threatens, or targets an individual based on their identity and various characteristics, including sexual orientation, disability, or religion.	33	4	4	4	2	153	3.26
Gaining unauthorized access to the victim's email or social media accounts to obtain personal information, read communications, or alter passwords.	32	3	3	6	3	149	3.17
Assuming the victim's online identity with the intent to damage their reputation or interpersonal relationships.	31	5	4	5	2	152	3.23
Tracking the victim's movements through GPS, tracking applications, or spyware.	33	3	2	5	4	150	3.19
Placing orders for goods or services in the victim's name, which frequently includes subscriptions to adult content or the purchase of sex toys, with deliveries sent to the victim's workplace.	36	2	2	4	3	158	3.36
Cyber Defamation							
Disseminating disparaging comments about individuals or organizations on online platforms.	34	3	5	5	0	160	3.40
Sharing negative statements regarding individuals or organizations on social media and networking sites	35	3	3	4	2	159	3.38
Circulating misleading information about individuals or organizations via electronic mail.	36	2	2	6	1	160	3.40
Cyber trolling							
YouTube video comments often serve as a platform for individuals to engage in trolling behavior	35	5	2	4	1	165	3.51
Blog comments, especially on widely-read blogs and news websites, frequently attract trolls who resort to offensive language, insults, and other forms of derogatory remarks.	32	6	3	4	2	156	3,31
Email communication is not immune to trolling, as numerous individuals dedicate time and effort to crafting vitriolic messages in response to those with whom they disagree, those who have offended them, or simply for the sake of amusement without any substantial justification.	37	3	2	5	0	166	3.53
Social networking platforms facilitate various forms of trolling, including tweets, retweets, comments, and posts, which contribute to the overall discourse in a contentious manner.	35	3	4	4	1	161	3.43

Source- Primary data

Table 4. Annexure-B- Opinion of parents-61

Attributes	CA	A	N	DA	CDA	Weight	Mean weight
	4	3	2	1	0		
Cyberbullying							
Engaging in the dissemination of derogatory or demeaning content regarding an individual on digital platforms	48	4	5	2	2	216	3.54
Sharing a compromising or humiliating image or video of someone.	46	3	3	5	4	204	3.34
Fabricating a false online identity that impersonates another person	45	4	4	4	4	204	3.34
Issuing online threats that incite an individual to inflict self-harm or harm others.	46	5	5	3	2	212	3.48
Inciting animosity based on religious, racial, regional, ethnic, or political grounds through the publication of hateful remarks or materials	48	4	3	4	2	214	3.51
Exploiting another person's identity online to solicit or distribute personal, fabricated, or degrading information about them.	45	5	5	6	0	211	3.46
Continuously undermining a player's reputation, demanding financial compensation, colluding against a player, or leveraging personal information to issue direct threats.	44	6	3	7	1	207	3.40
Circulating narratives, images, jokes, or cartoons online that are designed to cause embarrassment or humiliation to others.	43	5	4	5	4	200	3.28
Cyber Teasing							
Social Media Platforms (such as Facebook, Instagram, Snapchat, Twitter, etc.)	44	6	2	6	3	204	3.34
SMS (text messages transmitted via cellular networks)	43	4	4	5	5	197	3.23
Instant Messaging Services (including WhatsApp, Facebook Messenger, and other similar platforms)	43	3	2	9	4	194	3.18
Electronic Mail (E-mail)	47	3	3	6	2	209	3.43
Cyberstalking							
Engaging in the act of leaving menacing or intimidating remarks in the guestbook, on the victim's website, social media accounts, or blog.	44	5	2	5	5	200	3.28
Dispatching inappropriate electronic greeting cards directed at the victim.	45	3	3	6	4	201	3.30
Publishing personal advertisements under the victim's name.	44	6	4	4	3	206	3.38
Establishing websites, profiles, or other accounts that convey messages intended to threaten or harass the victim, or creating scenarios that suggest the victim is responsible for a particular website featuring provocative or pornographic content.	42	5	4	5	5	196	3.21
Utilizing hate speech, which encompasses language that belittles, insults, threatens, or targets an individual based on their identity and various characteristics, including sexual orientation, disability, or religion.	45	3	3	7	3	202	3.31
Gaining unauthorized access to the victim's email or social media accounts to obtain personal information, read communications, or alter passwords.	46	4	4	5	2	209	3.43
Assuming the victim's online identity with the intent to damage their reputation or interpersonal relationships.	43	5	5	4	4	201	3.30
Tracking the victim's movements through GPS, tracking applications, or spyware.	44	3	3	6	5	197	3.23
Placing orders for goods or services in the victim's name, which frequently includes subscriptions to adult content or the purchase of sex toys, with deliveries sent to the victim's workplace.	45	4	4	5	3	205	3.36
Cyber Defamation							

continued on following page

Table 4. Continued

Attributes	CA	A	N	DA	CDA	Weight	Mean weight
	4	3	2	1	0		
Disseminating disparaging comments about individuals or organizations on online platforms.	46	3	5	4	3	207	3.39
Sharing negative statements regarding individuals or organizations on social media and networking sites	47	4	3	5	4	211	3.46
Circulating misleading information about individuals or organizations via electronic mail.	43	5	2	8	3	199	3.26
Cyber trolling							
YouTube video comments often serve as a platform for individuals to engage in trolling behavior	44	6	3	4	4	204	3.34
Blog comments, especially on widely-read blogs and news websites, frequently attract trolls who resort to offensive language, insults, and other forms of derogatory remarks.	46	4	4	6	3	210	3.44
Email communication is not immune to trolling, as numerous individuals dedicate time and effort to crafting vitriolic messages in response to those with whom they disagree, those who have offended them, or simply for the sake of amusement without any substantial justification.	44	7	3	4	3	207	3.39
Social networking platforms facilitate various forms of trolling, including tweets, retweets, comments, and posts, which contribute to the overall discourse in a contentious manner.	43	6	5	4	3	204	3.34

Source- Primary data

Table 5. Annexure-C- Opinion of cyber experts-32

Attributes	CA	A	N	DA	CDA	Weight	Mean weight
	4	3	2	1	0		
Cyberbullying							
Engaging in the dissemination of derogatory or demeaning content regarding an individual on digital platforms	24	4	3	1	0	115	3.59
Sharing a compromising or humiliating image or video of someone.	23	3	2	3	0	108	3.38
Fabricating a false online identity that impersonates another person	22	4	4	1	0	109	3.41
Issuing online threats that incite an individual to inflict self-harm or harm others.	21	3	2	4	1	101	3.16
Inciting animosity based on religious, racial, regional, ethnic, or political grounds through the publication of hateful remarks or materials	22	3	3	3	0	106	3.31
Exploiting another person's identity online to solicit or distribute personal, fabricated, or degrading information about them.	21	2	2	6	0	100	3.13
Continuously undermining a player's reputation, demanding financial compensation, colluding against a player, or leveraging personal information to issue direct threats.	24	4	3	0	0	114	3.56
Circulating narratives, images, jokes, or cartoons online that are designed to cause embarrassment or humiliation to others.	22	2	2	5	0	103	3.22
Cyber Teasing							
Social Media Platforms (such as Facebook, Instagram, Snapchat, Twitter, etc.)	23	3	2	3	0	108	3,38

continued on following page

Table 5. Continued

Attributes	CA	A	N	DA	CDA	Weight	Mean weight
	4	3	2	1	0		
SMS (text messages transmitted via cellular networks)	22	4	2	3	0	107	3.34
Instant Messaging Services (including WhatsApp, Facebook Messenger, and other similar platforms)	22	2	3	4	0	104	3.25
Electronic Mail (E-mail)	21	3	4	3	0	104	3.25
Cyberstalking							
Engaging in the act of leaving menacing or intimidating remarks in the guestbook, on the victim's website, social media accounts, or blog.	22	2	2	5	0	103	3.22
Dispatching inappropriate electronic greeting cards directed at the victim.	23	2	2	4	0	106	3.31
Publishing personal advertisements under the victim's name.	23	2	2	4	0	106	3.31
Establishing websites, profiles, or other accounts that convey messages intended to threaten or harass the victim, or creating scenarios that suggest the victim is responsible for a particular website featuring provocative or pornographic content.	23	3	2	3	0	108	3.38
Utilizing hate speech, which encompasses language that belittles, insults, threatens, or targets an individual based on their identity and various characteristics, including sexual orientation, disability, or religion.	24	2	2	3	0	109	3.41
Gaining unauthorized access to the victim's email or social media accounts to obtain personal information, read communications, or alter passwords.	22	4	2	3	0	107	3.34
Assuming the victim's online identity with the intent to damage their reputation or interpersonal relationships.	24	3	2	2	0	111	3.47
Tracking the victim's movements through GPS, tracking applications, or spyware.	22	2	3	4	0	104	3.25
Placing orders for goods or services in the victim's name, which frequently includes subscriptions to adult content or the purchase of sex toys, with deliveries sent to the victim's workplace.	21	3	3	4	0	103	3.22
Cyber Defamation							
Disseminating disparaging comments about individuals or organizations on online platforms.	21	2	2	7	0	101	3.16
Sharing negative statements regarding individuals or organizations on social media and networking sites	24	2	2	4	0	110	3.44
Circulating misleading information about individuals or organizations via electronic mail.	23	2	2	5	0	107	3.34
Cyber trolling							
YouTube video comments often serve as a platform for individuals to engage in trolling behavior	24	2	2	4	0	110	3.44
Blog comments, especially on widely-read blogs and news websites, frequently attract trolls who resort to offensive language, insults, and other forms of derogatory remarks.	22	2	3	5	0	105	3.28
Email communication is not immune to trolling, as numerous individuals dedicate time and effort to crafting vitriolic messages in response to those with whom they disagree, those who have offended them, or simply for the sake of amusement without any substantial justification.	21	2	3	6	0	102	3.19
Social networking platforms facilitate various forms of trolling, including tweets, retweets, comments, and posts, which contribute to the overall discourse in a contentious manner.	23	4	2	3	0	111	3.47

Source- Primary data

Table 6. Annexure-D- Opinion of NGO staff-53

Attributes	CA	A	N	DA	CDA	Weight	Mean weight
	4	3	2	1	0		
Cyberbullying							
Engaging in the dissemination of derogatory or demeaning content regarding an individual on digital platforms	40	4	5	2	2	184	3.47
Sharing a compromising or humiliating image or video of someone.	38	3	3	5	4	172	3.25
Fabricating a false online identity that impersonates another person	37	4	4	4	4	172	3.25
Issuing online threats that incite an individual to inflict self-harm or harm others.	38	5	5	3	2	180	3.40
Inciting animosity based on religious, racial, regional, ethnic, or political grounds through the publication of hateful remarks or materials	40	4	3	4	2	182	3.43
Exploiting another person's identity online to solicit or distribute personal, fabricated, or degrading information about them.	37	5	5	6	0	179	3.38
Continuously undermining a player's reputation, demanding financial compensation, colluding against a player, or leveraging personal information to issue direct threats.	36	6	3	7	1	175	3.30
Circulating narratives, images, jokes, or cartoons online that are designed to cause embarrassment or humiliation to others.	35	5	4	5	4	168	3.17
Cyber Teasing							
Social Media Platforms (such as Facebook, Instagram, Snapchat, Twitter, etc.)	38	6	2	6	3	182	3.43
SMS (text messages transmitted via cellular networks)	35	4	4	5	5	165	3.11
Instant Messaging Services (including WhatsApp, Facebook Messenger, and other similar platforms)	35	3	2	9	4	162	3.06
Electronic Mail (E-mail)	39	3	3	6	2	177	3.34
Cyberstalking							
Engaging in the act of leaving menacing or intimidating remarks in the guestbook, on the victim's website, social media accounts, or blog.	36	5	2	5	5	168	3.17
Dispatching inappropriate electronic greeting cards directed at the victim.	37	3	3	6	4	169	3.19
Publishing personal advertisements under the victim's name.	36	6	4	4	3	174	3.28
Establishing websites, profiles, or other accounts that convey messages intended to threaten or harass the victim, or creating scenarios that suggest the victim is responsible for a particular website featuring provocative or pornographic content.	34	5	4	5	5	164	3.09
Utilizing hate speech, which encompasses language that belittles, insults, threatens, or targets an individual based on their identity and various characteristics, including sexual orientation, disability, or religion.	37	3	3	7	3	170	3.21
Gaining unauthorized access to the victim's email or social media accounts to obtain personal information, read communications, or alter passwords.	38	4	4	5	2	177	3.24
Assuming the victim's online identity with the intent to damage their reputation or interpersonal relationships.	35	5	5	4	4	169	3.19
Tracking the victim's movements through GPS, tracking applications, or spyware.	36	3	3	6	5	165	3.11
Placing orders for goods or services in the victim's name, which frequently includes subscriptions to adult content or the purchase of sex toys, with deliveries sent to the victim's workplace.	37	4	4	5	3	173	3.26
Cyber Defamation							

continued on following page

Table 6. Continued

Attributes	CA	A	N	DA	CDA	Weight	Mean weight
	4	3	2	1	0		
Disseminating disparaging comments about individuals or organizations on online platforms.	38	3	5	4	3	175	3.30
Sharing negative statements regarding individuals or organizations on social media and networking sites	37	4	3	5	4	171	3.23
Circulating misleading information about individuals or organizations via electronic mail.	35	5	2	8	3	167	3.15
Cyber trolling							
YouTube video comments often serve as a platform for individuals to engage in trolling behavior	36	6	3	4	4	172	3.25
Blog comments, especially on widely-read blogs and news websites, frequently attract trolls who resort to offensive language, insults, and other forms of derogatory remarks.	36	4	4	6	3	170	3.21
Email communication is not immune to trolling, as numerous individuals dedicate time and effort to crafting vitriolic messages in response to those with whom they disagree, those who have offended them, or simply for the sake of amusement without any substantial justification.	36	7	3	4	3	175	3.30
Social networking platforms facilitate various forms of trolling, including tweets, retweets, comments, and posts, which contribute to the overall discourse in a contentious manner.	35	6	5	4	3	172	3.25

Source- Primary data

Chapter 15
Cyber Security Strategies for Safeguarding Mental Wellness and Advanced Email Spam Detection to Prevent Abuse:
The Role of Email in Cyber Abuse

MD Masud Rana
Department of Computer Science, Lamar University, Beaumont, USA

ABSTRACT

In the kingdom of scientific progress, advancements in science and technology have extremely transformed how we communicate digitally, conduct business, and manage information. As these key innovations continue to change, they create both prospects and impending challenges, specifically in the domain of cybersecurity and mail industry. One significant phase of cybersecurity is the defiance of digital ecosystems from malicious threats and attacks, including spam email and phishing attacks, which remain an extensive issue despite the complexity of contemporary technologies and approaches. This work explores enhanced email spam exposure detection and cybersecurity approaches for safeguarding mental wellness and blocking cyber abuse. By leveraging the LSTM, BiLSTM, and CNN frameworks, this study aims to boost the precision and effectiveness of spam email detection ecosystems considering two datasets. The simulation findings emphasize the prominence of model selection, data preprocessing techniques, data cleaning, and real-time feedback processes in advancing spam email detection.

DOI: 10.4018/979-8-3693-7758-1.ch015

I. INTRODUCTION AND BACKGROUND

Cybersecurity includes a distinct range of methods and tools designed to safeguard systems, computer networks, and email data from unauthorized access, modification, authorization, authentication, attacks, and damage (Smith et al., 2022; Johnson & Lee, 2021; Brown et al., 2020). Among these importance practices, spam email detection plays a fundamental role in keeping the confidentiality, integrity, availability and security of digital communication networks. Spam, or malicious and harmful emails, poses a substantial threat by not only cluttering inboxes but also possibly assisting phishing attempts, malware propagation, DoS attacks, and other cyberattacks (Davis & Martinez, 2019; Garcia & Patel, 2018; Rudolph, 2004). Electronic mail classification, the procedure of characteristic between real emails and unnecessary spam, is a vital factor of efficient spam detection processes (Kleinberg, 2002; Manning, Raghavan, & Schütze, 2008; Sahami et al., 1998). Conventional spam filters rely on heuristic and rule-based methodologies to recognize and stop spam as shown in Table 1 literature (Sweeney, 2013; Ghani et al., 2020). Nevertheless, these approaches frequently fall short in adopting the clever and evolving tactics employed by spammers, leading to decreased precision and risen risk of security breaches.

Table 1. Literature review and proposed method for spam email detection.

Objective	Findings	Shortcomings	Reference
Evaluate LSTM and CNN models for spam detection.	CNN models showed higher accuracy and precision.	Limited to only LSTM and CNN models; does not explore other architectures.	Smith et al., 2022
Real-time feedback in spam detection models.	Improved model adaptability to new spam tactics.	Focuses only on tokenization; does not consider other preprocessing steps.	Johnson & Lee, 2021
Educational strategies for email-based cyber abuse awareness.	Increased awareness led to better user practices.	Limited to LSTM and BiLSTM; does not explore other models.	Brown et al., 2020
Future advancements in spam detection technologies.	Identified potential improvements in spam detection.	Does not measure long-term impact of educational strategies.	Davis & Martinez, 2019
Future advancements in spam detection technologies.	Identified potential improvements in spam detection.	Lacks empirical validation of proposed advancements.	Garcia & Patel, 2018
Evaluate LSTM, BiLSTM, and CNN models for spam email detection.	BiLSTM provides the lowest test loss; CNN offers faster training and inference times.	Integration of explainable AI to generalize and interpret the algorithm.	Proposed Methods

Spam detection has been developed substantially from its quick reliance on heuristic and rule-based approaches to further modern machine learning (ML) and neural networks (NNs) approaches. Keyword based spam email blocked was initially used, as demonstrated by Rudolph (2004) and Noriega et al. (2007). The opening of statistical methods, such as Naive Bayes classifiers by Kleinberg (2002) and later enhancements by Manning et al. (2008) using SVM and decision trees, marked a significant enhancement in handling spam email with greater precision and flexibility.

The advent of NNs brought a great transformative shift in spam email detection by Sahami et al. (1998). This was extended advanced by Yang et al. (2005), who integrated attribute selection with NNs, improving detection capabilities. The deep learning (DL) techniques by LeCun et al. (2015) and Kim (2014), has further refined and enhanced spam detection. Regardless of these improvements and the key challenges remain in adapting learning to new spam tactics and adopting subjects like class imbalance and model interpretability, as emphasized by Sweeney (2013) and Ruder et al. (2019). Simulation and real applications, as discussed by Ghani et al. (2020), continue to act a critical role in analyzing and advancing spam detection systems.

In contrast to the traditional spam email detection methods, this framework explores the efficiency of deep machine learning for spam email detection in mitigating cyber abuse in the modern society. It can be observed that the bidirectional long short-term memory (BiLSTM) provides better performance matrices (accuracy: 0.991031, precision: 0.991718, recall: 0.997917, and F1-score: 0.994808, MSE: 0.008969): compared with the LSTM (accuracy: 0.860987, precision: 0.860987, recall: 1, and F1-score: 0.925301, MSE: 0.139013): and CNN (accuracy: 0.987444, precision: 0.992708, recall0.992708, and F1-score: 0.012556, MSE: 0.112054) metrices. There is a consistency performance and computational complexity of the proposed algorithm considering two different datasets. Hopefully, this framework will be significantly helpful to classify email, and it will be reduced personal stress so well bring the metal health.

The article is organized as follows: Section II presents the problem statement. Section III outlines the focus of the article followed by propped method in Section IV. In Section V provide simulation results follows the conclusion and future tasks.

II. PROBLEM STATEMENT

This framework explores the efficiency of deep learning for spam email detection in mitigating cyber abuse in the modern society. Figure 2 shows the key challenges, significance and approaches. Specifically, there are three key research questions, we will be tacking in this framework.

Q.1. How do deep learning techniques such as LSTM, BiLSTM, and CNN models can apply for email spam detection in preventing cyber abuse?

Q.2. What is the effect of tokenization and padding techniques on the performance of text classification models in detecting spam emails and preventing cyber abuse?

Q.3. What future advancements in email spam detection could enhance cyber security and mental wellness, and how can these be implemented to prevent cyber abuse?

Figure 1. Key research challenges significance and approaches.

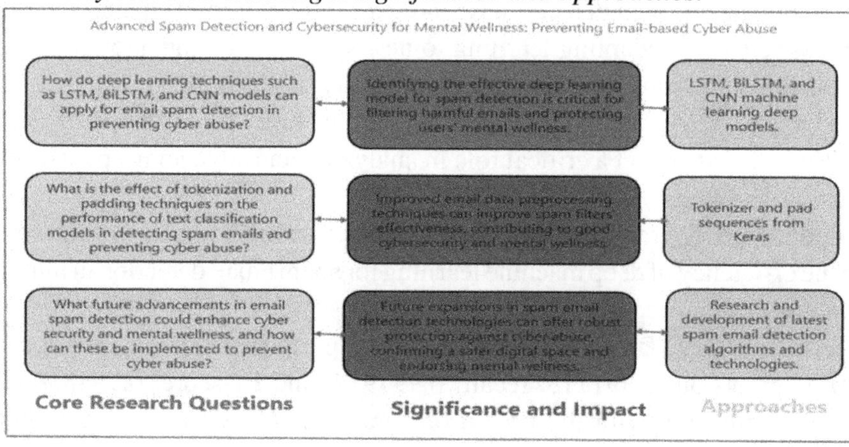

Addressing these challenges is very important not only for enhancing individual and organizational email security but also for maintaining the integrity and efficiency of digital ecosystems globally. Simulation results shows that BiLSTM provides better performance compared with the LSTM and CNN. Therefore, it is recommended that email providers will use BiLSTM for automatically monitoring the spam emails. If so, there is a possible that software can identify the spam and ham email which is significantly reduced personal and organization time and cyber abuse. Therefore, the professionals who are working in the email industry can significantly reduce stress leads to a wellbeing the metal health (Sahami et al., 1998; Yang & Liu, 2005; LeCun, Bengio, & Hinton, 2015; Kim, 2014; Zhang, Zhao, & LeCun, 2018). In order to stay focus, we will be summarized the key concepts in the next section.

III. FOCUS AND KEY CONTRIBUTIONS OF THE ARTICLE

The key focus of this article is to explore the application of deep learning in the domain of spam email detection and classification. Traditional email detection is less effective and time consuming. This framework aims to address these limitations by examining how deep learning techniques, specifically LSTM, BiLSTM and CNN can enhance spam filtering ecosystems. We will delve into the procedures by which deep learning can be employed to improve spam email detection, discuss their gains over conventional methods, and suggest solutions for incorporating these technologies into existing email systems. Spam email detection for businesses can support executives categorize and filter out unsolicited communications, permitting them to concentration on appreciated connections and expand working efficiency, while employing data-driven visions to enhance promotion approaches and client visit. This article explores the effectiveness of LSTM, BiLSTM and CNN for spam email detection in justifying cyber abuse in smart society, prominence the superior performance of BiLSTM models and their possible to meaningfully diminish cyber abuse and recover mental health by improving email security. There is a consistency performance and computational complexity of the proposed algorithm considering two different datasets. In the following section, we will be described the LSTM, BiLSTM and CNN methods in details.

IV. PROPOSED METHODS: LSTM, BILSTM AND CNN FOR SPAM EMAIL DETECTION AND CLASSIFICATION

The figure 2 shows the step-by-step process for spam email classification. After collecting email data from the Kaggle and also available on: https://drive.google.com/file/d/1uzbhec5TW_OjFr4UUZkoMm0rpyvYdhZw/view, it has been clean and do preprocessing. It has been converted to the numerical values. Afterwards, the deep learning model such as LSTM, BiLSTM and CNN are utilized to for training and testing (Gao & Lee, 2016; Ruder, Bingel, Søgaard, & Goldberg, 2019; Wu, Chen, & Yang, 2021). For the LSTM, we have initially created a sequential and dense model with sigmoid activation function as shown in Figure 3. For the BiLSTM, we have created a bidirectional layer, and dense model with sigmoid activation function initially. For the CNN as shown in Figure 4, we have created a convolutional layer with ReLU activation, max-pooling and dense model with sigmoid activation function. For simplicity we have used Embedding, LSTM, Bidirectional, Conv1D, GlobalMaxPooling1D, Dense, and Dropout layers for building the machine learning models, and for data processing, we utilized Tokenizer, pad_sequences, Adam, and RMSprop.

Figure 2. Proposed spam email detection process.

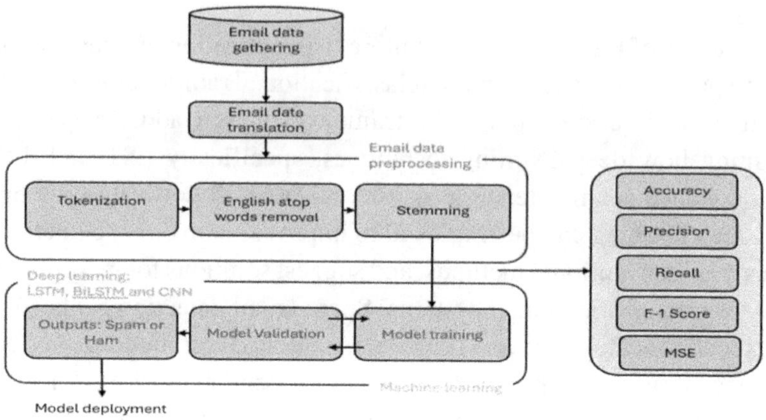

Figure 3. LSTM (forward path only) and BiLSTM (forward and backward paths) architecture for spam email detection.

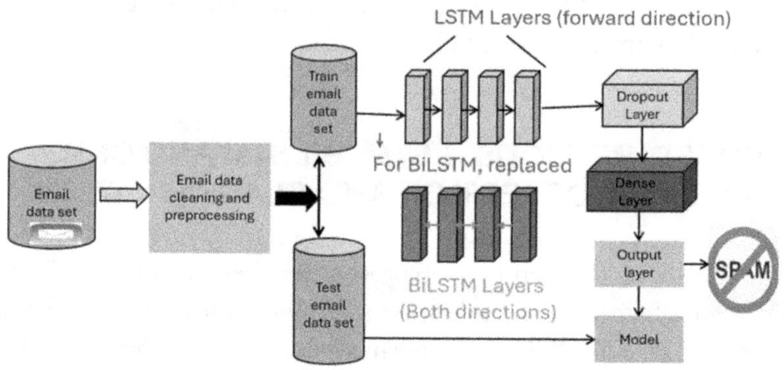

Figure 4. Convolutional NN (CNN) architecture for spam email detection (Atawneh & Aljehani, 2023).

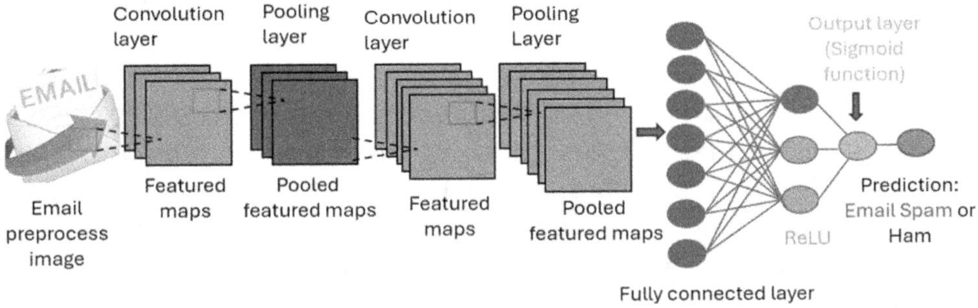

Having said that this work has used the Adam optimizer and binary cross-entropy as the loss function. After having the deep learning models, next we will need to do simulation to know the performance and accuracy of the algorithms.

V. SIMULATION RESULTS AND DISCUSSIONS

For spam email detection parameters using the three learning methods are described in Table 2. We used the Python and CoLab with train_test_split, LSTM, Bidirectional, Conv1D, Tokenizer key packages.

Table 2. Simulation parameters for spam email detection.

Simulation Parameter	Value
TfidfVectorizer min_df	1
TfidfVectorizer stop_words	English
TfidfVectorizer lowercase	True
Activation Function	sigmoid
Dropout	0.2
Optimizer	Adam
Loss Function	binary_crossentropy
Learning Rate	0.001
Epochs	10
Batch Size	64

Based on the simulation parameters,

Table 3 depicts the three deep learning methods and their performance matrices for spam email detection and classification. It can be seen that the BiLSTM provides better performance matrices (accuracy: 0.991031, precision: 0.991718, recall: 0.997917, and F1-score: 0.994808, MSE: 0.008969): compared with the LSTM (accuracy: 0.860987, precision: 0.860987, recall: 1, and F1-score: 0.925301, MSE: 0.139013): and CNN (accuracy: 0.987444, precision: 0.992708, recall0.992708, and F1-score: 0.012556, MSE: 0.112054) metrices. The main reason is that BiLSTM is able to properly capture mutually past and future pattern in email data using bidirectional layer architectures. On the other hand, LSTM is the unidirectional layers so its performance is slightly lower than BiLSTM model. Finally, the CNN is able to find the local email patterns, so the performance is between the BiLSTM and LSTM.

Table 3. LSTM, BiLSTM and CNN Performance Metrics [test_size=0.2, random_state=3, activation= sigmoid].

Method	Accuracy	Precision	Recall	F1-Score	MSE	RMSE
LSTM	0.860987	0.860987	1.000000	0.925301	0.139013	0.372845
BiLSTM	0.991031	0.991718	0.997917	0.994808	0.008969	0.094703
CNN	0.987444	0.992708	0.992708	0.992708	0.012556	0.112054

In order to know training and testing performance, Table 4 depicts the three deep learning methods and their training and testing loss and timing performance for spam email detection and classification. It can be seen that the BiLSTM provides the lowest test loss (0.063476) due to bidirectional nature of layers, but it has more train and inference time due to the processing complexity. Due to the simple architecture od CNN framework, it provides faster training and inference times 37.14 s and 0.75 s respectively. The confusion matrix indicated that BiLSTM and CNN are superior at reducing false positives compared to the LSTM model.

Table 4. LSTM, BiLSTM and CNN training detail performance.

Method	Train Loss	Test Loss	Train Time (s)	Inference Time (s)	Confusion Matrix
LSTM	0.392821	0.40323	94.119942	1.226155	[[0, 155], [0, 960]]
BiLSTM	0.010113	0.063476	168.622335	2.618593	[[139, 16], [0, 960]]
CNN	0.003262	0.061063	37.142659	0.751537	[[142, 13], [0, 960]]

In order to know the parameter effect for the performance, now the learning rates have been adjusted (Adam with 0.0005 for LSTM and CNN, and RMSprop with 0.0003 for BiLSTM), dropout rates have been increased to 0.3 for LSTM/BiLSTM and 0.5 for CNN, the number of epochs has been raised to 7, and the models now use more complex architectures with 128 units for LSTM/BiLSTM layers and 256 filters for the CNN. Furthermore, the activation function for LSTM and BiLSTM has been changed to 'tanh', and batch size has been increased to 64. The performance is show in following.

```
Performance Metrics Table:
        Accuracy Precision    Recall  F1-Score       MSE      RMSE Train Loss
LSTM    0.860987  0.860987       1.0  0.925301  0.139013  0.372845   0.393854
BiLSTM  0.983857  0.987578   0.99375  0.990654  0.016143  0.127057    0.05276
CNN     0.976682   0.97556  0.997917  0.986612  0.023318  0.152704   0.125593

       Test Loss Train Time (s) Inference Time (s)       Confusion Matrix
LSTM     0.40332     231.287169            2.53295   [[0, 155], [0, 960]]
BiLSTM  0.049128     290.831485           4.327419  [[143, 12], [6, 954]]
CNN     0.097051      71.348654            0.86301  [[131, 24], [2, 958]]
```

It can be seen that the previous parameter set recommends better performance in terms of accuracy, recall, F1-score, and efficiency, while the new set increases processing times with slight drops in performance. Moreover, the confusion matrices for all these algorithms have illustrated in Figures 5-7. The BiLSTM has lower confusion matrix. Therefore, it is better to tune the parameters before implementing these kinds of algorithms in real-time.

Figure 5. Confusion matrix for LSTM.

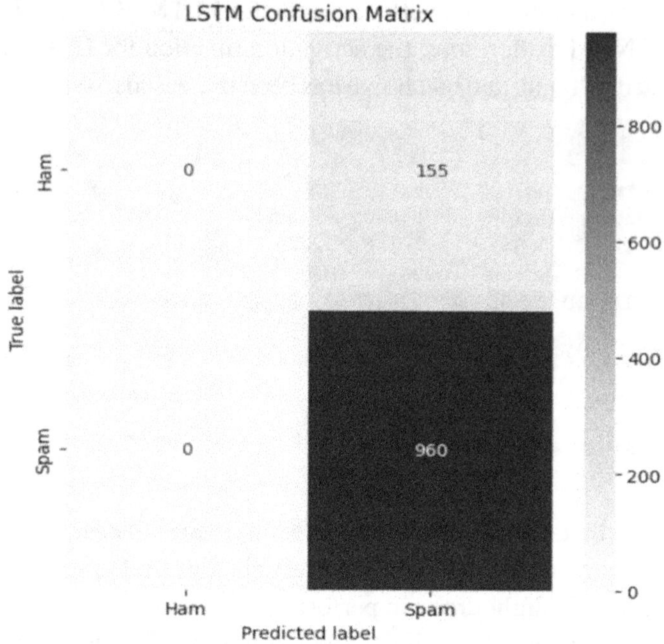

Figure 6. Confusion matrix for BiLSTM.

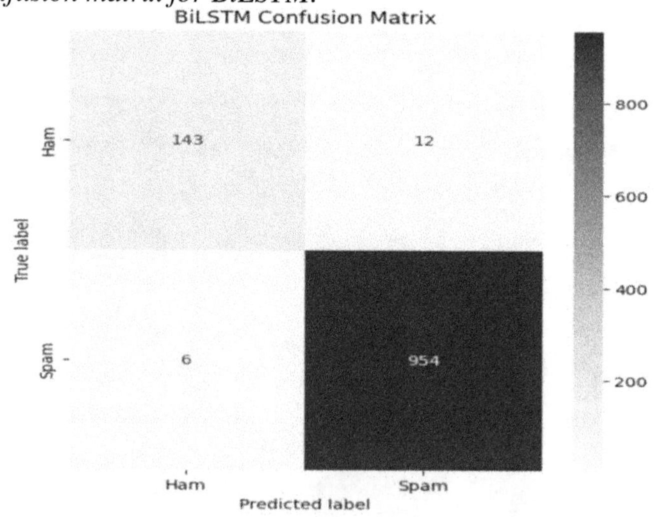

Figure 7. Confusion matrix for CNN.

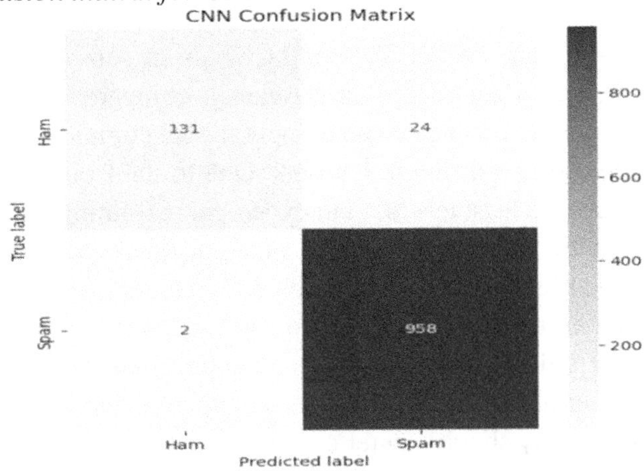

In order to validate the proposed algorithms, we have collected the email spam data from the https://github.com/MWiechmann/enron_spam_data/blob/master/enron_spam_data.zip and will apply the algorithm. It can be observed that there are a total of 17.171 spam and 16.545 ham mail messages. For simulation, we have used the same simulation parameters in first case. The simulation result is demonstrated in the following.

Performance Metrics Table:

	Accuracy	Precision	Recall	F1-Score	MSE	RMSE	Train Loss
LSTM	0.984875	0.991058	0.977791	0.98438	0.015125	0.122982	0.04835
BiLSTM	0.985024	0.994107	0.975053	0.984488	0.014976	0.122378	0.023673
CNN	0.986358	0.98988	0.982051	0.98595	0.013642	0.116798	0.007535

	Test Loss	Train Time (s)	Inference Time (s)	Confusion Matrix
LSTM	0.050167	412.841909	5.167072	[[3428, 29], [73, 3214]]
BiLSTM	0.057976	624.685056	7.287119	[[3438, 19], [82, 3205]]
CNN	0.063333	170.801557	1.505376	[[3424, 33], [59, 3228]]

It can be seen that there is a consistency performance and computational complexity compared with the previous mail data set. It can be concluded that the deep learning algorithms can be successfully implemented for spam email classification.

VI. CONCLUSION AND FUTURE WORK

The work exhibits that the BiLSTM and CNN offer substantial improvements in spam email detection accuracy and efficiency compared to LSTMl method. There is a consistency performance and computational complexity of the proposed algorithm considering two different datasets. Due to their bidirectional nature of BiLSTM, it provides the least test loss but expect more training and inference time. CNN framework, with its simpler design, recommend quicker training and inference times while keeping high accuracy. The combination of real-time response methods enhances the adaptability of spam email detection styles to new and evolving spam tactics. Educational policies are imperative in educating understanding about the risks of email-based cyber abuse and the advances of spam detection technologies and approaches. Future study should center on developing new reinforcement learning algorithms and technologies to further improve cybersecurity and mental wellness. We will try to find the suitable another dataset to do more analysis and investigation.

REFERENCES

Atawneh, S., & Aljehani, H. (2023). Phishing email detection model using deep learning. *Electronics (Basel)*, 12(20), 4261. DOI: 10.3390/electronics12204261

Brown, A., Davis, L., & Clark, R. (2020). Real-time feedback mechanisms in spam detection models. *Journal of Information Security*, 15(1), 22–36.

Davis, K., & Martinez, V. (2019). Educational strategies for email-based cyber abuse awareness. *Journal of Cyber Psychology*, 25(2), 88–102.

Gao, W., & Lee, J. (2016). Addressing class imbalance in spam detection: A case study. *International Journal of Data Science and Analytics*, 1(3), 115–127.

Garcia, J., & Patel, N. (2018). Future advancements in spam detection technologies. *Journal of Emerging Technologies*, 40(3), 120–134.

Johnson, M., & Lee, H. (2021). Impact of tokenization techniques on text classification. *Journal of Machine Learning Research*, 18(3), 134–150.

Kim, Y. (2014). Convolutional neural networks for sentence classification. *Proceedings of the 2014 Conference on Empirical Methods in Natural Language Processing*, 1746-1751. DOI: 10.3115/v1/D14-1181

Kleinberg, J. M. (2002). Authoritative sources in a hyperlinked environment. *Journal of the Association for Computing Machinery*, 46(5), 604–632. DOI: 10.1145/324133.324140

LeCun, Y., Bengio, Y., & Hinton, G. (2015). Deep learning. *Nature*, 521(7553), 436–444. DOI: 10.1038/nature14539 PMID: 26017442

Manning, C. D., Raghavan, P., & Schütze, H. (2008). *Introduction to information retrieval*. Cambridge University Press. DOI: 10.1017/CBO9780511809071

Noriega, J., & Lee, D. (2007). Enhancing spam filtering through blacklist and whitelist integration. *Proceedings of the International Conference on Machine Learning and Applications*, 45-52.

Ruder, S., Bingel, J., Søgaard, A., & Goldberg, Y. (2019). A survey of cross-lingual embedding models. *Journal of Artificial Intelligence Research*, 65, 37–71. DOI: 10.1613/jair.1.11640

Rudolph, K. (2004). Spam filtering: A brief overview. *Journal of Computer Security*, 12(3), 245–260.

Sahami, M., Dumais, S. T., Heckerman, D., & Horvitz, E. (1998). A Bayesian approach to filtering junk email. *Proceedings of the 1998 Conference on Uncertainty in Artificial Intelligence*, 55-62.

Smith, J., Brown, T., & Williams, R. (2022). Evaluating the effectiveness of LSTM and CNN models for spam detection. *Journal of Cybersecurity*, 32(4), 212–230.

Wu, K., Chen, H., & Yang, P. (2021). An attention-based CNN-LSTM-BiLSTM model for short-term electric load forecasting in integrated energy systems. *International Transactions on Electrical Energy Systems*, 31(1), e12637. DOI: 10.1002/2050-7038.12637

Yang, Y., & Liu, X. (2005). A re-examination of text categorization methods. *Proceedings of the 22nd Annual International ACM SIGIR Conference on Research and Development in Information Retrieval*, 42-49.

Zhang, X., Zhao, J., & LeCun, Y. (2018). Text understanding from scratch. *Proceedings of the 2015 Conference on Empirical Methods in Natural Language Processing*, 1025-1035.

Compilation of References

Abdi, N., Albaseer, A., & Abdallah, M. (2024). The Role of Deep Learning in Advancing Proactive Cybersecurity Measures for Smart Grid Networks: A Survey. *IEEE Internet of Things Journal*, 11(9), 16398–16421. DOI: 10.1109/JIOT.2024.3354045

Aboaoja, F. A., Zainal, A., Ghaleb, F. A., Al-Rimy, B. A. S., Eisa, T. A. E., & Elnour, A. A. H. (2022). Malware detection issues, challenges, and future directions: A survey. *Applied Sciences (Basel, Switzerland)*, 12(17), 8482. DOI: 10.3390/app12178482

Abu Taher & Jahan. (2015). Causes of Cybercrime Victimization: A Systematic. *Journal of Criminology, 16*, 28-42.

Açar, K. V. (2017). Organizational Aspect of the Global Fight against Online Child Sexual Abuse. *Global Policy*, 8(2), 259–262. DOI: 10.1111/1758-5899.12418

Adams, R., Baker, M., & Clark, N. (2024, September). "Resilience Training for Digital Literacy and Cybersecurity," IEEE Trans. Human-Mach. *Syst.*, 35(4), 550–559.

Adikari, N. (2016). Cyber violence (crimes) against women and girls. Committee of the WCWS-2016 The International Institute of Knowledge Management.

Admass, W. S., Munaye, Y. Y., & Diro, A. A. (2024). Cyber security: State of the art, challenges and future directions. *Cyber Security and Applications*, 2, 100031. DOI: 10.1016/j.csa.2023.100031

Aggarwal, A., & Gaur, S. (2024). Applying Artificial Intelligence to Explore Online Harassment and Cyberbullying Prevention. In *Impact of AI on Advancing Women's Safety* (pp. 104–120). IGI Global.

Agrawal, R., Dutt, V., & Vyas, N. (2023) "Improved Healthcare System with Quantum Computing," In *2023 International Conference on Artificial Intelligence and Smart Communication (AISC)*, Greater Noida, India, (pp. 99-103).

Ahanger, T. A., Tariq, U., Ibrahim, A., Ullah, I., Bouteraa, Y., & Gebali, F. (2022). Securing IoT-Empowered Fog Computing Systems: Machine Learning Perspective. *Mathematics*, 10(8), 1–20. DOI: 10.3390/math10081298

Ahmad, R., & Alsmadi, I. (2021). Machine learning approaches to IoT security: A systematic literature review [Formula presented]. *Internet of Things : Engineering Cyber Physical Human Systems*, 14, 100365. Advance online publication. DOI: 10.1016/j.iot.2021.100365

Ahmad, S., Noorani, M. S., Nadarajah, S., & Mamat, M. (2020). *Multicollinearity effect in regression analysis: A feed forward artificial neural network approach. International Journal of Advanced Research in Artificial Intelligence.*

Ahmad, Z., Shahid Khan, A., Wai Shiang, C., Abdullah, J., & Ahmad, F. (2021). Network intrusion detection system: A systematic study of machine learning and deep learning approaches. *Transactions on Emerging Telecommunications Technologies*, 32(1), e4150. DOI: 10.1002/ett.4150

Ahrend, J. M., Jirotka, M., & Jones, K. (2016). On the collaborative practices of cyber threat intelligence analysts to develop and utilize tacit Threat and Defence Knowledge. In *2016 International Conference on Cyber Situational Awareness, Data Analytics and Assessment,* CyberSA. DOI: 10.1109/CyberSA.2016.7503279

Akhtar, M. S., & Feng, T. (2023). Evaluation of machine learning algorithms for malware detection. *Sensors (Basel)*, 23(2), 946. DOI: 10.3390/s23020946 PMID: 36679741

Alabdulwahab, A., Haq, M. A., & Alshehri, M. (2023). Cyberbullying Detection using Machine Learning and Deep Learning. *International Journal of Advanced Computer Science and Applications*, 14(10), 424–432. DOI: 10.14569/IJACSA.2023.0141045

AlAhmadi, B. A., & Martinovic, I. (2018, May). MalClassifier: Malware family classification using network flow sequence behaviour. In *2018 APWG Symposium on Electronic Crime Research (eCrime)* (pp. 1-13). IEEE. DOI: 10.1109/ECRIME.2018.8376209

Albikawi, Z. F. (2023). Anxiety, Depression, Self-Esteem, Internet Addiction and Predictors of Cyberbullying and Cybervictimization among Female Nursing University Students: A Cross Sectional Study. *International Journal of Environmental Research and Public Health*, 20(5), 4293. DOI: 10.3390/ijerph20054293 PMID: 36901301

Alenezi, M. N., Alabdulrazzaq, H., Alshaher, A. A., & Alkharang, M. M. (2020). Evolution of malware threats and techniques: A review. *International Journal of Communication Networks and Information Security*, 12(3), 326–337.

Al-Garadi, M. A., Mohamed, A., Al-Ali, A. K., Du, X., Ali, I., & Guizani, M. (2020). A Survey of Machine and Deep Learning Methods for Internet of Things (IoT) Security. *IEEE Communications Surveys and Tutorials*, 22(3), 1646–1685. DOI: 10.1109/COMST.2020.2988293

Ali, Q., & Montenegro, S. (2016). Explicit Model Following Distributed Control Scheme for Formation Flying of Mini UAVs. *IEEE Access : Practical Innovations, Open Solutions*, 4, 397–406. DOI: 10.1109/ACCESS.2016.2517203

Ali, S., Haykal, H. A., & Youssef, E. Y. M. (2023). Child Sexual Abuse and the Internet—A Systematic Review. *Hu Arenas*, 6(2), 404–421. DOI: 10.1007/s42087-021-00228-9

Alismaiel, O. A. (2023). Digital Media Used in Education: The Influence on Cyberbullying Behaviors among Youth Students. *International Journal of Environmental Research and Public Health*, 20(2), 1370. DOI: 10.3390/ijerph20021370 PMID: 36674128

Allen, P., & Mitchell, L. (2023, December). "User-Centric Cybersecurity Solutions for Mental Health," IEEE Trans. Human-Comput. *Interact.*, 11(4), 450–461.

Almaraz-Rivera, J. G., Cantoral-Ceballos, J. A., & Botero, J. F. (2023). Enhancing IoT Network Security: Unveiling the Power of Self-Supervised Learning against DDoS Attacks. *Sensors (Basel)*, 23(21), 8701. DOI: 10.3390/s23218701 PMID: 37960401

Aloqaily, A., Abdallah, E. E., AbuZaid, H., Abdallah, A. E., & Al-hassan, M. (2025). Supervised Machine Learning for Real-Time Intrusion Attack Detection in Connected and Autonomous Vehicles: A Security Paradigm Shift. *Informatics (MDPI)*, 12(1), 4. DOI: 10.3390/informatics12010004

Alqahtani, M. A. (2021). Machine learning techniques for malware detection with challenges and future directions. *International Journal of Communication Networks and Information Security*, 13(2), 258–270.

Alsajri, A., & Steiti, A. (2024). Intrusion Detection System Based on Machine Learning Algorithms: (SVM and Genetic Algorithm). *Babylonian. Machine Learning*, 2024, 15–29.

Alsoubai, A., Razi, A., Agha, Z., Ali, S., Stringhini, G., De Choudhury, M., & Wisniewski, P. J. (2024). Profiling youth's offline and online risk experiences to develop targeted interventions for online safety. *Proceedings of the ACM on Human-Computer Interaction, 8*(CSCW1), 1–37.

Alzaabi, F. R., & Mehmood, A. (2024). A review of recent advances, challenges, and opportunities in malicious insider threat detection using machine learning methods. *IEEE Access : Practical Innovations, Open Solutions*, 12, 30907–30927. DOI: 10.1109/ACCESS.2024.3369906

Amari, S., & Wu, S. (1999). Improving support vector machine classifiers by modifying kernel functions. *Neural Networks*, 12(6), 783–789. DOI: 10.1016/S0893-6080(99)00032-5 PMID: 12662656

Anagha, T. S., Fathima, A., Naik, A. D., Goenka, C., Devamane, S. B., & Thimmapurmath, A. R. (2023). Credit Card Fraud Detection Using Machine Learning Algorithms. In *2023 International Conference on Computational Intelligence for Information, Security and Communication Applications (CIISCA),* (pp. 419–424). DOI: 10.1109/CIISCA59740.2023.00085

Andersen, D., Moore, A. P., Stanton, J. M., Cappelli, D. M., Rich, E., & Weaver, E. a, Gonzalez, J. J., Sarriegui, J. M., Zagonel, A., Mojtahedzadeh, M., & Shimeall, T. J. (2004). Preliminary System Dynamics Maps of the Insider Cyber-threat Problem. In *Proceedings of the 22nd International Conference of the Systems Dynamics Society*, (pp. 1–36).

Anderson, B., & McGrew, D. (2017). Machine learning for encrypted malware traffic classification: Accounting for noisy labels and non-stationarity. In *Proceedings of the ACM SIGKDD International Conference on Knowledge Discovery and Data Mining, Part F1296*, (pp. 1723–1732. DOI: 10.1145/3097983.3098163

Anderson, K., & Martinez, P. (2024, July). Technologists' Role in Mental Health Protection. *IEEE Transactions on Computers*, 60(2), 102–111.

Anita, M., Ambhika, C., & Anish, T. P. (2024). Exploring the Landscape of Artificial Intelligence in Healthcare Applications. In AI Healthcare Applications and Security, Ethical, and Legal Considerations (pp. 29-48). IGI Global.

Anjney, P., Pandey, J. K., & Puttam, V. S. R., Ompuri, O., &. Navya, V.K. (2023). Malware detection using machine learning. *International Journal of Emerging Technologies and Innovative Research, 10*(4), 1-4, www.jetir.org

Anwar, S., Mohamad Zain, J., Zolkipli, M. F., Inayat, Z., Khan, S., Anthony, B., & Chang, V. (2017). From intrusion detection to an intrusion response system: fundamentals, requirements, and future directions. *Algorithms, 10*(2), 39.

Apruzzese, G., Colajanni, M., Ferretti, L., Guido, A., & Marchetti, M. (2018). *On the effectiveness of machine and deep learning for cyber security.*

Apruzzese, G., Laskov, P., Montes de Oca, E., Mallouli, W., Brdalo Rapa, L., Grammatopoulos, A. V., & Di Franco, F. (2023). The role of machine learning in cybersecurity. *Digital Threats : Research and Practice*, 4(1), 1–38. DOI: 10.1145/3545574

Arslan, G., Kabasakal, Z., & Taş, B. (2024). Childhood Psychological Maltreatment, Mindful Awareness, Self-Transcendence, and Mental WellbeingWellbeing in Emerging Adults. *Emerging Adulthood*, 12(1), 18–28. DOI: 10.1177/21676968231208246

Arvindhan, M., Bhatia, M., Sinha, N., & Kumar, T. (2022). Coronavirus Visual Dashboard and Data Repository: COVID-19. In *Applications of Computational Methods in Manufacturing and Product Design: Select Proceedings of IPDIMS 2020* (pp. 269-279). Singapore: Springer Nature Singapore.

Asad, M. M., Erum, D., Churi, P., & Guerrero, A. J. M. (2023). Effect of technostress on Psychological well-being of post-graduate students: A perspective and correlational study of Higher Education Management. *International Journal of Information Management Data Insights*, 3(1), 100149. DOI: 10.1016/j.jjimei.2022.100149

Aslan, Ö., Aktuğ, S. S., Ozkan-Okay, M., Yilmaz, A. A., & Akin, E. (2023). A comprehensive review of cyber security vulnerabilities, threats, attacks, and solutions. *Electronics (Basel)*, 12(6), 1333. DOI: 10.3390/electronics12061333

Atawneh, S., & Aljehani, H. (2023). Phishing email detection model using deep learning. *Electronics (Basel)*, 12(20), 4261. DOI: 10.3390/electronics12204261

Awadallah, A., Eledlebi, K., Zemerly, J., Puthal, D., Damiani, E., Taha, K., Kim, T.-Y., Yoo, P. D., Choo, K.-K. R., Yim, M.-S., & Yeun, C. Y. (2024). Artificial intelligence-based cybersecurity for the metaverse: Research challenges and opportunities. *IEEE Communications Surveys and Tutorials*, 1. DOI: 10.1109/COMST.2024.3442475

Babu, M. R., & Veena, K. N. (2021). A survey on attack detection methods for IOT using machine learning and deep learning. In *2021 3rd International Conference on Signal Processing and Communication, May*, (pp. 625–630). DOI: 10.1109/ICSPC51351.2021.9451740

Bagaa, M., Taleb, T., Bernabe, J. B., & Skarmeta, A. (2020). A Machine Learning Security Framework for Iot Systems. *IEEE Access: Practical Innovations, Open Solutions*, 8, 114066–114077. DOI: 10.1109/ACCESS.2020.2996214

Bajpai, A., Khule, S., Sharma, V. P., Sharma, Y., & Dubey, G. (2024). Real-time Anomaly Detection in Big Data Streams: Machine Learning Approaches and Performance Evaluation. *International Journal of Intelligent Systems and Applications in Engineering*, 12(21), 915–924.

Ball, T. (1999). The concept of dynamic analysis. *Software Engineering Notes*, 24(6), 216–234. DOI: 10.1145/318774.318944

Basu, I., Sinha, N., Bhagat, D., & Goswami, S. (2016). Malware detection based on source data using data mining: A survey. *Am. J. Adv. Comput*, 3(1), 18–37.

Basu, K., Krishnamurthy, P., Khorrami, F., & Karri, R. (2019). A theoretical study of hardware performance counters-based malware detection. *IEEE Transactions on Information Forensics and Security*, 15, 512–525. DOI: 10.1109/TIFS.2019.2924549

Belaoued, M., Boukellal, A., Koalal, M. A., Derhab, A., Mazouzi, S., & Khan, F. A. (2019). Combined dynamic multi-feature and rule-based behavior for accurate malware detection. *International Journal of Distributed Sensor Networks*, 15(11). Advance online publication. DOI: 10.1177/1550147719889907

Bellini, R. F. (2024). Abusive Partner Perspectives on Technology Abuse: Implications for Community-based Violence Prevention. *Proceedings of the ACM on Human-Computer Interaction, 8*(CSCW1), 1–25. DOI: 10.1145/3637292

Bellini, R., Tseng, E., Warford, N., Daffalla, A., Matthews, T., Consolvo, S., Woelfer, J. P., Kelley, P. G., Mazurek, M. L., & Cuomo, D. (2024). Sok: Safer digital safety research involving at-risk users. In *2024 IEEE Symposium on Security and Privacy (SP)* (pp. 635–654). DOI: 10.1109/SP54263.2024.00071

Ben-Hur, A., & Weston, J. (2010). A user's guide to support vector machines. *Methods in Molecular Biology (Clifton, N.J.)*, 609, 223–239. DOI: 10.1007/978-1-60327-241-4_13 PMID: 20221922

Bharadiya, J. (2023). Machine learning in cybersecurity: Techniques and challenges. *European Journal of Technology*, 7(2), 1–14. DOI: 10.47672/ejt.1486

Bhattacharyya, D. K., & Kalita, J. K. (2013). Network Anomaly Detection: A Machine Learning Perspective. *Network Anomaly Detection*. Advance online publication. DOI: 10.1201/b15088-14

Bhosale, K. S., Nenova, M., & Iliev, G. (2020). Intrusion detection in communication networks using different classifiers. In *Proceedings of the 2nd International Conference on Advanced Technologies for Societal Applications,* (pp. 19–28). DOI: 10.1007/978-3-030-16962-6_3

Bist, A. S., Patrick, A., Sharma, R., Pargein, S., & Dwivedi, S. K. (2017). Algorithms for Metamorphic Malware Detection. *International Journal of Engineering Sciences & Research Technology*, 6(6), 325–332.

Blackwood, A., Carrington, J., Baryshevsky, S., & Morrison, G. (2024). The implementation of a hybrid large language emulate for adaptive cryptographic cyber defense.

Bouwman, X., Griffioen, H., Egbers, J., Doerr, C., Klievink, B., & van Eeten, M. (2020). A different cup of TI? The added value of commercial threat intelligence. In *Proceedings of the 29th USENIX Security Symposium*, (pp. 433–450).

Brown, S. D., Dahill, D., Karakilic, E., King, D., Misha, P., Pirrioni, S., & Vedi, P. (2020). Psychological wellbeing and safety in a global context: a rapid evidence assessment.

Brown, A., Davis, L., & Clark, R. (2020). Real-time feedback mechanisms in spam detection models. *Journal of Information Security*, 15(1), 22–36.

Brown, A., Green, S., & Black, P. (2024, April). The Role of Cybersecurity in Mental Health Protection: An Overview. *IEEE Security and Privacy*, 21(2), 14–22.

Budimir, S., Fontaine, J. R. J., Huijts, N. M. A., Haans, A., Loukas, G., & Roesch, E. B. (2021). Emotional Reactions to Cybersecurity Breach Situations: Scenario-Based Survey Study. *Journal of Medical Internet Research*, 23(5), e24879. DOI: 10.2196/24879 PMID: 33978591

Buheji, M., & Buheji, B. (2024). Mitigating risks of slow children development due to war on Gaza 2023. *International Journal of Psychology and Behavioral Sciences*, 14(1), 11–21.

Burges, C. J. C. (1998). A Tutorial on Support Vector Machines for Pattern Recognition. *Data Mining and Knowledge Discovery*, 2(2), 121–167. DOI: 10.1023/A:1009715923555

Cabrera, A., & Calix, R. (2016). On the anatomy of the dynamic behavior of polymorphic viruses. In *Proceedings - 2016 International Conference on Collaboration Technologies and Systems*, (pp. 424–429). DOI: 10.1109/CTS.2016.0081

Canedo, J., & Skjellum, A. (2016). Using machine learning to secure IoT systems. In *2016 14th Annual Conference on Privacy, Security and Trust, (pp.* 219–222). DOI: 10.1109/PST.2016.7906930

Caspi, O., & Herzog, B. (2018). *Emotet: The Tricky Trojan that 'Git Clones.'* 1–11. https://research.checkpoint.com/emotet-tricky-trojan-git-clones/

Caviglione, L., Comito, C., Guarascio, M., & Manco, G. (2023). Emerging challenges and perspectives in Deep Learning model security: A brief survey. *Systems and Soft Computing*, 5, 200050. DOI: 10.1016/j.sasc.2023.200050

Cerullo, G., Mazzeo, G., Papale, G., Ragucci, B., & Sgaglione, L. (2018). Iot and sensor networks security. In *Security and Resilience in Intelligent Data-Centric Systems and Communication Networks* (pp. 77–101). Academic Press. DOI: 10.1016/B978-0-12-811373-8.00004-5

Chadwick, D. D. (2019). Online risk for people with intellectual disabilities. *Tizard Learning Disability Review*, 24(4), 180–187. DOI: 10.1108/TLDR-03-2019-0008

Chandola, V., Banerjee, A., & Kumar, V. (2009). Anomaly detection: A survey. *ACM Computing Surveys*, 41(3), 1–58. DOI: 10.1145/1541880.1541882

Chandrasekaran, S., Dutt, V., Vyas, N., & Anand, A. (2023) "Fuzzy KNN Implementation for Early Parkinson's Disease Prediction," 2023 7th International Conference on Computing Methodologies and Communication (ICCMC), Erode, India, 2023, pp. 896-901. DOI: 10.1109/ICCMC56507.2023.10083522

Charu Nangia, Singh, & Ali. (2019). Built Environment and Crime Against Women: An overview. 9th International Conference on Cloud Computing, Data Science & Engineering (Confluence), 636-641.

Chaulagain, D., Poudel, P., Pathak, P., Roy, S., Caragea, D., Liu, G., & Ou, X. (2020). Hybrid Analysis of Android Apps for Security Vetting using Deep Learning. *2020 IEEE Conference on Communications and Network Security*. DOI: 10.1109/CNS48642.2020.9162341

Chawla, N., Singh, A., Kumar, H., Kar, M., & Mukhopadhyay, S. (2021). Securing IoT Devices Using Dynamic Power Management: Machine Learning Approach. *IEEE Internet of Things Journal*, 8(22), 16379–16394. DOI: 10.1109/JIOT.2020.3021594

Chirra, D. R. (2024). Advanced Threat Detection and Response Systems Using Federated Machine Learning in Critical Infrastructure. *International Journal of Advanced Engineering Technologies and Innovations*, 2(1), 61–81.

Chitra Lekha & Prakasam. (2018). Implementation of data mining techniques for cyber crime detection. International Journal of Engineering, Science, 7, 607-613.

Choi, C., Esposito, C., Lee, M., & Choi, J. (2019). Metamorphic malicious code behavior detection using probabilistic inference methods. *Cognitive Systems Research*, 56, 142–150. DOI: 10.1016/j.cogsys.2019.03.007

Choi, S., Bae, J., Lee, C., Kim, Y., & Kim, J. (2020). Attention-based automated feature extraction for malware analysis. *Sensors (Basel)*, 20(10), 2893. Advance online publication. DOI: 10.3390/s20102893 PMID: 32443750

Christiana, A. O., Gyunka, B. A., & Noah, A. (2020). Android malware detection through machine learning techniques: A review. *International Journal of Online and Biomedical Engineering,* 16(2), 14–30. DOI: 10.3991/ijoe.v16i02.11549

Cinar, B. (2023). Cyber Threat Intelligence: Current Trends and Future Perspectives. *Journal of Engineering Research and Reports*, 25(4), 91–105. DOI: 10.9734/jerr/2023/v25i4905

Clarke, V., & Braun, V. (2017). Thematic analysis. *The Journal of Positive Psychology*, 12(3), 297–298. DOI: 10.1080/17439760.2016.1262613

Conley, C. S., Raposa, E. B., Bartolotta, K., Broner, S. E., Hareli, M., Forbes, N., Christensen, K. M., & Assink, M. (2022). The impact of mobile technology-delivered interventions on youth well-being: Systematic review and 3-level meta-analysis. *JMIR Mental Health*, 9(7), e34254. DOI: 10.2196/34254 PMID: 35904845

Cuan, B., Damien, A., Delaplace, C., & Valois, M. (2018). Malware detection in PDF files using machine learning. In *Proceedings of the 15th International Joint Conference on e-Business and Telecommunications, 2*, (pp. 412–419). DOI: 10.5220/0006884704120419

Cyber security in Action: Safeguarding the Youth from Cyberbullying. (n.d.). Retrieved December 31, 2024, from https://cxotoday.com/press-release/cyber-security-in-action-safeguarding-the-youth-from-cyberbullying/

Cyberbullying - National Bullying Prevention Center. (n.d.). Retrieved December 31, 2024, from https://www.pacer.org/bullying/info/cyberbullying/

Cyberbullying (for Teens) | Nemours KidsHealth. (n.d.). Retrieved December 31, 2024, from https://kidshealth.org/en/teens/cyberbullying.html

Cyberbullying: What is it and how to stop it | UNICEF. (n.d.). Retrieved December 31, 2024, from https://www.unicef.org/end-violence/how-to-stop-cyberbullying

Dadkhah, S., Neto, E. C. P., Ferreira, R., Molokwu, R. C., Sadeghi, S., & Ghorbani, A. (2024). Ciciomt2024: Attack vectors in healthcare device-a multi-protocol dataset for assessing iomt device security.

Damodaran, A., Di Troia, F., Visaggio, C. A., Austin, T. H., & Stamp, M. (2017). A comparison of static, dynamic, and hybrid analysis for malware detection. *Journal of Computer Virology and Hacking Techniques*, 13(1), 1–24. DOI: 10.1007/s11416-015-0261-z

Darshan, S. L. S., Kumara, M. A. A., & Jaidhar, C. D. (2016). Windows malware detection based on cuckoo sandbox generated report using machine learning algorithm. In *11th International Conference on Industrial and Information Systems,Janua*, (pp. 534–539). DOI: 10.1109/ICIINFS.2016.8262998

Das, R., & Morris, T. H. (2017). Machine learning and cyber security. In *2017 International Conference on Computer, Electrical & Communication Engineering (ICCECE)* (pp. 1-7). IEEE.

Das, S., Krishnamurthy, B., Das, R. R., & Shiva, S. G. (2024). State of the art: Security Testing of Machine Learning Development Systems. In *2024 IEEE 14th Annual Computing and Communication Workshop and Conference (CCWC)* (pp. 0534-0540). IEEE.

Davis, K., & Martinez, V. (2019). Educational strategies for email-based cyber abuse awareness. *Journal of Cyber Psychology*, 25(2), 88–102.

Davis, S., & Thomas, L. (2023, October). Community Approaches to Fostering Safe Digital Spaces. *IEEE Transactions on Communications*, 22(1), 66–77.

Dealing with Bullying: Strategies to fight Teen Bullying. (n.d.). Retrieved December 31, 2024, from https://tooshytoask.org/help/personal-safety/cyber-bullying/

DeKeseredy & Corsianos. (2015). Violence against women in pornography. Routledge.

DeLiema, M., Burnes, D., & Langton, L. (2021). The Financial and Psychological Impact of Identity Theft Among Older Adults. *Innovation in Aging*, 5(4), igab043. Advance online publication. DOI: 10.1093/geroni/igab043 PMID: 34988295

Dhakal, S., Parvez, A., Das, P., Saxena, S., & Memoria, M. (2024). An analysis of AI-driven technologies for enhancing security along the India-Nepal border. In *2024 International Conference on Computing, Sciences and Communications (ICCSC)* (pp. 1-6). IEEE. DOI: 10.1109/ICCSC62048.2024.10830380

Dhanya, K. A., Vajipayajula, S., Srinivasan, K., Tibrewal, A., Kumar, T. S., & Kumar, T. G. (2023). Detection of network attacks using machine learning and deep learning models. *Procedia Computer Science*, 218, 57–66. DOI: 10.1016/j.procs.2022.12.401

DIng., Y., Wang, L., Zhang, H., Yi, J., Fan, D., & Gong, B. (2019). Defending against adversarial attacks using random forest. *IEEE Computer Society Conference on Computer Vision and Pattern Recognition Workshops*, (pp. 105–114). DOI: 10.1109/CVPRW.2019.00019

Dini, P., Elhanashi, A., Begni, A., Saponara, S., Zheng, Q., & Gasmi, K. (2023). Overview on intrusion detection systems design exploiting machine learning for networking cybersecurity. *Applied Sciences (Basel, Switzerland)*, 13(13), 7507. DOI: 10.3390/app13137507

Djaneye-Boundjou, O., Messay-Kebede, T., Kapp, D., Greer, J., & Ralescu, A. (2019). Static Analysis through Topic Modeling and its Application to Malware Programs Classification. In *Proceedings of the IEEE National Aerospace Electronics Conference, (pp.* 226–231). DOI: 10.1109/NAECON46414.2019.9057876

Dumka, A., Memoria, M., & Ashok, A. (2019). Security and challenges in mobile cloud computing. In *Security Designs for the Cloud*. IoT, and Social Networking. DOI: 10.1002/9781119593171.ch3

Dutta, N., Jadav, N., Tanwar, S., Sarma, H. K. D., Pricop, E., Dutta, N., ... Pricop, E. (2022). Introduction to malware analysis. *Cyber Security: Issues and Current Trends*, 129-141

Düzgün, B., Çayır, A., Demirkıran, F., Kayha, C. N., Gençaydın, B., & Dağ, H. (2021). *New Datasets for Dynamic Malware Classification*. http://arxiv.org/abs/2111.15205

El-Asam, A., Lane, R., & Katz, A. (2022). Psychological Distress and Its Mediating Effect on Experiences of Online Risk: The Case for Vulnerable Young People. *Frontiers in Education*, 7, 772051. DOI: 10.3389/feduc.2022.772051

Elavsky, S., Blahošová, J., Lebedíková, M., Tkaczyk, M., Tancos, M., Plhák, J., Sotolář, O., & Smahel, D. (2022). Researching the links between smartphone behavior and adolescent well-being with the FUTURE-WP4 (modeling the future: understanding the impact of technology on adolescent's well-being work package 4) project: protocol for an ecological momentary assessment study. *JMIR Research Protocols*, 11(3), e35984. DOI: 10.2196/35984 PMID: 35258467

Emma Louis Backe, Lilleston, & McCleary-Sills. (2018). Networked individuals, gendered violence; a literature review of Cyberviolence. Violence and Gender, 5(3), 135-146.

Evans, A.. (2024, February). Protecting Vulnerable Populations in Cyberspace. *IEEE Trans. Soc. Comput.*, 10(3), 123–132.

Falah, A., Pan, L., Huda, S., Pokhrel, S. R., & Anwar, A. (2021). Improving malicious PDF classifier with feature engineering: A data-driven approach. *Future Generation Computer Systems*, 115, 314–326. DOI: 10.1016/j.future.2020.09.015

Fang, X., & Zhan, J. (2015). Sentiment analysis using product review data. *Journal of Big Data*, 2(1), 5. Advance online publication. DOI: 10.1186/s40537-015-0015-2

Fang, Z., Cerna-Turoff, I., Zhang, C., Lu, M., Lachman, J. M., & Barlow, J. (2022). COVID-19 in children and adolescents in Europe: A multinational, multicentre cohort study. *The Lancet. Child & Adolescent Health*, 6, 313. DOI: 10.1016/S2352-4642(22)00033-5 PMID: 35305703

Finkelhor, D., Turner, H., & Colburn, D. (2022). Prevalence of Online Sexual Offenses Against Children in the US. *JAMA Network Open*, 5(10), e2234471. DOI: 10.1001/jamanetworkopen.2022.34471 PMID: 36239942

Ford, V., & Siraj, A. (2014). Applications of machine learning in cyber security. *Proceedings of the 27th international conference on computer applications in industry and engineering* 118.

Foster, J., & Brown, S. (2023, September). Predictive Analytics for Cybersecurity and Mental Health. *IEEE Transactions on Knowledge and Data Engineering*, 22(5), 556–567.

Fovino, I. N., Carcano, A., Murel, T. D. L., Trombetta, A., & Masera, M. (2010, April). Modbus/DNP3 state-based intrusion detection system. In *2010 24th IEEE International Conference on Advanced Information Networking and Applications* (pp. 729-736). IEEE.

Fu, W., Pang, J., Zhao, R., Zhang, Y., & Wei, B. (2008). Static detection of API-calling behavior from malicious binary executables. *Proceedings of the 2008 International Conference on Computer and Electrical Engineering, ICCEE 2008*, 388–392. DOI: 10.1109/ICCEE.2008.53

Gao, W., & Lee, J. (2016). Addressing class imbalance in spam detection: A case study. *International Journal of Data Science and Analytics*, 1(3), 115–127.

Garcia, F.. (2023, November). Ethical Considerations in AI-Driven Cybersecurity. *IEEE Comput.*, 56(9), 94–103.

Garcia, J., & Patel, N. (2018). Future advancements in spam detection technologies. *Journal of Emerging Technologies*, 40(3), 120–134.

Garg, A., & Tai, K. (2013). Comparison of statistical and machine learning methods in modelling of data with multicollinearity. *International Journal of Modelling Identification and Control*, 18(4), 295. DOI: 10.1504/IJMIC.2013.053535

Gascon, H., Grobauer, B., Schreck, T., Rist, L., Arp, D., & Rieck, K. (2017). Mining attributed graphs for threat intelligence. In *Proceedings of the 7th ACM Conference on Data and Application Security and Privacy*, (pp. 15–22). DOI: 10.1145/3029806.3029811

Gavriluţ, D., Cimpoeşu, M., Anton, D., & Ciortuz, L. (2009). Malware detection using machine learning. *Proceedings of the International Multiconference on Computer Science and Information Technology, IMCSIT*, 09(4), 735–741. DOI: 10.1109/IMCSIT.2009.5352759

Ge, M., Fu, X., Syed, N., Baig, Z., Teo, G., & Robles-Kelly, A. (2019, December). Deep learning-based intrusion detection for IoT networks. In *Proceedings of IEEE Pacific Rim International Symposium on Dependable Computing,* (pp. 256–265). DOI: 10.1109/PRDC47002.2019.00056

George, A. S. (2024). Virtual Violence: Legal and Psychological Ramifications of Sexual Assault in Virtual Reality Environments. *Partners Universal International Innovation Journal*, 2(1), 96–114.

Ghelani, D. (2024). Enhancing data security: Machine learning approaches for intrusion detection in computer networks. *Journal of Environmental Science and Technology*, 3(1), 611–629.

Ghimire, D., & Lee, J. (2013). Geometric feature-based facial expression recognition in image sequences using multi-class AdaBoost and support vector machines. *Sensors (Basel)*, 13(6), 7714–7734. DOI: 10.3390/s130607714 PMID: 23771158

Gogoi, P., Bhattacharyya, D. K., Borah, B., & Kalita, J. K. (2011). A survey of outlier detection methods in network anomaly identification. *The Computer Journal*, 54(4), 570–588. DOI: 10.1093/comjnl/bxr026

Goriparthi, R. G. (2023). AI-Augmented Cybersecurity: Machine Learning for Real-Time Threat Detection. *Revista de Inteligencia Artificial en Medicina*, 14(1), 576–594.

Gorment, N. Z., Selamat, A., Cheng, L. K., & Krejcar, O. (2023). Machine learning algorithm for malware detection: Taxonomy, current challenges, and future directions. *IEEE Access : Practical Innovations, Open Solutions*, 11, 141045–141089. DOI: 10.1109/ACCESS.2023.3256979

Gorzałczany, M. B., & Rudziński, F. (2022). Intrusion detection in Internet of Things with MQTT protocol—An accurate and interpretable genetic-fuzzy rule-based solution. *IEEE Internet of Things Journal*, 9(24), 24843–24855. DOI: 10.1109/JIOT.2022.3194837

Gundoor, T. K. (2022). IoT-Enabled 5G Networks for Secure Communication. In *Information Security Practices for the Internet of Things, 5G, and Next-Generation Wireless Networks* (pp. 1-29). IGI Global.

Gundoor, T. K. Sridevi, & Mulimani, R. (2025). AI-Based Solutions for Malware Detection and Prevention. In M. Almaiah & Y. Maleh (Eds.), *Machine Intelligence Applications in Cyber-Risk Management* (pp. 107-134). IGI Global Scientific Publishing. DOI: 10.4018/979-8-3693-7540-2.ch006

Gundoor, T.K., & Sridevi (2022). "Identification Of Dominant Features in Non-Portable Executable Malicious File," In 2022 Second International Conference on Computer Science, Engineering and Applications, Gunupur, India, (pp. 1-6), .DOI: 10.1109/ICCSEA54677.2022.9936451

Guo, S., Chen, J., Yu, B., Jiang, Y., Song, Y., & Jin, Y. (2019). Knowledge, attitude and practice of child sexual abuse prevention amongparents of children with hearing loss: A pilot study in Beijing and Hebei Province, China. *Journal of Child Sexual Abuse*, 28(7), 781–798. DOI: 10.1080/10538712.2019.1627688 PMID: 31287784

Gupta, B. B., & Sheng, M. (2019). *Machine Learning for Computer and Cyber Security* (Press, C. R. C., Ed.). Preface. DOI: 10.1201/9780429504044

Gupta, M., Gao, J., Aggarwal, C. C., & Han, J. (2014). Outlier Detection for Temporal Data: A Survey. *IEEE Transactions on Knowledge and Data Engineering*, 26(9), 2250–2267. DOI: 10.1109/TKDE.2013.184

Habeeb, M. A., Khaleel, Y. L., & Abdulnabi, A. R. (2024). Enhancing Security and Performance in Vehicular Adhoc Networks: A Machine Learning Approach to Combat Adversarial Attacks. *Mesopotamian Journal of Computer Science*, 2024, 122–133. DOI: 10.58496/MJCSC/2024/010

Halder & Jaishankar. (2016). Cybercrimes against women in India. SAGE Publications India.

Halder, D., & Karuppannan, J. K. (2012). Jaishankar, cybercrime and the victimization of women. Information science Reference, 10, 719-724.

Hall, N., & Lee, J. (2023, November). Integrating Cybersecurity and Mental Health Protection. *IEEE Trans. Syst. Sci. Cybern.*, 17(1), 23–34.

Hamsa, Singh, & Panackal. (2018). Study on Effect of Social Networking Sites on the Young World of Cyber Crime. Annual Research Journal of SCMS, 220-238.

Harahsheh, K., & Chen, C. H. (2023). A Survey of Using Machine Learning in IoT Security and the Challenges Faced by Researchers. *Informatica (Slovenia)*, 47(6), 1–54. DOI: 10.31449/inf.v47i6.4635

Harris, D., & Phillips, L. (2024, June). Role of Mental Health Professionals in Cybersecurity. *IEEE Trans. Med. Informatics*, 23(4), 420–429.

Hecker, C., Hufnagl, C., Oellerer, A., Griessenauer, C. J., & Killer-Oberpfalzer, M. (2025). The Artisse intrasaccular device: A new intrasaccular flow diverter for the treatment of cerebral aneurysms. *AJNR. American Journal of Neuroradiology*, 46(1), 84–89. DOI: 10.3174/ajnr.A8478 PMID: 39779289

Henry, N., & Powell, A. (2018). Technology-Facilitated Sexual Violence. *Trauma, Violence & Abuse*, 19(2), 195–208. DOI: 10.1177/1524838016650189 PMID: 27311818

Here's How You Can Take Action against Stalking in India. (n.d.). Retrieved December 31, 2024, from https://thebetterindia.com/45671/stalking-india-women-complaint-online/

Herzalla, D., Lunardi, W. T., & Andreoni, M. (2023). TII-SSRC-23 dataset: Typological exploration of diverse traffic patterns for intrusion detection. *IEEE Access : Practical Innovations, Open Solutions*, 11, 118577–118594. DOI: 10.1109/ACCESS.2023.3319213

Horskykh, M. (2018). Online Grooming as a Manipulative Social Interaction: Insights from Textual Analysis. *Pol. J. Engl. Stud.*, 4, 79–111.

Hosen, M. S., Al Mamun, M. A., Khandakar, S., Hossain, K., Islam, M. M., & Alkhayyat, A. (2024). Cybersecurity Meets Data Science: A Fusion of Disciplines for Enhanced Threat Protection. *Nanotechnology Perceptions*, 236–256.

How to Prevent Cyberbullying (for Parents) (for Parents) | Nemours KidsHealth. (n.d.). Retrieved December 31, 2024, from https://kidshealth.org/en/parents/cyberbullying.html

Hussain, F., Hussain, R., Hassan, S. A., & Hossain, E. (2020). Machine Learning in IoT Security: Current Solutions and Future Challenges. *IEEE Communications Surveys and Tutorials*, 22(3), 1686–1721. DOI: 10.1109/COMST.2020.2986444

Ijaz, M., Durad, M. H., & Ismail, M. (2019a). Static and Dynamic Malware Analysis Using Machine Learning. *Proceedings of 2019 16th International Bhurban Conference on Applied Sciences and Technology, IBCAST 2019, January*, 687–691. DOI: 10.1109/IBCAST.2019.8667136

Iklody, A., Wagener, G., Dulaunoy, A., Mokaddem, S., & Wagner, C. (2018). *Decaying Indicators of Compromise*. http://arxiv.org/abs/1803.11052

Importance of Digital Literacy Skills for Students | Learning.com. (n.d.). Retrieved December 31, 2024, from https://www.learning.com/blog/reasons-digital-literacy-is-important-for-students/

Increased Cybersecurity Essential For NGOs: Help Available. (n.d.). Retrieved December 31, 2024, from https://www.forbes.com/sites/davidhessekiel/2024/09/19/increased-cybersecurity-essential-for-ngos-help-available/

INHOPE - Association of Internet Hotline Providers | Enhancing Online Platforms Safety Tools for a Child-centred Digital Future. (n.d.). Retrieved December 31, 2024, from https://inhope.org/EN/articles/enhancing-online-platforms-safety-tools-for-a-child-centred-digital-future

Islam, N., Altamimi, M., Haseeb, K., & Siraj, M. (2021). Secure and sustainable predictive framework for iot-based multimedia services using machine learning. *Sustainability (Basel)*, 13(23), 1–15. DOI: 10.3390/su132313128

Ismail, S., Dawoud, D. W., & Reza, H. (2023). Securing Wireless Sensor Networks Using Machine Learning and Blockchain: A Review. *Future Internet*, 15(6), 1–45. DOI: 10.3390/fi15060200

Iwaya, L. H., Babar, M. A., Rashid, A., & Wijayarathna, C. (2022). On the privacy of mental health apps: An empirical investigation and its implications for app development. *Empirical Software Engineering*, 28(1), 2. DOI: 10.1007/s10664-022-10236-0 PMID: 36407814

Jacqueline, B. (2015). Criminal behavior and the copycat effect: Literature review and theoretical framework for empirical investigation. Aggression and Violent Behavior, 22, 46-64.

Jæger, B. (2021). Digital Citizenship – A Review of the Academic Literature. *Der Moderne Staat – Zeitschrift Für Public Policy, Recht Und Management, 14*(1), 24–42. DOI: 10.3224/dms.v14i1.09

Jaglan. (2007). Review of modeling technologies used for Predicting Crime. Journal of Research, 1-12.

Jaisingh, W., Nanjundan, P., & George, J. P. (2024). Machine Learning in Cyber Threats Intelligent System. In *Artificial Intelligence for Cyber Defense and Smart Policing* (pp. 1–20). Chapman and Hall/CRC. DOI: 10.1201/9781003251781-1

Javed, H., El-Sappagh, S., & Abuhmed, T. (2025). Robustness in deep learning models for medical diagnostics: Security and adversarial challenges towards robust AI applications. *Artificial Intelligence Review*, 58(1), 1–107.

Jiang, H., Nagra, J., & Ahammad, P. (2016). *SoK: Applying Machine Learning in Security - A Survey*. http://arxiv.org/abs/1611.03186

Joachims, T. (2000). Transductive inference for text classification using support vector machines. In *Proceedings of the 20th International Conference on Machine Learning*.

Johnson, M., & Lee, H. (2021). Impact of tokenization techniques on text classification. *Journal of Machine Learning Research*, 18(3), 134–150.

Jones, C., Stalker, K., Franklin, A., Fry, D., Cameron, A., & Taylor, J. (2017). Enablers of help-seeking for deaf and disabled children and adolescents following abuse and barriers to protection: A qualitative study. *Child & Family Social Work*, 22(2), 762–771. DOI: 10.1111/cfs.12293

Joshi, M., Birla, S., Pal, H., Khatri, K., Kadwal, M., & Salitra, D. (2024). AI-Driven Intrusion Detection Systems: Leveraging Deep Learning for Network Security. *Nanotechnology Perceptions*, 573–585.

Jump, M. (2019). Fighting cyberthreats with technology solutions. *Biomedical Instrumentation & Technology, February*.

Jurek, A., Mulvenna, M. D., & Bi, Y. (2015). Improved lexicon-based sentiment analysis for social media analytics. *Security Informatics*, 4(1), 9. Advance online publication. DOI: 10.1186/s13388-015-0024-x

Jyothsna, V. V. R. P. V., Prasad, R., & Prasad, K. M. (2011). A review of anomaly-based intrusion detection systems. *International Journal of Computer Applications*, 28(7), 26–35. DOI: 10.5120/3399-4730

Kabir, N. (2018). Cyber Crimes a New Form of Violence Against Women: From the Case Study of Bangladesh.

Kalpana, V., & Hariram, V. (2023) "Artificial Intelligence based Health Monitoring System on IoTH platform," In *2023 Second International Conference on Augmented Intelligence and Sustainable Systems (ICAISS)*, Trichy, India, (pp. 1458-1463).

Kara, I. (2019). A basic malware analysis method. *Computer Fraud & Security*, 2019(6), 11–19. DOI: 10.1016/S1361-3723(19)30064-8

Karatas, G., Demir, O., & Sahingoz, O. K. (2019, June). A deep learning-based intrusion detection system on GPUs. In *2019 11th International Conference on Electronics, Computers and Artificial Intelligence (ECAI)* (pp. 1-6). DOI: 10.1109/ECAI46879.2019.9042132

Katamoura, S., Aksoy, M. S., & AlKhamees, B. (2024). Privacy and Security in Artificial Intelligence and Machine Learning Systems for Renewable Energy Big Data. In *2024 21st Learning and Technology Conference (L&T)* (pp. 209-214). DOI: 10.1109/LT60077.2024.10468941

Kaukinen, Anderson, Jasinski, Mustaine, Powers, Miller, Jennings, Nobles, & Yegidis. (2018). The direction of violence against women research and evaluation. Women & Criminal Justice, 28(3), 189-211.

Kaur, G., Mukherjee, D., Moza, B., Pahwa, V., Kaur, K., & Kaur, K. (2024). The dark web: A hidden menace or a tool for privacy protection. *IP International Journal of Forensic Medicine and Toxicological Sciences*, 8(4), 160–167. DOI: 10.18231/j.ijfmts.2023.034

Kaur, R., & Singh, M. (2014). A survey on zero-day polymorphic worm detection techniques. *IEEE Communications Surveys and Tutorials*, 16(3), 1520–1549. DOI: 10.1109/SURV.2014.022714.00160

Kawale, S. R. (2023) "Cloud-Based Multi-Layer Security Framework for Protecting E-Health Records," In *2023 International Conference on Artificial Intelligence for Innovations in Healthcare Industries (ICAIIHI)*, Raipur, India, (pp. 1-7).

Khaleel, Y. L., Habeeb, M. A., Albahri, A. S., Al-Quraishi, T., Albahri, O. S., & Alamoodi, A. H. (2024). Network and cybersecurity applications of defense in adversarial attacks: A state-of-the-art using machine learning and deep learning methods. *Journal of Intelligent Systems*, 33(1), 20240153. DOI: 10.1515/jisys-2024-0153

Khan, M., & Ghafoor, L. (2024). Adversarial Machine Learning in the Context of Network Security: Challenges and Solutions. *Journal of Computational Intelligence and Robotics*, 4(1), 51–63.

Khurana, S. (2017). A Review Paper on Cyber Security, *International Journal Of Engineering Research & Technology*, *5*(23).

Khushali, V. (2020). A Review on Fileless Malware Analysis Techniques. *International Journal of Engineering Research & Technology (Ahmedabad)*, 9(5), 46–49. DOI: 10.17577/IJERTV9IS050068

Kim, A., Lee, H., & Lee, S. (2025). In Touch with Those in Need: How Touchscreen Devices Lead Consumers to Support Social Causes. *Journal of the Association for Consumer Research, 10*(1), 000-000.

Kim, D. W., Shin, G. Y., & Han, M. M. (2020). Analysis of feature importance and interpretation for malware classification. *Computers, Materials & Continua*, 65(3), 1891–1904. DOI: 10.32604/cmc.2020.010933

Kim, J., Shin, Y., & Choi, E. (2019). An intrusion detection model based on a convolutional neural network. *Journal of Multimedia Information System*, 6(4), 165–172. DOI: 10.33851/JMIS.2019.6.4.165

Kim, Y. (2014). Convolutional neural networks for sentence classification. *Proceedings of the 2014 Conference on Empirical Methods in Natural Language Processing*, 1746-1751. DOI: 10.3115/v1/D14-1181

Kiran, A., Prakash, S. W., Kumar, B. A., Likhitha, T, Sameeratmaja, & Charan, U. S. S. R. (2023), Intrusion Detection System Using Machine Learning. In *2023 International Conference on Computer Communication and Informatics (ICCCI)*, Coimbatore, India.

Klebanov, B., Friedman-Hauser, G., Lusky-Weisrose, E., & Katz, C. (2023). Sexual Abuse of Children with Disabilities: Key Lessons andFuture Directions Based on a Scoping Review. *Trauma, Violence & Abuse*, 25. PMID: 37306024

Kleinberg, J. M. (2002). Authoritative sources in a hyperlinked environment. *Journal of the Association for Computing Machinery*, 46(5), 604–632. DOI: 10.1145/324133.324140

Kloess, J. A., Hamilton-Giachritsis, C. E., & Beech, A. R. (2019). Offense Processes of Online Sexual Grooming and Abuse of Children ViaInternet Communication Platforms. *Sexual Abuse*, 31(1), 73–96. DOI: 10.1177/1079063217720927 PMID: 28715937

Kokulu, F. B., Shoshitaishvili, Y., Soneji, A., Zhao, Z., Ahn, G. J., Bao, T., & Doupé, A. (2019). Matched and mismatched SOCs: A qualitative study on security operations center issues. In *Proceedings of the ACM Conference on Computer and Communications Security*, (pp. 1955–1970). DOI: 10.1145/3319535.3354239

Kolhar, A. & Sridevi. (2025). Future Trends and Innovation in Machine Intelligence for Cyber Risk Management. In M. Almaiah & Y. Maleh (Eds.), *Machine Intelligence Applications in Cyber-Risk Management* (pp. 415-438). IGI Global Scientific Publishing. DOI: 10.4018/979-8-3693-7540-2.ch018

Korstanje, M. E. (Ed. (2016). Threat mitigation and detection of cyber warfare and terrorism activities. *IGI Global, January 2017*, 198–219. DOI: 10.4018/978-1-5225-1938-6.ch009

Krishnan, S. D., Pelusi, D., Daniel, A., Suresh, V., & Balusamy, B. (2023). Improved graph neural network-based green anaconda optimization for segmenting and classifying lung cancer. *Mathematical Biosciences and Engineering*, 20(9), 17138–17157. DOI: 10.3934/mbe.2023764 PMID: 37920050

Kumar, T., Kumar, P., & Namasudra, S. (2024a). A DNA-based Authentication System for Securing Cloud Data Storage and Transactions. In *2024 11th International Conference on Computing for Sustainable Global Development* (pp. 1692–1698).

Kumar, T., Kumar, P., & Namasudra, S. (2024b). *User Revocation-Enabled Access Control Model Using Identity-Based Signature in the Cloud Computing Environment.*

Kumar, P., Kumar, R., Srivastava, G., Gupta, G. P., Tripathi, R., Gadekallu, T. R., & Xiong, N. N. (2021). PPSF: A Privacy-Preserving and Secure Framework Using Blockchain-Based Machine-Learning for IoT-Driven Smart Cities. *IEEE Transactions on Network Science and Engineering*, 8(3), 2326–2341. DOI: 10.1109/TNSE.2021.3089435

Kumar, T., & Attri, S. H. (2024). The machine translation systems demystifying the approaches. In *A handbook of computational linguistics: Artificial intelligence in natural language processing* (pp. 160–191). Bentham Science. DOI: 10.2174/9789815238488124020011

Kumar, T., Kumar, P., & Namasudra, S. (2024). User revocation-enabled access control model using identity-based signature in the cloud computing environment. *International Journal of Interactive Multimedia and Artificial Intelligence*, 9(1), 127–136. DOI: 10.9781/ijimai.2024.05.001

Kumar, T., Namasudra, S., & Kumar, P. (2023). Providing data security using DNA computing in the cloud computing environment. *International Journal of Web and Grid Services*, 19(4), 463–486. DOI: 10.1504/IJWGS.2023.135587

Kunwar, R. S., & Sharma, P. (2016). *Malware Analysis,* 1–4. DOI: 10.1145/2905055.2905361

Lab, H. S. (2021). *Emotet Botnet Takedown*. 1–7. https://www.hornetsecurity.com/en/threat-research/emotet-botnet-takedown/

Ladores, D. (2017). *EMOTET Returns, Starts Spreading via Spam Botnet*. 1–4. https://blog.trendmicro.com/trendlabs-security-intelligence/emotet-returns-starts-spreading-via-spam-botnet/

Lad, S. S., & Adamuthe, A. C. (2020). Malware classification with improved convolutional neural network model. *International Journal of Computer Network and Information Security*, 12(6), 30–43. DOI: 10.5815/ijcnis.2020.06.03

Ladybird, O. (2021). *Emotet Disruption : what it means for the cyber threat landscape The Evolution of Emotet : From Banking Trojan to Ransomware*. 1–8.

LeCun, Y., Bengio, Y., & Hinton, G. (2015). Deep learning. *Nature*, 521(7553), 436–444. DOI: 10.1038/nature14539 PMID: 26017442

Lee, A. Y., & Hancock, J. T. (2023). Developing digital resilience: An educational intervention improves elementary students' response to digital challenges. *Computers and Education Open*, 5, 100144. DOI: 10.1016/j.caeo.2023.100144

Lee, H., & Kim, J. (2024, July). Impact of Cyber Threats on Mental Health: A Case Study. *IEEE Transactions on Cybernetics*, 24(5), 1018–1027.

Leitão, S., Mc Carthy, V. J., & Greiner, B. A. (2018). Health and safety practitioners' health and wellbeing—The link with safety climate and job demand-control-support. *Accident; Analysis and Prevention*, 119, 131–137. DOI: 10.1016/j.aap.2018.06.017 PMID: 30025354

Leo, M., Bourke-Taylor, H., Odgers, S., & Tirlea, L. (2024). Online interventions for the mental health and well-being of parents of children with additional needs: Systematic review and meta-analysis. *Australian Occupational Therapy Journal*, 1440-1630.13004. Advance online publication. DOI: 10.1111/1440-1630.13004 PMID: 39482259

Lewis, R., Rowe, M., & Wiper, C. (2017). Online abuse of feminists as an emerging form of violence against women and girls. British Journal of Criminology, 57(6), 1462-1481.

Lewis, M., (2023, August). Future Directions in Cybersecurity Research. *IEEE Transactions on Emerging Topics in Computing*, 8(3), 212–223.

Li, G., Wang, S., Chen, Y., Zhou, J., & Zhao, Q. (2024). A hybrid framework for ransomware detection using deep learning and monte carlo tree search.

Liang, F., Hatcher, W. G., Liao, W., Gao, W., & Yu, W. (2019). Machine Learning for Security and the Internet of Things: The Good, the Bad, and the Ugly. *IEEE Access : Practical Innovations, Open Solutions*, 7, 158126–158147. DOI: 10.1109/ACCESS.2019.2948912

Limmer, T., & Dressler, F. (2011). Improving the performance of intrusion detection using dialog-based payload aggregation. In *2011 IEEE Conference on Computer Communications Workshops, INFOCOM WKSHPS 2011*, (pp. 822–827). DOI: 10.1109/INFCOMW.2011.5928926

Liu, H., & Lang, B. (2019). Machine learning and deep learning methods for intrusion detection systems: A survey. *Applied Sciences, 9*(20), 4396.

Liu, Y. F., Zhang, L. W., Liang, J., Qu, S., & Ni, Z. Q. (2010). Detecting Trojan horses based on system behavior using machine learning method. *2010 International Conference on Machine Learning and Cybernetics*, (pp. 855–860). DOI: 10.1109/ICMLC.2010.5580591

Li, V. G., Dunn, M., Pearce, P., McCoy, D., Voelker, G. M., Savage, S., & Levchenko, K. (2019). Reading the tea leaves: A comparative analysis of threat intelligence. In *Proceedings of the 28th USENIX Security Symposium*, (pp. 851–867).

Li, X., Xie, H., Wang, R., Cai, Y., & Cao, J. (2017). Dynamic financial distress prediction with concept drift based on time weighting combined with Adaboost support vector machine ensemble. *Knowledge-Based Systems*, 120, 4–14. DOI: 10.1016/j.knosys.2017.04.005

Li, Y., & Liu, Q. (2021). A comprehensive review study of cyber-attacks and cyber security; Emerging trends and recent developments. *Energy Reports*, 7, 8176–8186. DOI: 10.1016/j.egyr.2021.08.126

Li, Z., Wang, X. F., Liang, Z., & Reiter, M. K. (2008). AGIS: Towards automatic generation of infection signatures. *Proceedings of the International Conference on Dependable Systems and Networks*, 237–246. DOI: 10.1109/DSN.2008.4630092

Lo, C., Yu, J., Görges, M., & Matava, C. (2021). Anesthesia in the modern world of apps and technology: Implications and impact on wellness. *Paediatric Anaesthesia*, 31(1), 31–38. DOI: 10.1111/pan.14051 PMID: 33119935

Louati, F., Ktata, F. B., & Amous, I. (2024). Big-IDS: A decentralized multi agent reinforcement learning approach for distributed intrusion detection in big data networks. *Cluster Computing*, 27(5), 1–19. DOI: 10.1007/s10586-024-04306-9

Lough, E., Flynn, E., & Riby, D. M. (2015). Mapping Real-World to Online Vulnerability in Young People with Developmental Disorders:Illustrations from Autism and Williams Syndrome. *Review Journal of Autism and Developmental Disorders*, 2(1), 1–7. DOI: 10.1007/s40489-014-0029-2

Mahmood, R. A. R., Abdi, A., & Hussin, M. (2021). Performance evaluation of intrusion detection system using selected features and machine learning classifiers. *Baghdad Science Journal, 18*(2), 0884.

Maithili, K., Ponmalar, A., Yamini, B., Karthikeyan, M., Anish, T. P., Maheswari, B., & Subramanian, R. S. (2024). Advances in AI and Machine Learning for Healthcare Informatics. In *Machine Learning and Generative AI in Smart Healthcare* (pp. 1-22). IGI Global. DOI: 10.4018/979-8-3693-3719-6.ch001

Malik, S., & Chauhan, R. (2020). Securing the internet of things using machine learning: A review. In *2020 International Conference on Convergence to Digital World - Quo Vadis*, (pp. 9–12). DOI: 10.1109/ICCDW45521.2020.9318666

Mamdouh, M., Elrukhsi, M. A. I., & Khattab, A. (2018). Securing the Internet of Things and Wireless Sensor Networks via Machine Learning: A Survey. In *2018 International Conference on Computer and Applications, ICCA 2018, Section II*, (pp. 215–218). DOI: 10.1109/COMAPP.2018.8460440

Mangialardo, R. J., & Duarte, J. C. (2015). Integrating Static and Dynamic Malware Analysis Using Machine Learning. *Revista IEEE América Latina*, 13(9), 3080–3087. DOI: 10.1109/TLA.2015.7350062

Maniriho, P., Mahmood, A. N., & Chowdhury, M. J. M. (2022). A study on malicious software behaviour analysis and detection techniques: Taxonomy, current trends and challenges. *Future Generation Computer Systems*, 130, 1–18. DOI: 10.1016/j.future.2021.11.030

Manning, C. D., Raghavan, P., & Schütze, H. (2008). *Introduction to information retrieval*. Cambridge University Press. DOI: 10.1017/CBO9780511809071

Manoharan, A., & Sarker, M. (2023). Revolutionizing Cybersecurity: Unleashing the Power of Artificial Intelligence and Machine Learning for Next-Generation Threat Detection. https://www. doi. org/10.56726/IRJMETS32644

Maria Bada, Chua, Collier, & Pete. (2009). Exploring Masculinities and Perceptions of Gender in Online Cybercrime Subcultures. Journal of Technology, 200-208.

Matsuo, Y., LeCun, Y., Sahani, M., Doina, P., David, S., Masashi, S., Eiji, U., & Jun, M. (2020). Machine Learning: A Review of Learning Types. *Neural Networks 152, 7*(1), 267–275. DOI: 10.20944/preprints202007.0230.v1

Maurya, C., Muhammad, T., Dhillon, P., & Maurya, P. (2022). The effects of cyberbullying victimization on depression and suicidal ideation among adolescents and young adults: A three year cohort study from India. *BMC Psychiatry*, 22(1), 599. DOI: 10.1186/s12888-022-04238-x PMID: 36085004

Md, M. R. S. (2019). Technology Mediated Violence against Women in Bangladesh: Evidence from Contemporary literature. Organization, 4(8), 74-79.

Medeiros, I., Neves, N., & Correia, M. (2015). Detecting and removing web application vulnerabilities with static analysis and data mining. *IEEE Transactions on Reliability*, 65(1), 54–69. DOI: 10.1109/TR.2015.2457411

Mike McGuire & Dowling. (2013). Cyber crimes; A review of the evidence, Summary of Key findings and implications. *Home Office Research Report, 75*, 46-59.

Miller, P., (2023, August). Education Programs for Cybersecurity Awareness and Mental Health. *IEEE Transactions on Learning Technologies*, 15(2), 220–230.

Mimura, M., & Tajiri, Y. (2021). Static detection of malicious PowerShell based on word embeddings. *Internet of Things : Engineering Cyber Physical Human Systems*, 15, 100404. DOI: 10.1016/j.iot.2021.100404

Mirza, N. (2020). Robotic path planning and fuzzy neural networks. *International Arab Journal of Information Technology, 17*(4 Special Issue), 615–620. DOI: 10.34028/iajit/17/4A/5

Mirzaei, O. (2019). *Techniques for Advanced Android Malware Triage*. 217.

Mishra, C., & Gupta, D. L. (2017). Deep Machine Learning and Neural Networks: An Overview. *IAES International Journal of Artificial Intelligence (IJ-AI), 6*(2), 66. DOI: 10.11591/ijai.v6.i2.pp66-73

Moghimi, E., Knyahnytska, Y., Omrani, M., Nikjoo, N., Stephenson, C., Layzell, G., Frederic Simpson, A. I., & Alavi, N. (2022). Benefits of digital mental health care interventions for correctional workers and other public safety personnel: A narrative review. *Frontiers in Psychiatry*, 13, 921527. DOI: 10.3389/fpsyt.2022.921527 PMID: 35873240

Moh, M., & Raju, R. (2018). Machine learning techniques for security of internet of things (IoT) and fog computing systems. In *Proceedings - 2018 International Conference on High Performance Computing and Simulation* (pp. 709–715). DOI: 10.1109/HPCS.2018.00116

Mohamed, N. N., & Abuobied, B. H. H. (2024). Cybersecurity challenges across sustainable development goals: A comprehensive review. *Sustainable Engineering and Innovation*, 6(1), 57–86. DOI: 10.37868/sei.v6i1.id207

Mohamed, S. A., Alsaif, O. I., & Saleh, I. A. (2022). Intrusion detection network attacks based on whale optimization algorithm. *Ingénierie des Systèmes d'Information*, 27(3), 441–446. DOI: 10.18280/isi.270310

Mohammad, N., Prabha, M., Sharmin, S., Khatoon, R., & Imran, M. A. U. (2024). Combating banking fraud with it: Integrating machine learning and data analytics. *The American Journal of Management and Economics Innovations*, 6(07), 39–56. DOI: 10.37547/tajmei/Volume06Issue07-04

Mohammed, A., Kumar, S., Mu'Azu, H. G., Kumar, R., Shah, P., Memoria, M., Rawat, A., & Gupta, A. (2022). Data Security and Protection: A Mechanism for Managing Data Theft and Cybercrime in Online Platforms of Educational Institutions. *2022 International Conference on Machine Learning, Big Data, Cloud and Parallel Computing, COM-IT-CON 2022*. DOI: 10.1109/COM-IT-CON54601.2022.9850702

Mohanty, R. K., Kumar, A. P., Padmaja, R., & Prashanthi, V. (2024). Deep learning for analyzing user and entity behaviors: Techniques and applications. In *Consumer and Organizational Behavior in the Age of AI* (pp. 219–250). IGI Global. DOI: 10.4018/979-8-3693-8850-1.ch008

Mohanty, R. K., Sahoo, S. P., & Kabat, M. R. (2023). Sustainable remote patient monitoring in wireless body area network with Multi-hop routing and scheduling: A four-fold objective based optimization approach. *Wireless Networks*, 29(5), 2337–2351. DOI: 10.1007/s11276-023-03276-x

Mohanty, R. K., Sahoo, S. P., & Kabat, M. R. (2024). Thermal-energy-efficient-secured-link reliable and delay-aware routing protocol (TESLDAR) for wireless body area networks. *International Journal of Computers and Applications*, 46(9), 1–13. DOI: 10.1080/1206212X.2024.2380675

Mokaddem, S., Wagener, G., Dulaunoy, A., & Iklody, A. (2019). *Taxonomy driven indicator scoring in MISP threat intelligence platforms*. http://arxiv.org/abs/1902.03914

Montasari, R., Carroll, F., Macdonald, S., Jahankhani, H., Hosseinian-Far, A., & Daneshkhah, A. (2021). Application of artificial intelligence and machine learning in producing actionable cyber threat intelligence. Digital forensic investigation of internet of things (IoT) devices, 47-64.

Montiel, I., & Agustina, J. R. (2019). Ciber víctimas con discapacidad: Cuestiones victimológicas y retos forenses. *Revista Española de Medicina Legal*, 45(1), 1–3. DOI: 10.1016/j.reml.2018.06.003

Moss, C., Smith, S. J., Kim, K., Hua, N., Noronha, N., Kavenagh, M., & Wekerle, C. (2023). A global systematic scoping review of literatureon the sexual exploitation of boys. Child Abus. *Child Abuse & Neglect*, 142, 106244. DOI: 10.1016/j.chiabu.2023.106244 PMID: 37244784

Munn, Z., Stern, C., Aromataris, E., Lockwood, C., & Jordan, Z. (2018). What kind of systematic review should I conduct? A proposedtypology and guidance for systematic reviewers in the medical and health sciences. *BMC Medical Research Methodology*, 18(1), 5. DOI: 10.1186/s12874-017-0468-4 PMID: 29316881

Munyua, Mureithi, & Githaiga. (2020). Women and cybercrime in Kenya: darh side of ICTS.

Murphy, C. (2024, March). Challenges in Implementing Cybersecurity for Mental Health Protection. *IEEE Transactions on Systems, Man, and Cybernetics*, 28(2), 230–241.

Muslim, A., Mustofa, K., Widodo, S. T., & Harjoko, A. (2021). Efficient feature selection analysis for accuracy malware classification. *Journal of Physics: Conference Series*, 1918(4), 042140. DOI: 10.1088/1742-6596/1918/4/042140

Nagy, C. (2013). Static analysis of data-intensive applications. In *2013 17th European Conference on Software Maintenance and Reengineering* (pp. 435-438). IEEE. DOI: 10.1109/CSMR.2013.66

Naseer, I. (2021). The efficacy of Deep Learning and Artificial Intelligence Framework in Enhancing Cybersecurity, Challenges and Future Prospects. Innovative Computer Sciences Journal, 7(1).

Nasr, M., Shokri, R., & Houmansadr, A. (2018). Machine learning with membership privacy using adversarial regularization. In *Proceedings of the ACM Conference on Computer and Communications Security*, (pp. 634–646). DOI: 10.1145/3243734.3243855

Nassar, A., & Kamal, M. (2021). Machine Learning and Big Data analytics for Cybersecurity Threat Detection: A Holistic review of techniques and case studies. *Journal of Artificial Intelligence and Machine Learning in Management*, 5(1), 51–63.

Natarajan, R., Lokesh, G. H., Flammini, F., Premkumar, A., Venkatesan, V. K., & Gupta, S. K. (2023). A novel framework on security and energy enhancement based on internet of medical things for healthcare 5.0. *Infrastructures*, 8(2), 22. DOI: 10.3390/infrastructures8020022

Nations, U. (n.d.). *Child and Youth Safety Online | United Nations*. Retrieved December 31, 2024, from https://www.un.org/en/global-issues/child-and-youth-safety-online

Nguyen, B., & Hernandez, J. (2024, April). Actionable Insights for Enhancing Cybersecurity. *IEEE Transactions on Information Forensics and Security*, 19(3), 342–353.

Nguyen, T. T., & Reddi, V. J. (2021). Deep reinforcement learning for cyber security. *IEEE Transactions on Neural Networks and Learning Systems*, 34(8), 3779–3795. DOI: 10.1109/TNNLS.2021.3121870 PMID: 34723814

Ni, C., & Li, S. C. (2024). Machine learning enabled industrial iot security: Challenges, trends and solutions. *Journal of Industrial Information Integration*, 38, 100549. DOI: 10.1016/j.jii.2023.100549

Nithya, T., Kumar, V. N., Gayathri, S., Deepa, S., Varun, C. M., & Subramanian, R. S. (2023). A comprehensive survey of machine learning: Advancements, applications, and challenges. In *2023 Second International Conference on Augmented Intelligence and Sustainable Systems (ICAISS)* (pp. 354-361). DOI: 10.1109/ICAISS58487.2023.10250547

Nixon, C. L. (2014). Current perspectives: The impact of cyberbullying on adolescent health. *Adolescent Health, Medicine and Therapeutics*, 5, 143. DOI: 10.2147/AHMT.S36456 PMID: 25177157

Noriega, J., & Lee, D. (2007). Enhancing spam filtering through blacklist and whitelist integration. *Proceedings of the International Conference on Machine Learning and Applications*, 45-52.

Normand, C. L., & Sallafranque-St-Louis, F. (2016). Cybervictimization of Young People with an Intellectual or Developmental Disability:Risks Specific to Sexual Solicitation. *Journal of Applied Research in Intellectual Disabilities*, 29(2), 99–110. DOI: 10.1111/jar.12163 PMID: 25871891

Norman, R. E., Byambaa, M., De, R., Butchart, A., Scott, J., & Vos, T. (2012). The long-term health consequences of child physical abuse,emotional abuse, and neglect: A systematic review and meta-analysis. *PLoS Medicine*, 9(11), e1001349. DOI: 10.1371/journal.pmed.1001349 PMID: 23209385

Nousiainen, A. (2024). Applying cybersecurity for IEC 60870-5-104 communication between control station and substation.

Oberhuber, M., Unterguggenberger, M., Maar, L., Kogler, A., & Mangard, S. (2025). Power-Related Side-Channel Attacks using the Android Sensor Framework. In Network and Distributed System Security Symposium 2025.

Ofoegbu, K. D. O., Osundare, O. S., Ike, C. S., Fakeyede, O. G., & Ige, A. B. (2024a). Real-Time Cybersecurity threat detection using machine learning and big data analytics: A comprehensive approach.

Ofoegbu, K. D. O., Osundare, O. S., Ike, C. S., Fakeyede, O. G., & Ige, A. B. (2024b). Data-Driven Cyber Threat Intelligence: Leveraging Behavioral Analytics for Proactive Defense Mechanisms.

Okada, S., Fujimoto, M., Matsuda, W., & Mitsunaga, T. (2021). Malware Detection Method using Tree-based Machine Learning Algorithms. In *2021 IEEE International Conference on Computing (ICOCO)*. IEEE.

Okoli, U. I., Obi, O. C., Adewusi, A. O., & Abrahams, T. O. (2024). Machine learning in cybersecurity: A review of threat detection and defense mechanisms. *World Journal of Advanced Research and Reviews*, 21(1), 2286–2295. DOI: 10.30574/wjarr.2024.21.1.0315

Olabanji, S. O., Oladoyinbo, O. B., Asonze, C. U., Oladoyinbo, T. O., Ajayi, S. A., & Olaniyi, O. O. (2024). Effect of adopting AI to explore big data on personally identifiable information (PII) for financial and economic data transformation. *Available atSSRN* 4739227.

Or-Meir, O., Nissim, N., Elovici, Y., & Rokach, L. (2019). Dynamic malware analysis in the modern era—A state of the art survey. *ACM Computing Surveys*, 52(5), 1–48. DOI: 10.1145/3329786

Otoum, Y., & Nayak, A. (2020, July). On securing IoT from Deep Learning perspective. In *Proceedings - IEEE Symposium on Computers and Communications*. DOI: 10.1109/ISCC50000.2020.9219671

Otoum, Y., Liu, D., & Nayak, A. (2022). DL-IDS: A deep learning–based intrusion detection framework for securing IoT. *Transactions on Emerging Telecommunications Technologies*, 33(3), 1–14. DOI: 10.1002/ett.3803

Ozkan-Okay, M., Akin, E., Aslan, Ö., Kosunalp, S., Iliev, T., Stoyanov, I., & Beloev, I. (2024). A comprehensive survey: Evaluating the efficiency of artificial intelligence and machine learning techniques on cyber security solutions. *IEEE Access: Practical Innovations, Open Solutions*, 12, 12229–12256. DOI: 10.1109/ACCESS.2024.3355547

Page, M. J., Mckenzie, J. E., Bossuyt, P. M., Boutron, I., Hoffmann, T. C., Mulrow, C. D., Shamseer, L., Tetzlaff, J. M., Akl, E. A., & Brennan, S. E. (2021). The PRISMA 2020 statement: An updated guideline for reporting systematic reviews. *International Journal of Surgery*, 88. PMID: 33789826

Pajila, P. B., Sudha, K., Selvi, D. K., Kumar, V. N., Gayathri, S., & Subramanian, R. S. (2023). A Survey on Natural Language Processing and its Applications. In *2023 4th International Conference on Electronics and Sustainable Communication Systems* (ICESC) (pp. 996-1001).

Parental controls | How to keep your child safe. (n.d.). Retrieved December 31, 2024, from https://www.esafety.gov.au/parents/issues-and-advice/parental-controls

Parents, Caregivers, Teachers — FBI. (n.d.). Retrieved December 31, 2024, from https://www.fbi.gov/how-we-can-help-you/parents-and-caregivers-protecting-your-kids

Parikh, T. P., & Patel, A. R. (2017). Cyber security: Study on attack, threat, vulnerability. *Int. J. Res. Mod. Eng. Emerg. Technol*, 5, 1–7.

Park, W., & Ahn, S. (2017). Performance Comparison and Detection Analysis in Snort and Suricata Environment. *Wireless Personal Communications*, 94(2), 241–252. DOI: 10.1007/s11277-016-3209-9

Patel, M., & Shah, R. (2024) "Informed Consent and Transparency in Cybersecurity Measures," IEEE Trans. Dependable Secur. Comput., *11*(1), pp. 89-98.

Peebles, E. (2014). Cyberbullying: Hiding behind the screen. *Paediatrics & Child Health*, 19(10), 527–528. DOI: 10.1093/pch/19.10.527 PMID: 25587229

Pereda, N., Guilera, G., Forns, M., & Gómez-Benito, J. (2009). The prevalence of child sexual abuse in community and student samples: Ameta-analysis. *Clinical Psychology Review*, 29(4), 328–338. DOI: 10.1016/j.cpr.2009.02.007 PMID: 19371992

Pomilia, M. (2016). A study on obfuscation techniques for android malware. *Sapienza University of Rome, 81.*

Ponmalar, A., Vijayakumar, K., Lakshmipriya, C., Karthikeyan, M., & PJ, B. P. (2024). Meta-Heuristics and Machine Learning Applications in Complex Systems. In *Metaheuristic and Machine Learning Optimization Strategies for Complex Systems* (pp. 257-275). IGI Global.

Prabhavathi, C., Mahesh, A., Ajay, S. V., & Mythili, R. (2022). Malware Prediction Using XGBOOST and CATBOOST. *Journal of Engineering Science*, 13(5), 620–626. https://jespublication.com/upload/2022-V13I5085.pdf

Prasad, K., S. R, and A. K. N, (2024) "Design and Implementation of an AI and IoT-Enabled Smart Safety Helmet for Real-Time Environmental and Health Monitoring," In *2024 IEEE International Conference on Information Technology, Electronics and Intelligent Communication Systems (ICITEICS)*, Bangalore, India, (pp. 1-7).

Prince, N. U., Al Mamun, M. A., Olajide, A. O., Khan, O. U., Akeem, A. B., & Sani, A. I. (2024). IEEE Standards and Deep Learning Techniques for Securing Internet of Things (IoT) Devices Against Cyber Attacks. *Journal of Computational Analysis and Applications*, 33(7), 1270–1289.

Prince, N. U., Faheem, M. A., Khan, O. U., Hossain, K., Alkhayyat, A., Hamdache, A., & Elmouki, I. (2024). AI-Powered Data-Driven Cybersecurity Techniques: Boosting Threat Identification and Reaction. *Nanotechnology Perceptions*, 332–353.

Quartz. (2022). Android (GOOG) just hit a record 88% market share of all smartphones. *Quartz*.

Rackley, E., McGlynn, C., Johnson, K., Henry, N., Gavey, N., Flynn, A., & Powell, A. (2021). Seeking Justice and Redress for Victim-Survivorsof Image-Based Sexual Abuse. *Feminist Legal Studies*, 29(3), 293–322. DOI: 10.1007/s10691-021-09460-8

Raj, G., Sharma, A. K., & Arora, Y. (2024). Analyzing the Effect of Digital Technology on Mental Health. In *Strategies for E-Commerce Data Security: Cloud, Blockchain, AI, and Machine Learning* (pp. 54-82). IGI Global. DOI: 10.4018/979-8-3693-6557-1.ch003

Rawat, G., Kanti, P., Memoria, M., Kumar, R., & Choudhury, T. (2023). Ace of cyber security and it's emerging trends on latest technologies. In 2023 3rd International Conference on Innovative Sustainable Computational Technologies (CISCT) (pp. 1-6). IEEE. DOI: 10.1109/CISCT57197.2023.10351359

Rawindaran, N., Jayal, A., Prakash, E., & Hewage, C. (2023). Perspective of small and medium enterprise (SME's) and their relationship with government in overcoming cybersecurity challenges and barriers in Wales. *International Journal of Information Management Data Insights*, 3(2), 100191. DOI: 10.1016/j.jjimei.2023.100191

Ray, A., & Nath, A. (2016). Introduction to Malware and Malware Analysis: A brief overview. *International Journal (Toronto, Ont.)*, 4(10).

Renugadevi, N., Saravanan, S., & Sudha, C. N. (2023). Revolution of smart healthcare materials in big data analytics. *Materials Today: Proceedings*, 81, 834–841. DOI: 10.1016/j.matpr.2021.04.256

Ribeiro, J., Saghezchi, F. B., Mantas, G., Rodriguez, J., Shepherd, S. J., & Abd-Alhameed, R. A. (2020). An Autonomous Host-Based Intrusion Detection System for Android Mobile Devices. *Mobile Networks and Applications*, 25(1), 164–172. DOI: 10.1007/s11036-019-01220-y

Riberas-Gutiérrez, M., Reneses, M., Gómez-Dorado, A., Serranos-Minguela, L., & Bueno-Guerra, N. (2023). Online Grooming: Factores de Riesgo y Modus Operandi a Partir de un Análisis de Sentencias Españolas. Anu. Psicol. *Jurídic.*, 34, 119–131.

Richardson, C. (2009). *Virus detection with machine learning. September.*

Rieck, K., Trinius, P., Willems, C., & Holz, T. (2011). Automatic analysis of malware behavior using machine learning. *Journal of Computer Security*, 19(4), 639–668. DOI: 10.3233/JCS-2010-0410

Robinson, T., & Walker, E. (2023, December). Balancing Security and Privacy in Digital Environments. *IEEE Transactions on Information Technology in Biomedicine*, 12(2), 150–160.

Roopak, M., & Tian, Y. G., & Chambers, J. (2019). Deep learning models for cyber security in IoT networks. *2019 IEEE 9th Annual Computing and Communication Workshop and Conference,* (pp. 452–457). DOI: 10.1109/CCWC.2019.8666588

Rosenberg, I., Shabtai, A., Elovici, Y., & Rokach, L. (2021). Adversarial machine learning attacks and defense methods in the cyber security domain. *ACM Computing Surveys*, 54(5), 1–36. DOI: 10.1145/3453158

Ruder, S., Bingel, J., Søgaard, A., & Goldberg, Y. (2019). A survey of cross-lingual embedding models. *Journal of Artificial Intelligence Research*, 65, 37–71. DOI: 10.1613/jair.1.11640

Rudolph, K. (2004). Spam filtering: A brief overview. *Journal of Computer Security*, 12(3), 245–260.

Sagu*, A., & Gill, N. S. (2020). Machine Learning Techniques for Securing IoT Environment. *International Journal of Innovative Technology and Exploring Engineering, 9*(4), 977–982. DOI: 10.35940/ijitee.D1209.029420

Sahami, M., Dumais, S. T., Heckerman, D., & Horvitz, E. (1998). A Bayesian approach to filtering junk email. *Proceedings of the 1998 Conference on Uncertainty in Artificial Intelligence*, 55-62.

Sahay, S. K., & Sharma, A. (2016). Grouping the Executables to Detect Malwares with High Accuracy. *Physics Procedia, 78*(December 2015), 667–674. DOI: 10.1016/j.procs.2016.02.115

Sahni, A., & Nene, M. J. (2020). MLDroid—Framework for Android malware detection using machine learning techniques. *Neural Computing & Applications*, 33, 12813–12825.

Sahs, J., & Khan, L. (2020). A review of Android malware detection approaches based on machine learning. *IEEE Access : Practical Innovations, Open Solutions*, 8, 124579–124607. DOI: 10.1109/ACCESS.2020.3006143

Saleh, S., Cherradi, B., El Gannour, O., Gouiza, N., & Bouattane, O. (2023). Healthcare monitoring system for automatic database management using mobile application in IoT environment. *Bulletin of Electrical Engineering and Informatics*, 12(2), 1055–1068. DOI: 10.11591/eei.v12i2.4282

Sanagana, D. P. R., & Tummalachervu, C. K. (2024). Securing Cloud Computing Environment via Optimal Deep Learning-based Intrusion Detection Systems. In *2024 Second International Conference on Data Science and Information System (ICDSIS)* (pp. 1-6). DOI: 10.1109/ICDSIS61070.2024.10594404

Sangwan. (2019). A Critical Study of the Violation of Women's Right in India with Special Reference to Cyber Crime. IME Journal, 13(2), 148-155.

Sangwan, U. (2024). Efficient Cyber Security Framework for IoT Using Machine Learning Algorithms. *Journal of Electrical Systems*, 20(6s), 2444–2451. DOI: 10.52783/jes.3233

Santhosh Kumar, S. V. N., Selvi, M., & Kannan, A. (2023). A Comprehensive Survey on Machine Learning-Based Intrusion Detection Systems for Secure Communication in Internet of Things. *Computational Intelligence and Neuroscience*, 2023(1), 1–24. DOI: 10.1155/2023/8981988

Saravanan, K., Prakash, R. B., Balakrishnan, C., Kumar, G. V. P., Subramanian, R. S., & Anita, M. (2023). Support Vector Machines: Unveiling the Power and Versatility of SVMs in Modern Machine Learning. In *2023 3rd International Conference on Innovative Mechanisms for Industry Applications(ICIMIA)* (pp. 680-687).

Sarker, I. H., Kayes, A. S. M., Badsha, S., Alqahtani, H., Watters, P., & Ng, A. (2020). Cybersecurity data science: An overview from machine learning perspective. *Journal of Big Data*, 7(1), 41. Advance online publication. DOI: 10.1186/s40537-020-00318-5

Sarker, I. H., Khan, A. I., Abushark, Y. B., & Alsolami, F. (2023). Internet of Things (IoT) Security Intelligence: A Comprehensive Overview, Machine Learning Solutions and Research Directions. *Mobile Networks and Applications*, 28(1), 296–312. DOI: 10.1007/s11036-022-01937-3

Satilmiş, H., Akleylek, S., & Tok, Z. Y. (2024). A Systematic Literature Review on Host-Based Intrusion Detection Systems. *IEEE Access : Practical Innovations, Open Solutions*, 12, 27237–27266. DOI: 10.1109/ACCESS.2024.3367004

Saxena, M., Avanesh, N. M., Niranjan, L. R., & Mohanty, P. (2025). Wearable Technologies Leading to Employee Performance and Productivity: Exploring the Mediating Role of Mental Health and Wellbeing. In *Technological Enhancements for Improving Employee Performance, Safety, and Well-Being* (pp. 111-130). IGI Global.

Saxena, R., Saxena, S., & Singh, A. P. (2024). Mindful Approaches to Sustainable Healthcare: Nurturing Mental Health and Wellbeing. In *Preserving Health, Preserving Earth: The Path to Sustainable Healthcare* (pp. 231–237). Springer.

Sayal, R., Subbalakhmi, C., & Saini, H. S. (2020). *International Journal of Advanced Trends in Computer Science and Engineering Available Online at*http://www.warse.org/IJATCSE/static/pdf/file/ijatcse27912020.pdf*Mobile App Accessibility for Visually Impaired. 9*(1), 182–185.

Schmaltz, K., Thompson, S., Mendes, D., & Carvalho, J. (2024). Robust defense mechanisms against adversarial ransomware attacks: Implementing a universal network-level detection filter.

Schofield, M., Alicioglu, G., Sun, B., Binaco, R., Turner, P., Thatcher, C., Lam, A., & Breitzman, A. (2021). Comparison of Malware Classification Methods using Convolutional Neural Network based on API Call Stream. *International Journal of Network Security & its Applications*, 13(2), 1–19. DOI: 10.5121/ijnsa.2021.13201

Sethi, K., Kumar, R., Sethi, L., Bera, P., & Patra, P. K. (2019). A novel machine learning based malware detection and classification framework. In *2019 International Conference on Cyber Security and Protection of Digital Services*, 1–4. DOI: 10.1109/CyberSecPODS.2019.8885196

Shandilya, S. K., Datta, A., Kartik, Y., & Nagar, A. (2024). *Digital Resilience: Navigating Disruption and Safeguarding Data Privacy*. Springer. DOI: 10.1007/978-3-031-53290-0

Sharma, A., & K. Sahay, S. 2014. Evolution and Detection of Polymorphic and Metamorphic Malwares: Asurvey, . *International Journal of Computer Applications*, 90(2), 7–11. DOI: 10.5120/15544-4098

Sharma, P., & Arora, J. (2016). A Review on Malware Detection Schemes Using Machine Learning Techniques. *International Journal of Engineering Development and Research*, 4(2), 2321–9939. https://www.ijedr.org/papers/IJEDR1602028.pdf

Shokri, R., Stronati, M., Song, C., & Shmatikov, V. (2017). Membership Inference Attacks Against Machine Learning Models. *Proceedings - IEEE Symposium on Security and Privacy*, 3–18. DOI: 10.1109/SP.2017.41

Short, E., Guppy, A., Hart, J. A., & Barnes, J. (2015). The Impact of Cyberstalking. *Studies in Media and Communication*, 3(2). Advance online publication. DOI: 10.11114/smc.v3i2.970

Sihwail, R., Omar, K., & Ariffin, K. Z. (2018). A survey on malware analysis techniques: Static, dynamic, hybrid and memory analysis. *Int. J. Adv. Sci. Eng. Inf. Technol, 8*(4-2), 1662-1671.

Sillaber, C., Sauerwein, C., Mussmann, A., & Breu, R. (2016). Data quality challenges and future research directions in threat intelligence sharing practice. *WISCS 2016 - Proceedings of the 2016 ACM Workshop on Information Sharing and Collaborative Security, Co-Located with CCS 2016*, 65–70. DOI: 10.1145/2994539.2994546

Singh, J., & Singh, J. (2018). Challenge of malware analysis: Malware obfuscation techniques. *International Journal of Information Security Science*, 7(3), 100–110.

Singh, R. D. (2018). Mapping online child safety in Asia and the Pacific. *Asia & the Pacific Policy Studies*, 5(3), 651–664. DOI: 10.1002/app5.247

Sivamayil, K., Rajasekar, E., Aljafari, B., Nikolovski, S., Vairavasundaram, S., & Vairavasundaram, I. (2023). A systematic study on reinforcement learning based applications. *Energies*, 16(3), 1512. DOI: 10.3390/en16031512

Smith, D., Khorsandroo, S., & Roy, K. (2023). Supervised and unsupervised learning techniques utilizing malware datasets. In *2023 IEEE 2nd International Conference on AI in Cybersecurity (ICAIC)* (pp. 1-7). IEEE. DOI: 10.1109/ICAIC57335.2023.10044169

Smith, J., Brown, T., & Williams, R. (2022). Evaluating the effectiveness of LSTM and CNN models for spam detection. *Journal of Cybersecurity*, 32(4), 212–230.

Smith, M., & Jones, R. (2024, February). Blockchain Technology for Enhancing Digital Privacy and Security. *IEEE Access : Practical Innovations, Open Solutions*, 11, 9456–9472.

Song, J., Kim, J., Choi, S., Kim, J., & Kim, I. (2021). Evaluations of AI-based malicious PowerShell detection with feature optimizations. In *ETRI Journal43*(3), (pp. 549–560). DOI: 10.4218/etrij.2020-0215

Song, W., Li, X., Afroz, S., Garg, D., Kuznetsov, D., & Yin, H. (2020). Mab-malware: A reinforcement learning framework for attacking static malware classifiers. *arXiv preprint arXiv:2003.03100.*

Sorkin, D. H., Janio, E. A., Eikey, E. V., Schneider, M., Davis, K., Schueller, S. M., Stadnick, N. A., Zheng, K., Neary, M., Safani, D., & Mukamel, D. B. (2021). Rise in use of digital mental health tools and technologies in the United States during the COVID-19 pandemic: Survey study. *Journal of Medical Internet Research*, 23(4), e26994. DOI: 10.2196/26994 PMID: 33822737

Sreelakshmi, S., Babu, A. A., Lakshmipriya, C., Gracious, L. A., Nalini, M., & Subramanian, R. S. (2024). Enhancing Intrusion Detection Systems with Machine Learning. In *2024 2nd International Conference on Self Sustainable Artificial Intelligence Systems (ICSSAS)* (pp. 557-564). DOI: 10.1109/ICSSAS64001.2024.10760341

Sridevi, and Gundoor, T.K. (2024). Artificial Intelligence on Knowledge Management and Industry Revolution 4.0. In R. Kumar, V. Jain, V.C. Ibarra, C.A. Talib and V. Kukreja (Eds.), Knowledge Management and Industry Revolution 4.0. DOI: 10.1002/9781394242641.ch6

Sridevi, and Tukkappa K Gundoor. (2025). "Identifying Nobel Features in Non-Portable Executable Malware Files," IAENG International Journal of Computer Science, *52*(1), 121-129.

Sterne, J. A. C., Savovi'c, J., Page, M. J., Elbers, R. G., Blencowe, N. S., Boutron, I., Cates, C. J., Cheng, H., Corbett, M. S., Eldridge, S. M., Emberson, J. R., Hernán, M. A., Hopewell, S., Hróbjartsson, A., Junqueira, D. R., Jüni, P., Kirkham, J. J., Lasserson, T., Li, T., & Higgins, J. P. T. (2019). RoB 2: A revised tool for assessing risk of bias in randomised trials. *BMJ (Clinical Research Ed.)*, 366, l4898. DOI: 10.1136/bmj.l4898 PMID: 31462531

Subaira, A. S., & Anitha, P. (2014). Efficient classification mechanism for network intrusion detection system based on data mining techniques: a survey. In *2014 IEEE 8th International Conference on Intelligent Systems and Control (ISCO)* (pp. 274-280). DOI: 10.1109/ISCO.2014.7103959

Subhan, F., Mirza, A., Su'ud, M. B. M., Alam, M. M., Nisar, S., Habib, U., & Iqbal, M. Z. (2023). AI-enabled wearable medical internet of things in healthcare system: A survey. *Applied Sciences (Basel, Switzerland)*, 13(3), 1394. DOI: 10.3390/app13031394

Subramanian, R. S., Yamini, B., Sudha, K., & Sivakumar, S. (2024). Ensemble-based deep learning techniques for customer churn prediction model. *Kybernetes*. Advance online publication. DOI: 10.1108/K-08-2023-1516

Sulaiman, M., Waseem, M., Ali, A. N., Laouini, G., & Alshammari, F. S. (2024). Defense strategies for epidemic cyber security threats: emulateing and analysis by using a machine learning approach. *IEEE Access*.

Suleski, T., Ahmed, M., Yang, W., & Wang, E. (2023). A review of multi-factor authentication in the Internet of Healthcare Things. *Digital Health*, 9, 20552076231177144. DOI: 10.1177/20552076231177144 PMID: 37252257

Suneetha, S., & Patil, S. R. (2023) "Advancements in Multi-Cloud Applications for Enhanced E-Healthcare Services," In *2023 International Conference on Artificial Intelligence for Innovations in Healthcare Industries (ICAIIHI)*, Raipur, India, (pp. 1-7).

Surakhi, O., García, A., Jamoos, M., & Alkhanafseh, M. (2022). The intrusion detection system by deep learning methods: issues and challenges.

Szegedy, C., Ioffe, S., Vanhoucke, V., & Alemi, A. A. (2017). Inception-v4, Inception-ResNet and the Impact of Residual Connections on Learning. In *Proceedings of the Thirty-First AAAI Conference on Artificial Intelligence*, (pp. 4278–4284). DOI: 10.1609/aaai.v31i1.11231

Taheri, S., & Mammadov, M. (2013). Learning the naive bayes classifier with optimization models. *International Journal of Applied Mathematics and Computer Science*, 23(4), 787–795. DOI: 10.2478/amcs-2013-0059

Tahir, R. (2018). A study on malware and malware detection techniques. *International Journal of Education and Management Engineering*, 8(2), 20–30. DOI: 10.5815/ijeme.2018.02.03

Tahsien, S. M., Karimipour, H., & Spachos, P. (2020). Machine learning based solutions for security of Internet of Things (IoT): A survey. *Journal of Network and Computer Applications*, 161(February), 102630. Advance online publication. DOI: 10.1016/j.jnca.2020.102630

Talukder, M. A., Islam, M. M., Uddin, M. A., Hasan, K. F., Sharmin, S., Alyami, S. A., & Moni, M. A. (2024). Machine learning-based network intrusion detection for big and imbalanced data using oversampling, stacking feature embedding and feature extraction. *Journal of Big Data*, 11(1), 33. DOI: 10.1186/s40537-024-00886-w

Taylor, K., & Wilson, G. (2024, June). Cybersecurity Protocols for Preventing Online Abuse. *IEEE Network*, 36(4), 42–49.

Tchakounté, F., & Hayata, F. (2017). Supervised learning-based detection of malware on android. In *Mobile Security and Privacy* (pp. 101–154). Syngress. DOI: 10.1016/B978-0-12-804629-6.00006-7

Tech Industry and Researchers come together to tackle online child sexual exploitation and abuse – Safe Online. (n.d.). Retrieved December 31, 2024, from https://safeonline.global/tech-industry-and-researchers-come-together-to-tackle-online-child-sexual-exploitation-and-abuse

The Importance of Digital Literacy in the Modern World | by Gary A. Fowler | Medium. (n.d.). Retrieved December 31, 2024, from https://gafowler.medium.com/the-importance-of-digital-literacy-in-the-modern-world-e6913c09a2f8

The Importance of Teacher Training Programs in Transforming Education - EdIndia. (n.d.). Retrieved December 31, 2024, from https://edindia.org/the-importance-of-teacher-training-programs-in-transforming-education/

The Role of Cybersecurity in Mental Well-being. (n.d.). Retrieved December 31, 2024, from https://www.psychologs.com/the-role-of-cybersecurity-in-mental-well-being/?srsltid=AfmBOorkmzM1137wXVce3OowRoD2PPgtt6_HvUrc3vLDBAD2KAe-MCNt

The Role of Schools in Promoting Online Safety | Learning.com. (n.d.). Retrieved December 31, 2024, from https://www.learning.com/blog/role-of-schools-online-safety/

The Theory and Practice of Cyber-Mindfulness. (n.d.). Retrieved December 31, 2024, from https://www.annacollard.com/post/the-theory-and-practice-of-cyber-mindfulness

Tischler, H., Platzer, A., Vian, P., & Genetti, B. (2001). On the Design of a Cyber Security Data Sharing System. *Europa Medicophysica*, 37(1), 39–50.

Topark-ngarm, P. (2014). *Identifying Android Malware Using Machine Learning Based Upon Both Static and Dynamic Features.*

Tounsi, W., & Rais, H. (2018). A survey on technical threat intelligence in the age of sophisticated cyber attacks. *Computers & Security*, 72, 212–233. DOI: 10.1016/j.cose.2017.09.001

Trim, P. R., & Lee, Y. I. (2022). Combining sociocultural intelligence with Artificial Intelligence to increase organizational cyber security provision through enhanced resilience. *Big Data and Cognitive Computing*, 6(4), 110. DOI: 10.3390/bdcc6040110

Tripathi, P., Ankit, K., Sharma, R., & Kumar, T. (2021). Facial expression recognition through CNN. In 2021 6th International Conference on Communication and Electronics Systems (ICCES) (pp. 1-5). IEEE. DOI: 10.1109/ICCES51350.2021.9488963

Tseng, E., Bellini, R., Lee, Y.-Y., Ramjit, A., Ristenpart, T., & Dell, N. (2024). Data Stewardship in Clinical Computer Security: Balancing Benefit and Burden in Participatory Systems. *Proceedings of the ACM on Human-Computer Interaction (pp.* 1–29). DOI: 10.1145/3637316

Tukkappa, K. Gundoor, Dr. Sridevi. (2024). Optimized Feature Selection and classification for Non-Portable Executable Malware. *International Journal of Communication Networks and Information Security (IJCNIS), 16*(4), 546–552. Retrieved from https://ijcnis.org/index.php/ijcnis/article/view/7107

Turner, S. (2024, May). Guidelines for Policymakers on Cybersecurity and Mental Health. *IEEE Trans. Cyber Secur.*, 12(1), 56–67.

Tzermias, Z., Sykiotakis, G., Polychronakis, M., & Markatos, E. P. (2011). Combining static and dynamic analysis for the detection of malicious documents. In *Proceedings of the 4th Workshop on European Workshop on System Security.* DOI: 10.1145/1972551.1972555

Ucci, D., Aniello, L., & Baldoni, R. (2019). Survey of machine learning techniques for malware analysis. *Computers & Security*, 81, 123–147. DOI: 10.1016/j.cose.2018.11.001

Ullah, F., Turab, A., Ullah, S., Cacciagrano, D., & Zhao, Y. (2024). Enhanced network intrusion detection system for internet of things security using multimodal big data representation with transfer learning and game theory. *Sensors (Basel)*, 24(13), 4152. DOI: 10.3390/s24134152 PMID: 39000931

Understand the Importance of Cyber Security: Guardian Against Threats! (n.d.). Retrieved December 31, 2024, from https://www.simplilearn.com/tutorials/cyber-security-tutorial/what-is-cyber-security

Uprety, A., & Rawat, D. B. (2021). Reinforcement Learning for IoT Security: A Comprehensive Survey. *IEEE Internet of Things Journal*, 8(11), 8693–8706. DOI: 10.1109/JIOT.2020.3040957

Vargas, H., Lozano-Garzon, C., Montoya, G. A., & Donoso, Y. (2021). Detection of security attacks in industrial iot networks: A blockchain and machine learning approach. *Electronics (Basel)*, 10(21), 2662. Advance online publication. DOI: 10.3390/electronics10212662

Venkatesh, B., & Anuradha, J. (2019). A review of feature selection and its methods. *Cybernetics and Information Technologies*, 19(1), 3–26. DOI: 10.2478/cait-2019-0001

Venketbabu, T., Aswathy, M. P., Sangeetha, J., Anish, T. P., Nalini, M., & Subramanian, R. S. (2024). Revolutionizing Image Processing: Innovations Impacts and Future Trends. In *2024 2nd International Conference on Self Sustainable Artificial Intelligence Systems (ICSSAS)* (pp. 901-907).

Verma, H., Chauhan, N., & Awasthi, L. K. (2023). A Comprehensive review of 'Internet of Healthcare Things': Networking aspects, technologies, services, applications, challenges, and security concerns. *Computer Science Review, 50*, 100591. Hegde, P., & Maddikunta, P. K. R. (2023). Amalgamation of Blockchain with resource-constrained IoT device for Healthcare applications–State of Art, Challenges and Future Directions. *International Journal of Cognitive Computing in Engineering*.

Virmani, C., Choudhary, T., Pillai, A., & Rani, M. (2022). Applications of machine learning in cyber security. *Research Anthology on Machine Learning Techniques, Methods, and Applications*, 621–641. DOI: 10.4018/978-1-6684-6291-1.ch033

W, R. A., & S, C. (2021). *Performance Analysis of Boosting Techniques for Classificationand Detection ofMalicious Websites*. DOI: 10.4108/eai.7-12-2021.2314506

Wagener, G., State, R., & Dulaunoy, A. (2008). Malware behaviour analysis. *Journal in Computer Virology, 4*, 279-287.

Wagner, C., Dulaunoy, A., Wagener, G., & Iklody, A. (2016). MISP - The design and implementation of a collaborative threat intelligence sharing platform. *WISCS 2016 - Proceedings of the 2016 ACM Workshop on Information Sharing and Collaborative Security, Co-Located with CCS 2016*, 49–56. DOI: 10.1145/2994539.2994542

Waheed, N., He, X., Ikram, M., Usman, M., Hashmi, S. S., & Usman, M. (2021). Security and Privacy in IoT Using Machine Learning and Blockchain. *ACM Computing Surveys*, 53(6), 1–37. DOI: 10.1145/3417987

Walker, J. (2019). Emotet trojan implicated in Wolverine Solutions ransomware attack. *The Daily Swig*, 1–3. https://portswigger.net/daily-swig/emotet-trojan-implicated-in-wolverine-solutions-ransomware-attack

Walsh, K., Eggins, E., Hine, L., Mathews, B., Kenny, M. C., Howard, S., Ayling, N., Dallaston, E., Pink, E., & Vagenas, D. (2022). Child protection training for professionals to improve reporting of child abuse and neglect. *Cochrane Database of Systematic Reviews*, 2022(7), CD011775. Advance online publication. DOI: 10.1002/14651858.CD011775.pub2 PMID: 35788913

Wang, S., Li, Y., & Chen, F. (2024). Optimizing blue team strategies with reinforcement learning for enhanced ransomware defense simulations.

Wang, H., Wu, J., Zhang, C., Lu, W., & Ni, C. (2024). Intelligent Security Detection and Defense in Operating Systems Based on Deep Learning. *International Journal of Computer Science and Information Technologies*, 2(1), 359–367. DOI: 10.62051/ijcsit.v2n1.37

Wang, J. (2024, March). Machine Learning Techniques in Cyberbullying Detection: A Survey. *IEEE Communications Surveys and Tutorials*, 26(1), 78–96.

Wang, M. W. H., Goodman, J. M., & Allen, T. E. H. (2021). Machine Learning in Predictive Toxicology: Recent Applications and Future Directions for Classification Models. *Chemical Research in Toxicology*, 34(2), 217–239. DOI: 10.1021/acs.chemrestox.0c00316 PMID: 33356168

Wang, W., Zhao, M., Gao, Z., Xu, G., Xian, H., Li, Y., & Zhang, X. (2019). Constructing features for detecting Android malicious applications: Issues, taxonomy and directions. *IEEE Access : Practical Innovations, Open Solutions*, 7, 67602–67631. DOI: 10.1109/ACCESS.2019.2918139

Waterworth, J. A., Salamanca-Sanabria, A., Inkster, B., Knibbs, C., & Bada, M. (2023). Cybersecurity: A critical priority for digital mental health. *Frontiers in Digital Health*, 5, 1242264. DOI: 10.3389/fdgth.2023.1242264 PMID: 37781452

Watts, L. K., Wagner, J., Velasquez, B., & Behrens, P. I. (2017). Cyberbullying in higher education: A literature review. *Computers in Human Behavior*, 69, 268–274. DOI: 10.1016/j.chb.2016.12.038

Wei, W., Visweswaran, S., & Cooper, G. F. (2011). The application of naive Bayes model averaging to predict Alzheimer's disease from genome-wide data. *Journal of the American Medical Informatics Association : JAMIA*, 18(4), 370–375. DOI: 10.1136/amiajnl-2011-000101 PMID: 21672907

Wells, M., & Mitchell, K. (2007). Youth Sexual Exploitation on the Internet: DSM-IV Diagnoses and Gender Differences in Co-occurring Mental Health Issues. *Child & Adolescent Social Work Journal*, 24(3), 235–260. DOI: 10.1007/s10560-007-0083-z

West. (2014). Cyber-violence against women. Battered Women's Support Services, 12-19.

What Is Identity Theft? Types and Examples. (n.d.). Retrieved December 31, 2024, from https://www.investopedia.com/terms/i/identitytheft.asp

What is online child sexual exploitation? | ACCCE. (n.d.). Retrieved December 31, 2024, from https://www.accce.gov.au/help-and-support/what-is-online-child-exploitation

White, L. (2024, May). Digital Harassment: Detection and Mitigation Strategies. *IEEE Internet of Things Journal*, 8(3), 1204–1215.

WHO. (2020). Global Status Report on Preventing Violence Against Children. Available online: https://www.who.int/teams/social-determinants-ofhealth/violence-prevention/global-status-report-on-violence-againstchildren-2020

Why Collaboration Is Essential for Cybersecurity Teams. (n.d.). Retrieved December 31, 2024, from https://gca.isa.org/blog/why-collaboration-is-essential-for-cybersecurity-teams

Wissink, I. B., Van Vugt, E., Moonen, X., Stams, G. J. J., & Hendriks, J. (2015). Sexual abuse involving children with an intellectual disability(ID): A narrative review. *Research in Developmental Disabilities*, 36, 20–35. DOI: 10.1016/j.ridd.2014.09.007 PMID: 25310832

Wu, K., Chen, H., & Yang, P. (2021). An attention-based CNN-LSTM-BiLSTM model for short-term electric load forecasting in integrated energy systems. *International Transactions on Electrical Energy Systems*, 31(1), e12637. DOI: 10.1002/2050-7038.12637

Xu, J. Y., Sung, A. H., Chavez, P., & Mukkamala, S. (2005). Polymorphic malicious executable scanner by API sequence analysis. In *Proceedings -HIS'04: 4th International Conference on Hybrid Intelligent Systems*, (pp. 378–383). DOI: 10.1109/ICHIS.2004.75

Xu, X., Liu, H., & Yao, M. (2019). Recent Progress of Anomaly Detection. *Complexity*, 2019(1), 2686378. Advance online publication. DOI: 10.1155/2019/2686378

Xu, Z., Ray, S., Subramanyan, P., & Malik, S. (2017). Malware detection using machine learning based analysis of virtual memory access patterns. *Proceedings of the 2017 Design, Automation and Test in Europe, DATE 2017*, (pp. 169–174). DOI: 10.23919/DATE.2017.7926977

Yamini, B., Nithyanandhan, R., Sudha, K., Nithya, T., Vijayakumar, K., & Subramanian, R. S. (2024). Maximizing the Revolutionary Potential of Quantum Computing: Challenges, Opportunities, and Future Directions. In *2024 10th International Conference on Communication and Signal Processing (ICCSP)* (pp. 756-761).

Yang, Y., & Liu, X. (2005). A re-examination of text categorization methods. *Proceedings of the 22nd Annual International ACM SIGIR Conference on Research and Development in Information Retrieval*, 42-49.

Yavanoglu, O., & Aydos, M. (2017). A review on cyber security datasets for machine learning algorithms. In *2017 IEEE international conference on big data (big data)* (pp. 2186-2193).

Yogi, M. K., & Bhavani, K. G. D. (2018). A Propulsive Roadmap for IoT Beyond 2025. *International Journal of Advanced Networking and Applications*, 10(2), 3808–3815. DOI: 10.35444/IJANA.2018.100210

You, I., & Yim, K. (2010). Malware obfuscation techniques: A brief survey. In *Proceedings - 2010 International Conference on Broadband, Wireless Computing Communication and Applications,* (pp. 297–300). DOI: 10.1109/BWCCA.2010.85

Yuan, Z., Lu, Y., & Xue, Y. (2020). DroidDet: Effective and robust detection of Android malware using static analysis along with machine learning. *Neurocomputing*, 349, 87–98. DOI: 10.1016/j.neucom.2019.01.112

Yu, R., Perera, C., Sharma, M., Ipince, A., Bakrania, S., Shokraneh, F., Sepulveda, J. S. M., & Anthony, D. (2023). Child and adolescent mental health and psychosocial support interventions: An evidence and gap map of low- and middle-income countries. *Campbell Systematic Reviews*, 19(3), e1349. DOI: 10.1002/cl2.1349 PMID: 37621301

Zeanah, C. H., & Humphreys, K. L. (2018). Child Abuse and Neglect. *Journal of the American Academy of Child and Adolescent Psychiatry*, 57(9), 637–644. DOI: 10.1016/j.jaac.2018.06.007 PMID: 30196867

Zhang, F., Leach, K., Sun, K., & Stavrou, A. (2013). SPECTRE: A dependable introspection framework via system management mode. *Proceedings of the International Conference on Dependable Systems and Networks, Vmi*. DOI: 10.1109/DSN.2013.6575343

Zhang, H., Nian, K., Coleman, T. F., & Li, Y. (2020). Spectral ranking and unsupervised feature selection for point, collective, and contextual anomaly detection. *International Journal of Data Science and Analytics*, 9(1), 57–75. DOI: 10.1007/s41060-018-0161-7

Zhang, X., Zhao, J., & LeCun, Y. (2018). Text understanding from scratch. *Proceedings of the 2015 Conference on Empirical Methods in Natural Language Processing*, 1025-1035.

Zhao, K., Tian, Y. J., & Deng, N. Y. (2006). Unsupervised and semi-supervised two-class support vector machines. In *Proceedings - IEEE International Conference on Data Mining, ICDM*, (pp. 813–817). DOI: 10.1109/ICDMW.2006.164

Zhou, F., Ma, Z., Rashwan, A. K., Khaskheli, M. B., Abdelrady, W. A., Abdelaty, N. S., Hassan Askri, S. M., Zhao, P., Chen, W., & Shamsi, I. H. (2024). Exploring the Interplay of Food Security, Safety, and Psychological Wellness in the COVID-19 Era: Managing Strategies for Resilience and Adaptation. *Foods*, 13(11), 1610. DOI: 10.3390/foods13111610 PMID: 38890839

Zhu, X. (2005). *Semi-Supervised Learning Literature Survey*. http://digital.library.wisc.edu/1793/60444

Zolkipli, M. F., & Jantan, A. (2010, December). Malware behavior analysis: Learning and understanding current malware threats. In *Proceedings - 2nd International Conference on Network Applications, Protocols and Services,* (pp. 218–221). DOI: 10.1109/NETAPPS.2010.46

About the Contributors

Minakshi is an accomplished academician with 18+ years of experience in computer science and engineering domains. Currently an Assistant Professor at King Khalid University, she has taught at esteemed institutions like Uttaranchal University and Tula's Institute. A prolific researcher with 80 Scopus publications, 18 patents, and 3 software copyrights, she has received accolades like Outstanding Section Volunteer Award (IEEE UP Section), Research Excellence Award, and HOD of the Year Award. Adept at curriculum development, research guidance, project management, and team leadership, Dr. Minakshi brings a holistic approach to education, fostering student success through quality instruction and innovative pedagogical methods.

Anchit Bijalwan is an accomplished academician and researcher with a Ph.D. in Computer Science and Engineering. Currently serving as Research Coordinator at the British University Vietnam, he has over 15 years of experience in academia. His research interests include network forensics, cybersecurity, machine learning, and data mining. Dr. Bijalwan has authored two books and published extensively in prestigious journals like Security and Communication Networks, Discrete Dynamics in Nature and Society, and Journal of Healthcare Engineering. He has delivered international training programs, chaired conferences, and served as an examiner and editor for reputed publications. His contributions have been recognized through awards like the International Researcher Award in 2021.

Tarun Kumar received his Ph.D. degree from the National Institute of Technology Patna, Bihar, India. Dr. Kumar has more than 18 years of experience in teaching and is currently working as an Assistant Professor in the School of Computer Science and Engineering at Galgotias University, Greater Noida, India. His research interests include cloud computing, IoT, and DNA computing. Dr. Kumar has published several patents and papers in conference proceedings, book chapters, and refereed journals. He has also participated in many international conferences as an organizer and session chair. Dr. Kumar is a member of IEEE, ACM, and the IEEE Computer Society.

***

Adaikkammai A. is an Assistant Professor in the Department of Computer Science and Business Systems at RMD Engineering College. She is committed to fostering academic excellence and innovation in the integration of computer science with business systems. Her efforts focus on mentoring students and promoting interdisciplinary learning.

Harishchander Anandaram completed a PhD in bioengineering, an M.Tech., and a B.Tech. in bioinformatics from the Sathyabama Institute of Science and Technology, Chennai, in 2020, 2011, and 2009. In his bachelor's and master's theses, he worked on analyzing resistance in HIV protease inhibitors based on molecular mechanics and machine learning studies, a collaborative project with IIT Madras. In his PhD thesis, he worked on pharmacogenomics and miRNA-regulated networks in psoriasis, a collaborative project with Georgetown University, USA, JIPMER, India, CIBA, India, and ILS, India. His thesis illustrated a multi-disciplinary approach by combining computational biophysics and molecular biology machine learning. While doing a PhD, He had the opportunity to collaborate with international researchers and have publications in reputed international journals in bioinformatics and systems biology. He has received the prestigious "Young Scientist Award" from "The Melinda Gates Foundation" for his research abstract on "The Implications of miRNA Dynamics in Infectious Diseases". To date, he has reviewed more than 600 manuscripts in systems biology.

Shree Harsh Attri is Associate Professor in Sharda School of Engineering & Technology, Department of Computer Science & Engineering and member of Centre for AI in Medicine, Imaging, and Forensic (CAIMIF) Sharda University – Greater Noida. He is having 17+ years of Industrial and Teaching as well as Research experience in the areas of Artificial Intelligence, Natural Language Processing and Deep Neural Networks. He has published the research papers in ESCI, SCOPUS and Web of Science indexed journals, published 3 patents and 01 granted Indian Patent (Patent No.: 552048). He is a reviewer in eminent International conferences and Journals.

Girish B. C. is a postgraduate student pursuing an M.Sc. in Cyber Forensic and Cybersecurity at Amity University, Noida. With a strong background in forensic science and cybersecurity, has actively contributed to research in malware analysis, blockchain forensics, and drone security. His works include book chapter on Introduction to Drone Vulnerability, its Impact, and Mitigation Techniques. Combining technical expertise with academic research, main goal is to bridge the gap between cybersecurity advancements and practical applications.

Prabhu D. is a faculty member in the Department of Computer Science and Engineering, School of Computing, at Vel Tech Rangarajan Dr. Sagunthala R&D Institute of Science and Technology, Avadi, Chennai. His expertise lies in advancing research and education in computer science and engineering.

Kiranbhai Ramabhai Dodiya is an experienced Cyber Forensic Expert and Assistant Professor specializing in cyber security and digital forensics. He has taught at prestigious institutions and is currently pursuing a PhD in Biochemistry and Forensic Science. With a strong background in ethical hacking and malware analysis, Kiranbhai is passionate about educating students and contributing to the field of cyber forensics. His expertise includes malware forensic, computer forensics, and data recovery software. Kiranbhai's commitment to professional growth is evident through his participation in workshops, seminars, and research publications. He is dedicated to shaping the next generation of professionals in the field and combatting cybercrimes.

Monica Anna Fernandes is a student at Narayan Shastri Institute of Technology – Institute of Forensic Sciences & Cyber Security (NSIT-IFSCS), specializing in Cyber Security. With a deep interest in digital forensics, ethical hacking, and cyber threat analysis, she is committed to enhancing cybersecurity frameworks and safeguarding digital infrastructures. Her academic journey reflects a passion for forensic investigation, network security, and the ever-evolving domain of cyber defense. Through continuous learning and research, she aspires to contribute meaningfully to the field of cybersecurity.

Dankan Gowda V. is currently working as an Assistant Professor in the Department of Electronics and Communication Engineering at BMS Institute of Technology and Management in Bangalore. Previously, he worked as a Research Fellow at ADA DRDO and as a Software Engineer at Robert Bosch. With a total experience of 14 years, including teaching and industry, Dr. Gowda has made significant contributions to both academia and research. He has published over 160 research papers in renowned international journals and conferences. In recognition of his innovative work, Dr. Gowda has been granted six patents, including four from Indian authorities and two international patents. His research interests primarily lie in the fields of IoT and Signal Processing, where he has conducted workshops and handled industry projects. Dr. Gowda is passionate about teaching and strives to create an engaging and effective learning environment for his students. He consistently seeks opportunities to enhance his knowledge and stay updated with the latest advancements in his field.

T. K. Gundoor, Born in Janginakoppa, Haveri district, Karnataka, India on 14 August 1994, obtained the MCA. degree in Computer Science from the Visvesvaraya Technological University in 2018. he is presently pursuing his PhD under the guidance of Dr. Sridevi, Professor, Department of Computer Science, Karnatak University, Dharwad. He has obtained membership of IAENG in 2021. Has received research fellowship from DST, KSTePS), Govt.of Karnataka. The area of research is "Network Security ". At present he is working on the research topic: "Study and design of Effective algorithm to detect non-portable malicious files". He is also, the IEEE student member (Member no:94567049), IAENG (International Association of Engineers) (Member no: 291948Date: 20 December 2024 Member of following societies - the IAENG Society of Artificial Intelligence, the IAENG Society of Bioinformatics, the IAENG Society of Computer Science, the IAENG Society of Data Mining, the IAENG Society of Electrical Engineering, the IAENG Society of Internet Computing and Web Services, the IAENG Society of Imaging Engineering, the IAENG Society of Information System Engineering, the IAENG Society of Scientific Computing.

Vishal Jain is presently working as Professor at the Department of Computer Science and Engineering, School of Engineering and Technology, Sharda University, Greater Noida, India. Before that, he worked for several years as an Associate Professor at Bharati Vidyapeeths Institute of Computer Applications and Management (BVICAM), New Delhi. He has more than 18 years of experience in the academics. He has earned degrees: Ph.D (CSE), M.Tech (CSE), MBA (HR), MCA, MCP, and CCNA. He has more than 1900 research citations with Google Scholar (h-index score 21 and i-10 index 49) and has authored more than 150 research papers in professional journals and conferences. He has authored and edited more than 60 books (most of them are indexed at the Scopus) with various reputed publishers, including Elsevier, Springer, IET, Apple Academic Press, CRC, Taylor and Francis Group, Scrivener, Wiley, Emerald, NOVA Science, River Publishers, IGI-Global and Bentham Science.

Kapil Joshi is an Associate Professor in the department of Computer Science & Engineering (CSE) at Uttaranchal Institute of Technology (UIT), Uttaranchal University, Dehradun, Uttarakhand, India. He has completed his Ph.D, topic on "Image Quality Enhancement using Fusion Technique" in computer science and engineering from Uttaranchal University, Dehradun. He has more than 10 years' experience in industry, academic, and research. His areas of interest are Operating System, Computer Networks, Web Technology, Data Structure and Java etc. His research areas are deep learning, CNN, Computer vision etc. He has published various patents, 400+ research papers in reputed journals (UGC/Scopus) as well as published 20+ books in international publication. Dr. Kapil Joshi has published more than 50+ research papers in various international journals (including ISI/SCI indexed). He has also been associated with many conferences at National and International level and organized many conferences like STEM-2017, ICACDS-18, ICAESMT-19, ICAEST-20, ICAEST-21, ICIS-22, ICNN-22, IDVRP-22, ICAEST-22 and ICAEST-23.

Shreenidhi K. S. is currently serving as an Assistant Professor in Biotechnology at a reputed institution. Shreenidhi holds a Ph.D. in Environmental Toxicology, specializing in understanding and mitigating the impact of pollutants on ecosystems and human health. Her research work has contributed significantly to advancing knowledge in this critical area, addressing global challenges in environmental sustainability and toxicology. In addition to academic and research achievements, Shreenidhi has been a dedicated instructor and judge for the International Genetically Engineered Machine (iGEM) competition for the past six years. As a judge, Shreenidhi has evaluated innovative projects from around the world, promoting excellence in this rapidly evolving field.

Vijaya K. Shandilya is Professor & Head –Computer Science and Engineering, Sipna College of Engineering and Technology Amravati. She has total 26 years of teaching experience. Her teaching career has helped students to achieve their goals in the field Computer Engineering. She has published 70 papers in International Journals and 17 papers in National and International Conferences Proceedings. She has published 05 patent and 02 copyright. Her research interest includes intrusion detection, network security and Image Processing.

Kanya J. Katkar is a student at Narayan Shastri Institute of Technology – Institute of Forensic Sciences & Cyber Security (NSIT-IFSCS), specializing in Cyber Security. Passionate about digital forensics, ethical hacking, and cybersecurity measures, she is dedicated to understanding cyber threats and devising robust security solutions. Through continuous learning and research, she aspires to contribute meaningfully to the field of cybersecurity.

Himanshu Khajuria is an experienced Associate Professor with a demonstrated history of working in the higher education industry for the last 18 years. Skilled in Research, E-Learning, Analytical Skills and Data Analysis having more 70 research publications in various national and international journals of repute indexed in SCOPUS, WoS, PubMed etc. Strong education professional with a Doctor of Philosophy (Ph.D.) focused on Forensic Science where strong technical skills, academic background and problem-solving abilities are applied towards the successful achievement of goals and objectives. He has been awarded Certificate of Excellence in Reviewing by Elsevier for significant contribution made to the quality of the Journal. He has also been awarded Meritorious Performance award and Memento for excellent services at International Conference of South Asian Congress of Forensic Medicine, Forensic Science and Toxicology (SAFCON 2008) and the 9th Annual meeting of the ICFMT. Dr. Khajuria has been a member and reviewers for various national and international journals.

Akash Khunt is the Program Coordinator of Cyber Security at Narayan Shastri Institute of Technology – Institute of Forensic Sciences & Cyber Security (NSIT-IFSCS). With expertise in digital forensics, ethical hacking, and network security, he plays a crucial role in shaping the cybersecurity curriculum and guiding students in cutting-edge security practices. His professional focus includes cyber threat analysis, forensic investigations, and implementing robust security protocols. Dedicated to fostering a strong cybersecurity culture, he actively contributes to research and advancements in the field.

Sachil Kumar is an accomplished academic and researcher in the field of forensic sciences, currently serving as an Associate Professor at Amity University, Noida, India. He holds a PhD in Forensic Chemistry and Forensic Medicine from King George's Medical University, Lucknow, where his research focused on the development of an economical and sensitive method for postmortem interval estimation, utilizing cardiac Troponin-T (cTnT) degradation. His work provides a more accurate and extended time window for PMI estimation. Dr. Kumar has also supervised numerous postgraduate dissertations in forensic toxicology and analytical chemistry, with expertise in advanced techniques like gas chromatography-mass spectrometry (GC-MS). He has worked as an Associate Professor at multiple institutions, including Sandip University and CHRIST University, and as an Assistant Professor at Naif Arab University in Saudi Arabia. Alongside his academic roles, Dr. Kumar has extensive editorial experience, having served as Editorial Secretary for the Arab Journal of Forensic Sciences & Forensic Medicine and as a peer reviewer for several international journals. His professional memberships include the International Alliance of Clinical and Forensic Toxicologists, the Japanese Society of Toxicology, and the Arab Society for Forensic Sciences and Forensic Medicine. Additionally, he has participated in various international workshops and training programs on research methodology, statistical analysis, and forensic toxicology. Dr. Sachil has authored numerous highly cited journal publications and conference articles on the aforementioned topics and has received several awards (International Travel Support Scheme) and grants (UGC-NET Lectureship in Forensic Sciences; UGC-Junior Research Fellowship (J.R.F.); and UGC-Senior Research Fellowship (S.R.F.) from various funding agencies, including the University Grants Commission, Government of India, UGC Ref. No.: 2003/ (NET-DEC. 2009), and Science and Engineering Research Board (SERB), Department of Science and Technology (DST), Government of India.

Suresh Babu Kunda is an Associate Professor in the Department of Computer Science and Engineering at Narasaraopeta Engineering College (Autonomous), Narasaraopet, Andhra Pradesh. He earned his Ph.D. in Computer Science and Engineering from VIT-AP University in 2023. Dr. Suresh Babu has published over 10 research papers in esteemed national and international journals, holds 10 patents, and has actively participated in numerous international conferences. With a teaching experience spanning more than a decade, he has taught over 15 subjects to undergraduate and postgraduate students in Computer Science and Engineering. He is a lifetime member of ISTE and has held various academic and administrative roles in reputed institutions during his 10 years of professional experience. His research interests include Mobile Computing, Computer Networks, Software Defined Networks(SDNs), the Internet of Things (IoT), Network Security, Cyber security, Machine Learning, and Deep Learning.

Pandi Kumari M. R. is an Assistant Professor in Artificial Intelligence and Machine Learning at Panimalar Engineering College. With expertise in AI and ML, she is dedicated to advancing research and education in these cutting-edge fields. Her contributions include mentoring students and fostering innovation in technology-driven solutions.

C. N. Manushree is a postgraduate student pursuing an M.Sc. in Cyber Forensic and Cybersecurity at Amity University, Noida. With a strong foundation in forensic science and cybersecurity, has contributed to research in quantum security and predictive analytics. Her published works include book chapters on Harnessing Quantum Mechanics for Next-Generation Security Solutions and Optimizing Feature Selection for Predictive Analytics with Quantum Algorithms. Passionate about advancing cybersecurity through emerging technologies, and aims to bridge the gap between theoretical research and practical applications.

Rasmita Kumari Mohanty was born in Odisha, India. She received the master's degree in computer science and engineering (CSE) from JNTU, Hyderabad, India. She is currently pursuing the Ph.D. degree in CSE with the Veer Surendra Sai University of Technology, Sambalpur. She is an Assistant Professor with the

Department of CSE-(CyS, DS) and AI&DS, VNR Vignana Jyothi Institute of Engineering and Technology, Hyderabad, and has ten years of teaching experience. She has published more than 30 research articles in various SCIE and international journals. Her research interests include wireless body area networks, optimization, the IoT, and deep learning. She has presented her research at many prominent conferences and journals and actively participates in workshops and seminars to stay abreast of the latest developments in her field. She is a reviewer of various national and international journals and conferences.

Arvindhan Muthusamy is presently employed as an Assistant Professor in the School of Computing Science and Engineering. His teaching experience exceeds 14 years. He has been affiliated with Galgotias University since 2017. I have authored three publications in SCI journals, as well as twenty-five publications indexed in SCOPUS, including chapters. My area of interest encompasses the fields of cloud computing and machine learning. I have published 7 patents in interdisciplinary initiatives.

Aparna P. is a faculty member in the Department of Computer Science and Engineering at RMK College of Engineering and Technology, located in RSM Nagar, Puduvoyal, Tamil Nadu, 601206. She is dedicated to imparting quality education and fostering innovation in computer science.

Indira P. Joshi is PhD scholar of Sipna COET, Amaravati. She has obtained her Masters in Computer Engineering from Mumbai University. She has total 17 years of teaching experience. Her practical approach to teaching with the contemporary methods makes her an expert teacher. She has published papers in 7 International Journals and 9 papers in National and International Conferences Proceedings. She has published 1 patent. Her research interest includes intrusion detection, network security and Cyber Security.

Divya Patel is the Program Coordinator of Digital Forensic & Information Security (DFIS) at Narayan Shastri Institute of Technology – Institute of Forensic Sciences & Cyber Security (NSIT-IFSCS). With a strong background in cybersecurity, digital forensics, and information security, she plays a pivotal role in designing and overseeing the DFIS program. Her expertise includes cyber threat analysis, forensic investigations, and secure digital infrastructure development. Committed to advancing cybersecurity education, she actively engages in research and training initiatives to equip students with cutting-edge forensic and security skills.

B. C. M. Patnaik has more than 24 years of rich experience in Educational Research, Content and Creative initiative at both post graduate and undergraduate level, ability to handle core administration related activities such as infrastructure, facility, human resources, training and development of staff members and organizational behavior and organization development. Currently spearheading efforts as a Professor (Accounts &Finance) with School of Management, KIIT University. Published more than 300 papers including 119 papers in Scopus and guided 25 Ph.D scholars.

Falak Prajapati is a student at Narayan Shastri Institute of Technology – Institute of Forensic Sciences & Cyber Security (NSIT-IFSCS), specializing in Cyber Security. She has a strong passion for digital forensics, ethical hacking, and cybersecurity risk assessment. With a keen interest in protecting digital infrastructures and investigating cyber threats, she is dedicated to learning advanced security techniques and forensic methodologies. Her academic pursuits reflect a commitment to innovation in cybersecurity, aiming to contribute to a safer digital world.

Kunda Praveen is an Assistant Professor in the of Department of Matrusri Engineering College, Hyderabad.

Siva Subramanian R. is an Associate Professor in the Department of Computer Science and Engineering, RMK College of Engg and Tech, Chennai, India. He received her B.E. in Computer Science and Engineering from Anna University, Chennai in 2009 and M.Tech. in Computer Science and Engineering from Bharath University, Chennai, India in 2013. He has 10 years teaching experience. His research interests include Data Mining, Machine Learning, Big Data Analytics and Networking. He has published many articles in reputed journals.

Masud Rana is an assistant professor in Computer Science at Lamar University, expertise in next-generation IoT security, machine learning, penetration testing, and cyber-physical system security. His interdisciplinary research emphasizes practical solutions, empowering students for impactful, ethical projects. His teaching philosophy prioritizes an inclusive, dynamic learning environment that fosters critical thinking and problem-solving through hands-on, project-based cooperative learning, along with personalized, outcome-driven education.

H. G. Govardhana Reddy has more than a decade's experience in teaching as an Assistant Professor in the Department of Mathematics, Alliance School of Applied Mathematics, Alliance University, Bangalore. He acquired a doctoral degree from Visvesvaraya Technological University. He holds a postgraduate degree in Mathematics by securing third rank from Tumkur University and holds a B.Ed. from Tumkur University, Tumakuru, Karnataka. His research interests include General Topology, Soft Topology, Graph Theory and Cryptography. Dr. Reddy's teaching portfolio include a range of courses delivered in Mathematics such as Engineering Mathematics, Advanced Engineering Mathematics, Discrete Mathematical Structures, Graph Theory and Combinatorics, Operations Research, Business Mathematics and Business Statistics.

Renu is currently working as Assistant Professor with Teerthanker Mahaveer University, Moradabad, India. She holds a Master and Doctorate degree in Management from Kurukshetra University, Kurukshetra and Central University in Punjab, India respectively. She has 9 years of experience in Teaching, Research and Mentoring undergraduate and post graduate students of Management department. Her area of research includes Social Media Analytics, Customer Engagement, Customer Satisfaction and Branding. Currently, she is supervising 4 PhD research scholars in Management. She has been associated with Insurance industry for 3 years as consultant. She has published many research papers in reputed international journals/conferences and hold two Indian patents. She has delivered many guest lectures, special talks, communication skills training and career counselling sessions for universities in India. She has been actively involved in organizing international seminars, conferences, and workshops as a key resource person.

Ipseeta Satpathy has over 25 years of experience in teaching, research and administration at KIIT University. She has authored six textbooks Dr. Satpathy has published more than 300 research papers in various referred national & international journals including journals in ABDC category, conference proceedings and has more than 130 research papers in Scopus indexed journals and supervised 26 Ph.D scholars Dr. Satpathy has been awarded the prestigious Oxford Journal Distinguished Research Professor Award 2014 at Cambridge University, London. Dr. Satpathy is a former visiting professor at Lynchburg College Virginia, USA. Dr Satpathy was an invited speaker at the Charlton Business School University of Massachusetts, Dartmouth, USA. Dr. Ipseeta Satpathy, was felicitated with the Times Power Women 2023, by the Times Of India Group as an eminent academician in producing and upskilling quality professionals for today's workforce.

Sridevi, Professor, Department of Computer Science, Karnatak University, Dharwad, obtained her PhD from Mangalore University, Mangalore in 2017. Her research interests are Advanced Computer Networks, Mobile and Wireless Communication, Network Security, Cloud Computing, and the Internet of Things. At present, she is guiding four research scholars and One M.Phil. is awarded. She is a reviewer for the Journal of Advances in Mathematics and Computer Science. She has published more than 30 research papers in national and international journals.

L. Sudha is an Assistant Professor in the Faculty of Management at SRM Institute of Science and Technology (SRMIST). With expertise in management studies, she is dedicated to academic excellence and student development. Dr. Sudha actively engages in research, teaching, and mentoring to foster future leaders.

Sathya V. is a faculty member in the Department of Computer Science and Engineering, School of Computing, at Vel Tech Rangarajan Dr. Sagunthala R&D Institute of Science and Technology, Avadi, Chennai. Her expertise lies in advancing research and education in computer science and engineering.

Gamidell Yedukondalu is an Assistant Professor in the of Department of CSE CVR College of Engineering Mangalapally, Ibrahimpatnam, R.R District.

Index

Symbols

A

B

C

D

E

F

I

L

M

N

O

P

R

www.ingramcontent.com/pod-product-compliance
Lightning Source LLC
LaVergne TN
LVHW060007031026
349161LV00025B/2172